The Fiqh of Medicine
Responses in Islamic jurisprudence to developments in medical science

Ahmed Abdel Aziz Yacoub

Ta-Ha Publishers Ltd.
1 Wynne Road,
London SW9 0BB
UK

Copyright © Ahmed Abdel Aziz Yacoub

Published Rabi' al-Awwal 1422/June 2001 by:
Ta-Ha Publishers Ltd.
1 Wynne Road
London SW9 0BB
Website: http://www.taha.co.uk
Email: sales@taha.co.uk

All rights reserved. No part of this publication may be reproduced, stored in any retrieval system, or transmitted in any form or by any means, electronic or otherwise, without written permission of the publishers.

By: Ahmed Abdel Aziz Yacoub
General Editor: Afsar Siddiqui
Edited by: Abdassamad Clarke

British Library Cataloguing in Publication Data
Yacoub, Ahmed Abdel Aziz
Fiqh of Medicine, The
I. Title

ISBN 1 84200 025 X

Typeset by: Bookwright
Website: http://www.bogvaerker.dk/Bookwright
Email: bookwright@bogvaerker.dk

Printed and bound by: Deluxe Printers, London.
Website: http://www.de-luxe.com
Email: de-luxe@talk21.com

Contents

Foreword xi
Glossary & Abbreviations xiii
Acknowledgements xiv
Chapter One: Introduction 1
  1. Premise 1
  2. Purpose and justification 2
  3. Methodological considerations 4
  4. Structure of the Thesis 7
  Notes 10
Chapter Two: Islamic Fiqh 13
  1. Development and sources of Islamic jurisprudence 13
    1.1. Material sources 15
      i. The Qur'an 15
      ii. Abrogation in the Qur'an 17
      iii. The Sunnah 18
      iv. Ijma' 24
      v. Qiyas 25
    1.2. Formal sources 25
      i. Istihsan, ... 26
      ii. Istishab, ... 26
      iii. 'Urf, ... 26
      iv. Maslahah or istislah, ... 26
      v. Adh-Dhara'i 27
  2. Contribution of the fuqaha 28
    2.1 Ijtihad in action 32
    2.3. Fatawa (fatwa: sing.) 34
  3. Schools of thought in Islamic jurisprudence (fiqh) and their leaders ... 36
    3.1 Sunni schools 37
    3.2. Kharijite and Shi'ite schools 136 40
  4. In search of common ground for the laws 43
  Notes 52

Chapter Three: Responsibility and liability in Islam, ... 62
1. Responsibility and liability in Islam 62
   1.1 Responsibility in Islam 64
   1.2 Rescue in Islamic law 67
   1.3. Liability in Islam 69
      a. Strict liability 70
      b. Vicarious liability 72
      (i) Diya 73
      'Aqila 81 73
      (ii) Qasama 74
      (iii) Ahl ad-diwan 76
      c. The limit or cap of liability 76
2. The Islamic viewpoint on matters arising within medical practice 77
   2.1 Should people, in a Muslim context, preserve their health? 78
   2.2 Should people, in a Muslim context, seek treatment? 80
   2.3 Is there a necessity for the existence of the medical profession,
   according to Islam? 82
   2.4 Should the medical practitioner be well prepared for his job and
   execute it properly? 83
   5. Are there any limits to the methods employed in treatment? 84
   Summary of the views of al-Imam al-Ghazali on medical treatment175 85
   2.6 Are there any legal remedies for an injury caused to the patient
   during the course of the treatment received? 88
   Notes 90

Chapter Four: The rights and responsibilities of patients and those who treat them 100
1. An overview 100
2. Litigation in the medical field and medical negligence 102
   Mistake, error, misadventure, and negligence 104
3. The medical practitioner and negligence 106
   3.1 First: The basis of liability 109
   3.2 Second: Standard of care 111
   (1) The standard of care 112
   (2) Differences in opinions and novel procedures 113
   (3) The numbers involved to make 'a defence to a negligence allegation'
   113
   (4) Levels of skill: Is a special standard of care required? 114
   3.3 Third: Medical negligence and its redress 115
   (1) The competent unauthorised medical practitioner 116
   (2) The incompetent practitioner 117
   (3) Disciplinary Measures and Reimbursement 119
   Notes 122

Chapter Five: Muslim fuqaha's classification of liability of medical practitioners 127

1. Prologue 127
2. The competent practitioner who performs his duty according to the accepted methods of the profession and is authorised 128
   2.1 Liability 129
      (a) The Hanafi school 129
      (b) The Maliki school 130
      (c) Shafi'i school 131
      (d) Hanbali school 131
   2.2 Unforeseeable Reactions (Sirayah), ... 132
      Hanafi school 132
      Maliki school 132
      Shafi'i school 132
      Hanbali school 132
   2.3 Concluding Remarks 133
3. The authorised and competent practitioner who errs 138
   3.1 Error 140
      (a) The Hanafi school 140
      (b) The Maliki school, ... 140
      (c) Shafi'i school 141
      (d) The Hanbali school 142
   3.2 Non-Muslims 143
   3.3 Compensation (diya) 144
      The value of diya 145
4. The medical practitioner and criminal negligence 146
   4.1 Hadd 146
   4.2 Ta'zir 147
   4.3 Qisas 147
   4.4 Criminal Negligence 148
5. Summary 151
Notes 153

Chapter Six: Euthanasia 159

1. Introduction and definition 159
2. Types of euthanasia 160
   (1) Active euthanasia 160
   (2) Passive euthanasia 160
   (3) Triad of terms: voluntary, involuntary, and nonvoluntary euthanasia. 160
3. Involuntary euthanasia 161
   (a) Relation to homicide 161
   (b) Definition of homicide 161

(c) Western view of involuntary euthanasia 162
(d) Islamic view of involuntary euthanasia 164
  (a) The Hanafi school 166
  b. The Maliki school 168
  c. The Shafi'i school 170
  d. The Hanbali school 170
4. Nonvoluntary euthanasia 172
  4.1 Brain-stem dead 173
  4.2 Patients in the permanent vegetative state (PVS). 174
  4.3 Coma 174
  4.4 Should persons in the permanent vegetative state and other mentally incompetents be fed? 175
    (a) Western views 175
    (b) Islamic views 176
    (i) Infanticide 176
    (ii) Killing of minors and those under care 177
    (iii) Killing, or terminating the life, of the unconscious 177
5. Voluntary euthanasia 178
  5.1 Western views 178
    The Netherlands 180
    Suicide and assisted suicide at common law 180
    Assisted suicide and Jack Kervorkian's (Kevorkian) suicide machine 181
    The Hospice system of care for the terminally ill 182
  5.2 Islamic views 183
    (a) The Hanafi school 185
    (b) The Maliki school 186
    (c) The Shafi'i school 188
    (d) The Hanbali school 188
6. Conclusions 190
Notes 193

Chapter Seven: The Prevention and Termination of Pregnancy 202

1. Introduction 202
  In the Hanafi school: 202
  The Maliki school defined it as: 202
  The Shafi'i school defined the transgression as: 203
  The Hanbali school define it as: 203
2. Children within Marriage 203
  2.1 Is it allowed to have fewer children in the family? 203
  2.2 Is it allowed to have smaller families by preventing pregnancy? ... 204
    (i) 'Azl 204
    Hanafi school 207
    Maliki school 207

Contents

Shafi'i school 207
Hanbali school 207
Shi'ite Zaydi school 207
Twelvers (Imamia) Shi'ite school, and the Ja'afari 207
Isma'aili Shi'ite school 207
Ibadia (Kharijite) school 207
Zahiri school, of Dawud adh-Dhahiri (d. 883 CE) 207
    (ii) Blocking the neck of the womb, as a method of contraception ... 208
    (iii) Other means 208
3. Can pregnancies be terminated lawfully, in accordance with Islamic fiqh? 210
    3.1 The views of Muslim fuqaha regarding permissibility of induced abortion 211
    (a) The Hanafi school 211
    (b) The Maliki school 211
    (c) The Shafi'i school 212
    (d) The Hanbali school 212
    3.2 Some special issues on terminations 212
    (i) Pregnancy and the 'mother' in health, sickness, and in rape cases 213
    (ii) The embryo (foetus) and abortion 217
    (iii) The husband's options, consent, and permission 217
4. Treatment of Abortion in the UK 218
5. Comparison of Islamic law and UK law on Abortion 219
    5.1. The welfare of other siblings as a reason to procure an abortion .. 219
    5.2. A time limit was set before which abortion could be performed ... 220
    5.3. The welfare of the mother 220
    5.4 Severe deformation of the foetus 220
    5.5 Is the husband's consent or permission necessary? 221
6. The consequences of termination of pregnancy in Islamic fiqh 221
    6.1 Termination of pregnancy with the consent of the woman in question 222
    6.2. Termination of pregnancy at the hands of a tortfeasor 222
    (i) Miscarriage of a dead foetus 222
    (ii) Miscarriage of a living foetus, that dies 223
    (iii) Death of the mother due to assault, followed by expulsion of a dead foetus 223
    (iv) What if a pregnant woman is killed and nothing is expelled 223
    (v) General considerations 223
7. Legislation and induced abortion, in the light of Islamic fiqh and common law. 224
Notes 226

The Fiqh of Medicine

Chapter Eight: Reproduction and cloning ... 233
- 1 Reproduction ... 233
  - 1.1 Infertility ... 233
    - (i) Primary infertility ... 233
    - (ii) Secondary infertility ... 234
  - 2. How does Islamic fiqh impinge on reproduction? ... 235
  - 3. What happens to surplus embryos in modern infertility techniques? 235
  - 4. Can a widow use stored fertilised ova of her late husband? ... 241
  - 5. Surrogate wives and polygamy ... 243
  - 6. Cloning ... 244
    - 6.1 Cloning and the laws ... 244
      - (i) Preamble ... 244
      - (ii) The existing 'laws' and the expected changes ... 245
    - 6.2 Implications for Human Cloning ... 247
    - 6.3 Islamic fiqh and the new challenges ... 248
  - Notes ... 250

Chapter Nine: Transplantation ... 254
- 1. Introduction ... 254
- 2. The Modern History of Transplantation ... 254
- 3. Evidence of permissibility of transplants in Islamic fiqh ... 256
- (1) Foetal Tissue Transplants and Genetically engineered organs ... 258
  - 3.1 Transplants from animals, dead and living ... 258
    - (i) Transplants from dead animals ... 258
    - (ii) Transplants from living animals ... 260
  - 3.2 Transplants from humans: ... 261
    - (i) Transplantation from a living donor ... 261
    - (ii) Cadaver donations, and parts from dead persons ... 263
    - Is it allowed to transplant one testicle from a donor? ... 267
    - (iii) Transplantation from the brain dead ... 268
    - (iv) Anencephalic Infants as Organ Donors91 ... 271
  - 3.3.. Foetal tissue transplants and genetically engineered organ donation 272
- 4. Conclusion ... 273
- Notes ... 275

Chapter Ten: Conclusion ... 281
- Notes ... 292
- Appendices ... 294

Appendix A.1: The Hippocratic Oath ... 295

Appendix A.2: International Code of Medical Ethics ... 296
- International Code of Medical Ethics ... 296

Duties of Doctors in General 296
Duties of Doctors to the Sick 296
Duties of Doctors to each other 297

Appendix A.3: Declaration of Geneva, A modern restatement of the Hippocratic Oath 1947 298

Appendix A.4 Islamic Code of Medical Ethics 300
Doctors' Oath 300

Appendix B: The Declaration of Helsinki, Human experimentation 301
Introduction 301
I. Basic Principles 302
II. Medical research combined with professional care (clinical research) 303
III Non-therapeutic biomedical research involving human subjects (non-clinical biomedical research) 304

Appendix C: Declaration of Oslo 1970 305

Appendix D: Declaration of Tokyo, Torture and other cruel, inhuman or degrading treatment or punishment 307
Preamble 307
Declaration 307

Appendix E: (a) Opinion of the Group of Advisors on the Ethical Implications of Biotechnology to the European Commission 28 May 1997 309
Ethical Aspects of Cloning Techniques… 309
1. Whereas 309
Concerning Human Implications 310
Concerning Human Implications 310
Notes 311

Appendix F: European Parliament 1997-1998. Minutes of the sitting of Wednesday 12 March 1997 312
9. Cloning animals and human beings 312
Notes 313

Appendix G: Hukm al-maskuti'anhu (Rules when Shari'ah is silent about a matter). 314
The First Viewpoint: 314
A. The Qur'an: 314
B. The Prophetic Sunnah 315

C. Reasoning (al-'aql) 316
The Second Viewpoint: 316
(1) The Qur'an, (Q. 16:116) 316
(2) The Sunnah 317
(3) Reasoning (al-'aql) 317
The Third Viewpoint is that of those who "Do not know" 317
Notes 318

Appendix H: Some Resolutions of Al-Majami' al-Fiqhia and Fatwa. 319
Resolution No. (3) Al-Ijtihad 319
Resolution No.(4) D 3/7/86 Test Tube Babies 319
Resolution No. 1 D 4/08/88 Organs Transplant 319
Resolution No. (58/76) The Use of Foetal Tissue in Transplantation 319
Resolution Number Four: Termination of pregnancy when the foetus is seriously deformed 320
Fatwa: Islamic Fiqh on Donating and Receiving Blood 320

Bibliography and Bibliographical Abbreviations 321
European Titles 321
Arabic Titles 328

Index 339

Arabic Newspaper Article 348

Foreword

For more than a decade the author of this work, Dr. Ahmed Abdel Aziz Yacoub, worked very hard in two different fields. First, as a specialist heart surgeon he continued to perform his professional duties; and in the course of his wide and long medical career he directly encountered and also witnessed other members of the profession encounter similar problems, all associated with the development and progress in medical science. Second, he embarked on the study of law as an undergraduate student at Cairo University (Khartoum Branch), and as a postgraduate student at the University of Khartoum. As expected, he performed very well, earning Bachelor's and Master's degrees.

The author then proceeded to study for a doctoral degree at the University of London, where his research and analysis of vast material on medical science and law earned him a PhD in jurisprudence, in July 2000.

This book, *The Fiqh of Medicine*, is based on the author's doctoral thesis, *Responses in Islamic Jurisprudence to Developments in Medical Science*. It examines some of the most burning and complex issues of the last four decades of the twentieth century in the field; and which will preoccupy religious thinkers, the legal and medical professions, throughout the twenty-first century and beyond. The subject of concern is, in the author's words, "the compatibility of Islamic jurisprudence with present-day laws".

He examines in depth a wide range of legal and moral aspects of responsibility and medical liability within the context and the scope of the Islamic faith, with particular reference to subjects of great concern namely: euthanasia, prevention and termination of pregnancy, reproduction and cloning, and transplantation.

What are the juristic bases, the moral and religious codes that guide medical practitioners in their daily work as they avail themselves of the results of progress and developments in medical science?

Is there room and justification for re-examination of some of the interpretations of issues addressed by some of the jurisprudential literature within the domain of the Islamic faith, itself firmly anchored on the Shari'ah and the Sunnah?

It is abundantly evident in this work that the author has benefited from rich literature, standard references, and authoritative views the sources of which have been well researched. He provides a number of ideas regarding developments and progress in medical science, which he views as consistent with the Islamic faith.

He has provided readers with a remarkable piece of work. He has been enabled to achieve this due to his multi-disciplinary background: a renowned medical practitioner, and now an accomplished jurist in his own right.

Dr. Ahmed Abdel Aziz has provided the legal and medical professions with what may well prove to be a standard reference, as medical science conquers new fields and makes them available for the human race.

Abel Alier,
Former Judge of the Sudan Judiciary,
Former Member of the Law Revision Committee,
Member of the Permanent Court of Arbitration at The Hague,
Legal Practitioner, Khartoum, Sudan.
January 2001

Glossary and Abbreviations

In editing the work which follows and preparing it for publication, we have assumed a certain familiarity with Arabic terms and names as we have seen that this is increasingly commonplace not only among Western educated Muslims but among English speaking people generally.

Throughout, and even sometimes in quotes from other authorities, we have in general chosen to use the divine name Allah in preference to God, and this in particular where the authority is in turn quoting in translation from the Messenger of Allah ﷺ, or one of the people of knowledge.

Most Arabic terms are defined in the text. A number recur repeatedly throughout, and so are defined here.

Allah   the All-Knowing, All-Powerful and All-Seeing Creator Who is not connected to His creation in any way and Who is not indicated by any metaphor, and Who is endowed with all the attributes of perfection. The word 'god' or 'God' only indicates an – or the – object of worship and is cognate with the Arabic *ilah* – god – or *al-ilah* – God, but not necessarily with Allah.

ﷺ   *salla'llahu 'alaihi wa sallam*, may Allah bless him and grant him peace, said upon mention of the Messenger of Allah.

AS   *'alaihi as-salam* – peace be upon him, said upon mention of one of the prophets.

ayah pl. *ayat*   a verse of Qur'an, a sign, a miracle.

deen   'religion' but in the wider sense that embodies moral values, fear of Allah, and its embodiment in all walks of life not only in acts of worship. Deriving from a root for 'debt', it indicates the debt owed the Crea-

	tor and is better translated as 'life-transaction'.
fatwa	a judgement from a person of knowledge on a matter at hand; later came to mean matters relating to law exclusively.
faqih pl. *fuqaha*	profoundly knowledgeable person on the practical rulings of the shari'ah; a jurist.
fiqh	Literally 'understanding', it is a deep knowledge of serious matters, and responsibility towards what is right. Later came to mean judicial matters exclusively (jurisprudence firmly linked to moral values).
iman	belief in Allah and His Messengers, as well as affirmation both verbally and in action.
Injil	the revelation granted 'Isa – Jesus the son of Mary – peace be upon both of them. 'Gospel' is not the exact meaning.
surah	a chapter of the Noble Qur'an.
Tawrah (Torah)	the revelation granted Musa – Moses – peace be upon him. It is not necessarily the same as the Torah of today or the books of the Old Testament.

Acknowledgements

I am indebted to those who taught me in all stages. I am particularly indebted to Mr. Ian Edge, Barrister at Law, part-time lecturer in Law at SOAS, University of London, who supervised my work.

I appreciate fully the post-examination remarks of Dr. Doreen Hinchcliffe, of London University, and Dr. Sheila Dziobon, of Sussex University. Their remarks on the work were useful, and were a great source of encouragement for me to wade into the realm of publishing.

Professor Dr. Yasin Dutton, of Edinburgh University, went through the work and threw a lot of light on issues, which guided me in the final preparation for publication. I am very thankful and indeed very grateful to him.

To my publishers Mr. A. Siddiqui and Mr. A. Clarke are due special thanks for their effort in the production of the book, and their understanding of my reticence on occasions.

Ahmed Abdel Aziz Yacoub, MS, FRCS, FRCS (Ed.), FRCP (Ed.)

London, August 2001

Chapter One
Introduction

1. Premise

This thesis concerns Islamic responses to developments in medical science.

There is a resurgence of interest in Islamic fiqh as many Muslim communities seek to govern themselves according to their own Islamic law.

Technical advances are continuously expanding the field of medical practice, and as a result medical practitioners, the legal profession, and society, are faced with legal and ethical situations of increasing complexity. Progress in methods of diagnosis and treatment of ailments has caused medicine to undertake complicated procedures resulting in increased risks. Advances in research have opened up avenues that have left the laws governing the profession stretched or found it unprepared.

In the Western world, where much of the new advances in medicine are taking place, moral, ethical, and legal questions arise every day. Debate and confrontation, some of it violent, are frequent occurrences. Muslim communities are no different. Health matters are the concern of everyone.

Muslim countries which are eager to legislate in accordance with their, mostly religion-based, culture, customs, and traditions want to consult the field of Islamic medical fiqh to find solutions to the questions posed. Some countries insist on applying Islamic shari'ah forthwith but the question arises as to what that Islamic shari'ah is on such matters.

Thus medical fiqh becomes an important and an urgent issue. For Muslims it must be discussed in the light of the teachings of Islam, but in comparison also with the generally accepted codes of behaviour, professional conduct, and medical ethics worldwide. These codes generally have their origins in the Hippocratic Oath,[1] and its modifications.[2]

Are these codes necessarily at variance with Islamic shari'ah? The main purpose of this work is to examine such a question, as conforming to the accepted trends in a community is necessary for co-existence.

2. Purpose and justification

This thesis is primarily addressed to medical practitioners who may be interested in the rulings of Islam on their practice. But it is hoped that it will be of some use to fuqaha (jurists) who are involved in this area. Although I am not one,[3] I am encouraged by what the Prophet, *salla'llahu 'alaihi wa sallama*, said:

> God will grant prosperity to His servant who hears my words, remembers them, guards them, and hands them on. Many a transmitter of law is no lawyer himself, and many may transmit law to others who are more versed in the law than they.[4]

It is also hoped that all those who are interested in the revival that Islam is having will find interesting and useful its views on the rights and responsibilities of patients, and those who treat them. Islam governs all aspects of life. This is an area of interest to all.

The thesis brings together and analyses a wide range of data in a select domain of the medical field: this is the all-encompassing field of responsibility and medical liability. However there is also a discussion of certain special matters pertaining to life and death situations: that is euthanasia, prevention and termination of pregnancy, reproduction and cloning, and transplantation. Practical considerations have dictated the selection. But the methodology adopted in furnishing the rules for these examples may be extended to other areas.

Those in the medical profession will be able to compare and contrast the rulings of Islam with present day ethical codes, mores, and laws. It is hoped that some of the rulings, locked up in ninth century methodology, can be opened up by my work to add to the sparse literature in the field.

It is also hoped that fuqaha will find in this work a response to the criticism levelled against the works of former Muslim fuqaha, in that:

In the main these works discussed questions of law on a case-by-case basis, presenting solutions from the different relevant sources of law and arguments for their application, and then indicating the solution for their particular school.

None of these works attempts analysis of law and legal rules from first principles and few formulate general rules of law from the mass of particular instances.

Very little of this vast array of material is available in English.[5]

The general readers, Muslims or non-Muslim, may be helped to fill in a gap in their assembly of a whole, about the rulings of Islam in the different aspects of life and law. Islam is, to a great extent, the law.

Islam has a common heritage with Judaism and Christianity.[6] Its people built a great civilisation helped by, Iranian, Indian, and Greek culture and philosophy. Those civilisations themselves had their roots in religions. Islamic civilisation was also passed on to the West, which kept alive its Greek and Roman heritage.

> Many in Europe would agree in despairing at mistakes – even perversity – of some recent European and US policy stances towards certain events relating to the Muslim world. But. The western press is not monolithically anti-Muslim; the Churches are not united in anti-Islamic missionary zeal. And even the foreign policy establishment in Washington DC includes significant elements sympathetic to Arab and Muslim perspective…

> It could be suggested that Christian Europe suppressed the Islamic-Arabic dimension of its parentage,…[7]

It is very important to address this last group. It represents the mass of public opinion. The field is in great need of legislation, which could adopt the norms of medical ethics without violating the Muslim faith or alienating non-Muslims.

Secular laws do not have special clauses for coping with matters arising within the professions; these are subject to the general law. This may need improvement. The salient point is that they are man-made and can be reviewed. Shari'ah, to Muslims, is God's given law. It stipulates the permissible and the impermissible. But not every act is listed. Many matters are left out. It is not because they were forgotten. It is an accommodation to the frailty of man. **"Allah desires to make things lighter for you. Man was created weak."**[8]

The Prophet said:

> Let me be if I do not order you not to do things; too much questioning has brought misery on peoples before you. Only if I forbid you doing something then it is forbidden.[9]

He also said,

> The worst crime of a Muslim is to continue probing and questioning

about something, which was not forbidden until it becomes so.[10]

Medical problems can arouse emotional tensions. These tensions can sometimes result in violence. A good example of this in the West has been the actions of some proclaiming the pro-life cause, willing to commit crimes to further their ends.

In this study I examine certain problems of present day medical practice in the light of the Qur'an and the teachings of the Prophet *(Sunnah)*. I also consider the ideas of pious, learned Muslim fuqaha: whether that may be in 'schools,' or as individuals. Some fuqaha have given their views as legal responses *(fatwa)*.

I examine the extent to which contemporary medical practice is acceptable from an Islamic viewpoint, and whether the unacceptable is perceived to be punishable in this world, in the Hereafter, or in both.

My aim is to analyse the relation between Islamic medical fiqh and modern Western secular laws as represented by Anglo-American common law; to seek similarities and common concepts; to assess to what degree they are comparable now, and the extent to which involvement of Islamic fiqh in modern day medical practice is possible or present; and to determine the possibilities for future legislation in the field in a manner which is compatible with the acceptable rules and ethics of the world community and developments in medical science.

It is hoped that some jurists, Muslims and non-Muslims can produce a document on 'Islamic Medical Fiqh' based on the true and unadulterated spirit and letter of Islam. Islam is not restrictive; as on the whole "all is allowed except for what was, specifically, rendered impermissible" *(al-aslu fi'l-ashya'i al-ibaha)*.

*

This introductory first chapter is intended to fulfil three tasks: to introduce the work, to make clear the methodological considerations which have guided it, and lastly to lay out the structure of the thesis.

3. Methodological considerations

The use of Arabic words in Romanised form is essential for this thesis in that it denotes a special meaning to the word which may not be rendered in English. The use of Arabic vocabulary may make for difficult reading but it provides the reader with the exact word, and whenever possible I produce as good a gloss as possible.

Ramadan quotes Justice Robert Jackson, "the barrier of language

Introduction 5

presents more than the usual difficulty of comparative law studies in the case of Islamic law."[11]

Spelling Arabic words in English can be done in various ways, some of which are governed by typing facilities. There are certain accepted ways of transliteration. I will conform to these as often as possible; but in some places this may be supplemented by my own, where the Arabic phonetic may be better rendered, or the grammar may dictate.

Quotes from the Qur'an were referenced in the footnotes as follows: (Q. 1:1) to denote the first verse *(ayah)* of the first chapter *(surah)*. I have confined myself, except for a few times, to two of the most popular English translations of the meaning of the Qur'an: Muhammad Marmaduke Pickthall, and 'Abdullah Yusuf 'Ali, which are noted as (tr. Pickthall) and (tr. Y. 'Ali). [The editors have substituted the recently published Bewley translation for its greater fidelity, accuracy and felicitous use of English language.]

A few important Arabic words are dealt with here:

Sunnah literally means 'something of frequent occurrence' which may be bad or good. It can mean habit, or normative legal custom. But *Sunnah* in Islam, has come to be defined as the deliberate instructions of the Prophet, whether by word, deed, or by the silent acceptance of what was done by others.

Hadith literally means speech, talk, or saying, but it has come to be defined as the spoken part of *Sunnah*. Arabic is a language rich in simile and metaphor. There are occasions when the part is used to name the whole and others when the whole can mean a specific part.

Ash-Shahawi explains:

> *Sunnah* and *Hadith* are interchangeable; and on occasions *al-Khabar* which literally means the news, and *al-Athar* which literally means what is left behind or the trace, can all mean the same thing: namely the Prophetic *Sunnah*. *Sunnah* includes the sayings, and the acts, which were meant as religious instruction.[12]

Ahkam literally means judgements, rules, or categorisations; but it can have a very special meaning. It can mean Allah's word or ruling on a matter. All actions need to be judged, this is the crux of the Muslim faith. Actions fall in one of five categories: (1) obligatory *(fard* or *wajib)*; (2) forbidden *(haram)*; (3) detested acts, but for which there is no punishment if committed, *(makruh)*; (4) praiseworthy acts, but not compulsory, *(mandub)*; and (5) indifferent acts *(mubah)*.[13]

The knowledge of categorisations *(al-ahkam)* is called *fiqh* or *'ilm*.

This knowledge is the way for the worship of Allah, which is the sole purpose of the creation.[14]

The Prophet (SAAS) said:

> Nothing is graver than allowing what is not allowed, or disallowing what is allowed. Communities before you perished *(halaka)* when they put one part of the Qur'an on collision course with another.[15]

Ash-Shafi'i said,

> The rule of Allah, *al-ahkam*, based on Qur'an and *Sunnah* never escaped the mass of the people of knowledge *('ulama')* at any time, as ignorance of it is inconceivable.[16]

Shari'ah means what people are used to. It literally means a well-trodden path to a source, a 'watering hole.' It has come to mean 'Sacred Islamic law, based on the Qur'an and *Sunnah*.'

Usul means sources, foundations, roots, basis, origins, crux, and the knowledge of what is right and what is wrong, all in one.

The above are the most important points in respect of Arabic usage in the thesis. The glossary documents the usage and explanation of other words and abbreviations.

The Arabic names of the authors and the publications warrant a special consideration for reference purposes. The names of the authors, and the titles of their contributions have been used in the footnotes on their first appearance as a mode of identification; thereafter an abbreviated form is used for the more important and recurring ones. That is because there is lack of standardisation of Arabic 'surnames,' and some reference texts are devoid of essential bibliographical data: date and place of publication, publishers name and address, and ISBN.[17]

The same plan has been adopted for the other references as well to standardise the format of the thesis. But the basic plan is author, date, etc.

The European and Arabic titles were rendered separate in the bibliography. The Arabic article *al-* (the), with its fourteen variants such as *ad-, an-, as, ash-, at-, az-* *(al-ahruf ash-shamsia)*, was attended to in the text but is neglected in the alphabetical arrangement of the bibliography. Its significance is like writing 'an historic' instead of 'a historic.'

The work is firmly based on a selective analysis of empirical data on Islamic fiqh. Data has been obtained from a number of sources.

First, and most importantly, from the Qur'an and the Prophetic *Sunnah*. Unless there is no express ruling in them regarding the issue in question no other source should be sought. Second, the acts, the rulings, and the narratives attributed to the Prophet. The methodological implications of relying intensively on these two sources will be discussed in detail in Chapter Two. It is not always easy to separate the sources from the methods in Islamic fiqh.[18] Third, the vast array of material left by the Islamic fuqaha. The difficulties associated with sifting through the material and gleaning the necessary rulings is also detailed below. Fourth, contemporary views of fuqaha and men of science. These fall into two categories; (a) official, as expressed in laws, circulars, court actions, codes, and legal responses *(fatwas)* which were adopted officially; and (b) non-official contributions, in books, journals, newspapers, meetings, teaching, and *fatwas*. Fifth, events and practices in hospitals and medical centres. These also are in two categories: (a) reported ones and (b) the author's own contact with personnel and events in the field, mostly open to every authorised person.

The rulings of Shari'ah on some actions are stated and discussed. Other actions for which no rule exists will have been closely examined, and by analogy some rulings for them were suggested. The third group of actions for which analogy was not applicable were carefully subjected to the doctrines of: (1) if something is not expressly forbidden *(haram)*, it could then be allowed; (2) that public interest, and community welfare, are reasons to find solutions to novel problems providing that they are not contrary to the Qur'an and *Sunnah*; and (3) that necessity, even for an individual, can dictate measures which, though detestable or distasteful *(makruh)*, are not overtly forbidden *(haram)*.[19]

4. Structure of the Thesis

The thesis is divided into ten chapters.

Chapter Two deals with Islamic fiqh under a number of subtitles: developments and sources, the schools of thought therein, and the search for common ground between Islamic fiqh and modern Western laws.

For this purpose it is important to reiterate the definition of some words as used in this thesis to establish a referral locus.

Shari'ah is contained in the 'revealed' sources of the Qur'an and Sunnah. Islamic fiqh contains elements from Shari'ah and the contribution of fuqaha: from the time of the Prophet and his companions until the Day of Judgement, **"Then every self will be paid in full for what it earned."**[20]

Shari'ah does not change; but Islamic fiqh responds to circumstances. Shari'ah must never be violated, when responding to the needs of the times, and formulating elements of Islamic fiqh.

Chapter Three deals with: Responsibility, and liability in Islam, and Islamic viewpoints on matters arising within medical practice.

The general major guidelines in Islamic fiqh are:"enjoining the right and forbidding the wrong,"[21] and the necessity of preserving the five essentials in life: iman (faith), self (life), intellect, property, and offspring.[22]

Islamic fiqh adopts the principle of non-malfeasance as an element of conduct and ethics. The Prophet (SAAS) said, "do no harm, nor reciprocate hurt" *(la darar, wa la dirar)*.[23] A corollary of which is the responsibility to redress harm *(ad-darar uzal)*.

Honesty, responsibility, and the execution of one's duty to the best of one's ability, after thorough preparation, are required.[24]

Negligence cannot be assumed, it must be proved. No fault, no compensation. Negligence has many facets, some result in moral blame but liability is attached to all of them.

The Prophet (SAAS) ruled over medical liability per se:

> He, who sets himself up for the treatment of others without knowledge, is liable if life, limb, or function is injured, or lost.[25]

Liability incurred pecuniary compensation, except for criminal behaviour. Fairness in litigation, compassion, and forgiveness are encouraged."Blessed is the one who is fair when he buys, sells, or litigates."[26] Sanctity of life, and respect for the human being, who is honoured by Allah, and was made **"a khalif (viceroy) on the earth,"**[27] are an integral part of Muslim iman and law.

> **Verily We have honoured the children of Adam. We…have preferred them above many of those whom We created with a marked preferment."**[28]

Chapter Four deals with the rights and responsibilities of patients and those who treat them.

Chapter Five deals with Muslim fuqaha's classification of liability of medical practitioners.

Chapters Six, Seven, Eight and Nine deal with euthanasia, prevention and termination of pregnancy, reproduction and cloning, and transplantation respectively.

Termination of life, except for what Allah has ordained, is a crime, which may never be forgiven in the Hereafter, but the worldly punishment may be modified by forgiveness, or a doctrine of consent.

Termination of pregnancy when 'allowed' is entirely the right of the mother. The husband cannot compel her to maintain the pregnancy or vice versa.

Reproduction is only allowed within the marriage bond. But marriage can sometimes be polygynous. Can one wife donate ova to be fertilised by the shared-husband's sperm and then implanted into the other wife's womb? Can cloning, at any of its stages, be allowed within the married family?

Are all forms of transplantation allowed?

The concluding chapter summarises the focal issues in question, and analyses the findings for areas of compatibility and incompatibility between Islamic fiqh and modern laws. The results and contributions are stated.

The closeness of Islamic medical fiqh to the dictates of the medical codes of behaviour as seen in the Hippocratic Oath and current accepted values of professional conduct are scrutinised.

The ethical problems posed as a result of the rapid developments in the techniques of medical practice have been highlighted. The response is no different from that of the community and the profession at large: perplexity at the pace of change, with a willingness not to hinder progress but with determination not to compromise the sanctity of life or the rights of *all* humans involved in the equation.

Notes

[1] Hippocratic Oath: An English translation of a version of the oath is rendered in appendix A.1
Hippocrates (460-370 BC) of Cos, Greece, student of Plato, is the father of Greek medicine. The ethical codes of medical practice which he approved dominate the profession to the present day. Some medical faculties and schools include 'taking the oath' in their graduation ceremony. 1987, 252-253, and 286. {Henceafter quoted as, *Risala* (tr. Khadduri), 1987}; and al-Hakim *al-Mustadrak 'ala 'l Sahihain fi 'l Hadith*, Hydar Abad, 1st. ed., 1334 AH., vol. 1:88.

[2] The World Medical Association's International Code of Medical Ethics, London 1947-1949 revised 1968 and 1983 (Text is in appendix A.2); Declaration of Geneva 1947 (a modern restatement of the Hippocratic Oath: see appendix A 3); and the following appendices for:
The Declaration of Helsinki, 1964, revised 1975 and 1983.
The Declaration of Lisbon, 1981.
The Declaration of Sydney, 1968, revised 1983.
The Declaration of Oslo, 1970, revised 1983.
The Declaration of Tokyo, 1975, revised 1983.
The Declaration of Hawaii, 1977, revised 1983.
The Declaration of Venice, 1983.
The World Health Organization: *Ethics in Medicine,* Cab. Mass & London, MIT Press, 1977:552.

[3] I am a member of the medical profession who was involved in the creation of the Medical Association, the Doctors' Union, and the General Medical Council in the Sudan, and I have been one of its presidents. I am interested in studying Islamic Law (Shari'ah) for the purposes, inter alia, of professional regulations; and therefore in more detail than the essential needs for a Muslim individual. The prerequisites for a Master's Degree in Shari'ah at the University of Khartoum are: a basic law degree (LL.B.), and a Diploma in Shari'ah following an academic year's course. The (LL.M.) in Shari'ah follows a twelve months taught course. This was completed in 1994. I found this education invaluable as there is a scarcity of actual applications of Shari'ah-based laws to problems of medical practice and behavior.

[4] Banna, al-Banna (al-Sa'ati), *Al-Fath al-Rabani fi Tartib Musnad Ahmad ibn Hanbal al-Shaybani*, 1396 AH, vol. 1, pp. 164, and 165. {Henceafter, *al-Fath al-Rabani fi Musnad Ahmad*}. See also *Sahih al-Bukhari*, 1981, vol. 1:24-25; and Khadduri's translation: in al-Shafi'i, al-Imam Muhammad ibn Idris,

Introduction 11

al-Risala fi Usul al-Fiqh, (tr.) Majid Khadduri, 1987, 252-253, and 286. {Henceafter quoted as, *Risala* (tr. Khadduri), 1987}; and al-Hakim *al-Mustadrak 'ala 'l Sahihain fi 'l Hadith,* Hydar Abad, 1st. ed., 1334 AH., vol. 1:88.
[5] Edge, Ian, (ed.), *Islamic Law and Legal Theory,* 1996: xxviii.
[6] Q. 2:135, **"Say, 'We have iman in Allah and what has been sent down to us and what was sent down to Ibrahim and Isma'il and Ishaq and Ya'qub and the Tribes, and what Musa and 'Isa were given, and what all the Prophets were given by their Lord. We do not differentiate between any of them. We are Muslims submitted to Him.'"** (translation: Bewley); and Q. 87:18-19, **"This is certainly in the earlier texts, the texts of Ibrahim and Musa."** (tr. Bewley).
[7] Nielsen, J. S.,'Islam and Europe,' February 1996, pp. 1-10, at pp. 5 and 6. Unpublished paper read at the Janadirya Meeting in Riyadh, Saudi Arabia, March 1996; and personal communication. (Nielsen, J. S., Centre for the Study of Islam and Christian-Muslim Relations, Selly Oak Colleges, Birmingham, UK).
[8] Q. 4:28.
[9] Jakni, *Zad al-Muslim fi ma rawahu al-Bukhari wa Muslim,* 1967, vol. 1:193. {Henceafter referred to as Jakni, *Bukhari and Muslim,* 1967}.
[10] Jakni, *Bukhari and Muslim,* 1967, vol. 1:70*"hurrima min ajl masa'latahu."*
[11] Ramadan, Said, *Islamic Law,* 1970:27.
[12] Shahawi, *Kitab al-Shahawi fi Mustalah al-Hadith,* 1966:8.
[13] Qadri, *Islamic Jurisprudence* 1973:241. Also Weiss, Bernard G., *The Search for God's Law:*1992:3.
[14] Q. 51:56.
[15] Suyuti, *al-Jami'i as-Saghir* 1969, vol. 1:417.
[16] Shafi'i, *Kitab al-Umm,* 1993, vol. 7:494.
[17] Ash-Sharq Al-Awsat, (Arabic Daily Newspaper, London et. al.), 27 May 1999, Sawsan al-Abtah wrote,"Is Beirut Still the Foremost Arabic Publisher?"P. 19 (upper half), columns 1-6.
She referred to'lack of attention to bibliographical data,'in column 2; and that,'in Lebanon, and in other Arab countries, printers become publishers and distributors, with no regard to copy rights and professional acumen,'in column 4; she reiterated that,'the problems of republishing (Heritage Books) with pretences of editing, but without any real contribution or care for bibliographical data, approach piracy,' in column 5; and that, 'the situation is not better in other Arab countries,'in column 6. (Author's translation).
[18] Mayer,'The Shari'ah: A Methodology or a Body of Substantive Rules?'in Heer, (ed.), *Islamic Law and Jurisprudence,* 1990:177.
[19] Ramadan, *Islamic Law,* 1970:68, and 71.
[20] Q. 2:28, (tr. Bewley). This verse has the very last words revealed in the

Qur'an, but they were inserted in chapter 2, which is of an earlier descent. It was number 87 in order of descent; 27 chapters followed it.

[21] Q. 3:104, 110, 114; Q. 9:71, 112, et. al.

[22] Shatibi, (d. 790/1388), *al- Muwafaqat fi ash-Shari'ah*, 1975, vol. 2:8-11, at p. 10.

[23] *Sunan Ibn Majah*, 1953, vol. 2:784.

[24] Q. 5:1, **"fulfil your contracts"**; also *hadith*: *Sunan Ibn Majah*, 1952, vol. 1:84,"sincerity in performing duties"; and Jarrahi, *Kashf al-Khafa*, Maktabat at-Turath al-Islami, Halab, (n.d.), vol. 1:285, *Hadith* No. 747,"Allah loves it when one perfects his job"; and in Cairo edition, Maktabat Al-Qudsi, (1351 AH), p.240.

[25] Hindi, *Kanz al-'Ummal*, 1971, vol. 10:32.

[26] *Sunan Ibn Majah*, 1953, vol. 2:742.

[27] Q. 2:29, (tr. Bewley).

[28] Q. 17:70, (tr. Bewley).

Chapter Two
About Islamic Fiqh (Jurisprudence)

Now, one hears too often from one's Arab colleagues the dictum, "No, we have civil courts in our country; the Shari'ah is not relevant."

That is, of course, a dangerous non sequitur; the crucial matter is not the label put on the courts, but the law, which those courts are directed to apply.

…To a large extent, this issue, embarrassing to regimes, which have perforce adopted in the last two decades Western codes and, even more importantly, become absorbed into the Western economic system, has been swept under the rug. I do not believe that it will continue to be so.

…the swing back to the Shari'ah is apparent in current legislation. It is the duty of the practising lawyer always to point out the possibility of its application.[1]

Since Islam is for every person everywhere, and for all times, it becomes necessary to examine the sources of Islamic fiqh; the dynamism therein; the role of humans in legislating for their affairs; the integration of Muslims and non-Muslims in one community, and hence the common grounds for the laws.

1. Development and sources of Islamic Fiqh

Islam considers that each and every action of human behaviour is accountable and will be judged according to **"He has laid down the same deen for you as He enjoined on Nuh: that which We have revealed to you and which We enjoined on Ibrahim, Musa and 'Isa:" "This is certainly in the earlier texts, the texts of Ibrahim and Musa."**[2]

No Muslim is immune to these laws.[3] The rights of non-Muslims in a Muslim community must be guarded; "they have the same rights and obligations as us"[4] [i.e. their rights are guaranteed by the contract of the *dhimmah*. Ed].

The sources of Islamic fiqh can be divided, as with modern Western laws,[5] into: 1. Material sources, and 2. Formal sources.

Material sources are the Qur'an and Sunnah.

Formal sources are the product of the fuqaha's endeavours to find the laws by: *qiyas* which is juristic reasoning by analogy, *ijma'* (consensus) when all jurists agree to a ruling (both are based on the Qur'an and/or Sunnah (*nass* or text)), and other methods and criteria for elaboration of legal rules *(ijtihad)*.

In a sense *qiyas* and *ijma'* should belong to the material sources, as they are firmly anchored in the Qur'an and Sunnah. On the other hand they are the exercise of human reason to ascertain a rule of Shari'ah, which is *ijtihad*.

Other formal sources are: (1) *istihsan*, the principle of fiqh where equitable considerations may override the results of strict analogical reasoning; (2) consideration of public welfare or interest, which is expressed variously as *istislah* or *maslahah*, or *adh-dhara'i* (mitigating factors) in the elaboration of legal rules; (3) custom *('urf)* of a community or trade; (4) *istishab*, the presumption in the laws of evidence that a state of affairs known to exist in the past continues to exist until the contrary is proved; (5) the laws of our predecessors *(shar'u man qabluna)*: as in the scrolls of Ibrahim and Musa, peace be upon them, the *Torah* (revelation to Musa (Moses)) and the *Injeel* (revelation to 'Isa (Jesus)); (6) the narrative of a single companion of the Prophet ﷺ *(qawl as-sahabi al-wahid)*.

The latter two sources require special consideration. If these are accepted as authentic they really should belong to the category of material sources.

This is broadly consistent with the classification of Professor Madkour, former Head of the Department of Shari'ah, Cairo University, who renders the sources into: Textural *(naqlia)*, the Qur'an and Sunnah, and Intellect-linked *('aqlia)* which include the others.[6] The late Professor Abu Zahra, of Al-Azhar University, has a comparable classification also.[7] Other modern authors have classified the sources into primary and secondary sources.[8]

Ramadan is one such author. About his adopted classification he said:

…this classification of sources is by no means a decisive or [an] authoritative one.[9]

According to the Prophet ﷺ :

The Qur'an, and Sunnah are the source (sources), they will guide you as though you were in broad daylight: any other is a grace.[10]

Ash-Shafi'i, (d. 820 CE), said:

The sources are the Qur'an, the Sunnah, and the consensus based on them. Then exercising one's own judgement *(ijtihad)* to model on their guidance by analogy *(qiyas)*.[11]

Ghazali, (d. 1111 CE), said:

The (source) is one, it is what Allah says. What the Prophet ﷺ says is not a ruling, it is not binding. The Prophet ﷺ is the messenger who says Allah has ordained so and so. But the ruling is that of Allah only. As for consensus *(ijma')* it is the evidence of Sunnah, which in its turn is the evidence of Allah's rule, as we can only know the revelation through the Prophet ﷺ.[12]

Shahrastani, (d. 1153 CE), said:

The sources are: the Qur'an, Sunnah, consensus, and analogy. Probably we should say two, because consensus on the whole must be based on a stipulation *(nass)* from the Qur'an or Sunnah; and so is analogy *(qiyas)*.

Thus the four sources are reduced to two, or even to one: the word of Allah.[13]

Be that as it may, all fuqaha are agreed that four sources are in the forefront: (a) Qur'an, (b) Sunnah (c) *ijma'* (consensus), and (d) *qiyas* (analogy).[14]

1.1. Material sources

i. The Qur'an

The Qur'an is meant to provide a system to govern all actions of a Muslim.

Strictly speaking the whole of the Qur'an is law in the Islamic sense of law, as belief, and as a set of obligations on the individual as to the ideal conduct required by God. Little distinction is therefore made between the moral and the legal in the Western sense.

The Qur'an – the word of God – purports to regulate the whole of man's life; the word 'Muslim' refers to submission to the deen of Islam and its concomitant obligations.[15]

But it is not meant as a comprehensive listing of acts, articles, and codes.

It is a **"guidance and mercy and good news for the Muslims;"**[16] …who are prepared to think, analyse, and deduce.[17]

Only 500 verses (*ayat*) of the Qur'an out of 6236 are directly concerned with *ahkam*-rulings.[18] Coulson observed that there were:

> six hundred verses of Qur'anic legislation and the vast majority of these are concerned with the religious duties and ritual practices of prayer, fasting, and pilgrimage. No more than approximately eighty verses deal with legal topics in the strict sense of the term.[19]

Hitti said:

> All Allah's commandments - about ritual, civil, and other matters - with their punishments are recorded in the Koran. Of the roughly six thousand verses therein, some two thousand are strictly legislative.

> They are mostly embraced in surahs (chapters) 2 and 4.[20]

There may be little difference amongst all the aforementioned versions, if the content rather than the form is viewed. A single word or two is often an verse (ayah),[21] whereas over 135 words (all about law) are also a single verse.[22]

Throughout the Qur'an the message is of **"enjoining the right and forbidding the wrong"**:[23] this is repeated over and over again. Its aim is to teach, educate, encourage, and warn against the pitfalls of greed, selfishness, insensitivity, and criminality.

Professor Alfred Guillaume said:

> The Qur'an is one of the world's classics, which cannot be translated without grave loss. It has a rhythm of peculiar beauty and a cadence that charms the ear. Many Christian Arabs speak of its style with warm admiration, and most Arabists acknowledge its excellence.

> In sickness the Qur'an is the Muslim's stand-by…The bereaved find their consolation in reading it. Muslims are prone to quote verses from the Qur'an in all the manifold circumstances of life.[24]

But if no more than approximately eighty verses (ayat) deal with legal topics in the strict sense of the term as Coulson has stated above, this is not necessarily a negative criticism. It leaves a wide berth for Muslims to make their own laws, providing they are in accord with the Sunnah and do not violate the 'few' restrictions in the eighty ayat.

It is accepted that the Qur'an, which is memorised in its entirety and recited every day by many Muslims was committed to writing during the life of the Prophet ﷺ; although not arranged in its final form.[25]

The Qur'an, in many places, asserts that the message is delivered, complete; that nothing is omitted, and that every thing, which is disallowed, is detailed.[26]

Muslims, throughout the ages and across the entire world believe that it is the word of Allah **"Who will preserve it"**[27] and that, **"falsehood cannot reach it from before it or behind it."**[28]

ii. Abrogation in the Qur'an

Laws need to be continually evaluated. That is because the changing of circumstances with time has the effect of making certain changes necessary. It is also possible that laws may have to be changed because they were unsuitable from their inception. This is not applicable to Allah's given law. The reason for abrogation is change of circumstance. Abrogation *(naskh)* is mentioned in the Qur'an:

Whenever We abrogate an ayah or cause it to be forgotten, We bring one better than it or equal to it.[29]

There are several examples of abrogation in the Qur'an and Sunnah.

Muslims accept that abrogation is a change of a rule, or its modification because of differing circumstances. But the 'message' is in the deen (religion):

He has laid down the same deen (religion) for you as He enjoined on Nuh: that which We have revealed to you and which We enjoined on Ibrahim, Musa and 'Isa: 'Establish the deen and do not make divisions in it.'[30]

The essence and substance of the message has never been changed: "iman in Allah (faith in God), enjoining what is right, and forbidding what is wrong."[31]

The following are some examples of abrogation in the Qur'an:

(a) Regarding facing the *Ka'bah* in Makkah at prayers, instead of al-Quds (Jerusalem) in Q. 2: 114 **"so wherever you turn, the Face of Allah is there"** the legal sense of which was abrogated by the ayah 143 of the same Chapter 2, **"Turn your face, therefore, towards the Masjid al-Haram [at the Ka'bah in Makkah]. Wherever you all are, turn your faces towards it."**[32]

(b) Regarding the period following the dissolution of a marriage after which a divorcee is allowed to re-marry *('iddah)*, Q. 2: 226 stated that, **"Divorced women should wait by themselves for three menstrual cycles."** In certain circumstances, this was abrogated, in Q. 33: 49 **"... when you marry believing women and then divorce them before you have touched them, there is no *'iddah* for you to calculate for them,"** and provision was made for women who were menopausal, or were not menstruating, or were pregnant, in Q. 65: 4: **"In the case of those of your wives who are past the age of menstruation, if you have any doubt, their *'iddah* should be three months, and that also applies to those who have not yet menstruated. The time for women who are pregnant is when they give birth."** [33]

(c) Regarding the punishment for impermissible sexual intercourse,

If any of your women commit fornication, four of you must be witnesses against them. If they bear witness, detain them in their homes until death releases them or Allah ordains another procedure for their case.

If two men commit a like abomination, punish them. If they make tawba [turn to Allah from the wrong action] and reform, leave them alone (Q. 4:15, and 16).

This was abrogated by, **"A woman and a man who commit fornication: flog both of them with one hundred lashes"** in Q. 24:2.[34] This was further abrogated by an ayah of Qur'an [whose recitation was later abrogated. Ed.] where the punishment became stoning to death.

There are about twenty situations where abrogation took place;[35] other examples of which are found in inheritance: Q. 4:8, was abrogated by Q. 4:11, 12, and 176.

Abrogation was witnessed when the Prophet ﷺ allowed graves to be visited, having previously forbidden it.[36] The Qur'an decries visiting graveyards as a show of worldly might and strength in numbers,[37] but visiting as a reminder of human frailty and that life is not eternal is commended.

iii. The *Sunnah*

The reliability of the data collected from the Sunnah depends to a large extent on the soundness of the methodology of Muslim scholars or fuqaha.

Ash-Shafi'i, in debating the viewpoint of fuqaha who claimed that, since they were sure that every word in the Qur'an was exactly what was revealed to the Prophet ﷺ, they were going to stick to the Qur'an as the one and only source for the rules of Shari'ah *(al-ahkam)*, has argued that, if the Prophetic Sunnah was not inconsistent with the Qur'an, then it should also be taken as a source in its own right.[38] Arguing this point in his *Risala*, Ash-Shafi'i said:

I have replied as follows:…as for the Sunnah, which he laid down on matters for which a text is not found in the Book of Allah, the obligation to accept them rests upon us by virtue of the duty imposed by Allah to obey the [Prophet's] orders.[39]

Mutraf ibn Abdullah ibn ash-Shakheer was told by some to quote the Qur'an as his only source; he said, "There is no substitute to the Qur'an; but we would like to know from the one who knows the Qur'an better than us."[40]

The Prophet ﷺ has foretold this in a hadith:

> There will come a time when some will say, 'stick to the Qur'an only to find the rules as regards what is permissible and what is not.' Let it be known that what I say should also be followed, for I only tell you what was revealed.

Al-Khattabi commented, 'it is only the infidels who would say the Qur'an is the only source.'[41]

The Qur'an had been learnt and committed to writing as it was revealed. Prophetic Sunnah came to be written later: though a very little might have been written during the life of the Prophet ﷺ.

Muslim, on the authority of Abu Sa'id al-Khudri, quotes the Prophet ﷺ as saying, "Do not write anything except for the Qur'an, and if someone has already written anything other than the Qur'an, he is to wipe it out." This narrative was supported by Ibn 'Umar, Ibn Mas'ud, Zayd ibn Thabit, Abu Musa al-Ash'ari, Abu Hurairah, Ibn 'Abbas, and others. Quoting of this hadith was rebutted by those who said that this happened early in Islam for fear of a mix up between the Qur'an and Sunnah, but as the Qur'an became learnt by heart, the hadith was abrogated. There were also those who qualified the Prophet's ﷺ prohibition, by saying that it meant that Qur'an and hadith were not to be written on the same 'page'; and there were those who said that the prohibition was meant for those who could remember things, and that those unable to retain what they heard were excused.

The supporters of the view that hadith were written at the time of the Prophet ﷺ quoted several incidents and hadith. It is narrated that at the time when Makkah was opened to Islam, a companion named Abu Shah requested that a hadith should be written for him lest he forget it. The Prophet ﷺ said, "Write for Abu Shah." (Narrated by al-Bukhari and Muslim). There was another occasion when Ibn 'Umar [himself] asked the Prophet ﷺ whether he should write what the Prophet ﷺ says even when the Prophet ﷺ was angry. The Prophet ﷺ said, "Yes, do: because it is always the truth which I say" (narrated by

Abu Dawud and al-Hakim). Al-Bukhari quotes Abu Hurairah as saying, "none of the Prophet's companions passed on more hadith than myself, except for Ibn 'Amr (the grandfather of 'Amr ibn Shu'aib ibn 'Amr) as he could write." At-Tirmidhi quotes Abu Hurairah as saying; "The Prophet ﷺ directed one of the Ansar (the Helpers) to write down what he fears to forget of his hadith." ...Al-Hakim quotes Anas that the Prophet ﷺ said, "Document knowledge (*'ilm*) by writing." And ad-Dailami quoted 'Ali ibn Abi Talib as saying, "Should you write hadith it must be properly referenced."[42]

Authentication of hadith became an essential science or craft in Islam, because of the numerous false ones that were introduced to corrupt the faith or for political reasons. Some were written for material gain and others were concocted out of professional jealousy. Ash-Shahawi informs us:

One, Abu Isma Nuh ibn Maryam said that, "when people became engrossed in the fiqh of Abu Hanifah, and the parables of Muhammad ibn Ishaq, I became fearful that they would stop learning the Qur'an. So I conjured up some hadiths about the rewards of reading the Qur'an, seeking Allah's favour."[43]

But it was much more serious than that. By the time of al-Mahdi (d. 785 CE), father of Harun ar-Rasheed, there were more than 14,000 falsified hadith;[44] and al-Bukhari (d. 870 CE) said that he knew 100,000 authentic hadith and 100,000 inauthentic ones (*ghair sahih*).[45]

The authenticity of hadith is always crucial to the knowledge of the rulings *(ahkam)*, or to their deduction.

Goldziher maintained that hadith were invented as required, either to document the differing views, or to justify existing local usages.[46]

Coulson observed:

> This would... be the most appropriate point at which to explain...the attitude, which has been adopted in this book towards the controversial problem of the authenticity of Traditions from the Prophet.

> We take the view that the thesis of Joseph Schacht is irrefutable in its broad essentials and that the vast majority of the legal dicta attributed to the Prophet are apocryphal and the result of the process of "back-projection" of legal doctrine...At the same time,...the Qur'an itself posed problems which must have been of immediate concern to the Muslim community, and with which the Prophet himself,...must have been forced to deal. When, therefore, the thesis of Schacht is systematically

developed to the extent of holding that "the evidence of legal traditions carries us back to about the year AH 100 [sc. AD 719] only," and when the authenticity of practically every alleged ruling of the Prophet is denied, a void is assumed, or rather created, in the picture of the development of law in early Muslim society. From a practical standpoint, and taking the attendant historical circumstances into account, the notion of such a vacuum is difficult to accept.

> …it is suggested that the substance of many Traditions, particularly those which deal with the obvious day-to-day problems arising from the Qur'anic laws, may well represent at least an approximation to a decision of the Prophet which had been preserved *initially by general oral tradition*. If this practical premise is accepted then it is a reasonable principle of historical enquiry that an alleged ruling of the Prophet should be tentatively accepted as such unless some reason can be adduced as to why it should be regarded as fictitious.[47]

It may be argued that, though the preservation of the Qur'an and Sunnah including hadith might have been "initially by general oral tradition," at the same time, the Qur'an and Sunnah, to Muslims, are articles of faith. They are much more important than a mere source of fiqh, or case law, or an object of historical enquiry. They are learnt, recited every day, and practised. Their preservation came about from being a part of life.

This argument finds support in what Joseph Schacht, himself, said on another occasion:

> Islamic law is the epitome of the Islamic spirit, the most typical manifestation of the Islamic way of life, the kernel of Islam itself.[48]

So, the Qur'an, and Sunnah, including hadith must have been constantly and continuously reiterated. Ash-Shafi'i, on discussing consensus based on the Qur'an and Sunnah, stated that:

> The rule of Allah based on the Qur'an and Sunnah never escaped the mass of fuqaha at any time; as ignorance of it is inconceivable. The differences amongst the fuqaha as regards the Sunnah were in its finer details or in something pertaining to a special circumstance.[49]

Al-'Asqalani, in the *"Introduction"* to his book, *Fath al-Bari bi Sharh Sahih al-Bukhari*, quotes Muslim as an authority in saying that the Sunnah was not written during the era of the companions of the Prophet ﷺ; nor was it written at the time of their followers. The writing of hadith was discouraged in the beginning, unless there was a pressing reason, lest it got mixed up with the Qur'an. Besides "most of the learning was by rote and practice; as few could read." But when many started falsifying hadith it became necessary to write down authenticated hadith.[50]

It was at the time of 'Umar ibn 'Abd al-'Aziz (681-720 CE), the just Umayyad Caliph, that compiling, documenting, and authenticating of hadith and Sunnah was started. It was feared that people were beginning to forget parts of Sunnah, and mix up others. Contact with the Iranian and Indian civilisations brought home to them the full value of maintaining records; and also paper became more available.[51]

Malik ibn Anas was among the first in the field. He took eleven years compiling his book on hadith, Sunnah, and fiqh called *al-Muwatta,'* from (148/764) to (159/775). He was commissioned by Caliph Abu Ja'far al-Mansur, and it was completed in the reign of Harun ar-Rasheed ibn al-Mahdi. When asked by Harun ar-Rasheed to make it the only reference he refused: saying that:

> The *'ulama* were dispersed all over the land. Many of them have their reliable sources, and they are more aware of their local conditions. The differences between them are a God-sent mercy to the people. Each of them is guided, and all of them seek Allah's approval.[52]

Malik was very thorough in his research. The text of hadith had to be impeccable and accurate. He started *al-Muwatta'* with 10,000 hadith. He continued his verification over forty years, during which time he let it be examined by seventy learned men until he settled upon 1,720 hadith.[53]

Altogether the narrators *(isnad)* had to be qualified with:

(1) *'Adalah*, which entailed: i. Islam, ii. maturity, iii. soundness of mind, having *taqwa* (fear of Allah), iv. being knowledgeable and learned, v. being well intentioned and free of will, vi. integrity and respectability *(al-khulu min khawarim al-muruwah)*. (2) A retentive memory. (3) Accuracy in delivery.[54]

The method of authentication was painstaking and unprecedented in its thoroughness. Hadith, Sunnah, and fiqh were collected and verified by the likes of Malik, ash-Shafi'i, Abu Hanifah, and Ahmad ibn-Hanbal. Still some would reject their work. But it should make no difference to the arguments quoting what those fuqaha have authenticated, as points can still be debated with people who do not believe that the Qur'an was revealed to the Prophet ﷺ.

The issue is what do Muslims believe, or accept as being a correct or an authentic source.

If I were to present a system of law based on the belief of a tribe 'x' in a god 'y,' then all that is necessary is to represent, accurately, their law. Whether their belief in 'y' is right or wrong is of no consequence.

If that law of theirs interacts with the rest of humanity or an area of common interest to produce or adopt "the accepted worldwide codes of behaviour, professional conduct and *medical* ethics; codes which have their origins in the Hippocratic Oath and its modifications,"[55] then the core of that belief should not detract from its pragmatic value.

The Prophet ﷺ upon his arrival in Madinah established the first Muslim community and its laws in the very first year of *hijrah* (Emigration): 1 AH. Evidence as to the existence of Sunnah concurrently with the Qur'an as bases of Islamic law is highlighted by Yasin Dutton in his re-examination of Malik's presentation of *'amal ahl al-Madina* (the practice of the people of Madinah: religion in action).[56]

Six hadith books dominate the field: *Sahih al-Bukhari* (d. 256/870), *Sahih Muslim* (d. 260/875), *Sunan Ibn Majah* (d. 273/887), *Sunan Abu Dawud as-Sijistani* (d. 275/889), *Jami' at-Tirmidhi* (d. 279/892), and *Sunan an-Nasa'i* (d. 303/915).[57]

Malik's *Muwatta'* is in a class by itself, as it encompasses hadith, fiqh and Sunnah.

Musnad Ahmad ibn Hanbal has more than 40,000 hadith;[58] some consider him to be like Malik in his combining of fiqh and hadith.[59]

There are also others in the field, e.g. *Sunan ad-Darimi, Sunan ad-Daraqutni, Sunan al-Baihaqi*.

The most reliable text of hadith is generally considered to be one which is found in both al-Bukhari and Muslim; then one that is in al-Bukhari alone, then one found in Muslim alone.

The most reliable chain of narrators *(isnad)* is the 'Golden Chain' of narrators: Malik, through Nafi,' through Ibn 'Umar to the Prophet ﷺ.[60]

"Ibn Khuzayma an-Nisaburi (223-311 AH) collected many hadith, which though authenticated by al-Bukhari and Muslim were not included in their compilations, in his own *Sahih*. His effort survived in the collection of his student, Ibn Hibban at-Tamimi al-Basti (276-356 AH), *Sahih Ibn Hibban*, who was the teacher of Muhammad ibn Abdallah ad-Dabbi an-Nisaburi (al-Hakim). Al-Hakim (321-405 AH.) published his *al-Mustadrak 'ala's-Sahihain fi 'l -hadith* (the record of what was left out by al-Bukhari and Muslim of the absolute authentic hadith which fulfils their criteria). Hence their work and collections were ranked in the same category as al-Bukhari and Muslim."[61]

At this juncture it is best to reconsider and detail the report of a single companion of the Prophet ﷺ *(khabar al-wahid)* when a person attributes a saying or an act to the Prophet ﷺ. If the narrative is authenticated it is really not different from Sunnah. This is the commonest source of the sayings of the Prophet ﷺ (hadith).

> …ash-Shafi'i clearly supported the position of the Hijazi traditionalists, who held that the narratives of the Prophet's companions were authoritative, since they had been in close association with the Prophet and understood the meaning of his Sunnah. He also accepted the opinions of the Successors, if there was agreement among them.[62]

The way ash-Shafi'i reasoned was to invoke a hadith that was being told at his time by Sufyan ibn 'Uyayna from 'Abd al-Malik ibn 'Umayr, from 'Abd al-Rahman ibn 'Abdallah ibn Mas'ud from his father, that the Prophet ﷺ said:

> God will grant prosperity to His servant who hears my words, remembers them, guards them, and hands them on. Many a transmitter of law is no lawyer himself, and many may transmit law to others who are more versed in law than they. The heart of a Muslim shall never harbor vindictive feelings against three: sincerity in working for God; faithfulness to Muslims; and conformity to the community of believers - their call shall protect [the believers] and guard them from [the Devil's] delusion.[63]

If *khabar al-wahid* is authentic, then it is a material source. Madkour mentioned that some jurists put it ahead of *qiyas*, others differed.[64]

iv. Ijma'

Ijma' may be viewed as a procedure to arrive at a result, a consensus; when everyone agrees on a categorisation *(hukm)* that an action is one of the following: obligatory *(wajib)*, recommended or meritorious *(mandub)*, permitted *(mubah)*, disapproved or reprehensible *(makrouh)*, or forbidden *(haram)*. For that to happen, there must be a sound base from the Qur'an and Sunnah, which only needs to be found.

Ash-Shafi'i said:

> The rule of God based on the Qur'an and Sunnah never escaped the mass of jurists at any time as ignorance of it is inconceivable. The differences amongst the jurists as regards the Sunnah were in its finer details or in something pertaining to a special circumstance.[65]

Ash-Shafi'i's interpretation of *ijma'* called for responses similar:

...the legal principle was considered to be permissible only after there was a consensus of the entire Islamic community, or *ummah*, on a particular legal issue. As this was virtually impossible to achieve, then, a possible source of law making, *ijma'*, was stillborn.[66]

The argument may take note of whether *ijma'* is discussed as a source or as a method, and whether the discussion concerns Shari'ah, or Islamic fiqh, as these factors are relevant. At the time of the Prophet ﷺ all of the people concerned had the chance to meet often, and know his teachings.

Muslims contend that consensus (*ijma'*) is based on the Qur'an and Sunnah.[67]

Abu Zahra explained:

Ijma' is the consensus about whether something is allowed or not with reference to the Qur'an and Sunnah. It does not create a sacred rule (*hukm:* plural, *ahkam*), as some European jurists think [sic.].[68]

Murad Hofmann said:

A Qur'anic injunction is not at the disposition of lawmakers and cannot be disposed of, even by consensus.[69]

Muslim fuqaha often debated what was meant by *ijma'* (consensus). *Ijma'* of whom, on what, and for how long?

Ijtihad (independent reasoning) and *ijma'* are sources of Islamic law.[70] *Ijma'* is the agreement of all Muslim learned persons at a time, after the death of the Prophet ﷺ, on a 'legal' matter (*hukum shar'i*).[71]

v. Qiyas

Qiyas is a method of finding the rules of Shari'ah from the source: the Qur'an and Sunnah. It literally means: to measure, to compare, 'to see if it fits.' Ash-Shafi'i used *qiyas* effectively in his building of fiqh. Although it is accepted and utilised by most fuqaha, those in the Dhahiri school (literalists) amongst the Sunnah and the *Imami* Shi'ite schools do not accept it.

Qiyas is further examined with the schools of Fiqh below.

1.2. Formal sources

Fuqaha have recognised three types of *ijtihad* (effort to find the rules): firstly, seeking a material source (*nass*), or an explanation thereof (*tafsir*); secondly, analogy (*qiyas*) firmly based on material sources: Qur'an, or Sunnah, on which there is consensus (*ijma'*); and thirdly, formal sources not reliant on a material source *(nass)* from the Qur'an or Sunnah, but capturing the spirit of Shari'ah, taking in consideration the welfare of the community, and expressed as *istihsan, maslahah*; just as a modern day judge who does not find a textual precedent *(nass)* resorts to equity, and natural justice.[72]

i. Istihsan

Istihsan is "the principle of jurisprudence that in particular cases not regulated by any incontrovertible authority of the Qur'an, Traditions or *ijma'*, equitable considerations may override the results of strict analogical reasoning."[73] Doi defines it as, "equitable preference to find a just solution."[74] It is the preference of a ruling other than the one arrived at by analogy *(qiyas)*, when that rule is found to be harsh or contrary to custom. Whereas *qiyas* is based on the Qur'an or Sunnah, *istihsan* needs only not to contravene them.

ii. Istishab

Istishab means legal presumption of continuance.

> On many legal topics, of course, the Qur'an is completely silent…
>
> It is a natural canon of construction, and one in full accord with the general tenor of the Qur'an that the status quo is tacitly ratified unless it is expressly emended.[75]

iii. 'Urf

'Urf embodies custom, tradition, local habit, and trade or professional code. This source is common to all other laws, even secular ones. It is a source in the sense of it being there to tap; but there must be an active effort to select from it what is consistent, or what is not at variance, with the Qur'an and Sunnah. Islamic fiqh does not negate all 'laws' that precede it. *Diya* (the payment of compensatory money for death or injury) and *qasamah* (the compurgation oath) are examples of what was adopted from pre-Islamic tribal ones.

iv. Maslahah or istislah

Maslahah or *istislah* is the consideration of community welfare, public interest, or legitimate personal right in formulating laws.

Hofmann observed that:

> It is clear that Islamic law thus remained flexible enough to take into account the requirements of public interest, but that it was also open to the reception of some pre-Islamic customs.[76]

Al-Ghazali said:

Maslahah means fulfilling what Shari'ah was meant for: the purpose of Shari'ah is that, people are required to preserve their deen, their life, their minds (faculties), their offspring, and their wealth. Any measure that preserves these fundamentals is *maslahah*, and anything that threatens them is *mafsadah* (corrupting and vitiating), and warding it off is *maslahah*.[77]

Ash-Shatibi (d. 790 AH), said:

The purpose of all the rules of Shari'ah *(takalif)* is to secure the interests of the individual and the community. These interests can be summed up under three titles: essentials, necessities, and complimentary requirements.

Essentials *(daruriyat)* are mandatory for the welfare of deen and society; otherwise there will be chaos, loss of life, and lack of security and safety. The essentials are five: preserving deen (law), life, offspring, property, and the mind (by avoiding whatever impairs reason or faculties).

Necessities *(hajiyat)*: their existence eases the stresses of life, and removes hardship. e.g.:

in transactions, by accepting fabrication contracts where the subject matter is non-existent *(istisna'a)*,

in homicide, by accepting *qasama*, and *diya* (instead of exacting the death penalty); and that the *diya* should be paid by *'aqila*, (a pre-Islamic custom),

and in torts by making craftsmen liable.

Complimentary requirements *(takmaliyat)* are exemplified by requiring decency in behaviour, elegance in appearance, good table manners, and doing more and more good.[78]

v. Adh-Dhara'i

Adh-Dhara'i literally means causes, reasons or means. It is usually used with a prefix such as *sadd bab adh-dhara'i* (closing the door to, or removing the cause), or *fath bab adh-dhara'i* (opening the door to, or finding a way).

Stratagems *(hiyal)* is a variant of it. The basis for it is in the Qur'an.[79]

Also, when the Prophet ﷺ decreed that someone should receive one hundred lashes, Sa'd ibn 'Ubadah told the Prophet ﷺ that the man was frail and would die. The Prophet ﷺ advised one stroke with a bunch of one hundred palm fronds.[80]

Many fuqaha consider *maslahah, istislah, adh-dhara'i,* and *hiyal* as similar to one another, and that they are provisions to make laws, that need only not to make the impermissible permissible, or vice-versa. They involve public interest, necessity, need, a legitimate personal right, or an accommodation. They are the corner-stones of adaptability.

*

The material sources may be viewed as the revealed sources, with a provision to include the acceptable narrative of a single transmitter of a hadith *(khabar al-wahid)*, and a Scripture revealed to past prophets.

The formal sources for Islamic fiqh are a mixture of non-revealed sources, and methods to find the rules. Finding rules is a mental faculty *(ijtihad)*, that utilises analogy *(qiyas)*, equitable preference *(istihsan)*, and legal presumption of continuance *(istishab)*. It draws from custom *('urf)* with all its ramifications of tradition, local habit, trade or professional code, with due consideration to public welfare, need, and necessity *(maslahah)*. Should an opinion transpire a consensus *(ijma')* is sought for. The forum for *ijma'* varies with locale, time, communication, and methods of enacting laws.

All of these processes are sources-cum-methods of finding or securing laws in all societies. But Islamic fiqh went into such great depth and detail in some of them, that they almost became identifiable with it, if not a monopoly.

Ann Elizabeth Mayer observed:

> In a modern legal setting, one can classify sources as primary sources, which one consults to find the actual texts of laws, and secondary sources, where one finds clarification of the rules that are set forth in the primary sources. These should be distinguished from remote sources of law, such as customary norms and the religio-cultural heritage from which the law ultimately derives. Understanding the historical background and the origins of legal rules, as found in the remote sources, enhances the understanding of primary and secondary sources, but one does not refer to the remote sources to find what the legal system actually treats as the definitive statements of legal rules.

> This hierarchical ranking of legal sources may seem oversimplified, and one could object that it does not adequately reflect the historical complexity in the relationships among different types of legal sources. Still, it can be used as a starting point for analyzing where one should turn to find the law.[81]

2. Contribution of the fuqaha

The sources, and the methods come to life, and become law through the contribution of fuqaha. Muslim fuqaha have excelled in their efforts to enrich Islamic fiqh.

Fuqaha's views are not difficult to find, what is needed is their consensus. Even at the time of the Prophet ﷺ there were occasions when what he had said had been interpreted differently. He once told a marching group to say their *'Asr* (afternoon) prayers at Bani Qurayza's place.[82] The time for prayers became due before they got there. Some of them said their prayers when it was time. Others stuck to the letter of the instruction and said the *'Asr* prayers at Bani Qurayza; but by then it was later than the beginning of the specified time for the prayers. This was narrated to the Prophet ﷺ: he was silent and did not say that either party was right or wrong.

The fuqaha concluded that both factions were right. One prayed at the correct time according to the general instruction to say prayers at the beginning of their times, interpreting the specific instruction as urging them to move fast. The other obeyed the specific direct instruction and prayed at the specified place.

Furthermore the fuqaha concluded that the whole episode could be taken as a method of instruction for other eventualities, and as a model of accepting different interpretations.

The views of fuqaha were important throughout the history of Islam. At the time of the Prophet ﷺ a person could voice an idea which could be different from that of the Prophet ﷺ [in the cases where it was clear that that view was not from revelation]; not only that, but on occasions the Prophet ﷺ accepted it. Examples of these may be found in the events of the Battles of Badr (2/624), when he accepted the view of an-Nu'man ibn al-Mundhir, which was contrary to his, as to how to conduct the war. At the battle of Uhud (3/625) the younger Muslims who missed the previous year's battle were keen to meet the enemy and fight. The Prophet ﷺ thought it better to remain within the fortifications of Madinah. But he accepted their view. Thus they waged the battle and lost. At the preparations for the third battle of *al-Khandaq*, which took place in the year 626 CE, (four or five of AH), Salman al-Farisi suggested to the Prophet ﷺ that they should not fight but dig a great trench to keep the massive enemy and their horses out. The Prophet ﷺ accepted his view and they were able to survive a siege of two months, after which the enemy gave up and went away.[83]

He even subjected himself to the jurisdiction of others, but never in matters of iman. On several occasions the Prophet ﷺ pointed the way to the methods to be adopted, if no ruling was expressed in the Qur'an and Sunnah. The Prophet ﷺ sanctioned exercising one's own judgement to find solutions. There is the story involving his emissary Mu'adh ibn Jabal, when he sent him as a *qadi* (judge) to the people of Yemen. It is rendered into question and answer form, in many of the references.

> The Prophet ﷺ asked Mu'adh, "How would you judge events"? Mu'adh said that he would judge on the basis of the contents of the Qur'an. The Prophet ﷺ then asked him, "and if there is no ruling in the Qur'an?" Mu'adh said that he would judge according to the Prophetic Sunnah. The Prophet ﷺ asked him furthermore, "and if there is none?" Mu'adh said, "Then I will exercise my own judgement *(ajtahid)* to no end." The Prophet ﷺ said, "Praised be Allah for guiding Mu'adh to what has pleased the Messenger of Allah."[84]

Ibn Hazm adh-Dhahiri (d. 456/1064), who was opposed to *ra'y* and *qiyas*, called it hadith *ghair sahih* (unsound).[85] Some Western authors also doubted the authenticity of the narrative.[86] But the issue is the concept of *ijtihad* in Islamic fiqh. This narrative is accepted and propounded by Muslim fuqaha, and it appears in *Sunan Abi Dawud* (202/817-275/888).[87]

The least that can be said is that *ijtihad* is an accepted concept in Islamic fiqh even if it is from the 9th century as some allege. Besides there are numerous other examples of Islam encouraging *ijtihad*.

The Qur'an says:[88]

> "Those among them who *are able to think out the matter* would have known it, *(la 'alimahu al-ladhina yastanbitunahu minhum)*." Q.4:83, and,

> "those who, when they are reminded of the Signs of their Lord, do not turn their backs, deaf and blind to them." Q.25:73, and,

> "Will they not then ponder the Qur'an or are there locks upon their hearts?" Q.47:24.

The Prophet ﷺ once asked 'Amr ibn al-'As to judge a case. 'Amr asked, "Should I do so in your presence?" The Prophet ﷺ said, "Yes; if a *hakim* (ruler) exercises his judgement *(yajtahid)* and errs, he will still be rewarded; and if he is right then he has double the reward."[89] The Prophet ﷺ showed that every legal detail could not be found in the

Qur'an and Sunnah, and that exercising one's own judgement or *ijtihad* was commendable.

There are references in the Qur'an that all prophets, including the Prophet Muhammad ﷺ adjudicated in the affairs of their communities.

> "No, by your Lord, they are not muminun (believers) until they make you their judge in the disputes that break out between them, and then find no resistance within themselves to what you decide and submit themselves completely." Q.4:64;

and,

> "We have sent down the Book to you with the truth so that you can judge between people according to what Allah has shown to you." Q.4:104.[90]

The Qur'an left those of other faiths the freedom of choice of accepting its judgement, or opting for their own law according to their 'Revealed Books,' which were guidance and light in their own right. The Qur'an says:

> "If they come to you, you can either judge between them or turn away from them. If you turn away from them, they cannot harm you in any way. But if you do judge, judge between them justly. Allah loves the just."

> "How can they make you their judge when they have the Torah with them which contains the judgement of Allah?..."

> "We sent down the Torah containing guidance and light, ..." [Torah is the revelation granted Musa. It is not necessarily the same as the Old Testament or the present Torah. Ed.]

> "We prescribed for them in it: a life for a life, an eye for an eye,..."

> "And We sent 'Isa son of Maryam following in their footsteps, confirming the Torah that came before him. We gave him the Injil containing guidance and light,..." [Injil is the revelation granted 'Isa. It is not necessarily the same as the Gospels. Ed.]

> "The people of the Injil should judge by what Allah sent down in it."[91]

Is there a nucleus for legal pluralism in the preceding ayat?

Can there be a provision for a system of 'law' within the 'system' – as found in club markets or merchant law within the state legal system? Can a confederate idea for constitutional law, be derived from them?

Caliph 'Umar ibn al-Khattab, on appointing Abu Musa al-Ash'ari as a *qadi* (judge), wrote guiding him:

> Use your own individual judgement about matters…about which neither an answer is found in the Qur'an and the Sunnah. Know the similitude and weigh the issues accordingly (here Abu Musa is asked to use…*qiyas* and *ijtihad*…).[92]

The Arabic word *(qis: qiyas)* used by Caliph 'Umar which was translated as "weigh" could also be translated more literally as "measure."

Ijtihad and *qiyas* are ordinary Arabic words. They have always been used: before the time of the Prophet ﷺ, during his time, and nowadays. It is virtually impossible for *any* Arabic-speaking person not to use these words, or to find a substitute for them. Why would one want to do so? They are the simplest, and the most direct words for the meanings embodied, or involved. They describe an innate and commonly shared human mental faculty.

2.1 *Ijtihad* in action

A woman won her argument against Caliph 'Umar in the mosque when he wanted to limit the dower *(mahr)*. She quoted the Qur'an, **'and have given your original wife a large amount (*qintar*), do not take any of it.'**[93] And said, "Allah gives us by the *qintar*, and you, 'Umar, bar us from collecting mere *dirhams*?" He backed off decrying himself, "The woman is right, 'Umar is wrong: everybody is more learned *(afqah)* than 'Umar."[94]

The '*himariyya*' is another example where some litigants argued successfully against his judgement.[95]

'Ali ibn Abi-Talib suggested raising the punishment for 'wine' drinking to eighty lashes. This was accepted by 'Umar the second Caliph, but 'Uthman ibn 'Affan, the third Caliph went back to forty lashes.[96]

'Ali ibn Abi Talib, himself, was uneasy about his *ijtihad*, he said:

> I would never pay *diya* compensation for anyone who comes to harm during *hadd* punishment, except for those involved in drinking: the Prophet ﷺ stipulated neither a fixed number, nor a manner of lashing. It is just our own doing.[97]

Ibn 'Umar and Ibn Abbas held the view that *mut'a* marriages were valid for over twenty years after that license was abolished, up to the time when 'Ali ibn Abi-Talib was Caliph.[98] Fuqaha never stopped their search for finding the 'rules,' or furnishing legal responses, for the enactment of laws; as this is a dynamic process necessitated by the changes in life.

Shahrastani (1076-1154 CE) states that:

Prescriptions and injunctions are limited, but occurrences are unlimited. Since the limited cannot cater for the unlimited, and since the Qur'an and Sunnah did not prescribe for every event, nor do we expect them to; it becomes mandatory to exercise our own judgement to find solutions to problems of our times.[99]

It was at the time of the Umayyad dynasty, and more so, in the Abbasid era that fuqaha documented much of their views. That is because of the spread of Islam, and the attendant complexity and variety of urban problems. At the same time they themselves became well versed in writing, and, as mentioned before, paper had become more available. It was the dawn of an era of great learning, a golden age of scholarship. The arts, the crafts, the sciences, music, medicine, poetry, and other pursuits flourished.

"In the beginning, the attendants of a 'teaching ring' or *majlis*, of some one like Ibn 'Abbas would recite the Qur'an, discuss Sunnah, narrate travel tales, sing poetry, and recount history of olden events. Legal matters presented themselves very often and cases were judged. In short any matter anybody cared to present was the subject of such gatherings. They were the heart and soul of the community. A mixture of all of this was written or read from the very same piece of paper or parchment, without any classification according to subject or speciality."[100]

Later jurists wrote proficiently and profusely. The scope covered was immense. But it is as though their contribution is doubly trapped. Firstly, in the language – which great as it is – is not presently the lingua franca of interaction, and secondly, in the attire in which it is shrouded.

The Qur'an requires for knowledge to be explained, spread, and made available (transparency).

"Those who hide the Clear Signs and Guidance We have sent down, after We have made it clear to people in the Book, Allah curses them, and the cursers curse them...." And,

"Allah made a covenant with those given the Book: 'You must make it clear to people and not conceal it.'"[101]

The Prophet ﷺ taught:

Cursed be the knowledge, which is trapped. The best amongst you is the one who learns and teaches.[102]

And:

'teach and do not hide knowledge': 'my heirs are those who teach.'[103]

2.3. Fatawa (fatwa: sing.)

Many Muslim fuqaha, through the ages, have rendered their views into legal responses *(fatawa)*. It is a great source of information, and is a very popular method of education as well as solving problems. Fuqaha often engaged in setting up hypothetical questions, and responded to them.

Fatwa literally means an opinion, but it usually means a considered opinion based on deep knowledge of the subject matter. Gradually it became almost specific for legal matters.

The origins of Islamic *fatwa* are in the Qur'an.[104] It was a favourite method of the Prophet ﷺ of imparting information. Madkour says:

> It is a method of great importance as it deals with queries and questions about actual problems of daily life. It is always about current concerns and it moves with time.[105]

Vardit Rispler-Chaim observes:

> I found, however, that contemporary legal responses *(fatwa)* largely provide the necessary information on most Islamic medical ethics. The *fatwa* literature, a branch of Islamic law, deals with many topics, not only medical. For the study of twentieth century Islam it is almost the only channel through which Muslim scholars' attitudes and legal opinions can be learned.[106]

This may be a consequence of the chronic problem of the lack of formulating general rules of law from the mass of specific solutions to specific questions, "General principles, if evident at all, are found by a consideration of specific solutions to specific questions based upon answers in the texts of the divine law."[107] This was because fuqaha's attitudes and legal opinions had been individualistic for many years, and did not progress into formulated laws. The cause might have been that, it is only recently that some governments proclaiming Islam have come into power again.[108]

A parallel to that may be found in the progression of English 'law.'

> But four centuries before 1470, at the time of the Norman conquest, England had neither judicature nor legislature in any developed sense.

There were decision-making bodies,...but decisions can be made without following or making fixed rules,...Decisions settled the matter in hand and were not expected to do more;...Good decisions are guided by custom and wise counsel as to what is reasonable. Even so, good order, custom and due deliberation are not quite the same as 'law.'

...the learned men among the Britons preferred to pass on their traditions by word of mouth rather than commit them to writing.[109]

The legal responses *(fatawa)* of some fuqaha during different times were rendered into collections. Notable among these were:

(i) *Fatawa* Ahmad ibn-Taymiyya (d.1328 CE) of the Hanbali school. All Sunni Muslims accept Ahmad ibn Hanbal as a great compiler of authentic hadith, but many think that he has no school. He said:

Do not copy me *(la tuqallidni)*, or Malik, or ash-Shafi'i, or ath-Thawri; go to the source whence they got their information.[110]

(ii) The Grand *Fatwas* of Ibn Hajar (d. 974/1568) of the Shafi'i school.[111]

(iii) The Indian collection of the Hanafi school, *al-Fatawa al-Hindiya* (1670), which was commissioned by Sultan Alamgir hence the other name *al-Fatawa al'Alamkiriya*. It was contributed to by a consensus of 500 Hanafi fuqaha, *'Jam'at ash-Shaikh Nizam.'*[112]

The evolution of the Islamic Republic of Iran (Ithna- 'asharite Shi'ites) since 1979 has brought to the front discussion of the *fatwa* of the Supreme Imam and state law.[113]

Recently, the Ayatollah Hussein Ali Muntaziri has explained that the introduction of the status of the Supreme juriconsult *(Imam)* in the constitution of post revolution Iran was his engineering, but that he has changed his mind as regards that status because it has acquired more authority than the advisory guidance role he intended for it.[114]

Many Muslim countries have constituted councils for legal responses *(fatawa)*. There are also non-governmental bodies and universities with collections and facilities for such purposes. *Fatwas*, basically, are academic, religious explanations or opinions. They are made available for individual or personal needs. But the authorities can adopt suitable *fatwas* to make laws.

Relevant fatwas and the laws of some Muslim countries, which have declared Islamic constitutions, are included in the analysis in this thesis.

Islam has made allowance for exercising one's own judgement to find rules that govern actions for which there is no express ruling, *ijtihad*. This has to be guided by faith, good will, knowledge of Shari'ah, and the knowledge of the views of learned persons on the issue in question *(mujtahid fi masa'la)*.[115]

3. Schools of thought in Islamic fiqh and their leaders

Fiqh literally means understanding, knowledge and wisdom. The Prophet ﷺ said,"If Allah wishes someone well, He will make that person learned in matters of religion *(man yuridi'llahu bi hi khairan yufaqqihhu fi 'd-din)*."[116]

It later acquired the meaning of 'Islamic jurisprudence,' and all useful knowledge.[117]

With the spread of Islam, the diversification of life, and the differences in times and locale, different views or judgements started to appear among Muslim fuqaha.

Throughout the Umayyad dynasty (40/661-132/750),[118] and by the early Abbasid era (132/750-750/1258) there had come to be more than thirteen schools of thought. Those of: Abu Hanifah, Malik, ash-Shafi'i, Ibn Hanbal, al-Awza'i, ath-Thawri, al-Layth ibn Sa'd, adh-Dhahiri, al-Bisri, Sufyan ibn 'Uyaynah, Abu Thawr, Ibn Rahwayh, and at-Tabari.[119] These, later, came to be called *madhahib* (sing. *madhhab*).

Many of the fuqaha were dead when schools attributable to them came into being, like Abu Hanifah, al-Layth ibn Sa'd and al-Awza'i; others refused that nomenclature, like Malik, ash-Shafi'i, and Ibn Hanbal.

Even in the same school the views can be very different; for example in the Hanafi school the views of Abu Yusuf, ash-Shaybani, and Zufar did not always coincide neither with those of Abu Hanifah nor with one another. Ash-Shafi'i had two schools of thought, the old (when he was at Kufa – in Iraq) and the new (when he became resident in Cairo – in Egypt).[120] It is their followers who turned the ideas, discussions, and debates into, schools, cults, and sects.

The ideals adhered to by the different schools were sometimes a product of regional customs or traditions. The fuqaha who founded these schools were divided into two main groups, *ahl ar-ra'y* and *ahl al-hadith*.[121] One group resolved to find their own solutions for problems, even if the problem was not covered by the contents of the Qur'an and Sunnah. The only restriction was that their independent reasoning must not contravene the Qur'an or the Sunnah. They became *ahl ar-ra'y* (independent reasoning).

3.1 Sunni schools

Abu Hanifah (80/697-150/767) was the leader of this group. His ideas were influenced by the needs of the urban community of Iraq where he lived. He relied on analogy *(qiyas)*, and further more on equitable preference *(istihsan)*.

He was the master architect of the latter method. He was of Iranian descent, well versed in religions, philosophy, and he was argumentative to begin with, as he described himself. He was a rich silk merchant, familiar with the business world, elegant in dress, knowledgeable and having *taqwa* (fear of Allah). These elements enabled him to excel in finding solutions to problems.[122]

The other group was firmly based on the Qur'an, Sunnah, and hadith *(ahl al-hadith)*. Malik (93/710-179/796) was the founder in the sense that he was one of the first to compile, and authenticate hadith.

Malik was born, raised, and died in Madinah. His ideas were a product of Madinah's rural, non-cluttered atmosphere. Every place had the trace of the Prophet ﷺ – *athar* – every thought echoed his words, and every act had a precedent in his deeds. Yet Malik was a great supporter of *istihsan*, he said, "*Istihsan* is nine-tenths of knowledge."[123] It does not do justice to Malik to deny him his due in being *ahl ar-ra'y* as well.

Ash-Shafi'i (150/767-204/820) was both a student of Malik, and of Abu Hanifah's pupils. He was well travelled: born in Gaza *(Ghazza)*, raised in Makkah, and studied in Madinah. He travelled to Yemen (where his uncle, his father's brother, was a judge) and to Iraq before settling in Egypt where he died. His ideas were a product of his encyclopaedic knowledge of the Qur'an and Sunnah, and his interaction with different cultures and customs of the various communities he contacted. Despite that ash-Shafi'i was very opposed to *istihsan*, he maintained that:

> The rules, *al-ahkam*, should be gleaned from the Qur'an, and Sunnah, or reasoned by analogy *(ijtihad)* based on them. *Istihsan* was not founded on the Qur'an and Sunnah; hence, those who use it have made Shari'ah, which should not be done.[124]

Ash-Shafi'i did not pick one school or another; but he enhanced and crystallised the laws of deduction by analogy *(qiyas)*, then limited its use.

In adherence to these laws he was known to change his views upon the presentation of different and more reliable evidence. In reference to this he said, "If a (hadith) is correct then that is my school *(madhhabi)*."[125]

Coulson said:

> The great jurist Shafi'i, for example, the father of Muslim jurisprudence himself, consistently repudiated the notion of a new school of law based upon passive acceptance of his teaching.[126]

Shafi'i's main theses include the following summary from *Risala*:

> The sum total of what Allah has declared to His creatures in His book, by which He invited them to worship Him in accordance with His prior decision, includes various categories …

> One of these is what He has declared to His creatures by texts [in the Qur'an], …A second category consists of [those duties] the obligation of which He established in His book, but the modes of which He made clear by the tongue of His Prophet, …

> A third category consists of that which the Messenger of Allah established, by example or exhortation, but in regard to which there is no precisely defined rule from Allah [in the Qur'an]…

> A fourth category consists of what Allah commanded His creatures to seek through *ijtihad* (personal reasoning)…(pp. 67-68).

> No one - other than the Prophet - is allowed to make a decision except by *istidlal*…, nor should any man make use of *istihsan* (juristic preference), for to decide by *istihsan* means initiating something himself without basing his decision upon a parallel example (p. 69)…

> No one at all should [give an opinion] on a specific matter saying: It is permitted or prohibited, unless he is certain of [legal] knowledge, and his knowledge must be based on the Qur'an and the Sunnah, or [derived] from *ijma'* (consensus), and *qiyas* (analogy) (p.78).

> Analogy is [the method of reasoning] through which indications are sought from parallel precedents in the Qur'an or the Sunnah – since these are the authoritative sources of the truth - (p. 79).[127]

Ahmad ibn Hanbal (164/780-241/855) was a staunch pillar of hadith. He collected over 40,000 hadith in his book *al-Musnad*.[128]

His school, (Sunnah), was revived by Ahmad ibn Taymiyya (d. 1328

CE), and Muhammad ibn 'Abd al-Wahhab (1703-1765). It is now the school of thought adopted by Saudi Arabia.[129]

Dawud ibn 'Ali al-Asbahani or al-Asfahani (200/816-270/886) of Iraq was an avowed critic of *qiyas*. He based his doctrine on strictly adhering to the literal and apparent meaning of the words of the Qur'an and Sunnah; so much so that his doctrine of favouring what is apparent, "*adh-Dhahiri*" (literalist) became the name by which his school became known. Although extinct now, the school is an interesting source of dogmatic views.

Coulson said:

> By the end of the ninth century the sharp conflicts of principle which ash-Shafi'i's thesis had engendered had largely died away, and the place of the Sunnah or practice of the Prophet in Muslim jurisprudence was established. On the one hand extremist support for the Traditions was tempered by the recognition that, in the elaboration of the law, it was necessary in practice to use human reason in the shape of analogical deduction *(qiyas)*. (This at least, was the case with the Hanbali school; the Zahiris adhered rigidly to their original principles, and as a result became extinct in the Middle Ages.) On the other hand the established schools, having succeeded in formally justifying their established doctrine, were now quite prepared to acknowledge, as a matter of principle, the authority of the Traditions.

This development, initiated by ash-Shafi'i, determined the whole future course of Islamic law.[130]

But there was Islamic law and legal literature *before* the major change of methodology propounded by al-Shafi'i,...

As Brunschvig suggested as long ago as 1950...'If we could free ourselves from the hold of al-Shafi'i, whose ingenious synthesis has falsified our perspectives for a long time indeed...we would perhaps see the origins of fiqh with new eyes.'[131]

And the perspective of some of his devoted students was not falsified. Ahmad ibn Hanbal (d. 855 CE) admired his intellectual juristic abilities but had his reservations about *riwayatihi* (his narrations).[132]

"Many others shared Ibn Hanbal's views. Shafi'i's school of thought was not a great success in Iraq, hence his journey to Egypt. But it remains a fact that he was the generator of Islamic jurisprudence, as it was mentioned by al-Fakhr ar-Razi: *'assala al-usul, wa qa'ada al-al-qawa'id; wa as-sabqu liman sabaq* – He was the first to lay down the foundations and erect the pillars of jurisprudence: the first always leads'."[133]

Several other schools of thought were founded based on local traditions and teachings at different times. The ideals of Abu Hanifah changed in the hands of his followers; Abu Yusuf, Muhammad al-Hassan ash-Shaybani, and Zufar, all of whom, sometimes, held different views from him and from one another.

Abu Yusuf who became chief justice of the Islamic domain, in the era of Caliph al-Hadi and throughout the reign of Harun ar-Rasheed (166-182 AH) was responsible for 'Abu-Hanifa's school' coming to dominate the courts in the Islamic world. But at the same time the school began to embrace the hadith and Sunnah more than it did under Abu Hanifah. Amin states,

> Although the views of Abu Hanifah, sometimes philosophical, influenced others, it was his students, mainly Abu Yusuf and Shaybani, who brought more hadith to influence their school. The influence became so great that, in the end, *all* the schools became similar to one another.[134]

Jackson notes that,

> For, whereas in theory all of the Sunni schools were recognized as equally authoritative,…they were not all equidistant from the source of power…[135]

But at any time, anywhere, some persons, even in the same cabinet, are closer to the source of power than others.

3.2. Kharijite and Shi'ite schools [136]

The Kharijites were initially supporters of 'Ali ibn Abi-Talib. They left him after the battle of Siffin, which was fought against Mu'awiyyah ibn Abi Sufyan (37/657). *Kharijite* is derived from the word to leave *(kharaja)*. They may be viewed as political dissidents. "Presently there are some of them as *Ibadia* in *al-Maghrib* (West part of North Africa) who are not fanatical about their views of others."[137]

Mu'amar wrote about *Ibadia* in Libya, Tunisia, and particularly in Algeria (*al-Maghrib al-Awsat*).[138]

Some of those who remained with 'Ali, after the Kharijites, constituted the *Shi'ites* (the partisans).[139] They later became divided according to the names of descendants of the Prophet ﷺ, through 'Ali, whom they followed. Those who followed Zayd ibn 'Ali ibn al-Hussein ibn 'Ali ibn Abi Talib became Zaydi Shi'ites *(Zaydites)*. Zayd directed his followers to respect the companions of the Prophet ﷺ including Abu

Bakr and 'Umar, but they all loved 'Ali more. There is very little difference between them and the *Sunnis.* Most of the Zaydi Shi'ites are in Yemen.

The main group of the Shi'ites, who dominate about one fifth of the Islamic world, are the Imami Shi'ite *(Ja'fari).* They have a succession of twelve imams, descendants of 'Ali ibn Abi Talib, through Ja'far as-Sadiq and his son Musa al-Kazim down to the twelfth imam al-Mahdi who went into *ghayba* (disappearance) in 874 CE; and to them he will reappear as the 'awaited Mahdi.' Hence, the name the 'twelvers,' *ithna-asharites.*[140]

Another smaller division of Shi'ites followed the *imams* who descended from the other son of Ja'far as-Sadiq, Ismail. The Ismaili Shi'ites ruled North Africa, Egypt, ash-Sham, and Hijaz between 909 and 1171 CE, as the Fatimids.

Through a continuum of twenty-two *imams,* the *Imam* Caliph al-Mustansir billah, in 1094 CE, was succeeded by his two sons: Must'ali billah, and Nizar. The *imam* of the Must'ali branch also went into *ghayba.* The descendants of the Nizar branch retain their *imamate,* as the Agha Khan family of today.

The sources for the Shi'ites are the Qur'an, Sunnah,[141] consensus, and *'aql* (intellect). But for them, the Sunnah, and consensus *(ijma)* must have been narrated or relayed through members of the Prophet's household *(ahl al-bayt).* They do not accept analogy *(qiyas),* just like the Dhahiris *(Sunni).* Exercising judgement, *ijtihad,* is the prerogative of the *Imam.*[142]

Coulson observes:

> Nevertheless it is difficult to agree with the eminent authority (Schacht) that the Kharijite and Shi'ite systems "do not differ from the doctrines of the Sunnite Schools of law more widely than these last differ from one another."
>
> For while this is generally true of Kharijite law, Shi'ite law in its final form possesses certain distinctive characteristics, which stand in sharp contrast to, the principles recognised by the Sunnite system as a whole.[143]

Muhammad al-Ghazali, (d. 1996 CE), the Egyptian jurist, said:

> The sources of Islamic rulings, *ahkam,* for Imami Shi'ites are the Qur'an, the Prophetic Sunnah, the consensus, and human intellect. The Prophetic Sunnah must have been delivered by one of the descendants of the Prophet ﷺ, from his household *(ahl-al-bayt).* Consensus *(ijma')* is likewise, the preserve of the descendants of the Prophet ﷺ. They refute

deduction by analogy, *qiyas*; and exercising ones' own judgement is the prerogative of their leaders, *the imams*. (quoting Muhammad Jawwad Mughniyah, and Muhammad Taji al-Qummi, from their book, *Ma'a ash-Shi'a al-Imamia*). [144]

Abu Hanifah, the prolific generator of Islamic fiqh, who is a *Sunni* scholar, was a student of Zayd ibn 'Ali Zayn al-'Abidin for two years. He also communicated with Muhammad al-Baqir ibn 'Ali Zayn al-'Abidin and his son Ja'far as-Sadiq;[145] all of whom are highly respected by Shi'ite and Sunni groups.

The vast contribution of the majority of Muslim fuqaha was not intended for the creation of schools. Abu Hanifah's school appeared after his death when Abu Yusuf, his foremost understudy, became chief justice.[146] Malik refused Harun ar-Rasheed's request for his book *al-Muwatta'* to be the only reference for *al-ahkam*. Ash-Shafi'i dealt with issues differently when he was in Iraq and when he settled in Egypt. Ahmad ibn Hanbal's contribution was to examine about 500,000 sayings attributed to the Prophet ﷺ and select about 30,000 of them for his *Musnad*, according to the reliability of the transmitter or reference (*musnad* = with a full *isnad*). Some authors have quoted 40,000, others 80,000; the variation can be accounted for by the repetition of some hadith, as the same hadith may have more than one reliable source.

None of them was anxious to carve a school for his ideas. Ash-Shawkani, summarises the critique of the most prominent fuqaha of their own contributions: [147]

"Abu Hanifah said:

"'This is what I was able to do. Should someone else produce a better treatise, he should be followed.' When he was asked whether what he was saying was correct? He responded, 'I do not know, it could be otherwise.'

"Malik said:

"'Be critical of my deductions; adopt that which agrees with the Qur'an and the Sunnah only.'

"Ash-Shafi'i told his follower, ar-Rabi':

"'Do not follow what I say without examination; it is your responsibility and duty to be critical of what you hear. If something contrary to what I have been teaching is proven to be correct then it should be followed, for that would be my way *(madhhabi)*: (my school).'

"Ahmad ibn Hanbal said to his followers:

"'Do not follow Malik, or me or ash-Shafi'i, or ath-Thawri; go to the source whence they got their information.'"

> How strange that in every special case
> one praises one's own way!
> If Islam means 'surrender to God's will'
> it's in Islam that we all live and die.
> *(Johan Wolfgang von Goethe)*[148]

4. In search of common ground for the laws

At the outset it must be pointed out that legislation in Islam is guided by "the five cardinal rules":[149]

(1) Intent is all-important in actions, based on the Prophet's ﷺ saying:

> The reward of deeds depends upon the intentions and every person will get the reward according to what he has intended.[150]

(2) Do no harm: harm must be removed or compensated.[151]

(3) The doctrine of legal presumption of continuance,[152] based on the hadith, "The plaintiff is to produce evidence, or else denial on oath is an accepted rebuttal by the defendant *(shahidak aw yaminuhu).*"[153] An important question attached to it is, "What is to be assumed when there is no rule? Is the matter in question allowed or prohibited? The leaning may be towards it being allowed if there is no clear prohibition."[154]

(4) Hardship calls for a license *(al-mashaqqah tajlibu at-tayseer).*[155]

A corollary of which is, "Need or necessity makes for allowing what is prohibited" *(ad-darurat tubihu al-mahzurat).*[156]

(5) Custom is the rule (in the absence of a ruling) *(al-'adah muhkamah).*[157]

These cardinal rules lead fuqaha to think of Islamic fiqh as the subject of five conceptions: first, few obligations *(takalif)*; second, gradualism in the promulgation of laws, to take into account all the circumstances of a situation; third, making the burden lighter when making and executing laws; fourth, hardship is avoided, and necessity is taken into account; and fifth, justice and equality must prevail.[158] **"Allah desires ease for you;"**[159] **"Allah desires to make things lighter for you. Man was created weak;"**[160] **"He has selected you and not placed any constraint upon you in the deen; the religion** of your forefather Ibrahim."[161] "We have not omitted anything from the Book;"[162] "Your Lord does not forget."[163]

It may be opportune at this juncture to point out that the whole message of Islam is to inform, and spread the word. Islam is for everyone, everywhere and for all times.[164] Islamic law is living, dynamic, and relevant. *Ijtihad* is an integral part of Islamic fiqh.[165] That some opted not to do so, at a certain period and for specific reasons *(qafl bab al-ijtihad)* remains a form of *ijtihad* in itself; open to question and open to reversal. It is non-Islamic to stop thinking about solutions, or responses to developments or new occurrences. Events have overtaken such concepts.[166] The tools of research, methods of communication, and retrieval of information have advanced.

Finding the sacred rule of Shari'ah, for every act, is the objective of every Muslim. If it is spelled out in the Qur'an or in the teachings or commands of the Prophet ﷺ then the goal is accomplished. Otherwise it may be found in the consensus of learned persons *(ijma')*, or in analogy *(qiyas)*; both based on the Qur'an and Sunnah.

It is when there is no express rule, no consensus, and no model for analogy that the methodology of finding an answer is called into action. The corner-stone of this is not to contravene the stipulations of the Qur'an and Sunnah. A common denominator, in the views of fuqaha, is aimed for. The dogmas of splinter groups and cults are not helpful in working for consensus *(ijma')*.

The Prophet ﷺ has delivered the *completed* message of Islam embodying the Shari'ah before these groups appeared. If none is found, a personal view is advanced. This may be helpful in individual situations. But to make laws, a consensus must be reached *(ijma')*.

> The whole process of Muslim fiqh, from the definition of the sources of law to the derivation of substantive rules therefrom, was a speculative effort of the human intellect. And it was the *ijma,'* and the *ijma'* alone, which gave the necessary authority to this process…But the conclusion that an individual jurist might reach, in terms of a substantive doctrine derived from the recognised sources, was in the nature of a conjecture. Whether he was deciding upon the precise meaning of a Qur'anic text or resolving a novel problem, his conclusion could only amount to a tentative, or probable, statement of the divine law. But where the rule concerned was the subject of a general consensus, then its status was transformed into that of a certain and inconvertible statement of the divine law; for the consensus was infallible.[167]

Not divine law, but Islamic jurisprudence perhaps. It may be opportune to repeat what had been quoted before:

> A Qur'anic injunction is not at the disposition of lawmakers and cannot be disposed of, even by consensus.[168]

This work is not concerned with the making of divine law. It is concerned with finding the rulings of the divine law on matters presented. If such a rule does not exist, then the objective is to suggest one that does not contravene either the Qur'an or the Sunnah. When such rules have been found it is assumed that, the ones to be adopted would follow due process of law, involving the relevant form of *ijma'* (consensus), to be promulgated.

There is a strong desire to establish religion-friendly constitutions in many states, including some non-Muslim ones. There is room for those versed in a field to contribute: especially if it leads to better understanding amongst communities across nation-state borders, and arriving at comparable rules that govern fields of shared interest, without clashing with their beliefs.

Islamic fiqh needs to legislate for present day concerns. How can this be done? Fuqaha's law? or codified Islamic fiqh?

I have intentionally avoided the term "codified *Shari'ah*" because of the misunderstanding it may cause. It is important to reiterate that *Shari'ah* is taken to mean 'Allah-given law': it is already there in the Qur'an and the authentic Sunnah. Some of it is spelt out; qualified fuqaha, from the text of Qur'an and Sunnah, can deduce other rules of Shari'ah.[169]

Their contribution can be a part of Islamic fiqh, or law, or a code. All of which can be challenged or changed by other fuqaha. There is no one simple answer, as opposed to a multifaceted approach, to questions like "the Shari'ah: a methodology or a body of substantive rules?"[170]

Joseph Schacht said:

> Islamic law, being a doctrine and a method rather than a code is by its nature incompatible with being codified, and every codification must subtly distort it.[171]

Anderson said:

> ...the Shari'ah - as an uncodified, divine law, which had an authority, inherent in itself, over every Muslim from Caliph to slave...[172]

The Shari'ah, as embodied in the Qur'an and Sunnah, on occasions, clearly spells out certain transgressions and stipulates their punishment; examples of which are theft, accusation (*qadhf*) of illicit sexual intercourse, adultery and fornication.[173] But it also describes itself as "a guide, a light, and a mercy."[174] The Shari'ah is not the promulgation of rules under the hegemony of self-appointed national dictators, even when their policies are called *siyasah shar'iyyah*,[175] or under foreign yoke.

It is stated in the Qur'an that, as regards *al-ahkam* (rulings), that nothing is omitted,[176] what is forbidden is detailed,[177] all things are explained,[178] the message is completed and perfected,[179] *Shari'ah* is for everyone, everywhere, and for *all* times.[180] Fuqaha are honoured in Islam; they are considered "the heirs and successors to the prophets."[181] "The ink that flows from their pens is as valuable as the blood of the martyrs."[182]

George Makdisi observes:

> For nowhere in the world of the Middle Ages did this phenomenon first come into being except in classical Islam, in the sole field of the religious law. The doctorate, as just described, was that of the Muslim doctor of the law, the jurisconsult, called *faqih, mujtahid*, and *mufti*…As a master-jurisconsult,…the doctor had the authority to profess opinions regarding the law, based on his own personal research. There was no higher authority, religious or secular, which could force him to submit his opinions for approval before professing them (p. 119)

> …the licence to teach was the product of an individualistic system;…It was specifically the product of a guild…whose authority once granted, was independent of all outside forces, and above which was no other authority. Consequently, it could not have developed in Christianity with its ecclesiastical hierarchy, or in Judaism where the higher authority of the Gaon was recognised, (p. 120)

> Nor could the doctorate, as described, have originated in Shi'ite Islam, which may be described as a "church of authority" in contrast to Sunni Islam, a "church of consensus" (p. 121).[183]

Why give up such freedom and latitude, of being able to ask questions and pose problems on the one hand, and being able to answer, or respond, or make suitable laws that suit the circumstances on the other?

This liberty should be guarded as one of the foremost of human rights. This does not preclude the formulation of ordinances, laws, charters, and whatever is necessary in the machinations of an up-to-date community.

About Islamic Fiqh (Jurisprudence)

Playing up to temporal rulers to codify material, outside the realm of the consensus or parliament-like organs, is un-Islamic. The Qur'an stipulates that the believers are those who conduct their affairs by mutual consultation *(wa amruhum shura baynahum)*.[184]

Asad,[185] translated the ayah thus:

"Their [the Believers'] communal business *(amr)* is to be [transacted in] consultation among themselves,"

and expounded:

This *nass* injunction must be regarded as the fundamental, operative clause of all Islamic thought relating to state craft. It is so comprehensive that it reaches out into almost every department of political life, and it is so self-expressive and unequivocal that no attempt at arbitrary interpretation can change its purport…It makes the transaction of all political business not only consequent upon, but synonymous with, consultation: which means that the legislative powers of the state must be vested in an assembly chosen by the community especially for this purpose.

Arguments to the contrary, invoking the "general duty owed by citizens to obey those in power and what the latter proclaim as law,"[186] must receive careful consideration, as they are the cause of great misunderstanding and confusion. These arguments stem from misinterpreting or misreading, ayah fifty-eight of surah four in the Qur'an:

You who have iman! obey Allah and obey the Messenger and those in command among you. If you have a dispute about something, refer it back to Allah and the Messenger, if you have iman in Allah and the Last Day. That is the best thing to do and gives the best result.[187]

But the Qur'an, as any document, must be taken as a whole. The Qur'an anticipated this:

Do you, then, believe in one part of the Book and reject the other? What repayment will there be for any of you who do that except disgrace in the dunya? And on the Day of Rising, they will be returned to the harshest of punishments. Allah is not unaware of what you do.[188]

The Qur'an says, "you are, 'unbelievers,' 'wrongdoers,' and 'rebels'[189]…if you do not rule yourselves according to what is *detailed* therein.[190]

It removes any pretext for confusion by stating, **"Whoever obeys the Messenger has obeyed Allah."**[191] That means that any message from the Prophet ﷺ was Allah's revealed orders.

The revelation has finished with the death of the Prophet ﷺ, (632 CE), and no further commands will come. Qadri explains:

> God is God and man is man. The Prophet ﷺ was a bearer of Revelations, which terminated with the Prophet's passing away. The Shari'ah laws, which he left behind, are the laws of Allah. They are not God. In contrast to the Western concept of "theocracy" Islam is a revolt against all anthropormorphic implications in the realm of faith. With the Muslim concept, religion is not entirely a private affair between man and God. Nevertheless, with privacy, the individual is ruled by a code of law, which is binding on all, without establishing any kind of sanctity in a man or a class of men.[192]

Caliph Abu Bakr as-Siddiq, in his acceptance speech said:

> O people! I have been made the successor to the Prophet ﷺ. I am not the best of you; obey me if I am obedient to Allah in my actions: if not, do not obey me.[193]

The "general duty owed by citizens to obey those in power, and what the latter proclaim as law" also includes in modern day terminology as obeying everyday laws: Highway Code, traffic ordinances, and school regulations, etc.

There is the responsibility of the community to mend the ways of the errant: be they rulers or ruled. The Qur'an orders:

Let there be a community among you who call to the good, and enjoin the right, and forbid the wrong. They are the ones who have success.[194]

The Prophet ﷺ said:

The highest kind of *jihad* is to speak up for truth in the face of a ruler who deviates from the right path *(sultan jai'r)*.[195]

And:

If any of you sees something evil, he should set it right by his hand; if he is unable to do so then by his tongue; and if he is unable to do even that, then within his heart - but this is the weakest form of faith.[196]

 And:

If people see a wrongdoer but do not stay his hand, it is most likely that Allah will encompass them all with His punishment.[197]

The Qur'an praises those, "who conduct their affairs by mutual consultation," *"amruhum shura baynahum."*[198]

The Qur'an, also, says, **"You are not in control of them,"** [199] and points out that, **"We have appointed a law and a practice for every** one of you."[200] But the verse actually says, *"li kullin ja'alna minkum shir'atan wa minhaja,"* which may be translated into, "For each We have ordained, *from within yourselves*, a law and a way."

That 'way' includes a consideration of the others' viewpoint, as there is no compulsion in deen – life-transaction.[201] Tolerance is advocated, **"We have appointed a law and a practice for every one of you. Had Allah willed, He would have made you a single community"**;[202] consequently arguments should be conducted with decency and grace, **"Only argue with the People of the Book in the kindest way."**[203] The Qur'an mentions the People of the Book (Scripture) in this ayah *(ahl al-kitab)*; but the Prophet ﷺ on coming in contact with the Zoroastrians of Bahrain in the year 631 CE, asked for them to be treated like 'People of the Book, because they were likewise,' *(sunnu bihim sunnata ahl al-kitab, li annahum fi ma'nahum)*.[204]

Consequently when 'Umar ibn al-Khattab conquered Iran in 637-641 CE, he decreed that its people, the Zoroastrians, would be treated as *ahl-al-kitab*, when 'Abd ar-Rahman ibn 'Awf told him that he had actually heard the Prophet ﷺ say, "Treat them as *ahl-al-kitab*."[205]

Jews, Christians, Zoroastrians, and Sabians should not be killed or converted by force,…and when, in the year 712, Muhammad ibn al-Qasim conquered the lower Indus Valley he extended the same treatment to Hindus and Buddhists.[206]

The first to suggest codifying the laws in a Muslim community was Ibn al-Muqaffa' (724-759 CE) to the Abbasid Caliph al-Mansur.[207] Malik was asked for *al-Muwatta'* to be the sole source of Islamic law; but he declined the offer,[208] and he quoted the Prophet ﷺ:

> The differences of opinion among the learned within my community are [a sign of] Allah's mercy.[209]

It is noteworthy that Ibn al-Muqaffa' was later killed and burnt beyond recognition by Sufyan ibn Mu'awiyyah on the instigation of Caliph al-Mansur when they differed politically.[210]

Malik was incarcerated and beaten up on the order of, the same, al-Mansur because he said, "divorce, pronounced under duress is not operative, and is inconsequential." It was taken analogously to mean that people should not be forced to 'elect' a person, i.e. that allegiance pledged under coercion is not legally binding.[211]

It is stated in Jackson that:

> In a nation-state, the state is itself the only true repository of legal authority, …

This applies a bit less of course to Civil Law countries where private legal scholars or jurists have a significantly greater impact on the substance of the law than they do in the Common Law tradition. But even here it has been observed that "Unless some jurists are officially 'licensed' to give particularly authoritative opinions, as seems to have happened in the early Roman Empire, no opinion of an individual jurist *qua* jurist can be binding." As such, the authority to determine what is and what is not legally binding remains the exclusive preserve of the state...By contrast, legal authority, or the ability to declare what is and what is not law, is not, in the tradition of classical Islamic law, the exclusive preserve of the state.[212]

But there is nothing in *Shari'ah* to bar the formulation of 'laws' according to the wish of the people, concerning their affairs. Islamic fiqh remains a field for the fuqaha, for all times. It should not be Fuqaha's law versus Codified law. It is Fuqaha's law: which may be codified according to 'due process of law'; for each locale, time, and duration of a session. In such a way it is always open for debate, subject to amendment, or change.

Islamic fiqh does not condone the introduction of an 'Islamic law,' or 'Islamisation of laws,' to suit the whims of a self-appointed ruler.[213] The Qur'an has vested that authority equally in every one, and for the benefit of all.[214] The only proviso is that the laws should not contravene *Shari'ah*.

Fuqaha or *muftis* are free to give their views on any matter. In matters of religious observance *('ibadat)*, every individual is free to adopt the *fatwa*, which appeals to his conscience. But it should still be possible for the state, through the will of the people, and suitable channels, to have a binding system for "every legislative, interpretative and executive function."[215]

Professor Anderson observed:

> Always and everywhere, the law has constituted the basic science of Islam; but it has remained throughout a lawyer's law, finding its most authoritative expression in the compendia of jurists, rather than a judge's law, resting on a system of case law or the principle of *stare decisis*.[216]

And in the footnote, he quoted the guiding letter of Caliph 'Umar ibn al-Khattab to the qadi Abu Musa al-Ash'ari, telling him:

> "If you have given a judgement yesterday and today you may arrive at a correct opinion upon rethinking, you must not feel prevented from retracting your first judgement, because justice is primeval, and it is

About Islamic Fiqh (Jurisprudence)   51

better to retract than continue in error." (Another part of the letter was quoted for *qiyas* at p.44).

But this can be interpreted as a way to judicial review, and at the same time giving some permanence to adjudicated matters. And as far as precedents are concerned the letter, in a following sentence, instructs, "Know the similitude and weigh the issues accordingly."[217]

In as much as, "whatever may have been the position in practice over recent years, the trend towards a reassertion (of Shari'ah) is quite apparent,"[218] it may be stated that Muslim physicians had no misgivings adopting the Hippocratic Oath when they ranked supreme in the profession. They literally took the oath then. Ibn Abi Usaybia (d. 668/1267) had an Arabic translation of the Hippocratic Oath in his book, *'Uyun al-Anba' fi Tabaqat al-Atibba.'*[219]

And as far as the present:

> Despite the unique problems, which the Muslim doctor and patient may encounter in their mutual search for a cure, the First International Conference on Islamic Medicine (held in Kuwait January 1981) drew up the *Islamic Code of Medical Ethics*, which surprisingly included *no* clause, which is solely Islamic.[220]

But one may argue that it is Islamic so long as there is no violation of the Qur'an and Sunnah,[221] and that legislation is possible and permissible within Islamic doctrine as long as it takes into account Islamic prohibitions and considerations.

Notes

1. Ballantyne, "A Reassertion Of The Shari'ah:" in Heer, (ed.), *Islamic Law*, 1990:151, and 159.
2. Q. 42:13, and Q. 87:18-19 (tr. Bewley).
3. Q. 4:123-124; 14:51; 20:15; 34:28.
4. Q. 2:256, **"There is no compulsion where the deen is concerned"** (tr. Bewley); Q. 60:8, **"Allah does not forbid you from being good to those who have not fought you in the deen or driven you from your homes, or from being just towards them. Allah loves those who are just."** (tr. Bewley); and for the rule, "they have the same rights and obligations as us," see Sabiq, *Fiqh us Sunnah*, 1995, vol. 3:50 (*'aqd adh-dhima,*'Ali ibn Abi Talib said, their blood and their moneys are like our blood and moneys, on that basis fuqaha have adopted the rule, "*lahum ma lana, wa 'alaihim ma 'alaina*").
5. English Law began with the unification of local customs to form the common law. The formulation of the common law took place when there were few statutes or other forms of written law...It has been developed down to the present day by judges' decisions (the doctrine of precedent), and Acts of Parliament to make Statute law (legislation). In Marsh & Soulsby, 1995:5, and 8.
"When, in 1470, an English sergeant-at-law maintained that the common law had been in existence since the creation of the world, it is not improbable that he believed it literally. There was even a veneer of truth upon the notion, inasmuch as English law represented an unbroken development from prehistoric time. There had been no conscious act of creation or adoption." In Baker, *An Introduction to English Legal History*, 1990:1.
6. Madkour, *al-Madkhal lil Fiqh al-Islami*, (1386/1966), pp. 199-231, and 232-253. {Henceafter, Madkour, *al-Madkhal*, 1966}.
7. Abu Zahra, *Usul al-Fiqh*, 1958, pp. 57-59. {Henceafter, Abu Zahra, *Usul*, 1958}.
8. Doi, *Shariah:* 1984, pp. 21-63, and 64-84; see also Ramadan, *Islamic Law*, pp. 33-36; and Mayer, 'The Shari'ah:' in Heer, (ed.), *Islamic Law*, 1990:177-198.
9. Ramadan, *Islamic Law*, p. 33.
10. Rida, (ed.), *Majmou'at al-Hadith an-Najdia:* (1383 AH), pp. 235-236; also in *Sunan Ibn Majah*, 1952, vol. 1:21.
11. Ash-Shafi'i, *al-Umm*, 1993, vol. 7:492-494.
12. Ghazali, (d. 1111CE) *al-Mustasfa* 1906, vol. 1:100-101.
13. Shahrastani, (d.548/1153), *al-Milal wa'n-Nihal*, 1968, vol. 2:3-4.

14. Ash-Shafi'i, *al-Umm*, 1993, vol. 7:492-494; Doi, 1984:64; Ramadan, *Islamic Law*, 1970:33; Madkour, *al-Madkhal*, 1966:90, and 196; Abu Zahra, *Usul*, 1958:14.
15. Edge, Ian, (ed.), *Islamic Law*, 1996: xvi-xvii.
16. Q. 16:89.
17. Q. 4:83; 16:43; 29:43; 30:22; 35:28.
18. Abu Zahra, *Usul*, 1958:303, Madkour, *al-Madkhal*, 1966:47-58.
19. Coulson, N. J., *A History of Islamic Law*, (Reprint 1994), p. 12. {Henceafter, Coulson, *A History*, 1994}.
20. Hitti, *Islam*, 1970:42.
21. Q. 36:1; and Q. 80:1-42 et. al.
22. Q. 2:282,"transactions." Goitein, S. D.,"The Birth-Hour Of Muslim Law?" *The Muslim World*, vol. 50, 1 (1960), p. 24 refers to the same argument about different lengths of verses.
23. Q. 3:104, 3:110, 3:114, 7:157, 9:71, 9:112, 22:41, 31:27, et. al.
24. Guillaume, Alfred, *Islam*, 1973:73.
    (Guillaume, Alfred, was Head of the Department of Near and Middle East in S.O.A.S., and Professor of Arabic in the University of London. (d. 1965)).
25. Madkour, *al-Madkhal*, 1966:168,"The Prophet ﷺ chose some of his companions to write the Qur'an as it was revealed to him. Amongst them were: Zayd ibn Thabit,'Ali ibn Abi Talib,'Uthman ibn 'Affan, Ibn Mas'ud, Anas ibn Malik, Ubayy ibn Ka'b, Mu'awiyyah ibn Abi Sufyan, az-Zubayr ibn al-'Awwam,'Abdullah ibn al-Arqam, Ibn Rawahah, and others."
26. Q. 5:3; 6:38; 6:111 et. al.
27. Q. 15:9, (tr. Bewley).
28. Q. 41:41, (tr. Bewley).
29. Q. 2:105, (tr. Bewley).
30. Q. 42:11, (tr. Bewley).
31. Q. 3:103-104; Q. 3:110; et. al.
32. Q. 2:115 and 144 (tr. Bewley).
33. Q.2: 228, Q.33: 49, and Q.65: 4 (tr. Bewley).
34. Q. 4: 15, 16, and Q. 24:2 (tr. Bewley).
35. Abu Zahra, *Usul*, 1958:148.
    See Dutton, *The Origins of Islamic Law*, 1999:121-125, for *Naskh* (Abrogation), and *Takhsis* (making an exception); and 125-130 for *Asbab al-nuzul* (the knowledge of when particular parts or ayat of the Qur'an had been revealed).
36. Jakni, *Bukhari and Muslim*, 1967, vol. 2:28; also in Hakim, *al-Mustadrak*, (1334 AH), vol. 1:376.
37. Q. 102:1-2.
38. Ash-Shafi'i, *al-Umm*, 1993, vol. 7:494.
39. Ash-Shafi'i, *Risala*, (tr. Khadduri), 1987:180.

40 As-Salih, Sobhi, *'Ulum al-Hadith wa Mustalahu*, 1984:296, "Mutraf ibn 'Abdullah ibn ash-Shakheer (d. 87 AH) was a trusted *(thiqa)* Basran faqih."

41 Banna, (al-Sa'ati), *al-Fath al-Rabani li Musnad Ahmad*, (1396 AH), vol. 1:191-192; and *Sunan Ibn Majah*, 1952, vol. 1:6-7.

42 Shahawi, *Mustalah al-Hadith*, 1966:117-119, see also As-Salih, *'Ulum al-Hadith*, 1984:19-30.

43 Shahawi, *Mustalah al-Hadith*, 1966:55.

44 Shahawi, *Mustalah al-Hadith*, 1966:52.

45 Ibn al-Sallah, *'Ulum al-Hadith*, 1998:20.

46 Burton, *An Introduction to the hadith*, 1994: xvi.

47 Coulson, *A History*, (Reprinted), 1994:64-65. See Dutton, *The Origins of Islamic Law*, 1999:2-3, concerning *'Madinan 'Amal,'* (implementation of the Prophet's ﷺ teachings).

48 Schacht, Joseph, *An Introduction to Islamic Law*, (First Published OUP, 1964), Reprinted, 1966, 1971:1.

49 Ash-Shafi'i, *al-Umm*, 1993 vol. 7:494.

50 Al-'Asqalani, *Fath al-Bari al-Bukhari*, 1988, vol. Introduction *(al-Muqadima)*, p. 4.

51 Amin, *Doha al-Islam*, 1938, vol. 2:106, "Ummayad era 41-132 AH., Abbasid era 132-656 AH."

52 Abu Zahra, *Malik:* 1964:214, and p. 210.

53 Abu Zahra, *Malik,* 1964:214-217; and Malik, *al-Muwatta,'* Saad, 1983, pp. 7-10.

54 Shahawi, *Mustalah al-Hadith,* 1966:123-125, and 139, "One, Shu'bah, was asked why he did not consider the narrative of a certain person? He replied, 'I saw him on the back of a galloping mule' ." For more on *isnad* see ash-Shafi'i, *al-Umm*, 1993, vol. 7:495-496.

55 See p. 2, and p. 7, of this thesis and Appendices, A.1, A.2, and A.3.

56 Dutton, The *Origins of Islamic Law*, 1999:1-3.

57 Madkour, *al-Madkhal*, 1966:177, Madkour named the six books, but he quoted ash-Shafi'i as saying, "No book on earth is more correct than Malik's *al-Muwatta,'* except for the Qur'an."

58 Madkour, *al-Madkhal*, 1966:158; Coulson, *A History*, 1994:71, said, "*Musnad* (has) more than 80,000 *hadiths*," Abu Zahra, *Ibn Hanbal*, 1947:170, said: "Abdullah heard 30 000 *hadith*, and 80 000 *tafsirs*."

59 Abu Zahra, *Ibn Hanbal*, 1947:33, and 170. (Reprinted 1981).

60 Shahawi, *Mustalah al-Hadith*, 1966:16; (in this page Shahawi said Ibn 'Umr instead of Ibn 'Umar; but he has it correct on page 244; this tallies with common knowledge and also in Malik, *al-Muwatta,'* 1983:940.

61 *Sahih Ibn Hibban*, 1952, pp. 5-7, and 9, and 11.

62 Ash-Shafi'i, *Risala*, (tr. Khadduri), 1987:23.

[63] Ash-Shafi'i, *Risala*, (tr. Khadduri), 1987:252.
[64] Madkour, *al-Madkhal*, 1966:91.
[65] Ash-Shafi'i, *al-Umm*, 1993, vol. 7:494.
[66] Edge, Ian, (ed.), *Islamic Law*, 1996:xviii-xix.
[67] Ash-Shafi'i, *al-Umm*, 1993, vol. 7:492; Ghazali, *al-Mustasfa*, (1322 AH.), vol. 1:100.
[68] Abu Zahra, *Usul*, 1958:165-166. See Coulson, *Conflicts*, 1969:23.
[69] Hofmann, *Islam 2000*, 1996:50.
[70] Madkour, *al-Madkhal*, 1966:78-79
[71] Madkour, *al-Madkhal*, 1966:218.
[72] Madkour, *al-Madkhal*, 1966:72-73.
[73] Coulson, *A History*, (Reprinted), 1994:237.
[74] Doi, *The Shari'ah*, 1984:81.
[75] Coulson, *A History*, (Reprinted) 1994:19.
[76] Hofmann, Murad, *Islam: The Alternative*, 1993:121.
[77] Ghazali, *al-Mustasfa*, 1935, vol. 1:139.
[78] Shatibi, *al-Muwafaqat*, 1975, vol. 2:8-11, at p. 10.
[79] Q. 38:44. (The story of the prophet Ayyub (Job). He was angry with his wife and promised Allah that he would lash her one hundred lashes. When he came to, he was sad that he made such a promise. Allah revealed to him that he should take a bunch of one hundred reeds and strike but once). In, *Tafsir al-Imam at-Tabari*, of Surah 38 *(Sad)* ayah44, and Abdullah Yusuf'Ali's fn. 4202, commenting on the verse: 1989.
[80] *Sunan Ibn Majah*, 1953, vol. 2:859.
[81] Mayer,"The Shari'ah:"in: Heer, (ed.), *Islamic Law*, 1990:177-198, at p. 184.
[82] Jakni, *Bukhari and Muslim*, 1967, vol. 5:390.
[83] Ibn al-Qayyim, *Zad al-Ma'ad* ,1979, vol. 3, pp. 175, 193, and 271; and in Madkour, *al-Madkhal*, 1966:67.
[84] *Sunan Abi Dawud*, 1973, vol. 4:18-19; Madkour, *al-Madkhal*, 1966:68, and 333; Doi, *The Shari'ah*, 1984:71.
[85] Ibn Hazm az-Zahiri, *al-Muhalla*, (1347 AH), vol. 1:55-59.
[86] Madkour, *al-Madkhal*, 1966, pp. 333, and 338 where he responds to Goldziher's viewpoint.
[87] *Sunan Abi Dawud*, 1973, vol. 4:18-19.
[88] Q. 4:83, Q. 25:73, and Q.47:24, (tr. Bewley).
[89] Jakni, *Bukhari and Muslim*, 1967, vol. 1:28; and Ash-Shafi'i, *al-Umm*, 1993, vol. 7:492.
[90] Q. 4:65, and Q. 4:105, (tr. Bewley).
[91] Q. 5:42; 43; 44; 45; 46; and 47, (tr. Bewley). These ayat were never abrogated. They were revealed only a few months before the Prophet ﷺ died.
[92] Doi, *The Shari'ah*, 1984:14; Madkour, *al-Madkhal*, 1966:66, 337 with the full Arabic text of the letter.

56   The Fiqh of Medicine

   Ibn Hazm adh-Dhahiri called this narrative untrue, *al-Muhalla*, (1347 AH), vol. 1:59, and p. 44.
93 Q. 4:20; (Surat an-Nisa'): (tr. Bewley, and see Y. 'Ali's explanations: fn. 529, treasure: *qintar* = a talent of gold, and fn. 354 to Q. 3:14, a talent of 1200 ounces of Gold. *Qintar* = **100 lbs**.)
94 Sarakhsi, *al-Mabsut*, 1958, vol. 10:153; and Bultaji, *Minhaj 'Umar*, 1970:90, and 117.
95 Madkour, *al-Madkhal*, 1966:306, fn. 2, "'Umar gave the husband of a deceased woman half of her estate, her mother was given a sixth, and he divided the remainig 2/6 between the maternal brothers, leaving out the full brothers because they were *'asibs*. They protested saying, "asume that our father is a donkey *(himar)* we still have the same mother." Also Ibn Rushd, *Bidayat*, (1233 AH), vol. 2:289, Coulson, *A History*, 1994:25.
96 *Sahih al-Bukhari*, (ed.), Siddique, A., 1993:137; and *Sunan Ibn Majah*, 1953, vol. 2:858, "Anas ibn Malik said, 'The Prophet ﷺ used to hit with shoes and palm fronds, no specified number'."It became forty lashings, then eighty, and it went back to forty.
97 *Sunan Ibn Majah*, 1953, vol. 2:858.
98 Jakni, *Bukhari and Muslim*, 1967, vol. 5:520; *Sahih Muslim*, 1987, vol. 8:61.
99 Shahrastani, *al-Milal wa'n-Nihal*, 1968, vol. 2:4.
100 Amin, *Doha al-Islam*, 1938, vol. 2:10, and pp. 14 -22.
101 Q. 2:159, and Q. 3:187; (tr. Y. 'Ali).
102 *Sunan Ibn Majah*, 1953, vol. 2:1263; Suyuti, *al-Jami' al-Saghir*, 1969, vol. 1:401.
103 Ghazali, (d. 505/1111), *Ihya' 'Ulum al-Din*, Cairo, (n.d), vol. 1:20, and 22. {Henceafter, Ghazali, *Ihya'*}.
104 Q. 4:127; 4:176; 12:41; 12:43; 12:46; 18:22; 27:32; 37:11; 37:149.
105 Madkour, *al-Madkhal*, 1966:187.
106 Rispler-Chaim, Vardit, *Islamic Medical Ethics*, 1993:3.
107 Edge, (ed.), *Islamic Law*, 1996: xviii.
108 This work is primarily about Muslim juristic views as they impinge on the development of rules. It is not concerned with laws, which were developed in countries with Muslim populations at times of foreign rule. Such efforts did not claim that they were Islamic. So they are not relevant for this work.
109 Baker, *An Introduction to English Legal History*, 1990:1-2.
110 Shawkani, *Risalat al-Qawl al-Mufeed fi 'Adilat al-Ijtihad wa at-Taqleed*, (1347/1928), p. 25.
111 Madkour, *al-Madkhal*, 1966:188.
112 'Ali, 'Al-Madhhab 'ind al-Hanafia,' *Dirasat J.*, vol. 26, pp. 56-139; Omran, *Family Planning*, 1992:229.
113 Jackson, *Islamic Law and the State*, 1996:xv-xvi, and 145.

About Islamic Fiqh (Jurisprudence) 57

[114] Ash-Sharq Al-Awsat (Arabic Newspaper), London 19 November 1997, p.1 column 1.
[115] Qadri, *Islamic Jurisprudence*, 1973:257-259; see also Jackson, *Islamic Law* 1996:75-129; and Weiss, *God's Law*, 1992:717-718.
[116] *Sahih al-Bukhari*:English translation, Khan, 1994:86, see also *Sunan Ibn Majah*, 1952, vol. 1:80.
[117] Ghazali, *Ihya,'* vol. 1 pp. 44, 45, and 51.
[118] The Umayyads continued to dominate Spain until (887/1492). Ummayad era 41-132, Abbasid era 132-656.
[119] Amin, *Doha al-Islam*, 1938, vol. 2:173; Qadri, *Islamic jurisprudence*, 1973:148-150; Crone, Patricia, *Roman, provincial and Islamic Law*, 1987:19-22.
[120] Coulson, *A History*, (Reprinted), 1994:50.
[121] Coulson, *A History*, 1994:52; Crone, *Roman*, 1987:19-22; and Madkour, *al-Madkhal*, 1966:121, 125.
[122] Amin, *Doha al-Islam*, 1938, vol. 2:179.
[123] Shatibi, *al-Muwafaqat*, 1975, vol. 4:118; Abu Zahra, *Malik*, 1964:352.
[124] Ash-Shafi'i, *al-Umm*, 1993, vol. 7:492-494.
[125] Abu Zahra, *Ash-Shafi'i*, 1948, pp. 327 and 349.
[126] Coulson, *Conflicts*, 1969:42.
[127] Ash-Shafi'i, *Risala*, (tr. Khadduri), 1987:67-79.
[128] Madkour, *al-Madkhal*, 1966:158; Abu Zahra, *Ibn Hanbal*, 1981:170, "Ibn Hanbal collected 30,000 *hadith*, and 120, 000 *Tafsir* (explanations); Coulson, *A History*, (Reprint), 1994:71, said,"80, 000."
[129] Qadri, *Islamic jurisprudence*, 1973:147.
[130] Coulson, *A History*, (Reprint), 1994:72-73).
[131] Dutton, *Islamic Law*, 1999:4-5.
[132] Abu Zahra, *Ibn Hanbal*, 1947:101-102.
[133] Amin, *Doha al-Islam*, 1938, vol. 2:223, 226, 231, 228-229.
[134] Amin, *Doha al-Islam*, 1938, vol. 2:241-242.
[135] Jackson, *Islamic Law*, 1996:xxv.
[136] For a general reference see, Shahrastani, *al-Milal wa 'l Nihal*, 1968, vol. 1:13-31, and 62-172, also in English, Shahrastani, *Muslim Sects and Divisions*, 1984.
[137] Shahawi, *Mustalah al-hadith*, 1966:55.
[138] Mua'mar, *al-Ibadia fi Mawkib at-Tarikh*, 1979, pp. 6-7, and 323-458.
[139] But the seeds of the Shi'ite movement were sown when 'Ali did not become the first Caliph, in 632 CE.
[140] Shahrastani, *al-Milal*, 1968, vol. 1:169-172.
[141] Madkour, *al-Madkhal*, 1966:177. (Shi'ites call Prophetic *hadith*, *al-akhbar*. It is found in collections like: *al-Kafi*, by Muhammad ibn Ya'qub al-Kalbi (d. 228 AH.); *man la yahduruhu al-Faqih*, by Ibn Babawayhi (d. 381 AH.); *al-Istibsar*, by at-Tusi (d. 411 AH.); and *tahzeeb al-Ahkam*, also by at-Tusi.

58   The Fiqh of Medicine

[142] Makdisi, "Magisterium…"in Heer, (ed.), *Islamic Law*, 1990:121; see also Madkour, *Usul*, 1966:177.
[143] Coulson, *A History*, (Reprinted), 1994:105.
[144] Ghazali, *Laysa min al-Islam*, 1963:73-85.
[145] Qadri, *Islamic Jurisprudence*, 1973:91; Abu Zahra, *Abu Hanifah:* 1947, (Reprint) 1977:70-72.
[146] He was appointed by Caliph al-Hadi al-'Abbasi, and confirmed by Caliph Harun ar-Rasheed a year later.
[147] Shawkani, *Risalat al-Qawl al-Mufeed,* 1928, p. 15'Abu Hanifah and Malik,' p. 17'Malik,' p. 21'Abu Hanifah and Malik,' p. 22, 23'Shafi'i,' p. 23, 24, and 25'Ibn Hanbal'; also Madkour, *al-Madkhal*, 1966:92.
[148] Quoted by Annemarie Schimmel in, *Islam: An introduction*, 1992: v.
[149] Borno, *al-Wajiz*, 1998, pp. 8, and 63.
[150] Jakni, *Bukhari and Muslim,* 1967, vol. 1:7; *Sahih al-Bukhari*, (tr. Khan), 1994:49, and 79.
[151] Hadith, *(la darara wa la dirar),* in *Sunan Ibn Majah*, 1953, vol. 2:784; adopted in *al-Majalla* Article 19.
[152] Borno, *al-Wajiz*, 1998:172, citing Suyuti and Ibn Nujaim, *al-Ashbah*, and *al-Majala,* Articles 4, 5).
[153] *Sahih al-Bukhari*, (ed.), al-Bugha, (1410/1990), vol. 6:2528; *Sunan Ibn Majah*, 1953, vol. 2:778; *Sunan al-Tirmidhi (al-Jami'al-Sahih)*, 1983, vol. 2:398-399. {Henceafter, al-Tirmidhi, 1983}.
[154] Q. 2:28 **"It is He who created everything on the earth for you."** Q. 7:31 **"Say: 'Who has forbidden the fine clothing Allah has produced for His slaves and the good kinds of provision?'"** Q. 6:145 **"Say: 'I do not find, in what has been revealed to me, any food it is haram to eat except…'"** (tr. Bewley).
[155] Supported by Q. 2:184 **"Allah desires ease for you; He does not desire difficulty for you;…"**; Q. 2:285 **"Allah does not impose on any self any more than it can stand."**; Q. 4:28 **"Allah desires to make things lighter for you. Man was created weak."** Q. 22:76 **"He has selected you and not placed any constraint upon you in the deen;"** all ayat (tr. Bewley). Also many of the Prophet's *hadith* bear the same meaning,*"inna ad-dina yusr"* (Religion is ease) in *Sahih al-Bukhari*, 1981, vol. 1:25, and *Sahih Muslim*, 1987, vol. 4:492.
[156] Borno, *al-Wajiz*, 1998:234; and in *al-Majalla*, Article 21; based on Q. 6:119, **"…He has made clear to you what He has made haram for you except when you are forced to eat it"** (tr. Bewley).
[157] Borno, *al-Wajiz*, 1998:270, and in *al-Majalla*, Article 36; (based on"Whatever Muslims consider as good, is so to God," *(ma ra'ahu al-Muslimun hasanan fa huwa 'ind'Allahi hasan)*. It is attributed to the Prophet ﷺ, but its narration *(isnad)* stops at'Abdullah ibn Mas'ud, as per *Musnad Ahmad ibn*

About Islamic Fiqh (Jurisprudence)

Hanbal, in *Kitab al-Sunnah*: Borno, *al-Wajiz*, 1998:270).

[158] Madkour, *al-Madkhal*, 1966:12-20.
[159] Q. 2:185.
[160] Q. 4:28
[161] Q. 22:76.
[162] Q. 6:39, et. al.
[163] Q. 19:64.
[164] Q. 34:28.
[165] Q. 4:83, *(yastinbitunahu)* "those among them able to think out the matter would have known it."
[166] Madkour, *al-Madkal*, 1966:297, "Ijtihad is for always, for all times; it is an Islamic duty." (He quotes the Qur'an, the Sunnah, ibn al-Qayyim, al-Amidi in *al-Ahkam*, vol. 4:313, and others).
[167] Coulson, *Conflicts*, 1969:23.
[168] Hofmann, *Islam 2000*, 1996:50.
[169] Q. 4:83.
[170] Mayer, "The Shari'ah:" in Heer, (ed.), *Islamic Law*, 1990:184. (My definition of Shari'ah is that it is Allah's given law: it is not to be mixed or confused with Islamic fiqh).
[171] Schacht, "Problems of Modern Islamic Legislation," *Studia Islamica* 12 (1960):108, cited by Mayer, "Shari'ah," in Heer, (ed.), *Islamic Law*, 1990:177; and Jackson, *Islamic Law and the State*, 1996: xvii.
[172] Anderson, *Law Reform in the Muslim World*, 1976:17.
[173] Q. 5:38 **"As for thieves, both male and female, cut off their hands."** Q. 24:4 **"But those who make accusations against chaste women…flog them with eighty lashes,"** *(qadhf)*. Q. 24:2 **"A woman and a man who commit fornication: flog both of them with one hundred lashes,"** (tr. Bewley).
[174] Q. 5:44-46"
[175] *Siyasa shar'iyya* belongs to the confines of administrative law. The issue to be determined is constitutional: it is how does the ruler come to power and not what he promulgates.
[176] Q. 6:38.
[177] Q. 6:119.
[178] Q. 17:12.
[179] Q. 5:3.
[180] Q. 7:158.
[181] *Sahih al-Bukhari*, 1981, vol. 1:25.
[182] Ghazali, *Ihya,'* vol. 1:16; and Borno, *al-Wajiz*, 1998:5 citing Jarrahi, *Kashf al-Khafa*, Halab, vol. 2:400.
[183] Makdisi, "Magesterium…" in Heer, (ed.), *Islamic law*, 1990:119-121.
[184] Q. 42:39.

[185] Asad, *The Principles of State and Government in Islam*, (Reprinted), 1993:44-45.
[186] Mayer, "The Shari'ah:" fn. 9 at page 187. In Heer, (ed.), *Islamic Law*, 1990.
[187] Q. 4:58, (tr. Bewley).
[188] Q. 2:84, (tr. Bewley).
[189] Q. 5:44-47.
[190] Q. 6:38; and Q. 17:12.
[191] Q. 4:80.
[192] Qadri, *Islamic Jurisprudence*, 1973:271.
[193] Kandhloy, *Hayat al-Sahaba*, 1987, vol. 2:186; Haykal, Muhammad Hussein, *Al-Siddiq Abu Bakr*, 1361 AH, p. 67; al-Najjar, Abd al-Wahab, *Al-Khulafa' ar-Rashidun*, 1986:42.
[194] Q. 3:104, (tr. Bewley).
[195] *Sunan Ibn Majah*, 1953, vol. 2:1329, translation by Asad, 1993:77.
[196] *Sunan Ibn Majah*, 1953, vol. 2:1331; *Sahih Muslim*, (ed.), Abd al-Baqi, 1983, vol. 1:69, translation by Asad, 1993:77.
[197] *Musnad al-Imam Ahmad ibn Hanbal*, 1946, vol. 1:153, and 163, translation by Asad, 1993:81.
[198] Q. 42:38.
[199] Q. 88:22, (tr. Bewley) of "*lasta 'alaihim bi musaytir.*"
[200] Q. 5:48, (tr. Bewley); Y. 'Ali translated it as, **"To each among you have We prescribed a law and an open way."** Author's own translation highlights, *minkum* (from within yourselves).
[201] Q. 2:256.
[202] Q. 5:48, (tr. Bewley).
[203] Q. 29:46, (tr. Bewley).
[204] Baihaqi, *al-Sunan al-Kubra*, (1356 AH), vol. 9:185-186, and 189.
[205] Malik, *al-Muwatta,'* 1988, vol. 1:183; see also al-Qaradawi, *The Lawful*, 1960:62, "Qaradawi, speaking about Zoroastrians or Parsees (*Majus*), said that the Prophet ﷺ said, 'Treat them as you treat the People of the Book.'" And Khadduri said, "*Ahl al-Kitab*…are those who possess a Scripture. They include Christians, Jews, Samaritans, Sabians, and Magians (Zoroastrians)" in Khadduri, *Risala,* 1987:58, at fn. 5. See also Sabiq, *Fiqh us Sunnah*, 1995, vol. 3:51, *(ahlu al-Kitab wa yulhaqu bihim al-Majus)*.
[206] Schimmel, Annemarie, *Introduction to Islam*, 1992:70.
[207] Jackson, *Islamic Law*, 1996: xviii; Mayer, "The Shari'ah:" in Heer, (ed.), 1990:179.
[208] Abu Zahra, *Malik*, 1964:210, and 214; see also Mayer, "The Shari'ah:" in: Heer, (ed.), *Islamic Law*, 1990:179, fn. 3.
[209] Hindi, *Kanz al-'Ummal*, 1971, vol. 10:136, with no *sanad* (chain of narrators).
[210] Ibn al-Muqaff'a, *Kitab Kalila wa Dimna*, (ed.) al-Manfalouti, 1966:9.

About Islamic Fiqh (Jurisprudence)   61

[211] Abu Zahra, *Malik*, 1964:72; (citing *Tarikh ibn Kathir*, vol. 10:84).

[212] Jackson, *Islamic Law*, 1996: xiv-xv.

[213] Mayer, "The Shari'ah:" in Heer, (ed.), *Islamic Law*, 1990, at pp. 177-178, and 186-187.

[214] Q. 42:38.

[215] Jackson, *Islamic Law*, 1990: xiv.

[216] Anderson,'Law as a Social Force in Islamic Culture and History'*Bulletin of SOAS*, 20, pp. 20-21.
An English translation of the main points of 'Umar ibn al-Khattab's letter is in Doi, 1984:14-15.

[217] Ibn Hazm challenged the authenticity of the letter, *al-Muhalla*, 1347 AH. vol. 1:59, see p. 44 and fn. 120.

[218] Ballantyne, "A Reassertion of Shari'ah..."in Heer, (ed.), *Islamic Law* 1990:150.

[219] Ibn Abi Usaybia, *'Uyun al-Anba' fi tabaqat al-Atibba,'* p. 45.

[220] Rispler-Chaim, *Islamic Medical Ethics*, 1993:69.

[221] Presently graduates of all medical faculties in the Sudan take the Hippocratic Oath, under the auspices of the General Medical Council, before they embark on their professional careers. A practice, which has continued since 1928 with the first graduates of the Kitchener School of Medicine, Khartoum (currently Faculty of Medicine, University of Khartoum, since 1956).

Chapter Three
Responsibility and liability in Islam,
and Islamic viewpoints on matters arising within medical practice

This chapter is intended to fulfil two tasks: to define responsibility and liability in Islam, and to highlight some Islamic viewpoints on matters arising within medical practice.

Since the over-riding concern of this thesis is to examine the compatibility of Islamic medical fiqh with present day laws, a process of comparing and contrasting the two is essential. I have chosen English-based laws to relate to, because they are accessible, and because they are representative of an already accepted system of laws in the global community.[1] This is not meant to be a study of comparative law but it is useful and helpful to use a modern system of laws to relate to as a model for comparison. The Anglo-American common law has a common heritage, which is not so dissimilar to the civil law of Europe, particularly on questions of liability. Common law and civil law rules are neither congruent nor identical in every detail but they are compatible with one another in the sense that they produce similar solutions to similar problems.

Is Islamic fiqh similarly compatible?

1. Responsibility and liability in Islam

A distinction has been made between responsibility and liability in this work. Islamic fiqh does not require it, but it is not against it. The distinction was called for to explain situations where damage may be done without the perpetrator being required to compensate for it.

Responsibility in Arabic is *mas'uliyah* (duty, accountability, trustworthiness, reliability, stability, efficiency, capability, capacity, all wrapped up).

Liability is *daman* (indemnity, reimbursement, reparation, compensation, damages, restitution). Translations do not match the connotations always. The two are not congruent all the time.

Salmond uses them as alternatives in his definition of wrong:

He who commits a wrong is said to be liable or responsible for it. Liability or responsibility is the bond of necessity that exists between the wrongdoer and the remedy of the wrong.[2]

English law separates crimes and torts. Islamic law does not make this distinction. English law defines a crime as:

...a legal wrong the remedy for which is the punishment of the offender at the instance of the state.[3]

or,

...a crime (or offence) is a legal wrong that can be followed by criminal proceedings, which may result in punishment.[4]

As for tort:

...here we are at once in a thicket of difficulties; for it is perhaps impossible to give an exact definition of "a tort," or "the law of tort" or "tortious liability," and as a corollary, it is certainly impossible to give a definition which will satisfy every theorist who has taken any interest in the topic.[5]

Atiyah said:

Although the details are complex, in its essentials the subject is straightforward and not difficult to understand even for those with no knowledge of the law, or the legal system...

The first thing that must be grasped is that the law of damages, or more accurately, the law of civil liability, is not generally designed to *punish* anyone. Punishment is the function of criminal law; compensation is the function of civil law...

In general terms the law provides that any person who is injured by the fault of another can claim damages for those injuries...

In simple cases there is nothing esoteric about the legal concept of fault – lawyers define it as a failure to take reasonable care according to all the circumstances of the case...it does not require all possible care nor does it generally impose legal liability where damage or injury is caused by pure accident...

It must be stressed that negligence is a very minor kind of fault, in the legal sense...Although negligence can sometimes be followed by devastating consequences...lawyers insist – and rightly insist – that consequences like this are often more or less accidental,

In addition to liability for negligence, lawyers recognise another form of liability, which they call "strict liability." In these cases it is not necessary to prove negligence at all to claim damages.[6]

But Atiyah also described 'fault' as a very complex notion[7] and tort law as disorganised and ramshackle:

> More usually problems are classified partly according to the nature of the plaintiff's interest, and partly according to the way in which the injury was caused, whether intentionally, maliciously, negligently or without fault.
>
> The result of all this is that the conceptual structure of tort law is disorganized and ramshackle.[8]

As for Islamic law, crimes and torts are found inter-woven under the Islamic legal system. Although other legal systems had tried to distinguish between civil and criminal wrongs by means of proceedings, it is still unsettled among these legal systems whether a categorical dividing line can be drawn between the two branches of the law. So, often a wrong may be both civil and criminal and capable of being made the subject of the two proceedings.[9]

Glanville Williams said:

> An act can be either a civil wrong (wrongful by the civil law) or a crime; or it can be both…The part of civil law bearing the strongest resemblance to the criminal law is the law of tort. Its effect is primarily to give an action for damages (compensation).[10]

1.1 Responsibility in Islam

The fundamental basis of responsibility in Islam is the principle of **"enjoining what is right, and forbidding what is wrong."**[11] Justice, equity, and good conscience, are stressed in the Qur'an: **"Allah commands justice and doing good…and giving to relatives. And He forbids indecency and doing wrong and tyranny…"**[12] The teachings of the Prophet ﷺ reiterates these values.[13]

The Qur'an holds human beings responsible for their actions, because they enjoy intellectual capacity, the power to reflect,[14] and to think about the purpose of the creation: which is to know Allah and to worship Him,[15] **"enjoin the right, forbid the wrong and have iman in Allah."**[16] **"Allah commands justice and doing good…and giving to relatives. And He forbids indecency and doing wrong and tyranny…"**[17]

The Prophet ﷺ said:

> Behold, every one of you is a shepherd; and every one is responsible for

Responsibility and liability in Islam 65

his flock. Thus the imam (ruler) that has been placed over the people is a shepherd and is responsible for his flock; and every man is a shepherd over his family, and is responsible for his flock; and the woman is a shepherdess over her family and is responsible for them; and the servant is a shepherd over his master's property, and is responsible for it. Behold, every one of you is a shepherd and is responsible for his flock.[18]

Responsibility requires knowledge of what is permitted and what is not permitted (*al-ahkam*: categorisations or judgments). All human actions fall within five categories:
(1) *wajib* or *fard*, obligatory, which must be done,
(2) *mandub* or recommended, which when done is praiseworthy but for which there is no penalty if it is not done,
(3) *mubah*, permissible or neutral,
(4) *makruh*, or detested for which there is no penalty when committed, but which it is praiseworthy if it is not committed, and
(5) *haram* or forbidden, which must not be done at the pain of punishment, in this life, or the Hereafter, or both.[19]

Once these categorisations are known, one must act accordingly. This is based on submission to Allah's law as embodied in the message to Nuh, Ibrahim, Musa, and 'Isa,[20] (peace be upon them) and in the Tawrah, the *Injeel* (the revelation to 'Isa), and the Qur'an.[21]

Responsibility in Islam is personal, and is individualised; punishment is meted out only after a warning.

The Qur'an provides:

> Whoever is guided is only guided to his own good. Whoever is misguided is only misguided to his detriment. No burden-bearer can bear another's burden.[22]

And,

> No burden-bearer can bear another's burden. If someone weighed down calls for help to bear his load, none of it will be borne for him, even by his next of kin.[23]

This is true of criminal responsibility, but does it also apply to tortious liability? There are occasions in the *Shari'ah* (as we shall see) when relatives of the tortfeasor, who were not involved in the wrongdoing, or even some sectors of the community, are made responsible to redress the damage or compensate the aggrieved.

Allah is always there to forgive all the wrong actions of those who believe in Him and are repentant.[24] But if errors are committed against fellow humans, then the record must be set right, unless one is forgiven by the aggrieved.[25] Allah encourages one to forgive, **"Would you not love Allah to forgive you?"**[26]

The Prophet ﷺ said:

> Forgive the *hudud* wrong actions amongst yourselves, for if such is reported it becomes incumbent upon me to impose the punishment.[27]

And elsewhere,

> Blessed is the one who is noble and courteous when he conducts his business, or goes for litigation.[28]

Professor Antony Duff, in discussing criminal justice, has spoken of the need for the community to be inclusive of every one of its members (even criminals), and that everyone must have the feeling that they are included in the community so that all, together, must feel the responsibility to obey the laws. A genuine obligation to obey the law is for the good of everyone.[29]

These feelings are present in Islamic doctrines and teachings. The Qur'an asks people never to despair of the mercy or forgiveness of Allah, whatever their crimes or wrong actions might have been. They are required to make amends and to determine not to revert to crime again, whereby they may be forgiven; not only that but overcoming their past wrong actions may be counted as good deeds to tip the scales in their favour on Judgement day.[30]

At the time of the Prophet ﷺ, someone was punished for being drunk. One of the companions cursed him. The Prophet ﷺ said:

> No! He has paid for his transgression, so do not banish him, do not deliver him unto Shaytan *(la tu'inu ash-shaytan 'alayhi)*.[31]

Ma'iz, confessed his adultery; he was being stoned to death when he broke loose and ran away. He was brought back to finish his sentence. When the Prophet ﷺ was told about it, he is quoted as having said:

> Why was he not left alone; perhaps he would have asked for Allah's forgiveness and he might have been granted it.

And:

> He was forgiven. His forgiveness is sufficient for a whole nation.[32]

On another occasion, the Prophet ﷺ prayed for the confessed adulteress, al-Ghamidiya, after her punishment: when he was questioned about that, he said:

Her redemption is so complete that it is enough to forgive the wrong actions of seventy more.[33]

Enjoining what is right and forbidding what is wrong entail attention to both community and personal needs. This is seen with good effect in the attitude of Islamic law to the notion of rescue. Is there a legal obligation to help a person in danger or distress?

1.2 Rescue in Islamic law

Sometimes rescue becomes obligatory; just like prayers *(fard 'ayn)*.[34] Legal obligations *(wajib* or *fard)* are either *fard 'ayn* or *fard kifaya*. *Fard 'ayn* is a personal duty which must be executed by the person himself, as, for example, performing prayers; *fard kifaya* is an obligation of the community, which if it is done by some they are rewarded and the rest of the community are absolved from penalty but are not rewarded; but if it is not done at all then all members of the community are punished. Rescuing or helping those in distress is an obligation, reaching the level of *fard 'ayn* depending on circumstances.

The Prophet ﷺ said:

> Allah does not approve of the actions of those, who allow someone to remain hungry amongst them. [35]

And:

> One of three types that Allah will not look kindly upon, and will torture on the day of reckoning, is a person who denies a fellow human a drink of water in the desert whilst he has enough.[36]

And:

> Seeking knowledge is a duty of every Muslim; and Allah loves it when those in straits are helped or rescued *(Allaho yohibo ighathat al-lahfan)*.[37]

The Prophet ﷺ taught about the "duties and obligations to 'the public way,' or behaviour in public: i. do not stare at people; ii. do no harm; iii. greet people; iv. enjoin right and forbid wrong; v. guide those who lost their way; vi. and help those in need *(aghithu al-malhuf)*."[38]

Since offering medical care can be a personal responsibility, or an obligatory duty of a medical practitioner, it may be concluded that there might be situations when responsibility and liability may not coincide. There may be no liability in services rendered, whatever the outcome, or whatever the state of consent or capacity. Legal permission negates tortious liability.[39]

A skilful physician who practices his craft properly, whose hand causes no harm [sic], yet from his action – permitted by the law, and by the one he was treating – there occurs injury to a limb or loss of life, or the loss of some faculty. [sic] Such a man is not held responsible. This is agreed.[40]

The medical practitioner in Islam may be obliged to undertake treatment of others, as in rescue situations. On other occasions, the medical practitioner himself may feel that he is responsible, or has the right, to treat others even in the face of opposition.

The duty of care in Islam is wider than in English law, as it clearly covers rescue. There was almost a hint to encourage rescue in English common law in the ruling *per* Brett MR in *Heaven* v. *Pender* (1883):

> Whenever one person is by circumstances placed in such a position with regard to another that everyone of ordinary sense who did think would at once recognise that if he did not use ordinary care and skill in his own conduct with regard to those circumstances he would cause danger of injury to the person or property of the other, a duty arises to use ordinary care and skill to avoid such danger.[41]

But about the actual state of the law, Lewis writes:

> Is a doctor under a duty to treat when the man next to him in the theatre is taken ill? An English court would say not.[42]

As for the viewpoint in the Health care system, Montgomery explains:[43]

> In general, professionals who pass a road traffic accident have no legal obligation to stop and minister to anybody who has been injured,[44] although they may have a professional obligation to so.[45]

Islam shares certain values with other religions and faiths. Family members have a particular responsibility to help their relatives.

"Give your relatives their due, and the very poor and travellers but do not squander what you have."[46]

and:

"those in whose wealth there is a known share for beggars and the destitute."[47]

The community has the responsibility to support and care for one another.

"Hold fast to the rope of Allah all together, and do not separate …Let there be a community among you who call to the good, and enjoin the right, and forbid the wrong."[48]

The Prophet ﷺ said, "There are obligations and dues in wealth other than *zakat,* which are the right of others."[49] He also said,"The Muslim community is like a structured building, each one supports the other;"[50] and that,"The Muslim community is like one body, if one part is diseased or disabled the other parts share in fever, malaise, and sleeplessness."[51]

With the notions of free trade and market economy persist, many in the West consider the ability to provide social safety nets and public services to cushion the impact of naked capitalism on people important.

So it is in Islam, **"those who, if We establish them firmly on the earth, will establish salat and pay zakat, and command what is right and forbid what is wrong."**[52] There is need to find a balance between the relentless pressure for short-term profits and broader social responsibilities. **"Give just *(qist)* weight – do not skimp in the balance."**[53] As it may not be possible to reverse the trend of the market economy, so a cure must stem from the responsibility of those who reap the benefits of free trade to fulfil their obligations. **"You who have iman! fulfil your contracts."**[54] They must put right any damage they may have caused, or adequately compensate for it. Particular examples are the tobacco industry, and activities responsible for deforestation, pollution, destruction of the environment, and others, which contribute to global warming.

The Prophet ﷺ said that,"All people have a communal share in three items: water resources, grazing land, and fire."[55]

Brahimi said,"Ibn Taymiyya believes in the free play of market forces but recommends state intervention to protect the population and to safeguard the general interest."[56]

Muslim fuqaha recognise the need for equitable distribution of wealth and the all-important role of economics in human welfare, and sustainable development. There are ideas other than communism or the harsher variants of market economy. Some Muslim fuqaha are examining possibilities for community friendly formulas that allow for private enterprise, a hall-mark of Islam.

1.3. Liability in Islam

In Islam,"Deen, law and morality are all one."[57] Hurting others is offensive to Allah as well. One is bound to keep within the bounds of law and not to breach his duty at the pain of bearing the consequences, depending on the circumstances.

The Prophet ﷺ said:

Harm and exchanging hurt are not allowed *(la darar wa la dirar)*.[58]

And the three salient features of medical liability (duty of care, breach of that duty and causing harm) are captured in the Prophet's *hadith*:

He, who sets himself up to treat people without proficiency, and causes damage to a part, or life, is liable *(damin)*.[59]

Each transgression (case) is dealt with according to its circumstances. There are mitigating factors for dealing with some wrongs, which take into consideration compensation for the aggrieved. The Qur'an says:

"Our Lord, do not take us to task if we forget or make a mistake!"[60]

The Qur'an also says:

"You are not to blame for any honest mistake you make but only for what your hearts premeditate."[61]

The Prophet ﷺ said:

My people *(ummah)* have been forgiven in cases of mistake, forgetfulness, and in what they were forced or compelled to do (coercion).[62].

But that does not lose the aggrieved party due compensation. The Qur'an says, **"A mumin should never kill another mumin unless it is by mistake"**[63] but if it so happens by mistake, compensation is due: so, retaliation is replaced by *diya* (compensation), because it was a mistake.

Should the transgression be intentional, in the sense of fighting with the intention of doing the other harm and resulting in death, then retaliation can be sought.

You who have iman! retaliation is prescribed for you in the case of people killed;...

But if someone is absolved by his brother, blood-money should be claimed with correctness and paid with good will. That is an easement and a mercy from your Lord. (Q.2:177).[64]

The ayah (verse) denotes that intentional transgressions are penalised by retaliation, unless the crime is forgiven gratuitously or for a consideration. This does not include the case of premeditated murder which comes under another ruling.

Some special features of liability will be examined in the light of Islamic fiqh: that is: (a) strict liability, (b) vicarious liability, and (c) the limit or cap put on damages.

a. Strict liability

Legal liability does not, always, coincide with responsibility in Islamic fiqh. There are situations when an act that has caused damage may not warrant compensation of the injured party. Generally fault *(ta'adi)* must be proved to warrant payment of an indemnity *(daman)*.

Strict liability in Anglo American law has become part of the tort law:

> The fault principle, as embodied in the concept of negligence, is not the only basis of legal liability for personal injuries and death...modifications to and departures from the fault principle...are often said to impose 'strict liability' as opposed to fault liability. But to draw a simple contrast between fault liability and strict liability in this way is misleading. In the first place, it may be possible to argue that just as the fault principle is ultimately based on some moral notion of personal responsibility for one's conduct, so strict liability is also based on some notion of fairness in the allocation of responsibility for risky activities. Secondly, while 'liability for fault' may...[indicate] that fault should generally be a necessary condition of liability, the phrase 'liability without fault' merely eliminates fault as a necessary condition of liability; it does not put anything else in its place...the term 'strict liability' implies no criterion for deciding on whom liability should rest.[65]

Huber discussed the modifications to and departures from the fault principle in the USA under the chapter title of 'Uncommon Law.'

> The tort tax is a recent invention. Tort law has existed here and abroad for centuries, of course. But until quite recently it was a backwater of the legal system,...the omnipresent tort tax we pay today was conceived in the 1950s and set in place in the 1960s and 1970s by a new generation of lawyers and judges. In the space of twenty years they transformed the legal landscape, proclaiming sweeping new rights to sue...Tort law, as we know it is a peculiarly American institution. No other country in the world administers anything remotely like it.

> ...compared with the cautious incrementalism with which the common law had changed in centuries past, an utter transformation over a twenty-year span can fairly be described as a revolution, and a violent one at that.

> The revolution began and ended with the wholesale repudiation of the law of contract.[66]

> It has far reaching consequences, notable amongst which is the award of staggeringly high 'compensations.'[67]

Ian Edge observes, "In fact, it is controversial whether Islamic law accepted the idea of strict liability at all."[68] This is of particular relevance to medical liability. In Islamic law an authorised, competent practitioner, who discharges his duties according to the accepted norms, where his intervention was called for, is not liable if his patient comes to harm or dies as a result. He is not liable even if he had promised a cure.[69]

But Islamic fiqh recognises that damage must be compensated in the majority of situations without asking for negligence to be proved, and at the same time without labelling the action negligent: it recognises mistake, or error as distinct from negligence. It also recognises negligence per se (which may call for more than compensation): and the fuqaha recognised the difficulty in separating error or mistake from negligence.[70] Furthermore Islamic fiqh recognises criminal negligence, which can be classified as an intentional crime.[71] (See Chapter Four).

The Prophet ﷺ said:

> The 'aqila do not bear the responsibility of compensation for intentional damaging acts, or for what is agreed upon between parties, or the result of confession *(la tahmilu al-'aqila 'amdan, wa la sulhan, wa la 'itrafan)*.[72]

b. Vicarious liability

Vicarious liability does not feature as such in Islamic fiqh. Responsibility is personal:

What each self earns is for itself alone. No burden-bearer can bear another's burden.[73]

But having said that, it must be mentioned that Islam takes into consideration the necessity of compensating the injured party, and the possibility that the party that caused the damage may not be solvent. In such cases other parties may be brought in to effect the settlement. Relatives of the tortfeasor (even though they were not involved in causing the damage) may be called upon to contribute in compensating for it, through the systems of *diya* and *qasama.* This is a function of the Islamic concept of family support, interdependence, community welfare and its collective responsibility for the wayward behaviour of its members. Should the relatives be poor or non-existent then the family-at-large of Muslims' network may be called upon to contribute, through the concept of *ahl ad-diwan.*

The doctrines of *diya, qasama,* and *ahl ad-diwan,* which are relevant in this context, need explanation.

(i) Diya

Diya literally means loss, and it also means compensation for some loss.[74]

It originates from customs *('urf)* of the Arabs before Islam.

The law of *diya* was referred to in the Qur'an.[75] Its value was reiterated and detailed in the sayings of the Prophet ﷺ.[76] The main guide line is one hundred camels of different ages, to be given over a period of time not exceeding three to four years, for unintentional injury; but more valuable camels are to be delivered promptly in cases of intentional assault.

Later on, Caliph 'Umar ibn al-Khattab, valued it at one thousand *dinars* of gold for those in Syria, and Egypt; and 12,000 *dirhams* of silver for those in Iraq,"as camels were not a feasible proposition for townspeople."[77] This was further extrapolated by the different schools of fuqaha to include as alternatives: 200 cattle, 2000 sheep, and 200 of two-piece cloth material.[78] But any sort of money offered of the same value was legitimate tender, and had to be accepted.[79] In modern day money it is about £ 33,000 or $ 50,000.[80]

Diya is usually translated, as 'blood money,' but the atmosphere for settlement must also reflect commiseration with the aggrieved, and the recognition that the mere fact of accepting the *diya* is an act of great magnanimity on their part.

Another name for *diya* is *'aql*, a derivation from *'aqila*, when it is payable by a group of persons, related to the tortfeasor through an agnatic tie.

'Aqila [81]

In Islam certain relatives stand to share in the inheritance of a particular person. These same relatives the *'aqila*, are obliged to contribute financially in case of need particularly in matters pertaining to *diya*. This is rooted in part of an ayah in the Qur'an. [82] The Prophet ﷺ accepted it, ordered its adoption, and implemented it.[83] He said,"Each group of relatives within a tribe bears the compensation for the injury caused by their relative" *('ala kulli batnin 'uquluhu.*"[84]

The *diya* payable for loss of life entails compensation by one hundred camels or their monetary equivalent. It may be substituted by similar values in gold, silver, cattle, sheep, or cloth. Injury to parts of the body is assessed according to a scale of values necessarily less than the full *diya*.

The tortfeasor is required to bear a certain portion of the compensation, which is usually about one third of the value of the full *diya*: approximately the value of thirty-four camels. Compensation in excess of the value of more than one third of *diya* is borne by the aforementioned group of relatives *('aqila)*.[85]

(ii) Qasama

Qasama is operative when someone, usually a lone foreigner to the surroundings, is slain and no specific person is accused of the slaying. Someone must have initially caused the death within a clan, or a certain group of people, in circumstances suggesting *prima facie* evidence of guilt *(lawth)* by a person unknown within the group.

Fifty able-bodied men of the clan or the group who are closely related to one another are selected. Each of them is called upon to declare under oath *(qasam)* {hence the name *qasama*}, that he did not kill, nor does he know, who killed the deceased. Despite that, they have to provide one hundred camels as a *diya* to the relatives of the deceased. *Qasama* is an example of liability without direct responsibility.

It is contrary to the requirements of *hadith*, "your two witnesses or his oath" *(shahidaaka aw yaminu hu)*,[86] which is always applicable in business transactions or property dealings. But the situation where a lone person gets killed in a community, which is not his, requires special treatment.[87]

The accusers, fifty of them, under oath are required to specify a single person as the culprit. If they do, that person may be executed *(qisas)*. But they were not there to witness the crime, otherwise the situation wouldn't have arisen, so the onus shifts to the community members (the suspects) to provide testimony that they did not do it, and to pay *diya* as well.

On one occasion (Mahisa and Huwaysa's case) the Prophet ﷺ was going to adopt its ruling, though it was in the laws of the Arabs before Islam, but the accusing party would not accept to start the accusation under oath, (because they did not witness the event), nor did they want to accept the denial, under oath, of the other party as they were Jews and not Muslims. So the Prophet ﷺ provided one hundred camels *(diya)* from the state coffers *(bayt al-mal)*; and maintained that life was sacred; that security was paramount; that a lone person or the few (minorities) are the responsibility of the community in which they dwell; and that 'no blood should be spilt, or lost, in Islam without consequences *(hadar)*."[88]

Muslim said, "*Al-Qasama, aslun min usul ash-Shar'a'* (*Al-Qasama* is an accepted part of the shari'ah). The Prophet ﷺ sanctioned it as it was in pre-Islam."[89]

Ibn Rushd said, "*Qasama*, was accepted as Sunnah by Abu Hanifah, Malik, ash-Shafi'i, and Ibn Hanbal; but Salim ibn'Abdullah ibn'Umar, 'Umar ibn'Abdul Aziz, and ibn Qilaba were doubtful about that."[90]

Al-'Izz ibn Abd as-Salam said, "*Qasama* came down from pre-Islam; it is not Shari'ah, but it is an accommodation: a nicety *(talatuf)*."[91]

Al-Baihaqi explained that when 'Umar ibn al-Khattab, the second Caliph, was on pilgrimage, he instituted the rule of *qasama* in the case of a murdered man who was found near the place of *Wadi'a* tribe. He made them take the oath of denial, then made them pay the higher compensation *(diya mughalaza)*: dearer camels, and prompt settlement. They protested, "Neither did the oath protect our moneys, nor did our moneys excuse us from taking the denial oath." Caliph 'Umar said, "So it is! *(kadhalak al-amr)*. Your moneys protected your blood: and no Muslim's blood is spilt for nothing."

One of them, called Sanan, asked, "Doesn't my oath absolve me from paying?" 'Umar said "No."[92]

'Umar ibn'Abd al-'Aziz, the just Ummayad Caliph, discussed *qasama* with the faqih Abu Qilaba who was adamant that it should not hold.[93] Al-Baihaqi stated that the Prophet ﷺ never allowed *qisas* (loss of life) on the strength of *qasama*.[94]

Qasama is a most interesting doctrine. It dispenses full *diya*, in a situation where responsibility is not proven; and an oath was not enough to shift the burden of liability.[95] There are many situations in medical practice where the patient is alone, and sometimes under an anaesthetic, amongst a group by whom he might be harmed, although it may be that it cannot be shown exactly which among them caused the harm. The notion of *qasama* might then have a role to play to protect the patient who has been harmed by an unknown hand within that group.

It may be of interest to note that 'Law and Custom in Early Britain' had a 'Communal' justice procedure and proof that may be compared with *qasama*:

> The 'moot' or folk-assembly, first mentioned in the Kentish laws of the eighth century, was of prehistoric origin...

The procedure in contentious matters was calculated to avoid reasoned decision-making. If the parties could not be persuaded to make a 'love-day' – to settle amicably – then resort could be had to proof by oath,...the plaintiff was required to establish a prima facie case; and this was the purpose of his 'suit' (secta), the group of followers whom he brought with him to back him up on oath. The suit had some affinity with witnesses, and they may have been subject to examination as to competence, but their testimony was only part of the interlocutory process and did not dispose of the matter. If the defendant was allowed the benefit of proof by oath, he proceeded to swear on the holy evangels to the truth of his case, in very general terms and without possibility of cross-examination. In the form of proof known to later generations as wager of law, he was expected to bring with him some neighbours as 'compurgators' or 'oath-helpers' to back up his word. If this lesser kind of proof was deemed inappropriate, usually because of the gravity of an accusation and the unreliability of the party's word, the oath might have to be proved by the physical test of an ordeal.[96]

(iii) Ahl ad-diwan

Ahl ad-diwan,[97] means, those of the meeting place, or the people who drew a stipend from, and were related to an 'office.' The treasury or *(bayt al-mal)* was one of the first public 'offices' created after the mosque. The Prophet ﷺ used *bayt al-mal* for financial affairs.

But it was the Caliph 'Umar ibn al-Khattab who introduced the concept of the organised group to be responsible for the concerns of a member of its own. He decreed that the members of the army, which included almost every one at his time, were *ahl ad-diwan* to the liabilities of one another.

It was the introduction of public responsibility and liability. This might be extrapolated in modern times to the National Health Services, or to the different medical defence organisations in the case of medical practice. Similar other bodies cover different walks of life.

Muslim fuqaha in discussing medical liability apportioned the damages in great detail: to the practitioner, the relatives, and/or the treasury *(ahl ad-diwan,* or *bayt al-mal)*.

c. The limit or cap of liability

Liability in Islam is limited by the value of the damage to property or, in cases of injury or loss of life, by the amount permitted as *diya*. In cases of murder or criminal injury the values involved are left to the parties. These limits, where they do not exceed the value of one hundred camels, may be compared and contrasted with the system of awards in countries, which adopt Western laws.

Awards for cases emanating from medical practice in the United States are considered, as they show the trend in the size of the awards, and the effect on medical practice. At the same time a consideration of the reasons as to why this is taking place may help others to avoid the same pitfalls and adopt corrective or more sound measures. An English law practitioner, Charles Lewis, criticises the magnitude of US awards, and attributes the cause to the jury system and the limited power of the trial judge to interfere on liability.[98]

It may be stated that trial by jury is not universal in Anglo-American common law[99] and the Western world. The non-existence of a jury system in Islamic fiqh is not in itself a reason for incompatibility with other laws.[100] Islamic fiqh relies on witnesses, and has complete regard for expert opinion of those in the 'trade' or the 'profession.' The judgement of one's professional peers can determine that the medical practitioner has acted as expected and according to the rules; in which case he will not be liable.[101]

The judge *(qadi)* decides upon the evidence before him. The award of compensation is their function but within the bounds of *diya* doctrine.

Even in the USA there has been a call for examining the way awards are made, and suggestions for compensation caps.[102] It was also said that:

> The inadequacies of the present day system for resolving malpractice claims through court-based adversarial litigation under the tort system have become apparent in recent years, as substantial increases in malpractice claim frequency, claim severity, and insurance costs have occurred.[103]

2. The Islamic viewpoint on matters arising within medical practice

The understanding of the Islamic viewpoint on matters arising within medical practice is facilitated by examining and analysing six questions. These questions are a personal distillation from forty years of medical practice – its technical, administrative, and conflict management domains – and a long standing interest in Islamic fiqh as it views medical matters.

These questions are:
(i) Should people, in a Muslim context, preserve their health?
(ii) Should people, in a Muslim context, seek treatment?
(iii) Is the medical profession necessary?
(iv) Is preparation of the medical practitioner required?
(v) Are there any limits to the methods employed in treatment?
(vi) Are there any legal remedies for an injury caused to the patient during the course of the treatment received?
These questions are addressed in order below.

2.1 Should people, in a Muslim context, preserve their health?

Islam considers the protection and preservation of life of paramount importance.[104]

Five values and matters are deemed essential and vital in life. If a Muslim dies fighting for their cause then that person is a shahid (witness to the truth) in the eyes of Allah.[105] They are: integrity of iman, preservation of life, soundness of mind, legitimacy of offspring and protection of property.[106] Three of these essentials are directly based on preservation of health: life, mind, and offspring.

The Prophet ﷺ put health foremost. He said:

Ask to be healthy: man was never bestowed with anything better, other than the peace of mind that goes with being resigned in iman.[107]

And:

The one who is fit in himself, secure in his company, and has enough to feed on: has everything.[108]

And:

Two inestimable gifts, not best utilised by many, are health and leisure.[109]

And:

There is nothing wrong with riches, if one has taqwa; but for the pious there is nothing better than health.[110]

The Prophet ﷺ dealt with health matters in two ways: First, by teaching preservation of health and prevention of sickness. Second, by strongly recommending the treatment of illnesses.

As regards the first, he initiated a whole system of personal hygiene, public health measures and quarantine regulations.

Personal hygiene and cleanliness are regarded as part of iman.[111]

Although the washing connected to acts of worship is not initiated for reasons of hygiene, there is no doubt of the tremendous effect it has on it. Muslims are required to wash hands, mouth, nose, face, arms, ears, and feet with water before prayers. Prayers are five times a day. It is almost obligatory to have a bath every week.[112] One hand is to be used for food and clean purposes, and the other for unclean and toilet purposes.[113] Hair on the head and in the beard and moustache should be trimmed, and it is recommended to cut the nails and remove bodily hair.[114] Unclean nails harbour dirt, which is harmful *(adha)*; so does the hair if it becomes infested with lice. Clothes should be clean, and the body should be washed and adorned with scent or perfumed, especially on Fridays and festive days.[115] Sweet smelling flowers welcome.[116]

He recommended cleaning the teeth and mouth with *miswak* (branches and roots of certain ubiquitous shrubs), at least once a day; and he said:

> I would have recommended *siwak* (cleaning the teeth) with every prayer, five times a day, had it not been for the hardship it may cause.[117]

Bathing is compulsory after sexual intercourse.[118] Penetrative sexual intercourse is to be avoided during menstruation, as it can be a cause of harm or illness *(adha)*;[119] but the woman herself should not be shunned and all other contact leading to relief is allowed.[120] Sexual relations are encouraged within marriage; they are to take place with adornment, tenderness, and foreplay. 'A'isha said that, "The Prophet ﷺ used to kiss her and suck her tongue." The Prophet ﷺ "discouraged intercourse without foreplay."[121] Illicit relations were forbidden, as, apart from being shameful, they lead to abomination.[122]

As for community and public health measures, the Prophet ﷺ recommended the cleaning of houses. Animals were to remain in their own domain, but people were to be kind to them (this included dogs). The Prophet ﷺ said:

> A man went into paradise because he gave water to a thirsty dog.

And:

> A prostitute from Bani Israel, was forgiven because she gave water to a thirsty dog.[123]

A person is not to urinate in, or otherwise soil, a non-running water supply. Streets should be kept clean and free from obstructions: harmful objects and thorns should be removed; holes and wells are not to be dug where they can form a hazard.[124]

People must not expose themselves unnecessarily to the heat of the sun or to cold in winter.[125] Trees must not be felled in an uncontrolled manner even in wartime.[126] *Halal* food and drink should be consumed in moderation.[127] Alcohol is not allowed.[128]

He encouraged the taking of exercise for physical fitness, and ordered that children must be taught, swimming, archery, and horse riding.[129] One should entertain oneself every-so-often because weariness blinds the mind, *(Rawihu al-quluba sa'atan fa sa'ah: fa inna'l-quluba idha kalat 'amiyat).*[130] And, "do not over-exert yourselves *(aklifu min al-'amali ma tutiqun)*"[131]

He warned against communicable diseases. About leprosy he said, "When talking to a leper, let there be a distance of the length of a spear or two between both of you."[132] We know now that leprosy is not transmitted by touch, milk, blood, or semen. It is transmitted by droplet infection: the fine moisture that leaves the mouth and nose (in droplet form) during speech, coughing, or sneezing. The droplets are spread several feet away.

On another occasion he ate with a leper from the same container, saying: "Eat in the name of Allah, trusting in Allah, and relying upon Him."[133] These *Hadiths* are not necessarily contradictory. They were said on different occasions. It is an established medical fact that some forms of leprosy are burnt out and are not infective, and that others are spread, but by droplet infection.

As for quarantine regulations, the Prophet ﷺ said, "If you hear about the plague in a town do not enter it, and if you are inside it already, do not leave it."[134] 'Umar ibn al-Khattab was on the verge of entering Syria, but on hearing that there was plague there, he refrained and decided to go back to Madinah. Khalid ibn al-Walid, one of the companions and the famed army general, challenged his decision, asking, "Are you running away from a fate that Allah has determined?" 'Umar said, "Yes, I am running away from a fate that Allah has determined, to a fate that Allah has also determined." At this juncture 'Abd ar-Rahman Ibn 'Awf, said, "I have heard that from the Prophet ﷺ myself."

This leads to the debate as to whether a Muslim should seek treatment from an illness, or should he do nothing about it, 'leaving matters in the hands of Allah,' as trust in and dependence *(tawakkul) upon Allah*. This leads to the second way in which the Prophet ﷺ dealt with health matters, that is, by the treatment of disease.

2.2 Should people, in a Muslim context, seek treatment?

The Prophet ﷺ treated himself, and allowed himself to be treated by others:

> Ibn 'Abbas narrated that the Prophet ﷺ decongested his nose,…and that he asked a barber to perform blood-letting on him, and then paid him for the service.[135]

And:

> Fatima, the daughter of the Prophet ﷺ, burnt a piece of a mat and applied the ashes to stop bleeding from a wound of the Prophet ﷺ.[136]

Hisham ibn 'Urwa quoted his father:

> I said to 'A'isha, the wife of the Prophet ﷺ, "You have taken the teachings *(Sunan)*, from the Prophet ﷺ, poetry and the Arabic language from the Arabs: but where did you learn your medicine?" 'A'isha replied, "The Prophet ﷺ was often sick, he was on many occasions visited by Arab medicine-men. I learnt from them."[137]

The Prophet ﷺ himself treated others:

> Jabir ibn 'Abdullah said, "Sa'd ibn Mu'adh was wounded at the battle of *al-Ahzab* (626 CE), on his ankle. The Prophet ﷺ cauterised the wound, with his own hands, using an arrow. It became swollen, he cauterised him a second time; and he said, 'put him in the tent for the wounded, under the care of Rufaida,[138] so that I may visit him frequently.'"[139]

And:

> Anas said that, "The Prophet ﷺ cauterised As'ad ibn Zurarah for a pain in his side."[140]

The Prophet ﷺ let it be known to people, in a way that was almost an order, that Muslims should seek treatment for illness:

> Seek treatment: for Allah has created a cure for every sickness. Some treatments are known, others are not.[141] And,

> Allah created sickness and cures. There is a cure for every sickness. Seek treatment, but do not use forbidden procedures *(haram)*.[142]

When he was asked whether precautionary measures and protective medicines would ward off what Allah has destined, he replied:

> All of these measures, themselves, are part of destiny. So be treated, and Allah will cure whomever He wants to cure.[143]

The Qur'an says, **"Allah has appointed a measure for all things."**[144]

This would include treatment and its result. What Allah has decreed may be met by measures, which He Himself has decreed. Allah is the Healer,[145] but methods of cure have been made available to people as the means. These methods comprise medicines and procedures for body ailments,[146] and the Qur'an for those of the soul (psychic ailments), although the Qur'an can also treat physical body ailments, which may be controlled by the brain.[147]

2.3 Is there a necessity for the existence of the medical profession, according to Islam?

The Prophet ﷺ submitted himself for treatment, including cupping (*hijama*).[148]

He ordered others to be treated,[149] and he actually undertook the treatment of some people himself, including cauterisation.[150] He was selective in his choice of practitioners,[151] and he paid them for the services rendered.[152]

Adh-Dhahabi said, "Medical treatment is Sunnah because the Prophet ﷺ did it and ordered that it should be done," and he quoted ash-Shafi'i as saying, "No knowledge is nobler than the knowledge of what is permitted and what is prohibited (*fiqh*); medicine is second to *fiqh*."[153]

Al-'Izz ibn Abd as-Salam said:

> "Medicine is like the law, it was laid out to bring about the benefits of security and well being; and to ward off the ills of trouble and disease."[154]

Al-Ghazali said,

> learning medicine is *fard kifayah*, as it is essential in life. Medicine and arithmetic are at the top of the list of knowledge that is useful and necessary to have in the community:

> …And if you ask why I have equated *fiqh* (the law) with medicine, I will give the edge to *fiqh* as it is needed by everyone whereas medicine is needed by those who are sick; though medicine is important for health which is necessary for performing one's duties including Allah's worship.[155]

The fuqaha inferred from this that learning the profession to fulfil a need is obligatory (*fard* or *wajib*). There is almost an order from the Prophet ﷺ for people to get treated, he said, "*tadawu*" (be treated, or seek treatment).[156]

The Prophet ﷺ also said:

> Give the way its rights and its dues: do not stare at people, do no harm, return greetings, enjoin right and forbid wrong, guide the lost, and give help to the ones in need (*aghithu al-malhuf*).[157]

This means that attending to, or rescuing a patient can be a responsibility, or a duty, or an obligation of those who are qualified. Because of this, there are occasions when performing this duty absolves one from any consequent liability."The rule is that there is no liability in performing one's duty" *(Sirayat al-wajib muhdara bi 'l itifaq)*.[158]

On some occasions lack of consent may be excused:

> But what if a qualified medical practitioner fails to secure consent of an adult, a child, or a mad person; and that person comes to harm? Some of our colleagues said he is liable, others said it is probable that he may not be liable at all as he was a gooddoer *(muhsin) wa ma 'ala al-muhsinin min sabeel*, (and there is no way to (blame) good-doers): but that needs to be looked into.[159]

2.4 Should the medical practitioner be well prepared for his job and execute it properly?

The preparation of the medical practitioner to perform his duties is catered for in two spheres. The first sphere is that of the general values of Islam as they impinge on'private'law. The medical practitioner, as all others, is bound according to the Qur'an to: **"enjoin what is right and forbid what is wrong"**;[160] The Prophet ﷺ said,"Allah wants one to perfect whatever work one does *(inn'Allaha yuhibbu idha 'amila ahadukum al-'amala an yutqinahu)."*[161]

The second sphere is the requirement of expertise and further refinement of the person's abilities to perform one's duties. Malik relates the story of two persons from Bani'Anmar, who came to examine a wounded patient. The Prophet ﷺ who was present, enquired of them as to which of the two was better at medical management *(ayyukuma atabb)*.[162] Ibn al-Qayyim commented that:

> This means that in each subject, or craft, the best should be consulted, or chosen to do the job: as success is more likely.[163]

It can be said from this that, in Islamic fiqh, if one is going to undertake the treatment of others, it becomes an obligation on the practitioner to master his craft. Al-Ghazali says,"What is essential for the performance of one's duty, becomes a duty in its own right."[164]

Islam requires one to do one's job well; the Prophet ﷺ asked two medical practitioners,"Which of you is better at medicine?," before delivering his patient for treatment.[165]

This was later developed into, formal medical education; and later still into examinations to certify the competence of practitioners. Thabit ibn Sanan ibn Qurrah, narrates the following tale,

> On the first day of Muharam of the year 306 A. H. [918] my father Sanan ibn Thabit, in accordance with the directive of Caliph al-Muqtadir billah opened up the *bymarstan* (hospital) at Suq Yahia. He took his place in it, made arrangements for the students of medicine, and admitted patients. The cost of running the place was 600 dinars monthly. Later that year my father asked the Caliph to open another *bymarstan* at Bab ash-Sham. The cost of running the new place came to 200 dinars monthly.
>
> In the year 319 A. H. (930 CE), it came to the notice of the Caliph that a patient met his death at the hands of one of the novices in the medical profession. So the Caliph decreed that none is to practice medicine save those examined and passed by his chief physician (my father).
>
> My father examined the applicants; there were over 860 of them from both sides of Baghdad. He assigned to every one of them what was within his capabilities. But those who were well known for their excellent abilities, together with the court physicians, were exempt from the examination.[166]

This can easily be extrapolated to the present day system of registration in the general medical councils and their speciality organs.

5. Are there any limits to the methods employed in treatment?

This refers to the questions as to what is to be treated and to its extent.

As the Prophet ﷺ has said:

"Allah never created a disease for which He did not create a cure; So seek treatment";[167] and "There is a cure for every malady; if it is hit upon – Allah willing – then sickness is gone;[168] and "For every sickness there is a cure, some cures are known, others are not."[169]

This led the fuqaha to divide ailments or treatment procedures into three categories:[170]

Category one. These are categories of illness where a cure is almost sure to occur, but whenever there is non-treatment then they will lead to certain death. In these situations treatment is imperative by the consensus of fuqaha. They invoke the Qur'an where it is ordained that one should not waste life; and where the saving of one life is the same as though one has saved all the human race.[171] Hence an attempt at arresting severe haemorrhage is a duty *(wajib* or *fard)*. It may even become, *fard 'ayn*, an absolute personal obligation just like prayer. It must be undertaken. If left out, it is *haram*.[172]

Category two. These are categories of illness where a cure is the expected result. In this group lie most of the diseases or conditions requiring medical attention. The arguments of the fuqaha for the treatment of this second group of ailments where the expected result is a cure are based on the fact that the Prophet ﷺ himself received treatment, applied it to others, and ordered for it to be done; knowing that nothing human is a certainty.[173]

Some other fuqaha, would say that it is best to leave matters in the hands of Allah without treatment.

Category three. These are a group of ailments in which a cure is not a realistic expectation, or the treatment entails extreme measures. These diseases form the basis of the views of *some* of those who are opposed to any attempts at treatment, and who advocate reliance on Allah *(tawakkul)* without any attempt at a cure on their part.

These attitudes have prompted Ibn al-Qayyim to say:

> Man should not call his lack of zeal or achievement, reliance on Allah, nor should reliance on Allah be a pretext for not attempting to achieve.[174]

As this attitude also is attributed to some of the *sufis*, I have specifically concentrated on the ideas of one of the great *sufis*, al-Ghazali, in this respect.

Summary of the views of al-Imam al-Ghazali on medical treatment[175]

Al-Ghazali recommended treatment of ailments following the example of the Prophet ﷺ. He explained that, ailments were of three kinds: First, curable ones or life-threatening situations: these must be treated, just, as one would take water for thirst and food for hunger. This group he called, 'where benefit of treatment is clear' *(maqtu'un bihi)*. He said that refusal of treatment in such circumstances is forbidden *(haram)*, if it results in loss of life. Second, are the group of diseases in which a cure is the expected outcome *(madhnun)* and these are the ones, which are amenable for treatment using the 'usual' methods. He pointed out that treating this group is not contrary to reliance on Allah *(tawakul)*, as the Prophet ﷺ encouraged seeking treatment of diseases in many

Hadiths. Thirdly, there are diseases in which a cure is a figment of the imagination *(mawhum),* or may entail hazardous measures like cauterisation; such diseases may be left alone. He quoted examples when some of the companions of the Prophet ﷺ declined treatment per se, as with Abu Bakr as-Siddiq, Abu ad-Darda,' and Abu Dharr al-Ghifari. But, he went on to say that although there are reports that the Prophet ﷺ asked people not to be cauterised, there are reports of occasions when the Prophet ﷺ had to resort to it himself, as when he cauterised As'ad ibn Zurarah, and Sa'd ibn Mu'adh.[176]

Al-Ghazali concluded, that seeking treatment is not contrary to reliance on Allah; and that the Prophet ﷺ explained that both the ailments and the means of their treatment are what Allah wills and ordains *(hiya min qadari'llah).*[177] That he gave an example of the Prophet ﷺ using cauterisation, shows that the Prophet ﷺ was inclined to extend the limits of treatment.

But it must be stated that there are those, who do not subscribe to this 'pseudo-classification' of ailments. They are adamant that things must be left in the hands of Allah *(tawakkul)* and that no treatment should be sought. They look upon medical intervention as a form of battery, and as a sign of non-resignation to the will of Allah on the part of the patient. They quote the saying of the Prophet ﷺ:

> There are those of my people, who will unquestionably attain paradise: they are the ones who do not seek treatment by *ruqa,*[178] the ones who do not consult talismans, the ones who do not allow themselves to be cauterised; and they leave matters in the hands of their Lord *(wa 'ala Rabbihim yatawakkalun).*[179]

This may be seen a selective viewpoint or a special interpretation of the deen, so as to discourage some measures practised in desperate situations or as evidence of a genuine abhorrence of intervention. Non-intervention is known among a number of different religious communities for example, among Christian Scientists and Jehovah's witnesses who refuse blood transfusions and other treatments even if it will result in death.[180] In Islam this attitude does not detract from the fact that there are many sayings and actions attributable to the Prophet ﷺ, which encourage the seeking of treatment.

It must also be remembered that in the seventh century CE, and at the times of those fuqaha, treatment measures and procedures were somewhat limited. The outcome was not predictable in many cases, and safety was a concern.

It is by research and experimentation that treatment has been secured for more and more illnesses, even among those in the third category of ailments. The Prophet ﷺ did venture into the more difficult areas of seeking cures, albeit with due care, as with performing cauterisation. He encouraged research into the finding of cures. Ibn al-Qayyim commented about the *Hadiths* which say, "For every ailment there is a cure, so seek treatment, as Allah has not created a sickness for which He did not create a cure, known to some and unknown to others."[181] He said,

On the one hand patients will always be hopeful of a cure, and on the other hand those in the medical profession are encouraged to research it.[182]

But the Prophet ﷺ did specify two limits which should not be transgressed: first, treatment must not use methods which are not allowed *(haram)* and second, treatment must not alter or change what Allah has created.[183]

The Prophet ﷺ said, "Seek treatment; but do not use unlawful methods, as Allah did not make them avenues of cure for the Muslim community."[184] As regards methods of treatment, the Prophet ﷺ mentioned many, preferring some to others. A few will be selected for arguing the point of the extent to which one may pursue lawful treatment methods.

The Prophet ﷺ is reported to have said, "Treatment can be with a scalpel (surgery), or with bee honey (medicine), or with cauterisation: I forbid my people to use cauterisation."[185] In another *hadith* he said, "Treatment can be with a scalpel, honey, or cauterisation: but I would not like to be subjected to cauterisation."[186] Notwithstanding that, when Ubayy ibn Ka'b, became sick, the Prophet ﷺ sent him a medical practitioner who cauterised him.[187] Furthermore the Prophet ﷺ himself cauterised Sa'd ibn Mu'adh twice when he was injured in *al-Ahzab* battle.[188] He is also reported to have cauterised As'ad ibn Zurarah, for a pain in his side *(dhat al-junb)*.[189] The Prophet ﷺ described cupping – both a superficial variety where capillaries and tiny vessels are cut through the skin *(hijama)*, and phlebotomy (where a vein is cut *(qat'u al-'ariq)*) – as accepted methods of treatment. He was always in favour of the first superficial variety *(hijama)*; it was often performed on him and he is said to have paid the one who did it, although there are also ahadith expressing disapproval of the wages of the cupper.[190]

He warned against phlebotomy saying that it is hazardous and that *hijama* was a better option, *(qat'u al-irqi musqama wa al-hijamatu khayrun minh)*.[191] Yet on one occasion he is said to have sent a medical practitioner to perform phlebotomy on Ubayy ibn Ka'b.[192]

This may show that some abhorrent or hazardous procedures may be used if or when they become necessary implements in medical practice.

The Prophet ﷺ delayed treatment by cauterisation until it became the last resort; because disease can change from one time to another, and so does the response to more conservative methods of treatment. The treatment of the same ailment can vary with age, time, custom, dietary habits, contingency plans, and resistance to illness.[193]

The Prophet ﷺ did not neglect psychological methods. He pointed out the cure inherent in using verses of the Qur'an as *(ruqa)* and *(ta'widh)* and in the simple recitation of the Qur'an, which is a cure for some.[194]

2.6 Are there any legal remedies for an injury caused to the patient during the course of the treatment received?

There are many guiding *hadiths* of the Prophet ﷺ in this respect, for example:

> He who undertakes the treatment of others, but is ignorant of medical knowledge, and causes loss of life or a part, is liable.[195]

Ibn al-Qayyim, (d. 751/1350), expounded on the Prophet's *hadith*:

> The ignorant medical practitioner by setting himself up to treat others, without due preparation has assaulted *(tahajama)* the patient with his ignorance, and with his reckless behaviour has caused injury. Such a practitioner is liable. Retaliation is not sought because he was not the sole party responsible for the act. The patient contributed by his consent.[196]

This question is such a vital issue that there is a vast literature on the subject by Muslim fuqaha, as it always constitutes the hub of medical law.

In this chapter it was shown that Islamic fiqh considers health care a necessity. Hence it is essential for the community to provide it. Sometimes it becomes a personal obligation or duty on individuals. This modifies liability, providing the service is rendered with due care.

On the other hand recipients of medical care should not be unreasonably demanding or litigant. The "rights and responsibilities of patients and those who treat them" will be subject to analyses in the following chapter, for which this chapter was the foundation.

Notes

1. "Inevitably the growing economic and political integration in Europe will lead to attempts to integrate the legal rules and the paralegal regulations, declarations, and statements that govern medical ethics." Soren Holm, 'A common ethics for a common market?' pp. 118-123, in Richards, Tessa, (ed.), *Medicine In Europe*, BMJ Publications, London, 1992, at p. 118.
2. Salmond, *Jurisprudence*, 1924:377.
3. Cross, and Asterly Jones, *An Introduction to Criminal Law*, 1959 p. 3.
4. Williams, *Textbook of Criminal Law*, 1983:27.
5. Winfield, *Textbook of the Law of Tort*, 1948:1.
6. Atiyah, *The Damages Lottery*, 1997 pp. 3-6.
7. Cane, Peter (ed.), *Atiyah's Accidents, Compensation and the Law*, 1993, Reprint 1997:8.
8. Cane, *Atiyah's*, Reprint 1997: 25-26.
9. Zubair, *An Outline of Islamic Law of Tort*, Lagos, 1990: xi-xii.
10. Williams, *Textbook of Criminal Law*, 1983:25.
11. Q. 3:104, 110, 114; et. al.
12. Q. 16:90, (tr. Bewley).
13. Ghazali, *Ihya*,' vol. 2:287-9, *Sahih Muslim*, 1987, vol. 1:100-1; Jakni, *Bukhari and Muslim*, 1967, vol. 1:247.
14. Q. 3:190, **"In the creation of the heavens and the earth, and the alternation of night and day, there are Signs for people with intelligence,"** (tr. Bewley); Q. 17:36, **"Do not pursue what you have no knowledge of. Hearing, sight and hearts will all be questioned."** (tr. Bewley).
15. Q. 51:56, **"I only created jinn and man to worship Me."** (Asad, in *Islam at the Crossroads*, 1987:19, points out that knowledge of Allah is understood in worship and translate it, **"...that they may [know and] worship Me"**).
16. Q. 3:110, (tr. Bewley).
17. Q. 16:89, (tr. Bewley).
18. Jakni, *Bukhari and Muslim*, 1967, vol. 1:302-3; *Sahih al-Bukhari*, Kazi Publications, 1986 vol. 2:8.
19. Qadri, *Islamic Jurisprudence*, 1973:241; and Weiss, *God's Law*, 1992:3.
20. Q. 42:13.
21. Q. 5:44-50.
22. Q. 17:15 (tr. Bewley). See also Q. 2:286, **"For it is what it has earned; against it, what it has merited"**; and Q. 6:164 **"What each self earns is for itself alone. No burden-bearer can bear another's burden."** (tr. Bewley);

Responsibility and liability in Islam 91

23 Q. 35:18. (tr. Bewley).
24 Q. 4:48, 4:110, and 39:53.
25 Q. 2:178, 5:45, 55:8, et. al.
26 Q. 24:22. (tr. Bewley).
27 Azimabadi, *'Aun al-Ma'bud Sharh Sunan Abi Dawud*, (1410/1990), vol. 12:27. {Henceafter, Azimabadi, *Sunan Abi Dawud*, 1990}; also in *Sunan Ibn Majah*, 1953, vol. 2:850.
28 *Sahih al-Bukhari*, (ed.), al-Bugha, 1990, vol. 4:730-731; Suyuti, *al-Jami al-Saghir*, 1986, vol. 1:107; and *Sunan Ibn Majah*, 1953, vol. 2:809, and 811.
29 Duff, Antony, (Sterling University), 'Inclusion and Exclusion, Citizens, Subjects, and Outlaws' UCL Series of 'Legal Theory at the End of the Millennium Lectures,' Bentham House London 26 February 1998.
30 Q. 25:70, 39:53 et al.
31 *Sahih al-Bukhari*, (ed.) al-Bugha, 1990, vol. 6:2488-9.
32 *Sahih Muslim*, (ed.) Abd al-Baqi, 1983, vol. 3:1322-3.
33 *Sahih Muslim*, (ed.) Abd al-Baqi, 1983, vol. 3:1324,
34 Abu Zahra, *Usul*, 1958:28; Qadri, *Islamic Jurisprudence*, 1973:241.
35 *Musnad al-Imam Ahmad Ibn Hanbal*, 1946, vol. 2:33.
36 *Sahih al-Bukhari*, Bugha, 1990, vol. 2:835; *Sahih Muslim*, Baqi 1983, vol. 1:113.
37 Hindi, *Kanz al-'Ummal*, 1971, vol. 10:131.
38 *Sunan Abi Dawud*, 1974, vol. 7:160-161.
39 Ibn al-Qayyim, *Zad al-Ma'ad*, 1979, vol. 4:139.
40 Johnstone, *Medicine of the Prophet* ﷺ, 1998:105.
41 (1883) 11 QBD 503, 509.
42 Lewis, *Medical Negligence*, 1998:158.
43 Montgomery, *Health Care Law*, 1997:168.
44 *F v. W. Berkshire HA* [1989] 2 All ER 545, 567. (Montgomery, *Health Care Law*, 1997:168).
45 *Good Medical Practice*, (GMC, 1995), para. 4; (Montgomery, 1997:168).
46 Q. 17:26, (tr. Bewley).
47 Q. 70:24-25, (tr. Bewley).
48 Q. 3:103, and 104, (tr. Bewley).
49 *Sunan at-Tirmidhi: al-Jami' al-Sahih*, (ed.), 'Awad, Beirut, vol. 3:48-49.
50 *Sahih al-Bukhari*, (tr.) Khan, 1994:957; and *Sahih Muslim*, 1987, vol. 5:160.
51 *Sahih al-Bukhari*, (tr.) Khan, 1994:955; and *Sahih Muslim*, 1987, vol. 5:161.
52 Q. 22:39.
53 Q. 55:9: (*qist:* Arabic = **just**; the balance used for weighing is *qistas*: Arabic = **justice** in Q. 17:35).
54 Q. 5:1.
55 *Sunan Ibn Majah*, 1953, vol. 2:826.
56 Brahimi, Abdelhamid, 'The Origin of Islamic Economics,' *ISLAMICA* vol. 2

No. 3 1996 p.7.
[57] Allott, *The Limits of Law*, 1980:27.
[58] *Sunan Ibn Majah*, 1953, vol. 2:784.
[59] Hindi, *Kanz al-'Ummal*, 1971, vol. 10:32; and *Sunan Ibn Majah*, 1953, vol. 2:1148.
[60] Q. 2:285, (tr. Bewley).
[61] Q. 33:5, (tr. Bewley).
[62] *Sunan Ibn Majah*, 1952, vol. 1:658; and p. 659.
[63] Q. 4:92. (tr. Bewley).
[64] Q. 2:178.
[65] Cane, *Atiyah's Accidents,*1993, Reprint 1997, p. 78.
[66] Huber, *Liability: The Legal Revolution and its Consequences*, 1988, pp. 4, 5, and 6.
[67] Huber, *Liability*, 1988:4, "at least $ 80 billion a year,...lawyers and other middlemen pocket more than half the take." See p. 11 for deleterious effect on medical services as well.
[68] Edge, Ian,'The Development of Decennial Liability in Egypt,'pp. 161-175, in Heer, (ed.), *Islamic Law*, 1990, at p. 173.
[69] Sarakhsi, *al-Mabsut*, 1958, vol. 26:147; and Ibn'Abidin, *Hashiyat*, 1966, vol. 6:65-66.
[70] Ibn Rushd (al-Hafid, d. 595/1198), *Bidayat al-Mujthid*, Maktabat al-Kuliat Al-Azhar, Cairo, vol. 2:454-5, {Henceafter , Ibn Rushd, *Bidayat*, al-Kuliat}.
[71] Ibn Rushd, *Bidayat*, al-Kuliat, vol. 2:255, 454-455; also Ibn al-Qayyim, *Zad al-Ma'ad*, 1979:139.
[72] Ibn Qudama, *al-Kafi*, 1982, vol. 4:119.
[73] Q. 6:166; (tr. Bewley. Y.'Ali in his explanatory footnote said, "Nor can any one *vicariously* atone for our sins." The same words *(la taziru waziratun wizra ukhra)*, recur in, Q. 17:15; Q. 39:7, and Q. 53:38.
[74] Ibn Manzur, *Lisan al-'Arab*, 1990, vol. 13:486.
[75] Q. 2:178, 4:92.
[76] *Al-Muwatta,'* (ed.), Sa'd, 1983:737. "*Diya* reference: the written message of the Prophet ﷺ to 'Amr ibn Hazm: one hundred camels for loss of life; one hundred for loss of a nose; one third of that for deep head wounds and abdominal injuries (healing must be awaited); fifty for each of the eye, hand, or leg; ten camels for one finger or toe; five camels for a tooth or for a head injury that has exposed the bone." Also in *Sunan Ibn Majah*, 1953, vol. 2:877-882.
[77] *Al-Muwatta,'* (ed.), Sa'd, 1983:737.
[78] Salih, *al-Qisas*, 1989:543-546.
[79] Ash-Shafi'i, *al-Umm*, 1993, vol. 6:148, and 149-150.
[80] For some present day *diya* values see p.181 below and its fn. No. 635, and p. 184.

[81] *'Aqila*, literally means those who restrain or tie; because these relatives are supposed to tie the *diya* camels at night close to the premises of the aggrieved party. Etiquette entails that no moneys should change hands. The rope with which the camels are restrained is called *'uqal*. It is circular and just goes around the bent knee of the camel. Camel shepherds carry it wound around their heads. To this day it is part of the Arab head dress as it restrains it from flying off. Even kings wear it. *'Aql* is one of the Arabic names for the mind, brain, or intellect; as it restrains one, and makes for responsible behavior.

[82] Q. 2:233. **"The same duty is incumbent on the heir"** [as would have been on the father]: *wa 'ala al-warithi mithlu dhalik* (tr. Bewley)": Although the ayah addresses issues of nursing mothers, it is also extrapolated to mean the liability of would-be heirs to shore up their benefactor, should there be a call for that.

[83] *Sunan Ibn Majah*, 1953, vol. 2:879, and 880.

[84] Baihaqi, *al-Sunan al-Kubra*, (1354 AH), vol. 8:107, and pp. 104-105.

[85] Hanafi school, Ibn 'Abidin, *Hashiyat*, 1966, vol. 6:68-69; Maliki school, al-Hattab, *Mawahib al-Jalil*, 1329 AH, vol. 5:431; Shafi'i school, the *'aqila* is responsible for all of *diya*, in Ramli, *Nihayat*, 1938, vol. 8:35; Hanbali school has different views, but the leaning is towards the Maliki school: "In cases of mistake or error the *'aqila* bears whatever is in excess of 1/3 of *diya*." Ibn Qudama, *al-Kafi*, 1982, vol. 4:121, and Ibn al-Qayyim, *Zad al-Ma'ad*, 1979, vol. 4:140.

[86] *Sunan Ibn Majah*, 1953, vol. 2:778.

[87] *Sunan Ibn Majah*, 1953, vol. 2:1301-1302.

[88] *Qasama* in: *Al-Muwatt'a*, English translation: by Bewley, 1989 p. 372; and *Al-Muwatta,'* (ed.), Sa'd, 1983:764-769; and in San'ani, *Subul al-Salam*, 1987, vol. 3:515-520, *(qasama)*, at p. 519.

[89] *Sahih Muslim*, (ed.), Abd al-Baqi, 1983, vol. 3:1291-1295

[90] Ibn Rushd, *Bidayat, al-Kuliat*, vol. 2:465.

[91] San'ani, *Subul al-Salam*, 1987, vol. 3:515-520, at p. 519.

[92] Baihaqi, *al-Sunan al-Kubra*, (1354 AH), vol. 8:124-125.

[93] Baihaqi, *al-Sunan al-Kubra*, (1354 AH), vol. 8:128.

[94] Baihaqi, *al-Sunan al-Kubra*, (1354 AH), vol. 8:129.

[95] *Sunan Ibn Majah*, 1953, vol. 2:778, *"al-bayyinatu 'ala al-mudda'i wa'l-yaminu 'ala al-mudda'i 'alayhi."*

[96] Baker, *An Introduction to English Legal History*, 1990:4-5.

[97] Malik, *al-Muwatta,'* (ed.), 1983, p. 755. *Diwan*, (noun) means 'office.' The Arabic verb means 'to register.' The Caliph 'Umar ibn al-Khattab introduced the registration of the troops and their dues, in the year 15 AH. (636). Later it was developed to recording the finances of the government, the treasury *(bayt al-mal)*. See Bultaji, *Minhaj 'Umar*, 1970:281-283;

94 The Fiqh of Medicine

and *The Encyclopaedia of Islam,* 1965, vol. ii, pp. 323-324.
[98] Lewis, *Medical Negligence,* 1994:8-10, observes that, "Awards in America are large and frequent…The main reason is that they have juries…The power of the trial judge to interfere on liability is very limited,…A US plaintiff aged 61 years was awarded over $ 8m for the death from Opren [sic] of his 82-year- old mother…In 1989 one US plaintiff was awarded $ 76m for health problems caused by asbestos exposure." However, Lewis, in the 4th. ed., 1998:13-14, restates the first parts…and says, about the medical profession in the UK, "Their defense against extravagant and unjustified claims lies in the good sense of our judges."
[99] The English litigant…is entitled to apply for jury trial under s.6 (1) of the Administration of Justice (Miscellaneous Provisions) Act 1933 and RSC O.33 r.5 (1)(see Supreme Court Act 1981 s.69), but the effect …has been nullified by the decision of the Court of Appeal in *Ward* v. *James* [1966] 1 QB 273, 'juries may be ordered only in exceptional cases, and the severity of the injuries suffered does not render a case exceptional…An example of an 'exceptional' case is *Hodges* v. *Harland &Wolff Ltd* [1965] 1 WLR 523, where the plaintiff's penis had been torn off by a revolving spindle (Lewis, *Medical Negligence,* 1998:13 fn. 16).
[100] The Times reported that, "Lord Bingham of Cornhill, the Lord Chief Justice calls for a jury-free trial option." The Times July 22 1999, p. 2, columns 5, 6, and 7 (middle of page) by Frances Gibb.
[101] Sarakhsi, *al-Mabsut,* 1958, vol. 16:10-14 and vol. 26:147; and Ibn 'Abidin, *Hashiya,* 1966, vol. 6:68.
[102] Kridelbaugh, William W., and Palmisano, Donald J., "Compensation Caps for medical malpractice," *American College of Surgeons Bulletin,* vol. 78, number 4, April 1993 pp. 27-30.
[103] Nora, P. F., (ed.), *Professional Liability/ Risk Management,* American College of Surgeons, 1997:101.
[104] Q. 2:195 "and be not cast by your own hands to ruin" (tr. Pickthall).
[105] *Sahih Muslim,* 1987, vol. 1:170; *Sunan Ibn Majah,* 1953, vol. 2:861-862.
[106] Ash-Shatibi, *al-Muwafaqat,* 1975, vol. 2:10; and al-Ghazali, *al-Mustasfa* (1322 AH), vol. 1:139.
[107] *Sunan Ibn Majah,* 1953, vol. 2:1265.
[108] *Sunan Ibn Majah,* 1953, vol. 2:1387.
[109] *Sunan Ibn Majah,* 1953, vol. 2:1396.
[110] Hakim, *al-Mustadrak,* (1340 AH), vol. 2:3.
[111] "Cleanliness is a part of iman": *Muwatta' Malik,* (ed.), 1983:35-69, all *Fiqh* books have chapters on the subject of cleanliness in (section) *bab at-Tahara* and *Wudu.*
[112] Jakni, *Bukhari and Muslim,* vol. 1:27, "Bathe yourselves every Friday"; and in p. 174 "it is a duty to Allah to bathe and wash the hair weekly."

[113] Jakni, *Bukhari and Muslim*, vol. 1:26.

[114] Jakni, *Bukhari and Muslim*, vol. 1:257-258, with the footnotes. Also in *Muwatta,'* (ed.), Sa'd, 1983:814.

[115] Q. 7:31, **"Children of Adam! wear fine clothing in every mosque,"** (tr. Bewley).

[116] *Sahih al-Bukhari*, 1981, vol. 7:61, "the Prophet ﷺ never refused scent"; Ibn al-Qayyim, *Zad al-Ma'ad*, 1979, vol. 4:278-279, *hadith*, "Accept *ar- rayhan*," a scented whitish flower; and in *Ibn Qayyim al-Jawziyya: Medicine of the Prophet* ﷺ, Translated by Penelope Johnstone, 1998:199, {Henceafter, *Medicine of the Prophet* ﷺ, Johnstone, 1998}; "Sweet scent makes the heart rejoice, pleases the soul and revitalizes the spirit."

[117] *Muwatta,'* (ed.), Sa'd, 1983:67-68; Jakni, *Bukhari and Muslim*, 1967, vol. 2:132.

[118] Jakni, *Bukhari and Muslim*, 1967, vol. 1:246, *Hadiths*, "Clean your teeth every day,""use perfume," and "bathe after intercourse as you would every Friday."

[119] Q. 2:222. (Pickthall's translation of *adha* as 'an illness' is supported from the Q. 2:196, **"If any of you are ill or have a head injury..."** *(adhan min ra'sihi)* (Tr: Bewley)

[120] The Prophet ﷺ had sexual contact with his wives ('A'ishah, Maymounah, and Um Salmah) while they were menstruating, but not intercourse. In *Sahih Muslim*, 1987, vol. 2:203-206; also *Sunan Abi Dawud*, 1969, vol. 1:183-187.

[121] Ibn al-Qayyim, *Zad al-Ma'ad*, 1979, vol. 4:253, "The narrator Muhammad ibn Dinar al-Azdi was said to be a poor learner; and his teacher Sa'd ibn Ars al-Abdi had some contested narrations *(aghaliyat)*, (in this respect the issue was the effect of saliva on fasting). He also quoted a second *hadith*, *"naha 'an al-muwaqa'ah qabl al-mula'abah"* (he forbade intercourse before foreplay)," Ibid. vol. 4:253. See also Azimabadi, *'Aun al-Ma'bud…Sunan Abi Dawud*, 1990, vol. 7:9, and *Medicine of the Prophet* ﷺ, Johnstone, 1998:183, "Abu Dawud related in his *Sunan*: 'he [the Prophet] used to kiss A'ishah and kiss heavily. It is related from Jabir ibn 'Abdullah that the Messenger of Allah ﷺ discouraged intercourse without foreplay."

[122] Q. 17:32 **"And do not go near to fornication. It is an indecent act, an evil way;"** (tr. Pickthall).

[123] Jakni, *Bukhari and Muslim*, 1967, vol. 1:152, and 154.

[124] Jakni, *Bukhari and Muslim*, 1967, vol. 1:153, and its footnote 3; see *Sunan Ibn Majah*, 1953, vol. 2:1214.

[125] Jakni, *Bukhari and Muslim*, 1967, vol. 1:21.

[126] *Muwatta' Malik*, 1988, vol. 1:289; Jakni, *Bukhari and Muslim*, 1967, vol. 1:87.

[127] Q. 7:29-30, (tr. Bewley, **"and eat and drink but do not be profligate. He does not love the profligate. Say: 'Who has forbidden the fine cloth-**

ing Allah has produced for His slaves and the good kinds of provision?'").

[128] Q. 5:90. Alcohol, from the Arabic *al-ghul* which means 'headache, or drunk.' (Fairozabadi, *al-Qamus al-Muhit*, 1994:1344). It is interesting to note that when the Arabs borrowed their own word back they rendered it as *(al-kuhul)* and not as *al-ghul*.

[129] Ibn al-Qayyim, *Zad al-Ma'ad*, 1979, vol. 4:246-248.

[130] Suyuti, *al-Jami' as-Saghir*, 1981, vol. 2:19.

[131] *Sunan Ibn Majah*, 1953, vol. 2:1417.

[132] Al-'Asqalani, (d. 1449 CE), *Fath al-Bari...al-Bukhari*, 1988, vol.10:130; *Al-Musnad li'l-Imam Ahmad Ibn Hanbal*, 1946, vol. 2:28, hadith No. 581; Ibn al-Qayyim, *Zad al-Ma'ad*, 1979, vol. 4:148; and in *Medicine of the Prophet* ﷺ, Penelope Johnstone, 1998:112

[133] *Medicine of the Prophet* ﷺ, Johnstone, 1998:112-113; *Sunan Ibn Majah*, 1953, vol. 2:1172.

[134] Jakni, *Bukhari and Muslim*, 1967, vol. 1:234, detailing the narrative of the Caliph 'Umar Ibn al-Khattab and the plague; see also *Sahih al-Bukhari*, 1981, vol. 7:21, and *Sahih Muslim*, 1987, vol. 4:405.

[135] Al-'Asqalani, *Fath al-Bari...al-Bukhari*, 1988, vol. 10:120.

[136] Al-'Asqalani, *Fath al-Bari...al-Bukhari*, 1988, vol. 10:126, and 141.

[137] Al-Hakim, *al-Mustadrak*, (1342 AH), vol. 4:197.

[138] Rufaida, perhaps the first lady nurse in Islam, other helpers were Umm 'Atiyah, Umm 'Umarah al-Maziniah, and Safiyah bint Abd al-Muttalib: Reference, Anwar al-Jindi, *al-Islam wa Harakat at-Tarikh*, 1980:43.

[139] *Sunan Abi Dawud*, 1973, vol. 4:200, "The Prophet ﷺ cauterized Sa'd ibn Mu'adh twice"; and in *Sunan Ibn Majah*, 1953, vol. 2:115-116.

[140] Al-'Asqalani, *Fath al-Bari...al-Bukhari*, 1988, vol. 10:126; Shawkani, *Nayl al-Awtar*, (1372 AH), vol. 9:95; and in *Sunan at-Tirmidhi*, (ed.), 'Abd al-Baqi, (1350 AH), vol. 3:263.

[141] Al-'Asqalani, *Fath al-Bari...al-Bukhari*, 1988, vol. 10:110; Shawkani, *Nayl al-Awttar*, (1372 AH), vol. 9:89; and Hakim, *al-Mustdrak*, (1342 AH)., vol. 4:197.

[142] Al-'Asqalani, *Fath al-Bari...al-Bukhari*, 1988, vol. 10:110; *Sunan Abi Dawud*, 1973, vol. 4:207; Shawkani, *Nayl al-Awttar*, (1372 AH), vol. 9:93. {Examples of forbidden methods would be, alcoholic drinks, and those in Q. 5:90: carrion, blood, swine flesh, and animals slaughtered in heathen rituals (voodoo, sorcery, satanic worship): in Q. 2:173, 5:3, 16:115; and for sorcery see: Q. 2:102. Sorcery in Islam is tantamount to association of partners with Allah *(shirk)*, the worst of all transgressions, Q. 4:48, 5:28. et. al.

[143] Al-'Asqalani, *Fath al-Bari...al-Bukhari*, 1988, vol. 10:111; Hakim, *al-Mustadrak*, (1342 AH), vol. 4:199. Hindi, *Kanz al-'Ummal*, 1971, vol. 10:5;

Responsibility and liability in Islam 97

[144] Q. 65:3, *(qad ja'ala'llahu li kulli shay'in qadra)*.
[145] O. 26:80 **"and when I am ill, it is He who heals me"** (tr. Bewley)
[146] Q. 16:69.
[147] Q. 17:82; 10:57; and 41:44.
[148] Ai'sha said, "The Prophet ﷺ was often sick, and Arab medicine men treated him: so I learned from them." Al-Hakim, *al-Mustadrak*, (1342 AH), vol. 4:197; "The Prophet ﷺ used nasal instillations, and subjected himself to cupping" in 'Asqalani, *Fath al-Bari...al-Bukhari*, 1988, vol. 10:123-126.
[149] Order: *tadawu* (be treated, or seek treatment), in *Sunan Abi Dawud*, 1973, vol. 4:192, and in *Sunan Ibn Majah*, 1953, vol. 2:1137. The Prophet ﷺ ordered Abu Tayba to do cupping *(hijama)* on his wife Umm Salamah. *Sunan Ibn Majah*, 1953, vol. 2:1152.
[150] *Sunan Abi Dawud*, 1973, vol. 4:200; Shawkani, *Nayl al-Awtar*, (1372 AH), vol. 9:95; and *Sunan at-Tirmidhi*, (1350 AH), vol. 3:263.
[151] *Al-Muwatta,'* (ed.), Sa'd, 1983: 812; also in: Ibn al-Qayyim, *Zad al-Ma'ad*, 1979, vol. 4:132; see also, *Medicine of the Prophet* ﷺ, (tr.) Penelope Johnstone, 1998:101.
[152] Al-'Asqalani, *Fath al-Bari: Sharh al-Bukhari*, 1988, vol. 4:123, "The Prophet ﷺ paid the barber who performed cupping on him" and in *Sahih Muslim*, 1987, vol. 14:194.
[153] Dhahabi, *at-Tibb an-Nabawi*, 1986:219, and 228.
[154] Ibn 'Abd al-Salam, (d. 660 AH), *Qawa'id al-Ahkam*, vol. 1:4.
[155] Ghazali, *Ihya'* vol. 1:27, and 30.
[156] *Sunan Ibn Majah*, 1953, vol. 2:1137.
[157] *Sunan Abi Dawud*, 1974, vol. 7:160-161.
[158] Ibn al-Qayyim, *Zad al-Ma'ad*, 1979, vol. 4:139.
[159] Ibn al-Qayyim, *Zad al-Ma'ad*, 1979, vol. 4:141, the last italicized sentence is in Q. 9:91.
Compare this with, "Is a doctor under a duty to treat when the man next to him in the theatre is taken ill? An English court would say not." Lewis, *Medical Negligence*, 1998:158.
[160] Q. 3:110; et al.
[161] Jarrahi, *Kashf al-Khafa*, (Halab) Syria, (n.d.), vol. 1:285; and Cairo edition, (1351 AH), vol. 1:240.
[162] Malik, *al-Muwatta,'* (ed.), Saad, 1983:812.
[163] Ibn al-Qayyim, *Zad al-Ma'ad*, 1979, vol. 4:132; and *Medicine of the Prophet* ﷺ, Johnstone, 1998:101.
[164] Al-Ghazali, *Ihya,'* vol. 1:27.
[165] Malik, *Al-Muwatta,'* (ed.), Sa'ad, 1983:812.
[166] Ibn Abi Usaybia, *'Uyun al-Anba' fi Tabaqat al-Atibba,'* p. 302. (Thabit ibn Sanan ibn Qurrah was educated by his father, Sanan ibn Thabit ibn Qurrah who was the court physician to Abbasid Caliphs, al-Muqtadir billah,

98   The Fiqh of Medicine

al-Qahir billah, and ar-Radi billah (918-930), ibid. pp. 300-301).
[167] *Sunan Ibn Majah*, 1953, vol. 2:1137.
[168] Al-'Asqalani, *Fath al-Bari: al-Bukhari*, 1988, vol. 10:110; *Sahih Muslim*, 1987, vol. 14:195.
[169] Al-'Asqalani, *Fath al-Bari: al-Bukhari*, 1988, vol. 10:110.
[170] Ghazali, *Ihya,*' vol. 4:300, and Ibn al-Qayyim, *Zad al-Ma'ad*, 1979, vol. 4:14-16.
[171] Q. 2:159; and Q. 5:32.
[172] Al-Ghazali, *Ihya,*' vol. 4:300-301.
[173] "There is a cure for every sickness" in; *Sahih Muslim*, 1987, vol. 14:195; and in *Sunan Ibn Majah*, 1953, vol. 2:1137.
[174] Ibn al-Qayyim, *Zad al-Ma'ad*, 1979, vol. 4:15
[175] Al-Ghazali, (d. 1111), *Ihya,*' pp. 300-310.
[176] *Sunan Ibn Majah*, 1953, vol. 2:1156.
[177] *Sunan Ibn Majah*, 1953, vol. 2:1137.
[178] *Ruqa* is a word which can be used in two different ways: it can be good, as when the Prophet ﷺ used the Qur'an for treatment, or it can be unacceptable as when it is used by sorcerers and black magicians. But *ruqa* from the scripture by *(ahl al-kitab)* were acceptable to the Prophet ﷺ, "There is nothing wrong with them, unless they contravene a rule: so let me see them first." Abu Bakr as-Siddiq said that they were acceptable *(ja'iz)*. In *Sahih Muslim*, 1987, vol. 14:169; *Sunan Abi Dawud*, 1973, vol. 4:214.
[179] *Sahih Muslim*, 1987, vol. 14:169; al-'Asqalani, *Fath al-Bari…al-Bukhari*, 1988. vol. 10:127-128.
[180] Court Of Appeal, Civil Division Per Lord Donaldson of Lymington MR, Butler-Sloss and Staughton LJJ 22, 23, 24, 30 July 1992: case 1. Butler-Sloss LJ [1992] 4 All ER 664 case 2. [1992] 4 All ER 668.
[181] *Sunan Ibn Majah*, 1953, vol. 2:1137-1138; and in al-'Asqalani, *Fath al-Bari…al-Bukhari*, 1988, vol. 10:110, with the lengthier version of "cures that are known to some and unknown to others."
[182] Ibn al-Qayyim, *Zad al-Ma'ad*, 1979, vol. 4:17; *Medicine of the Prophet* ﷺ, Johnstone, 1998:12.
[183] Q. 4:119, "…and they will change Allah's creation": 'illegitimate treatment and surgical correction.'
[184] Al-'Asqalani, *Fath al-Bari…al-Bukhari*, 1988, vol. 10:110; *Sunan Abi Dawud*, 1973, vol. 4:207; Hindi, *Kanz al-'Ummal*, 1971, vol. 10:53.
[185] Al-'Asqalani, *Fath al-Bari…al-Bukhari*, 1988, vol. 10:113; *Sunan Abi Dawud*, 1973, vol. 4:197-199, "perhaps dependent on circumstances, type of disease, and site to be cauterised"; also in *Sunan Ibn Majah*, 1953, vol. 2:1155.
[186] Al-'Asqalani, *Fath al-Bari…al-Bukhari*, 1988, vol. 10:115; and Shawkani, *Nayl al-Awtar*, (1372 AH), vol. 9:98.
[187] *Sahih Muslim*, 1987, vol. 10:194; *Sunan Ibn Majah*, 1953, vol. 2:1156.

[188] Al-'Asqalani, *Fath al-Bari al-Bukhari,* 1988, vol. 10:113; and *Sunan Ibn Majah,* 1953, vol. 2:1156.

[189] *Sahih at-Tirmidhi,* (1350 AH), vol. 3:263; Shawkani, *Nayl al-Awtar,* (1372 AH), vol. 9:95.

[190] Al-'Asqalani, *Fath al-Bari... al-Bukhari,* 1988, vol. 10:123; *Sunan Abi Dawud,* 1973, vol. 4:194; and *Sunan Ibn Majah,* 1953, vol. 2:732, and p. 1151.

[191] Azimabadi, *Sunan Abi Dawud,* 1969, vol. 10:337; *Sunan at-Tirmidhi,* (1350 AH), vol. 3:275.

[192] *Sahih Muslim,* 1987, vol. 10:194; *Sunan Ibn Majah,* 1953, vol. 2:1156.

[193] *Sahih Muslim,* 1987, vol. 14:169.

[194] Q. 17:82, **"We send down in the Qur'an that which is a healing and a mercy to the muminun..."** (tr. Bewley).

[195] Hindi, *Kanz al-'Ummal,* 1971, vol. 10:32; and Azimabadi, *'Aun...Sunan Abi Dawud,* 1969, vol. 4:195.

[196] Ibn al-Qayyim, *Zad al-Ma'ad,* 1979, vol. 4:139; *Medicine of the Prophet* ﷺ, Johnstone, 1998:105.

Chapter Four
The rights and responsibilities of patients and those who treat them

1. An overview

I have engaged in an "analysis of law and legal rules from first principles, to formulate [some] general rules of law."[1] This is in order to fill a gap, which is often referred to by western legal commentators. I have relied heavily on the standard references of classical Islamic fiqh without neglecting the works of Muslim fuqaha of modern times.

Cases in Islamic fiqh are often reported in the abstract form of hypothetical questions and answers, although often they derive from actual requests for *fatwa* and guidance. Very little was written up in the form of general rules of law. I hope that this work contributes to the filling of that gap in Islamic medical fiqh.

It is important that this work takes a balanced stand to present the viewpoint of Islamic fiqh from the side of the patient and from the side of those engaged in treatment. The Qur'an mentions 'the balance' in a judicial sense many times; in several of them it is an order to be just and equitable even if it is against one's own interest.[2]

This balance must be the aim: it is to be resorted to, and it must be restored if it is disturbed:

> We sent Our Messengers with the Clear Signs and sent down the Book and the Balance with them so that mankind might establish justice. And We sent down iron in which there lies great force and which has many uses for mankind...[3]

This is not an easy undertaking as 'Medical Law' is not well established even in today's communities.

Margaret Brazier, said, "I do evaluate the state of the law and too often find it sadly wanting."[4]

A modern English writer on health care law said,

> The academic study of health care law is still a relatively young discipline and no consensus has yet been reached as to its proper scope

...Kennedy and Grubb have argued that 'it is essentially concerned with the relationship between doctors (and to a lesser extent hospitals and other institutions) and patients.'[5]

Kennedy and Grubb explained in their book "Medical Law":

...the book remains firmly embedded in English Law...After all, there is very little in the way of European community law, which yet affects 'medical law.'[6]

Islamic medical law is even less developed. The classical approach of Muslim fuqaha was to advocate solutions to certain problems, actual or imagined, posed to them in the field of medicine. The lack of development was further compounded by the fact that these were not decided cases in courts but they were mostly answers to requests for *fatwa* or hypothetical situations. In many cases the situations and arguments led to no clear conclusion. Sometimes a particular faqih will have two different views on the very same situation. Moreover there are the differences among fuqaha in the same school of law *(madhhab)*, and further ones amongst the different schools *(madhahib)*.

Yet, on the other hand, the arguments posed and the avenues opened up were nothing short of impressive. The classical texts are a great resource for making modern laws.

Muslim fuqaha discussed the performance of medical practitioners in all the mundane events of their careers. However, certain fields were given extensive coverage. Lengthy debates centred on the mishaps that occurred in male circumcision, because it was the commonest surgical practice. Sometimes surgery led to the most dramatic complications including loss of the glans. Modern English law treats this as a serious tort.

[Trial by jury]...may be ordered only in exceptional cases, and the severity of the injuries suffered does not render the case exceptional...An example of an 'exceptional' case is *Hodges* v. *Harland & Wolf Ltd.* [1963] 1 WLR 523, where the plaintiff's penis had been torn off by a revolving spindle (though it is hard to see why a jury would be better suited to decide liability or quantum in such a case than a judge).[7]

Muslim fuqaha also discussed other surgical matters resulting from falls or fights; they discussed what happens if a woman aborts after a scuffle with her husband or a third party; they discussed birth control (*'azl*) and other contraceptive methods in which consent of the partner (or lack of it) was of great importance; they discussed what happens when someone asks for the son of his neighbour to be circumcised with his children (a chivalrous and commendable act) and then something goes wrong with the circumcision, for what makes the situation complex is that, because of custom, permission of the guardian of the injured child might not have been obtained; they gave detailed narratives on feeding a person some poison or prescribing it for him; and they discussed compensation for injured or lost organs. A single author in a single discourse, in great and interesting detail, may review all such matters, and more.

The system, which I have adopted, is to examine a specific problem, in the light of the views of the fuqaha, primarily represented in their schools of thought *(madhahib)*. The issues raised are discussed in the framework of: duty of care, standard of care, breach of that duty, loss, causation and remoteness of damage, and compensation; but also bearing in mind contributory negligence and consent.

Thus the actions of the medical practitioner are examined for negligence, recklessness, and criminal negligence with an eye on criminal behaviour at one end of the scale and no-fault arguments at the other.

The results are compared and contrasted when possible with situations and cases in English law.

2. Litigation in the medical field and medical negligence

The overwhelming majority of malpractice cases are brought under the law of negligence. To win a negligence case it is necessary to prove three things. The first is…(duty of care). The second issue concerns the standard of care given…essentially to act in a manner acceptable to their professional peers. Finally victims have to show that the injuries that they suffered were caused by the failure to practise properly.[8]

But there is dissatisfaction with this framework from almost every party involved.

The legal profession is not totally in agreement with the standard of care known as the Bolam test, which was established in a case in 1957 called *Bolam v. Friern Hospital Management Committee*. That case held that: "A doctor is not guilty of negligence if he has acted in accordance with a practice accepted as proper by a responsible body of medical men skilled in that particular art."[9] Lord Scarman in the House of Lords attacked the Bolam test for "Leaving the determination of a legal duty to the judgement of doctors."[10] And Sir John Donaldson MR protested:

The definition of the duty of care is a matter for the law and courts. They cannot stand idly by if the profession, by an excess of paternalism, denies their patients a real choice. In a word, the law will not permit the medical profession to play God.[11]

The doctor derives no comfort when he is told that negligence is a legal term, a way to award damages and not a reflection on his character.

However, it is clear that legal actions are now pleaded in negligence. Even though it can be argued that the doctrines of negligence have not always been strictly applied, it is clear that the courts use the language of negligence.[12]

He may be despondent when he learns that:

It is common knowledge among lawyers that mere negligence in itself is not a cause of action. To give a cause of action there must be negligence, which amounts to a breach of duty towards the person claiming. There are many cases where there has been clear negligence, in the absence of which damage would not have happened, and yet there was no liability under English law
(*per* Greer LJ in *Farr* v. *Butter Bros & Co.* [1932] 2 KB 606, 618).[13]

This is the law; but, still, the medical practitioner finds it difficult to justify, morally, that negligence "in the absence of which damage would not have happened" is without liability for some, whereas his well-intentioned and conscientiously executed efforts have to be branded negligent in order for the patient to collect damages. This is unnecessary as far as the patient is concerned, as all he would like to see is accountability in place and to gain compensation.

Montgomery summarises malpractice litigation as follows:

In general terms it can be seen as an avenue by which health care professionals can be held accountable for their actions…

A second function…is to…maintain a high standard of care…

Thirdly,…as a way of gaining retribution [sic]…

Finally, malpractice law is concerned with compensation…

…the way that the NHS handles claims means that the real defendant will almost always be an NHS trust or health authority, not the individual who made the mistake. As far as compensation is concerned, the rules of negligence are to some extent a lottery.[14]

The issues raised are 'basically legal' and must be resolved by the law; but difficulties and dissatisfaction are reflected within the legal profession as well. Lewis has said:

> Negligence does not exist *in vacuo* as some sort of clearly defined legal concept. It must always be related to a particular fact-situation. This is true of all law, but particularly so of the law of negligence. It is for that reason that judicial decisions in this field only infrequently create any precedent that will necessarily dictate the conclusion in a later case…
>
> One cannot but think that it might well be beneficial to all if there was some sort of academic input involved before important decisions were given…[15]

There may be a point in this. Academics and others may find a way to examine this particular situation because health is everybody's right and concern.

Muslim fuqaha in debating medical fiqh were necessarily academic. They distinguished negligence from mistake or error, and classified criminal negligence as an intentional crime.[16]

Taylor has said:

> It has been said many times by many judges that negligence should be distinguished from 'a mere error of judgement,' but the line is a very fine one and very difficult to draw.[17]

And Lord Denning summed up:

> …the uncertainties inherent in the practice of medicine were such that a doctor, aware of a law which regards errors of clinical judgement as negligent, would sense this as 'a dagger at his back' when undertaking treatment.[18]

Mistake, error, misadventure, and negligence

But how is mistake, error, or misadventure in Islamic law to be defined?

Where is the line to be drawn between them and negligence?

It may be helpful to coin a legal definition, which distinguishes mistake, error, or misadventure from the ordinary word of negligence; negligence then should have a congruent literal and legal meaning in its own right.

On another occasion Lord Denning sought to characterise such mistakes as errors of clinical judgement and, accordingly, not negligent. This view was categorically rejected by the House of Lords on the grounds that to state that the defendant made an error of judgement, whether clinical or otherwise, tells one nothing about whether the error was negligent or not. One consequence, perhaps, of judicial attitudes such as that of Lord Denning is that a claim for compensation by an injured patient is often perceived by doctors to be accompanied by denigration of the defendant's professional competence.[19]

This may be semantics for the lawyer, but it may clarify matters for the medical and lay populace. Mason and McCall Smith, a medical man and a legal man have said:

> There is no doubt, too, that the defining of a relationship, such as that of a doctor and patient, in legalistic terms leads to a subtle but important change in the nature of the relationship. What the law expects of the doctor may mirror closely what codes of medical ethics expect, but the basis of compliance in each case is essentially different. Trust and respect are more likely to flourish in a relationship which is governed by morality rather than by legal rules and, no matter how appropriate the law may be for the regulation of many of the ordinary transactions of life, the injection of formality and excessive caution into the relationship between doctor and patient is ultimately not in the patient's interest if it means that each sees the other as a potential adversary.[20]

There is scope and provision in Islamic fiqh to separate mistake and error from negligence. This may rightfully and easily compensate the patient who would not have to prove anything as the damage speaks for itself *(Res ipsa loquitur)*. The medical practitioner will feel no chagrin or humiliation. At the same time Islamic fiqh may make the practitioner personally liable for causing damage which will be compensable up to one third of the value of *diya* as indemnity;[21] this is payable *from his personal funds*. Compensation beyond one third is payable by others as we shall see. This will take care of the patient's demands for accountability and justice. It is also an instruction for those in the medical profession, to be even more careful or more proficient in the execution of their duties. It is an accepted Islamic concept that mistakes will happen; what is important, is to stand to be corrected and to atone for any mistakes. The Qur'an says:

Our Lord, do not take us to task if we forget or make a mistake!;[22]
And,
You are not to blame for any honest mistake you make but only for what your hearts premeditate.[23]

The Prophet ﷺ said, "Allah forgives acts committed in error, or under coercion; and forgetfulness."[24]

There is no wrong action in committing an error; but in all cases the damage is to be redressed.[25] The practitioner is obliged to bear the payment of compensation for damage up to one third of the total *diya*; larger sums are the responsibility of his relatives *('aqila)*, or the government's treasury *(bayt al-mal)*. The involvement of the community or the society, in the form of relatives sharing the indemnity, is a token of shared responsibility and not liability. The involvement of the government has the added moral of better supervision of the standards of education, training, and performance; which is the responsibility of the government as an authorising body. From all of these responsibilities a construct like vicarious liability can emerge.[26]

Within the framework of Islamic fiqh, the four functions of the purpose of malpractice suits, as stated in modern medical laws, may be fulfilled, that is: accountability, an incentive to maintain high standards of care, retribution, and compensation.

3. The medical practitioner and negligence

The ingredients of medical negligence in Islamic fiqh are compared and contrasted with what constitutes negligence in modern day laws. Again 'English law' is selected as an example.

The three ingredients of negligence in English law: "a duty of care, a breach of that duty, and loss occasioned by that breach,"[27] are easily traceable in some of the sayings of the Prophet ﷺ on the matter, e.g.:

He who undertakes the treatment of others, without preparing himself, and causes loss of life or damage is held liable.[28]

And:

He who sets himself up, and undertakes the treatment of others, but had not prepared himself well for medical practice *(tatabbaba)* and as a result has caused harm *('anata)*, is liable,[29]

which Ibn al-Qayyim, chose for his analysis. His analysis was as follows:

According to the *hadith* I found three seams worthy of note:

The first was linguistic concerning the Arabic word for medicine *(tibb)* which means, mending and correction with gentle care and excellence of ability.

But *tatabbaba* means struggling with the craft not knowing it...

The second was legal, which stipulates that an ignorant practitioner of medicine is liable for the harm done, because in his recklessness and accepting to do what he is not qualified to do, he has betrayed the patient's trust and harmed him. One's duty is not to deceive, and not to harm others; he was in breach of that.

The third point was that the Prophet ﷺ stated that the "unprepared practitioner who causes harm *('anata)* is liable," and from this *hadith*, I was able to classify those who engaged in medical practice into five categories:

The first is a practitioner, who is well trained, alert and keen, who has done his job well. He was authorised by the state and had the consent of the patient. Despite that, his patient succumbed or there was damage to a part or to one or more of his senses; such a practitioner is not liable. This is the view of almost all the fuqaha and all schools of Islamic fiqh *(ijma')*.

The second, is a practitioner, who is unqualified and has harmed his patient: there are two possibilities here, the first one is that the patient knew about the lack of qualification of his treating attendant yet he consented to the intervention; in this case the practitioner is not liable; but if the patient did not know, and he was deceived, then the practitioner is liable.

The third is a practitioner, who is qualified and was attentive but his hand has slipped and he has cut what he should not have; he is liable because he erred. But his liability is limited by a ceiling of one third of the full *diya*. If the damage is more than that, then the extra compensation is borne by his family relatives *('aqila)*. If he has no *'aqila* then it is the *bayt al-mal* which bears the compensation when possible, otherwise it is dropped.

The fourth category of practitioner is a qualified one, who has prescribed some medicine for a person, and that person died as a result of ingesting the medicine. In that case it is the *bayt al-mal* which is responsible for the full *diya* as *per* Ibn Hanbal in one of his sayings, or it is the duty of the practitioner's relatives *('aqila')* as *per* Ibn Hanbal in another of his sayings.

The fifth category of practitioners is the one who is qualified, and attentive but did his job without consent, in the case of a child or a mad person. There are two possibilities: either the intervention was successful or the patient came to some harm. If the intervention was successful then there are two situations to be considered: one is that he had no permission, so he is at fault and liable even if there was no damage, as this constitutes battery. The other consideration is that, the practitioner meant well and did well and there was no harm so he is not liable as it is a duty to do well. But if the intervention was followed by damage then the practitioner is liable for the damage per se in the first place. The lack of consent must be looked into as well. Should that warrant an extra liability or is the liability enveloped in the mistake? This is a question that begs for an answer [sic].[30]

This is the way many Muslim fuqaha debated legal matters. Questions and answers, which are themselves sometimes questions. At other times the question is left open with the possibilty of more than one answer. But none of the possibilities would have been in violation of Shari'ah.

Ibn al-Qayyim with his analyses, answers, and even questions covered a lot of the ground in medical practice, and negligence. His work coupled with that of Ibn Rushd,[31] the Maliki faqih, is almost a complete treatise on the matter from an Islamic fiqh viewpoint.

Ibn Rushd said:

> The medical practitioner, who errs, as in cutting off the glans in circumcision, is liable, as it is a mistake. He is liable for values less than one third of *diya* in his own resources; his relatives (*'aqila*) are responsible for values more than that. But if he is an impostor then he is lashed, and jailed, and he is also liable for *diya* in his *own* funds; but it is mentioned that his relatives may be responsible to pay it.

> There is a narrative attributed to Malik that the medical practitioner is not liable if he is known to be competent and knowledgeable.[32]

The Qur'an repeatedly orders one to care for, and not to harm others:

Whoever does an atom's weight of good will see it. Whoever does an atom's weight of evil will see it.[33]

but within the limits of one's ability,

Allah does not impose on any self any more than it can stand.[34]

A similar seam can be traced in the teachings of the Prophet; some *hadith* in that respect may be quoted:

> "Do no harm, and cause no hurt in seeking redress, *(la darar wa la dirar)*."[35]

> "One should do one's job well, and with sincerity to Allah."[36]

> "Whoever is paid to do a job is accountable."[37]

The rights and responsibilities of patients and those who treat them   109

'Ali ibn Abi Talib, who was a master faqih, coined his dictum; "labourers (craftsmen) are liable, as that is a better discipline for the people."[38] The Hanafi fuqaha interdicted the practise of three types of persons: The corrupt faqih *(mufti)*, the bankrupt merchant, and the ignorant doctor.[39] This may translate into suspension of registration or being struck off the medical register in modern times.

Focusing on medical negligence as a special issue, it will be considered under three main points: First, the basis of liability, the duty of care and the breach of that duty with its attendant harm. Second, the standard of care. Third, what constitutes negligence in Islamic fiqh and its redress?

3.1 First: The basis of liability

I will continue to compare and contrast Islamic fiqh with English law, but first it is necessary to establish the basis of liability for malpractice in Islamic fiqh. Although it is possible to contract medical services in Islamic fiqh, it is also possible to invoke failure to perform according to the accepted norms and standards as a cause for litigation.

It was stated in the beginning of chapter three, that comparative law as such is not my concern. But many Muslim countries were under colonial rule. Some of their laws were influenced by English law, such as Pakistan, Bangladesh, Sudan, Jordan, Yemen, and some other Arab countries. Other Muslim countries' laws were influenced by the Code Napoleon, like Egypt, Syria, Lebanon, Algiers, Morocco, and Tunisia. So it may be useful to point out the basis of malpractice cases generally, *la responsabilite contractuelle ou la resposabilite delictuelle*, as it is possible to follow either course according to Islamic fiqh.

In England, theoretically one could contract for medical services, so actions may be brought in contract law, at least, in private practice. Few people do. Montgomery observes:[40]

> The overwhelming majority of malpractice cases are brought under the law of negligence...
>
> In private medicine,...The patient would be able to sue in both negligence and contract. In theory it is possible for a health professional to contract to provide a standard of care that is higher than that required in negligence. However, the courts have shown themselves very reluctant to accept that they have done so. They have refused to accept that

surgeons have agreed to exercise closer personal supervision than is normal[41] or to guarantee success[42]

This is very similar to Islamic fiqh, (Hulwani's head injury case):

> Faqih Shams al-A'imma al-Hulwani was asked about a girl who fell off a roof and injured her head. Many attending surgeons said if you allow her head to be opened she would die. One of them said, "If you do not open her head, she will die today. I will do that and cure her." He opened her head. She died a day later. Is he liable? Hulwani said, "No." He was asked, "What if he had promised to cure her?" He replied, "even though."[43]

Ibn 'Abidin said that, 'promises to cure are not binding,' because in contract three things must be fulfilled: it must be possible *(maqduran)*, if it involves an object that object must have been delivered *(musalaman)*, and it must be permissible *(ja'izan)*. These are only relevant to solid objects.

The damage caused by injury rests partly on the resistance of the host. Compensation for hurt is not contractual; it is for transgression (tort).[44]

But despite that, some Muslim fuqaha find no objection to contracting medical services stipulating a cure from an ailment. Ibn al-Qasim said:

> Malik says that, 'If a medical practitioner is contracted, it means that he was contracted to effect a cure. When that happens then he deserves his fee; unless there was a *halal* (legal) condition attached to the contract.

> But I [Ibn al-Qasim] think it is also possible to rent the services of a practitioner for a specified period: a day or a month, to instil *kohl* in the eye, for a fee of one *dirham*. If the eye heals before the passage of the month, does the practitioner deserve a fee relative to the number of days at which the eye has healed, or are the parties obligated by whatever was set in the contract? I think the payment should be for 'the whole month's rent' because you may not contract for a cure, whereas you can contract someone to put *kohl* in a healthy eye.[45]

Malik's view may find support in a quote of Lord Templeton:

> The relationship between doctor and patient is contractual in origin, the doctor performing services in consideration for fees payable by the patient.[46]

But it leads to the same result of dissatisfaction associated with trying medical malpractice cases, which has led even those who would like to consider the relationship as contractual, to classify the contract as a contract to render a service rather than to accomplish a result.[47]

This is even reflected in the debate consequent upon Lord Templeton's speech in *Sidaway* v. *Governors of Bethlem Royal Hospital* [1985]:

> The doctor, obedient to the high standards set by the medical profession impliedly contracts to act at all times in the 'best interests of the patient...'

> [i]t is difficult to see how a duty to act in the patient's 'best interests' can differ in any substantive way from a doctor's duty to exercise reasonable care in practising the skills of medicine.[48]

The preference of negligence to contract in English law is also consistent with the views of the Hanafi faqih, (al)-Sarakhsi, who specifically discussed why medical services could not be the subject of contract:

> It is not possible to contract medical services, be it in humans or animals, as with dealing with piercing pearls where a contract is in order.

> Opening a wound is opening the gates of the soul, healing after that depends on nature's way of defending the body against the effect of the wound. It is not within the capabilities of humans, so it cannot be the subject of contract of exchange *(mu'awada)*. His duty was performed; he is not liable except if he transgressed or operated without due consent. I explain further, that what follows the wound is nature's course, while in non-living objects it should be possible to set the limits of the procedure, hence such work can be contracted.[49]

A duty of care is wider in scope in Islamic fiqh than in English law as it includes rescue as well;[50] but there is no difference in the basic definition as we saw from the quote of Ibn al-Qayyim.[51]

3.2 Second: Standard of care

In England that standard was 'established' in 1957, in the important case of *Bolam* v. *Friern Hospital Management Committee*. The plaintiff, John Bolam, underwent electroconvulsive therapy at the defendant's hospital. The staff administered no muscle relaxant, nor manual restraints. The patient suffered bilateral dislocation of the hip joints and fractured pelvic bones. Competing evidence was given as to the normal practice of doctors.

J. McNair:

> A doctor is not guilty of negligence if he has acted in accordance with a

practice accepted as proper by a responsible body of medical men skilled in that particular art...

A doctor is not negligent, if he is acting in accordance with such a practice, merely because there is a body of opinion that takes a contrary view. At the same time, that does not mean that a medical man can obstinately and pig-headedly carry on with some old technique if it has been proved to be contrary to what is really substantially the whole of informed medical opinion.[52]

Montgomery wrote:

The *Bolam* case was decided in 1957, it did not become the cardinal test for negligence until it was adopted by the House of Lords in *Whitehouse v. Jordan* in 1980. Cases before that date need, therefore, to be treated carefully.[53]

Dissatisfaction surrounds the *Bolam* test, as some have said that the House of Lords came close to allowing doctors themselves to set the standard of care required of them.[54]

The issues stirred by the case had also been considered by Muslim fuqaha. The following points are chosen for comparison:

(1) The standard of care
(2) Differences of opinions in practice, and as regards novel procedures
(3) The numbers involved to make 'a defence to a negligence allegation'
(4) Levels of skill: Is a special standard of care required?

(1) The standard of care

Lord Scarman stated the Bolam principle in these terms:

The Bolam principle may be formulated as a rule that a doctor is not negligent if he acts in accordance with a practice accepted at the time as proper by a responsible body of medical opinion even though other doctors adopt a different practice. In short, the law imposes the duty of care: but the standard of care is a matter of medical judgement.[55]

This may be compared with the views of Muslim fuqaha:

Ash-Shafi'i (d. 204/819) expresses it as, "If he did what is done by his acknowledged peers in the craft then he is not liable."[56]

As-Sarakhsi, (d. (? 483)/1090), the Hanafi faqih, explained that "if he performs within the known bounds, then he is not liable; in contradistinction to trades, because 'the living' have their own reaction to injury, and healing is a function of nature: a domain outside the control of the practitioner."[57]

Al-Muwaq, the Maliki faqih (d. 897/1492), used expressions, denying liability in situations, which can be translated as "what is done by those in the profession" or, "the accepted practice in the field."[58]

(2) Differences in opinions and novel procedures

McNair J. held in Bolam that a doctor may not be negligent merely because there was a body of opinion that takes an opposite view if he acted in accordance with accepted medical practice. Montgomery commented:

"This does not mean that innovative practice is negligent merely because it is unusual."[59] This may be compared with the Muslim faqih Hulwani's 'head injury case,' quoted previously concerning the girl who fell from the roof.[60]

(3) The numbers involved to make 'a defence to a negligence allegation'

Montgomery says that, even a small number of such experts supporting a particular position will suffice. This is further explained by saying that they hold responsible positions in relation to the relevant speciality.[61]

This may be compared to Muslim fuqaha's views:

Ash-Sharawani,[62] and Ash-Shubramulsi (d. 1087/1676)[63] both of the Shafi'i school said:

> A medical practitioner is not liable, at the pain of ignorance, if two just and qualified men in the field consider him knowledgeable. They certify that his competence is well known to them; and that he had cured many people according to their knowledge.

An-Najdi, from the Hanbali School, was very specific, he said:

> Medical practitioners are not liable if it is well known that they are competent, and they were taught the profession by known teachers, who gave them permission to practise *(ajazahu)*.[64]

These examples show a similarity of approach in relation to what is accepted practise between Islamic fiqh and present day English law.

(4) Levels of skill: Is a special standard of care required?

The standard of care must vary, to be fair, depending on circumstances.

A general medical practitioner is not to be judged against the standards of specialists, who themselves vary from one speciality to another and within the same speciality. Conversely it might be negligent for a generalist to undertake the work of a specialist.[65]

In Islamic fiqh the very same theme can be traced as the standard of care was brought up to match the circumstances.

The Prophet ﷺ personally undertook to treat a companion, Sa'd ibn Mu'adh, in the battlefield of *al-Ahzab* (626 CE) when he was wounded. He cauterised him twice to stop the bleeding.[66]

That might have been because there was no person more qualified in medicine to do the job. This is inferred because on another occasion the Prophet ﷺ was with an injured man. The man summoned two persons from Bani Anmar tribe to treat him. The Prophet ﷺ asked them: "Which of you is the better at medicine *(atabb)*?"[67]

Ibn al-Qayyim took this *hadith* to mean that:

> In every subject or craft one must choose the best available, as success is more likely then.[68]

Penelope Johnstone rendered it as:

> This *hadith* shows that it is necessary, concerning every science and craft, to seek the help of the person most skilful in it; the most skilful person will be the one most likely to find the best solution.[69]

> Later on it became a necessity to be educated, trained and certified by experts to practice medicine.[70]

Formal medical education was well established during the reign of the Abbasid Caliph al-Muqtadir billah in 918 CE at the hands of his chief physician, Sannan ibn-Qurrah. The examination, classification, and registration of qualified physicians was carried out by Sannan ibn-Qurrah in the year 930 CE at the time of Caliph ar-Radi billah when a patient died during treatment.[71]

This can be extrapolated to express itself in the duty to encourage good medical practice through ongoing training and specialisation, consequent upon which is the requirement of differing standards of care.

3.3 Third: Medical negligence and its redress

Broadly, whatever calls for *daman* (redress) can be included in the constituents of medical negligence, which is also applicable to other walks of life, namely: *ta'adi* (transgression), and *tajawuz al-hadd* (overstepping the limits of permission). But not on every occasion on which the medical practitioner is called upon for redress is he considered negligent. This view is not uncommon amongst modern Western jurists:

> Lord Denning sought to characterise such mistakes as errors of clinical judgement and, accordingly, not negligent.[72]

According to Muslim fuqaha, medical negligence can have any one of several forms. Ibn al-Qayyim listed twenty requirements to be observed:

> ...knowing the disease; its cause; its virulence; the resistance of the patient; the unusual factors affecting the situation; age of the patient; his habits; suitability of the time for the intervention; country of origin of the patient; climate at the time of sickness; weighing the possibilities of treatment; the hazards attached to it; the cure must not be worse than the illness; the simpler the treatment the better; some diseases are incurable, alleviation of the suffering is enough; to give the body its natural time of response to the ailment before, say, incising an inflamed area, and allow treatment measures time to act; to understand that not all sickness is purely physical; being gentle with, and kind to the patient as though dealing with a child; being imaginative in devising treatments; the twentieth point is the hallmark of good medical practice: aim at preserving what health the patient has, aim at ridding the patient of his sickness or ameliorate it, accepting the lesser harm to remove the greater harm,...[73]

These requirements complement and detail what was laid down by the consensus of Muslim fuqaha as regards sound medical practice, which is 'a defence to an allegation of negligence.' Accordingly the main features of transgression *(ta'adi)* are:
1. Failure to secure the consent of the patient or his guardian
2. Failure to secure the authorities' permission to practise
3. Not being prepared, or being ill-prepared, for the job
4. Taking on more than one is qualified for
5. Not taking due care: using an instrument or a procedure which causes undue pain or shock; choosing a bad time of the day or season of the year, not paying due care to the age of the patient.[74]

In any of those cases transgression leads to *daman* (compensation or redress); but other 'penalties' could be meted out. The fuqaha divided medical practitioners in the above categories (medical negligence) into two main types: first, the competent medical practitioner who fails to secure the due consent of the patient or the authorisation of the relevant governing body; second the incompetent practitioner; and they described disciplinary measures and reimbursement.

(1) The competent unauthorised medical practitioner

(a) In the Hanafi, Maliki, and Shafi'i schools, *(al-jumhur* i.e. the majority) are agreed that lack of consultation or authority constituted *ta'adi* (transgression), and *daman* (restitution) was the remedy for the battery, and its complications *(sirayah)* should any arise.[75]

The Malikis went further and demanded that the practitioner must be disciplined as well, lashed or imprisoned, depending on the facts of each case.[76] And the Shafi'is called for expiation *(kaffara)* as well as the *daman*.[77] Expiation could be giving alms or by fasting a number of days.

The fuqaha held that the offence was twofold: battery against the person, and an offence against the law of the land.

(b) Ibn al-Qayyim, from the Hanbali school, said:

> It all depends on the result of the intervention; if the result was beneficial and there was no loss then the practitioner is not liable. Because the practitioner meant no harm and did no harm; he was doing a service to the patient out of his goodness. **"There is no way open against good-doers, Allah is Ever-Forgiving, Most Merciful."**[78]

But the quotation taken from the Qur'an does not make it applicable to the situation, nor can it be taken as authorisation in Islamic fiqh to treat without consent. It is quoted out of context.

(c) The Duty to Warn

Should the medical practitioner explain every detail to his patient as regards the ailment and the implications of treatment, so as not to be negligent?

In other words, is there a duty to warn?

Islam is for truthfulness, there should be no deception in dealings; but Islam is also for gentle care and kindness. The Prophet ﷺ said:

> When you see a patient tell him that he can expect a long life *(nafisu lahu fi'l-ajal)*: that will not alter fate, but it will cheer him up.[79]

A surgeon may tell the patient every frightening detail of the disease or operative procedure. That would be unkind. But Islam is also for people being for one another. Some close relative should be informed. It all depends on the intention and the manner in which things are done.

The Prophet ﷺ also said:

> Actions are only by intentions, and each man has only that which he intends. Whoever's emigration is for Allah and His Messenger, then his emigration is for Allah and His Messenger. Whoever's emigration is for some worldly gain which he can acquire or a woman he will marry, then his emigration is for that for which he emigrates.[80]

Compare this with cases in English law where occasionally the courts have not found for the plaintiff when he or she was not told everything by medical staff. In *Sidaway* v. *Governors of Bethlem Royal Hospital*, Mrs Sidaway claimed that, the neurosurgeon, Mr. Falconer did not tell her everything. Her claim was rejected at all levels up to the House of Lords.[81]

(2) The incompetent practitioner

All Islamic fuqaha are unanimous *(ijma')* that such a practitioner is liable for any loss or harm, caused by his action, and all its complications.[82]

But they did not agree as to who bears the *diya* (compensation).

(a) The Hanafis are split amongst themselves over this; some of them (as per Ibn Mas'ud) think that he should bear one half of the *diya*, others in the school say that he should bear it all if the act was intentional.[83]

(b) All the Maliki fuqaha think that the tort-feasor should definitely bear liability for compensation up to one third of the full *diya* (value of thirty-three camels), but they are split over compensation in excess of that. Some think it is his sole responsibility, others think that the *'aqila* should bear whatever is more than one third of the *diya* as an instruction in the wayward behaviour of one of their kin.[84]

So, all the Hanafi and all the Maliki fuqaha are agreed that at least one third of the total value of the *diya* (33 camels worth) is unquestionably the personal obligation of the tort-feasor.

(c) The Shafi'is, say that it is the *'aqila* which should bear all the *diya*. If there are no relatives to qualify as *'aqila*, or if they cannot afford it, then the *bayt al-mal* may be called upon. But if there are not enough public funds for such purposes, then it becomes the obligation of the tort-feasor.

Such behaviour should have been monitored by the closer community of the extended family, and the wider brotherhood of the *ummah*, or nation. But if the *'aqila* and the *bayt al-mal* cannot afford it, then it is the obligation of the tort-feasor. Compensation should never be denied to the aggrieved.[85]

In modern times it can be taken that the *bayt al-mal* is not going to be able to meet these obligations. So the tort-feasor will be the principal compensator.

(a) The Hanbali school, although agreed on the liability of the practitioner, have differing views on who pays the *diya*. At the same time they have introduced an inclining towards 'informed consent,' and a leeway to euthanasia:

> Some of our friends say that a general rule is derived from the Prophet's *hadith* ﷺ,"He who sets himself up, and undertakes the treatment of others, while it is not known of him that he is proficient in medical knowledge, is liable; even if the patient knew of his ignorance, and permitted him; because the issue is that he is not entitled to practise, and he should not have been enabled to practise"…But some friends of our present day [sic] say,"That the practitioner should not pay any compensation if the patient knew of his ignorance, yet consented to the treatment. Because, even if the practitioner was not entitled to practise, the situation is similar to someone asking and permitting another to kill, or wound him." In that situation no liability ensues, as most fuqaha have agreed [sic].[86]

Ibn al-Qayyim, a Hanbali faqih, said:

> The matter judged from a legal viewpoint *(shari'ah)*, is that an ignorant medicine man is liable for the harm done, because he has assaulted *(tahajama)* the patient with his ignorance and harmed him, and he had been reckless in doing what he was not qualified to do. He has betrayed the patient's trust and deceived him, therefore he is obligated to compensate him: this is the consensus of the learned.

Al-Khattabi says,'the consensus is that he who transgresses *(ta'ada)* and causes loss to a patient, is liable *(damin)*. The one who undertakes what he does not know, be it knowledge or an assignment is a transgressor, if his act results in loss, then he is liable for *diya*. Retribution *(qisas* – the severer punishment) is not entertained because the patient contributed by his consent. The compensation *(daman)* is the responsibility of his *'aqila* according to the majority of the fuqaha.'[87]

But Ibn al-Qayyim, said, in the second of his categories of medicine men:

> The second, is an ignorant practitioner who 'treated' and harmed someone by the treatment; in this situation there are two possibilities to consider: one is that the patient knew about the ignorance of the practitioner and consented to treatment, in that case there is no *daman* (liability); the second is that the practitioner has deceived the patient by holding himself out as being a competent medicine man, in that case he is liable. But returning to the first consideration, "saying that the patient knew of the ignorance of the medicine man and consented must be examined," as the strength in which things are coached and the way information is packaged can be deceptive.[88]

Those who argue that if the patient 'knew' of the practitioner's ignorance yet consented to the treatment, and then the practitioner is not liable, will have to prove that the consent was 'informed.'

Even in this day and age, and in highly sophisticated communities, people do consult palmists, sorceresses, quacks, and people who make talismans. Some do not refrain from dabbling in black magic, voodoo-like activities, and mass hysteria of groups invoking the occult. There have been cases of pact suicides and mass murders at the instigation of some, where there has been 'consent.' Should such consent negate liability or culpability?

(3) Disciplinary Measures and Reimbursement

Islamic fiqh may not only provide for compensation in every case of medical negligence; according to the doctrine of *ta'zir* (discretionary punishment), cases may be 'punished' as well. The scale of *ta'zir* varies from admonishing, through reprimands, fines, lashing, and incarceration, to even the taking of life. Punishments have been suggested by different fuqaha for negligent medical practitioners.

(a) The Hanafi school suggests that, "the ignorant medical practitioner can be interdicted."[89] This can translate into temporary or permanent suspension of registration, thus barring the practitioner from practising the profession.

(b) In the Maliki school Ibn Rushd said:

> The ignorant practitioner is to be lashed, imprisoned, and *diya* is due on his own funds, but some said that it is to be met by the *'aqila* (relatives).[90]

(c) The Shafi'i school adds expiation *(kaffara)* when there is loss of life. This consists of fasting for two consecutive months (other than the one month of Ramadan): a constant reminder of the wrong done. If illness or other excuse makes fasting difficult then sixty of the poor must be fed for one day, or permutations thereof. The Prophet ﷺ said, "If your good deeds please you, and your bad ones sadden you, then you are a true mumin."[91]

Islamic fiqh has offered the principle of a remedy, in the concepts of *diya, 'aqila,* and *ahl ad-diwan*.[92]

At present the *'aqila* system may not be possible to implement financially, but the reason for it is not solely as a resource for money; it is meant as a resource of empathy as well. And the concept of 'relatives' may extend to bigger 'tribes' or the entire society. The Prophet ﷺ initiated it because,"One of you has erred (a hand amongst you) *(yadun min aydikum janat).*"[93]

The system of *ahl ad-diwan*,[94] in meeting the compensation in Islamic fiqh, could possibly be likened to that in the NHS whereby the NHS is held responsible for the shortcomings of its practitioners. It is also of some interest to examine the later role of guilds of professions in Islamic society in this respect. Montgomery comments that:

> [t]he way that the NHS handles claims means that the real defendant will almost always be an NHS trust or health authority, not the individual who made the mistake.[95]

There is also room to offset the criticism levelled at the NHS, that it is paying for the mistakes of practitioners, thus leading to unaccountability and lack of zeal to improve standards,[96] by making a practitioner pay his share of the compensation. That share could always be more than the value of one third of *diya* according to Islamic fiqh.

> 'Aqila does not bear the restitution of intentional harmful acts, or whatever is less than the value of one third of diya in consequences of error *(khatta').*[97]

In summary, therefore, Islamic fiqh accommodates all of the four functions of malpractice litigation mentioned by Montgomery: accountability, incentive to maintain a high standard of care, retribution, and compensation.[98]

In English law 'the overwhelming majority of malpractice cases are brought under the law of negligence.'[99] Muslim fuqaha, chose to treat the subject within their own constructs of what constitutes *ta'adi* (trans-

The rights and responsibilities of patients and those who treat them 121

gression) and *tajawuz al-hadd* (overstepping the limits of permission).

The 'law of negligence' does not encompass all the debate Muslim fuqaha had on issues relating to medical practice in this respect. Muslim fuqaha debated the consequences of the actions of medical practitioners in a theoretical manner, which gave equal emphasis to the different hypothetical situations they engineered; irrespective of their frequency.

The duty of care is wider in scale as it includes rescue and 'volunteering.' Error is distinct from negligence, and although the patient is nearly always compensated, sometimes the treating person is not liable; not only that but he is also entitled to his fee.[100]

Medical negligence in their writings was rendered within a theme, which dealt with different facets of the practice; an example of which is seen in the discourses of Ibn al-Qayyim and Ibn Rushd, where the three ingredients of negligence: "a duty of care, a breach of that duty, and loss occasioned by that breach," are easily traceable.[101]

So, I came up with a classification of my own, on similar lines to those of Ibn al-Qayyim, that would allow for all the situations envisaged by Muslim fuqaha to be compared and contrasted with English law. Otherwise, situations where no compensation is due even when the patient is harmed, and others where the medical practitioner may be called upon to redress the patient, without being called negligent, will be missed.

There are daunting problems that stand in the way of any comparative sociology of law, especially at the level of whole cultures or whole societies. But there may be little pieces we can profitably compare, including pieces of legal culture.[102]

Notes

1. Edge, Ian, (ed.), *Islamic Law*, 1996: xxviii.
2. Q. 4:135.
3. Q. 57:25, 'the balance' is also mentioned in: Q. 6:152, Q. 7:85, Q. 11:84, 42:17, 55:7-9.
4. Brazier, Margaret, *Medicine Patients And The Law*, 1992:x.
5. Montgomery, *Health Care Law*, 1997:1.
6. Kennedy, and Grubb, *Medical Law: Text and Materials*, 1994:v.
7. Lewis, *Medical Negligence*, 1998:13, footnote 16. Quoted before in f.n. 348, above 'jury trial.'
8. Montgomery, *Health Care Law*, 1997:166.
9. [1957] 2 All ER 118, 121.
10. *Sidaway v Board of Governors of the Bethlem Royal Hospital and the Maudsly Hospital* [1985] 1 All ER 643, 649, and 663.
11. [1984] QB 493, [1985] AC 871.
12. Montgomery, *Health Care Law*, 1997:167.
13. Lewis, *Medical Negligence*, 1998:156.
14. Montgomery, *Health Care Law*, 1997:165 and 190.
15. Lewis, *Medical Negligence*, 1998:157.
16. Ibn al-Qayyim, *Zad al-Ma'ad*, 1979, vol. 4:139-141; and Ibn Rushd, *Bidayat, al-Kuliyat*, vol. 2:255.
17. Taylor, *Doctors and the Law*, 1976:80.
18. *Hatcher v Black* (1954) *The Times*, 2 July 1954, cited in Davies, *Textbook on Medical Law*, 1996:87.
19. Jones, *Medical Negligence*, 1996:1 (in fn. 2), "The disagreement occurred in *Whitehouse v. Jordan* [1980] 1 All ER 650, C.A.; [1981] 1 All ER 267, H. L"; see also Jones, *Medical Negligence*, 1996:119.
20. Mason and McCall Smith, *Law and Medical Ethics*, 1994:16.
21. Value of about £10,000 in today's money. See *diya* above, pp. 99-101 (Full *diya* is 100 camels or their value).
22. Q. 2:285.
23. Q. 33:5.
24. Al-Hakim, *al-Mustadrak*, (1340 AH), vol. 2:198; *Sunan Ibn Majah*, 1952, vol. 1:658-659.
25. Borno, *al-Wajeez*, 1998:226, and 237 citing *Majallat al-Ahkam al-'Adliya*, vol. 1:55. {Henceafter *al-Majalla*}.
26. See Chapter Three of thesis for: *diya, 'aqila, qasama, ahl ad-diwan*, and *bayt al-mal*, at pp. 96-103.
27. Lewis, *Medical Negligence*, 1998:156.

The rights and responsibilities of patients and those who treat them 123

28 Hindi, *Kanz al-'Ummal*, 1971, vol. 10:32.
29 *Sunan Abi Dawud*, 1973, vol. 4:710-711.
30 Ibn al-Qayyim, *Zad al-Ma'ad*, 1979, vol. 4:138-141; see also *Medicine of the Prophet*, Johnstone, 1998:105-107. Ibn al-Qayyim, Shams ad-Din Muhammad ibn Abi-Bakr ibn Ayyub az-Zari'i ad-Dimashqi, ((Ibn al-Qayyim al-Jawziyya (691-751/1291-1350)), a great Hanbali *Faqih* (jurist), a medical man, and a student of Ibn Taymiyya (d. 728/1328).
31 Ibn Rushd, Abu al-Walid Muhammad ibn Ahmad ibn Muhammad ibn Rushd (520-595/1126-1198), the greatest philosopher of the Muslim West in the Middle Ages; was regarded as one of the greatest physicians of his time; (see Sheikh, *Islamic Philosophy*, 1982:131). He was also Chief Justice *(Qadi al-Qudah)*.
(The two briefs are juxtaposed for comparison of the two great fuqaha).
32 Ibn Rushd, *Bidayat, al-Kulliyat*, Cairo, vol. 2:255 and 454-455.
33 Q. 99:7-8 (tr. Bewley); see also Q. 9:106 **"Say: 'Act, for Allah will see your actions, and so will His Messenger and the muminun.'"** (tr. Bewley).
34 Q. 2:286 (tr. Bewley).
35 Malik in *Al-Muwatta*, (ed.) Sa'd, 1983:638; *Sunan Ibn Majah*, 1953, vol. 2:784; *al-Majalla*, article 19.
36 Jarrahi, *Kashf al-Khafa*, Halab, vol. 1:285, hadith No. 747 *(inn'Allah yuhibbu, idha 'amila al-'amilu an uhsin)*; and *Sunan Ibn Majah*, 1952, vol. 1:84 *(...wa ikhlasun li'llahi fi'l-'amal)*.
37 Hindi, *Kanz al-'Ummal*, 1971, vol. 10:29, hadith, "man akhadha ajran hasabahu' llahu bi'l-'amal."
38 An-Nawawi, *al-Majmu'a Sharh al-Muhadhdhab*, Dar al-Fikr, vol. 15:96-97, "la yasluhu an-nas illa bi dhak."
39 Kasani, *Badai'a*, 1910, vol. 7:169; Sarakhsi, *al-Mabsut*, 1958, vol. 24:157, Ibn 'Abidin, *al-Hashiya*, 1966, vol. 6:147.
40 Montgomery, *Health Care Law*, 1997:166.
41 *Morris v. Winsbury-White* [1937] 4 All ER 494.
42 *Thake v. Maurice* [1986] 1 All ER 497}.
43 *Faqih* al-Hulwani, 'Abd al-'Aziz ibn Ahmad ibn Nasr ibn Salih al-Bukhari (d. 456/1064), see Ibn Qadi Samawa, *Jami' al-Fusilin*, (1300 AH), vol 2:186. The same was attributed to Faqih Najm al-A'imma al-Halimi by Trabulsi, *Mu'in al-Hukkam*, (1393/1973):204. Cited by Mubarak, *al-Tadawi*, 1991:73 and 183.
44 *Hashiyat Ibn 'Abidin*, 1966, vol.6:66; 67; and 68-69. See also Sarakhsi, *al-Mabsut*, 1958, vol. 26:147.
45 Sahnun, *al-Mudawwanah* (1323 AH), vol. 9:422.
46 *Sidaway v. Bethlem Royal Hospital BG* [1985] AC 871 at 904; [1985] 1 All ER 643, 665; Devereux, *Medical Law*, 1997:100. (Contractual Negligence, see

    Morris v. *Winsbury-White* [1937] 4 All ER 494: 'Surgeons to exercise closer personal supervision than is normal': Refused; *Thake* v. *Maurice* [1986] 1 All ER 497 'failed vasectomy': Failed; *Eyre* v. *Measday* [1986] 1 All ER 488, 'Sterilisation of a woman followed by child birth': Failed, unqualified warranty).

47. Muhsin al-Bayh, (Contemporary Egyptian faqih), *Khatta' at-Tabib al-mujib li'l-mas'uliya al-madaniya* 'Medical Negligence,' 1990:156, citing Civ., 20 mai 1936, D. 1936, 1, 11.
48. [1985] 1 All ER 643x.
49. Sarakhsi, *al-Mabsut*, 1958, vol. 16:10-11.
50. Rescue is a duty in Islamic fiqh see pp. 87-88 above. It is not so in English law, F v. *West Berkshire HA* [1989] 2 All ER 545, 567. See Lewis, *Medical Negligence*, 1998:170.
51. Ibn al-Qayyim, *Zad al-Ma'ad*, 1979, vol. 4:139-141.
52. [1957] 2 All ER 118,121; [1957] 1 WLR 582, pp. 586-88. See McHale, Fox, and Murphy, *Health Care Law*, 1997:152; and Montgomery, *Health Care Law*, 1997:169-170.
53. Montgomery, *Health Care Law*, 1997:172; Whitehouse v. *Jordan* [1981] 1 All ER 267.
54. Sidaway v *Bethlem RHG* [1985] 1 All ER 643, 649, HL, Lord Scarman attacked the *Bolam* test for 'leaving the determination of a legal duty to the judgement of doctors.' See Montgomery, *Health Care Law*, 1997:171,
55. *Sidaway* v. *Governors of Bethlem Royal Hospital* [1985] AC 871, 881.
56. Ash-Shafi'i, *al-Umm*, 1993, vol. 6:239.
57. Sarakhsi, *al-Mabsut*, 1958, vol. 16:10-11.
58. Muwaq, *al-Taj wa'l-Iklil li*, (1329 AH)., vol. 6:321.
59. Montgomery, *Health Care Law*, 1997:170.
60. Ibn Qadi Samawa, *Jami' al-Fasilin*, 1300 AH., vol 2:186, see fn. 488.
61. Montgomery, *Health Care Law*, 1997:170. *Maynard* v. *W. Midland RHA* [1985] 1 All ER 635.
62. *Hawashi ash-Sharawani wa Ibn Qasim al-Abbadi 'ala at-Tuhfa Sharh al-Minhaj,* Dar Sadir, vol. 9:197.
63. Shubramulsi, *Hashiya 'ala Nihayat al-Muhtaj* (Ramli), (1104 AH), vol. 8:35.
64. Najdi, *Hashiyat ar-Rawd al-Muraba'a*, (1405 AH), vol. 5:337-339.
65. *Whitehouse* v. *Jordan* [1981] 1 All ER 267, 280; *Defreitas* v. *O'Brien* [1993] 4 Med. LR 281.
66. *Sunan Ibn Majah*, 1953, vol. 2:1156; and Azimabadi, *Aun...Sunan Abi Dawud*, 1969, vol. 10:347.
67. *al-Muwatta*, (ed.), Sa'd, 1983:812. See p. 113 above, "2.4 Should the medical practitioner be well prepared for his job and execute it properly?" and fn.411 for a different discussion of same *hadith*.
68. Ibn al-Qayyim, *Zad al-Ma'ad*, 1979, vol. 4:132. See fn. 412, and fn. 512 above.

69 *Ibn al-Qayyim al-Jawziyya: Medicine of the Prophet,* Johnstone, 1998:101.
70 Najdi, *Hashiyat ar-Rawd al-Murab'a,* 1405 AH, vol. 5:337-9; Shubramulsi, *Hashiya 'ala Nihayat al-Muhtaj li'l-Ramli,* (1104 AH), 8:35; *Hawashi Ash-Sharawani,* Dar Sadir, vol. 9:197.
71 Ibn Abi Usaybia,' *'Uyun al-Anba' fi Tabaqat al-Atibba,'* p. 302. See pp. 114-115, above and fn. 415, where the same caption was used for another part of the debate.
72 Jones, *Medical Negligence,* 1996:1, *Whitehouse* v. *Jordan* [1980] 1 All ER 650, CA; [1981] 1 All ER 267 HL.
73 *Medicine of the Prophet,* Johnstone, 1998:107-109; Ibn al-Qayyim, *Zad al-Ma'ad,* 1979, vol. 4:142-145.
74 General references 1-5 see ash-Shafi'i, *al-Umm,* 1993, vol. 6:82, and 239; and Ibn Muflih, *al-Adab,* vol. 2:473-475; for specifics in 5 see, Bahwati, *Kashaf* (1319 AH), vol. 4:34-35 (pain due to bad instruments) and (for bad timing); Ibn Qudama, *al-Mughni,* 1980, vol. 2:217 (causing undue pain and shock); Ibn al-Qayyim, *Zad al-Ma'ad,* 1979, vol. 4:142-145, (times for intervention, and the age of the patient).
75 Hanafi school, Sarakhsi, *al-Mabsut,* 1958, vol. 16:10-14, and vol. 26:147; Maliki school, Ibn Farhun, *Tabsarat al-Hukkam,* 1958, vol. 2:348; Shafi'i school, *al-Umm,* 1993, vol. 6:81-82.
76 Ibn Rushd, *Bidayat, al-Kulliyat,* vol. 2:255.
77 Ramli, *Nihayat al-Muhtaj,* (1357 AH), vol. 8:35.
78 Ibn al-Qayyim, *Zad al-Ma'ad,* 1979, vol. 4:141, quoting Q. 9:92, (tr. Bewley).
79 *Sunan Ibn Majah,* 1952, vol. 1:462.
80 *Hadith,* Jakni, *Bukhari and Muslim,* 1967, vol. 1:7; *Sahih al-Bukhari,* (this hadith tr. Abdassamad Clarke), 1994:49 and 79; and *Sunan Ibn Majah,* 1953, vol. 2:1413.
81 [1985] 1 All ER 643 (HL). The case was taken all the way to the House of Lords. Mrs. Sidaway's claim was rejected at all levels. The oldest case is that of *Beatty* v. *Cullingworth* [1896] 2 BMJ 1525 (November).
82 Hanafi school, Ibn 'Abidin, *Hashiyat,* 1966, vol. 6:68-69; Maliki school, Ibn Rushd, *Bidayat, al-Kulliyat,* vol. 2:255; Shafi'i school, Ramli, *Nihayat al-Muhtaj,* (1357 AH), vol. 8:35; Hanbali school, Ibn Muflih, *al-Adab al-Shari'ah,* al-Buhuth, Riyadh, vol. 2:274.
83 Ibn 'Abidin, *Hashiyat,* 1966, vol. 6:68-69.
84 Ibn Rushd, *Bidayat, al-Kulliyat,* vol. 2:255
85 Ramli, *Nihayat al-Muhtaj,* (1357 AH), vol. 8:35.
86 Ibn Muflih, *al-Adab,* al-Buhuth, Riyadh, vol. 2:473-475.
87 Ibn al-Qayyim, *Zad al-Ma'ad,* 1979, vol. 4:139; see also *Medicine of the Prophet,* Johnstone, 1998:103-104, at "Physicians and medical responsibility."

[88] Ibn al-Qayyim, *Zad al-Ma'ad*, 1979, vol. 4:140.
[89] *Kasani, Badi'a*, 1910, vol. 7:169; Ibn 'Abidin, *Hashiya*, 1966, vol. 6:147; and Sarakhsi, *al-Mabsut*, 1958, vol. 24:156-157. "The list also includes the corrupt faqih, and the bankrupt merchant."
[90] Ibn Rushd, *Bidayat, al-Kulliyat*, vol. 2:255.
[91] *Sunan Ibn Majah*, 1953, vol. 1:269; also in *Musnad Ibn Hanbal*, 1993, vol. 1:269.
[92] This was detailed at pp. 94-101 above. "Vicarious liability."
[93] Baihaqi, *Al-Sunan al-Kubra*, 1354 AH, vol. 8:105; see also p. 98 for vicarious liability, 'aqila,' " 'ala kulli batnin 'uquluhu," and the concept of *(ahl ad-diwan)*, (it is the whole tribe which is responsible).
[94] Malik, *al-Muwatta,'* (ed.), Sa'd, 1983:755; see also p. 103 of thesis.
[95] Montgomery, *Health Care Law*, 1997:187-188.
[96] Montgomery, *Health Care Law*, 1997:189-190.
[97] Ibn Qudama, *al-Kafi*, 1982, vol. 4:121.
[98] Montgomery, *Health Care Law*, 1997:165 and 190.
[99] Montgomery, *Health Care Law*, 1997:166.
[100] Ash-Shafi'i, *Al-Umm*, 1993, vol. 6:81-82, and 239.
[101] See above pp136-138.
[102] Friedman, L. M.,'The Concept of Legal Culture: A Reply'in Nelken, David, *Comparing Legal Cultures*, Aldershot, Dartmouth, 1997:35.

Chapter Five
Muslim fuqaha's classification of liability of medical practitioners

1. Prologue
Four classes of medical practitioners are recognised by Muslim fuqaha:
(1) The authorised and competent practitioner who performs his duty according to the accepted methods of the profession.
(2) The authorised and competent practitioner who erred, or was mistaken, or was involved in a situation of misadventure or accident.
(3) The negligent practitioner.
(4) The criminally negligent practitioner.

Using the material available to classify the actions of medical practitioners, or to draw legal rules, necessitated quoting parts of the texts more than once. Another factor leading to the same result is that the 'frames' of incidents used by Muslim fuqaha in their writings are the same in some instances. They tended to be copied, and recopied: but with additions, developments of views, and explanations by successive generations of fuqaha.[1]

There is a wealth of ideas generated by their academic endeavours to separate mistake, error, and misadventure, from negligence.[2] Also their views on 'no fault: no compensation' are morally appealing, and may be investigated for socially fair solutions; these take into consideration the plight of those afflicted, and how best to utilise the available resources.

Such 'academic' inputs may bring into prominence areas of agreement amongst rules and help to make equitable common 'laws.' They are the justification and purpose of such studies as the one at hand.

As a matter of fact the classification above is not very different, in essence, from English law.

The first category is, in reality, the other face of the coin of the Bolam test and principle. The second and third categories are academically separable in the Muslim fuqaha's classification, but factually difficult to separate from one another, but on the other hand there is sympathy for the separation amongst English law jurists. Criminal negligence, the fourth category, has common ground in both Islamic and English laws in its formulation; but it remains to look into retaliation as a punishment for some of the offences in Islamic fiqh. Muslim fuqaha have already done so, as will be shown below.

Negligence was, in a major part, the subject of the analysis in the previous chapter, particularly subsections two and three. In the following subsections of this chapter I examine the remaining categories of practitioners.

2. The competent practitioner who performs his duty according to the accepted methods of the profession and is authorised

The issue at hand in this subsection is a presumption by Muslim fuqaha of the existence of a category of medical practice, which may be attended by *sirayah*: complications or even death without there being any question of transgression *(ta'adi)*, incompetence, or negligence. Thus there is no liability attached to the action, even if the patient is harmed, and no compensation is due *(la daman)*.

The argument is that the practitioner is performing his duty *(wajib)*, for which he was trained, in the manner in which it is usually conducted. In the course of executing a duty one is only liable if one is not authorised or if one goes beyond the limits of such authorisation. The Islamic dictum is:"executing one's duty *(wajib)* does not entail a guarantee of safety nor success."[3] Medical treatment is a *necessity*, providing it is a *duty* of the society and individuals."The consensus is that there is no liability attached to the consequences of performing one's duty *(wajib): (Sirayat al-wajib muhdara bi'l-ittifaq)*."[4] So the medical practitioner in charge may not be liable,"by consensus of all fuqaha."[5]

In Islamic fiqh this is only applicable in cases of the living (be it human or animal life). It is a different situation for craftsmen who agree to pierce a pearl, or make a sword, or create pottery. In these situations the craftsman is bound to do the job without fault, and he is liable if he does not honour the contract *('aqd mu'awada)*."The difference is that elements of nature, beyond the control of the practitioner, govern the response to injury and consequent healing where there is life."[6]

2.1 Liability

Lack of competence, and deviation from accepted methods, if attended by harm, make the practitioner liable.

Lack of consent, even when not attended by harm, is battery and makes the practitioner in the overwhelming majority of cases liable.

Some specifics from the different schools are given below:

(a) The Hanafi school

Sarakhsi in *al-Mabsut* said:

> If a barber-surgeon *(hajam)* lets out blood, or incises an abscess, for a consideration; or if a veterinary worker *(bazagh)* treats an animal, for a fee; then if that person or animal dies, the performer is not liable.

> This is in contradistinction to the work of a tailor who spoils a dress: because he was contracted to deliver a piece of work without defect, which is within human competence. Whereas in the case of living objects the intervention opens up a door for the soul (reaction), a domain which is not under the control of the performer; as it unleashes elements of nature which may complicate the procedure *(sirayah)*. The contract of *mu'awada* (exchange) is not applicable where there can be unforeseeable results to the intervention. So in this situation the performer is not liable, if he did what he was asked to do, unless he transgresses or performs without consent.[7]

…But:

> If someone is asked to circumcise a child and he cuts off the glans, he is liable, as circumcision *(khatan)* should be limited to the prepuce only. So, by cutting off the glans he has transgressed.[8]

…Whereas:

> If he confines himself to the limits of what is required, but the patient dies because of consequences not within his control *(sirayah)* then he is not liable.[9]

Al-Kamal ibn al-Humam commented on this:

> [t]he unforeseen results of reaction to injury in animate objects, *shock*, leading to untoward effects or death. In such cases the practitioner, if he has operated within his bounds (cuts the prepuce only in circumcision, and does not include the glans), is not held liable, because it is inconceivable to take care of the unknown. "Obstacles should not be put in the way of useful occupations lest people become afraid of engaging in them, since they are a necessity and fulfil a need." It is not the same with inanimate objects, such as in tailoring. It should be possible

to predict the outcome of intervention in such cases, as they have no reaction of their own.[10]

Three points are worthy of note from these quotes:
a) The Islamic legal mind does not accept strict liability
b) There is a thought to guard against defensive medicine
c) Non-physical injury (shock) may be grounds for compensation.

As to this last, the shock referred to by al-Kamal ibn al-Humam, in the quote above, may be a reaction to injury (e.g. fainting), or infection (poisoning or septicaemia). These two types of shock, which do not necessarily involve 'negligence' may be added to a third type which was mentioned by Ibn Qudama, "when he charged the practitioner who uses an instrument or a procedure that causes undue pain and shock, with negligence and made him liable."[11]

Islamic fiqh knew and dealt with yet a fourth type of shock, 'psychological' shock, which features nowadays in some compensation claims.[12] It is narrated that a man (Sa'd ibn Sa'nah) who demanded settlement of a debt on the spot physically stopped the Prophet ﷺ. 'Umar ibn al-Khattab who was accompanying the Prophet ﷺ was enraged, and went for the man. The Prophet ﷺ said,

> No! Give him what is due to him, and more: because you have frightened him. Perhaps I should have settled earlier, and perhaps he should have been more courteous in his asking. *(wa yazidahu 'ishrina sa'an lima rawa'ahu).*[13]

This is compensation for psychological trauma without any tangible physical harm. There is another incident, where a woman was summoned to the Caliph 'Umar. She was so terrified that she dropped a foetus, which cried and died immediately. 'Ali ibn Abi Talib who was present told 'Umar to pay her the full *diya*.[14]

(b) The Maliki school

Ibn Rushd said:

> The essence of the principle in Imam Malik's school is that all craftsmen are liable for any damage that results from their handling of objects, whether it is burning, breaking, or tearing: be it piercing pearls, engraving stones, making swords, or baking bread.

> But with the physician and the veterinarian if death follows their intervention, there is no liability unless they have transgressed.[15]

He also said:

Fuqaha are agreed that a practitioner is liable if he errs and cuts the glans with the prepuce. But it is attributed to Malik that even then he is not liable if he is known to be proficient in his domain, otherwise he is liable.[16]

Al-Baji narrated that:

Ibn al-Qasim said, "The medical practitioner, the barber-surgeon, and the veterinary worker, if their action results in death, then there are two possibilities: that they have done what is usually done, in that case they are not liable; the reason being that they are required to do such jobs and are permitted...but if they err then they are liable.[17]

Al-Muwaq added, "This applies to the non-Muslim practitioner as well."[18]

(c) Shafi'i school

Ar-Rabi' said:

Ash-Shafi'i said that if someone asks another to let his blood, or to circumcise his son, or to treat his horse, as a result of which loss occurred then the situation is as follows: if the person did what is done by the people in the trade in such circumstances which is considered beneficial then there is no liability. But if his performance was at variance with what is the customary practice, then he is liable.

As regards the fee, it is definitely payable if the performance was in accordance with the methods adopted by those in the field even if there is loss of life or part.

But it has been said that it is even payable to the one whose methods were not in accordance with what is accepted in the field, although he is still liable. But the predominant view is that he deserves no fee. Ash-Shafi'i said, "All fuqaha are agreed that craftsmen are liable for all the losses incurred at their hands; but they are all also agreed that this does not apply, in all cases, to those who deal with animate beings. I find no explanation for that other than that the living body has its own reaction to actions."[19]

(d) Hanbali school

Ibn Qudama, and other Hanbali fuqaha, point out that medical practitioners, and veterinarians are not liable if they are proficient, execute their job according to the accepted manner in the trade and act within the bounds of the authorisation given.[20]

Ibn al-Qayyim explains:

A practitioner, is not liable if it is known of him that he is competent in the craft and his hand did not transgress; even when consequent upon his action, which was consented to by the patient and which was sanctioned by the authorities, there occurred loss of a part, or a function, or life. This is the view of the consensus of fuqaha: as it is an unforeseeable spread *(sirayah)* of a permitted act.[21]

2.2 Unforeseeable Reactions *(Sirayah)*,

On *sirayah* (unforeseeable reactions) the varying Muslim fuqaha's views are as follows:

Hanafi school

[i]n the case of the living, the intervention opens up a door for the soul to react, a domain, which is not under the control of the performer; as it unleashes elements of nature, which may complicate the procedure *(sirayah)*.[22]

And:

[t]he unforeseen results of reaction to injury in living objects (shock), leading to untoward effects or death. In such cases the practitioner, if he has operated within his bounds, is not held liable; because it is inconceivable to take care of the unknown.[23]

Maliki school

the principle in al-Imam Malik's school is that all craftsmen are liable for any damage that results from their handling of objects... But with the physician and the veterinarian if death follows their intervention, there is no liability unless they have transgressed...[24]

Shafi'i school

All fuqaha are agreed that craftsmen are liable for all the losses incurred at their hands; but they are all also agreed that this does not apply in all cases to those who deal with animate beings. I find no explanation for that other than that the living body has its own reaction to actions.[25]

Hanbali school

The view of the consensus of fuqaha is that, there is no liability, and there is no compensation *(muhdara)* for unforeseeable complications, or spread (sirayah) of a permitted act.[26]

Fuqaha have extended the rule applicable to the medical practitioner in this regard to include the actions of the *wali* (ruler) who also bears neither blame, nor liability when he is executing the commands of the law regarding a crime, which was justly tried.[27]

Compare this with modern laws, which count unforeseeable causes as a defence against awarding damages. The EC Product Liability Directive (85/374/EEC), Art. 7(e) in its 1985 explanatory note refers to "the reaction of the human organism as a mitigating factor of liability" just as was suggested in Islamic fiqh:

> The safety, which a person is entitled to expect, raises particularly complex issues in respect of medical products and adverse reactions to them. Establishing the existence of a defect in a medicine administered to a patient is complicated by the fact that not only is the human body a highly complex organism but at the time of treatment is already subject to an adverse pathological condition…[28]

In the United Kingdom, the Consumer Protection Act 1987 came into force on 1 March 1988, and the Government enacted the 'development risks' defence, so that it is a defence to show that the state of scientific and technical knowledge at the relevant time was not such that a producer of products of the same description as the product in question might be expected to have discovered the defect if it had existed in his products while they were under his control (s. 4(1)(e)). [29]

This is advancement. Lewis notes that, "The Swedish system does not cover misfortunes which were within the area of foreseeable risk of a medically justified act"[30].

2.3 Concluding Remarks

According to Muslim fuqaha competence and consent are a defence against liability.

Competence is a quality control procedure by the authorities, resulting in the recognition of the professional standard of the treating practitioner. Islam requires one to do one's job well. The Prophet ﷺ said, "Allah likes it when one does his job well *(inn'Allah yuhibbu min al-'amil idha 'amila an yuhsin)*."[31]

The Prophet ﷺ also laid the ground for the requirement of levels of skill, or specialised competence, when he asked, "Which of you is better at medicine?"[32]

The second component of the defence, consent, was considered by

Muslim fuqaha under the notion of 'authorisation' *(ma'dhunia)*, which embodies: consent of the patient or his guardian to the treatment, on the one hand, and permission to practise, on the other. Consent was considered above.[33] Permission to practise is a later development in the views of Muslim fuqaha. It presumes competence, which is measured against the yardstick of "what is done by others in the field."

Ash-Shafi'i said:

> If the medical practitioner's actions are similar to that of those in the trade whose actions are known to be beneficial then, he is not liable; but if his actions are not similar to those who are well versed in the trade then he is liable.[34]

Ash-Sharawani said:

> A medical practitioner is not liable, at the pain of ignorance, if two just and qualified men in the field consider him knowledgeable. They certify that his competence is well known to them, and that he had cured many people according to their knowledge.[35]

An-Najdi said:

> Medical practitioners are not liable if it is well known that they are competent, and they were taught the profession by known teachers, who gave them permission to practise *(ajazahu)*.[36]

> The standard required does not entail a guarantee of results, otherwise people would stop rendering a necessary service for which there is need,[37] because the practice of medicine may involve unforeseen elements beyond the control of the practitioner *(gharar)*.[38] If it is an essential and needed service in the community, rendering it may be mandatory *(wajib)*, and that does not always entail a guarantee of safety, and no liability is attached to it.

The Hanafi fuqaha, Ibn Nujaim (d. 1560 CE) and Ibn 'Abidin (d.1834 CE), related:

> If a practitioner performs within the usual bounds, then he has fulfilled his part of the agreement *('aqd)* of duty *(wajib)*, and no liability can be attached to executing a duty. *(ada'u al-wajib la yataqayyad bi shart as-salama: wa la yujami'ahu ad-daman)*.[39]

Permission to practice, as a separate issue from consent of the patient or the guardian, was an innovation of Muslim fuqaha in their era of advancements. It is more similar to 'Administrative law' rather than jurisprudence; but since it featured to a great extent in their writings it is dealt with here, briefly.

The Prophet's ﷺ hadith, in this respect, are general legal rules. The basis of liability is: the harm caused by the actions of someone who holds himself out to treat others without knowledge (due care); if there is no harm there is no liability. An example of such a hadith is:

> He who undertakes the treatment of others, without preparing himself, and causes loss of life or damage is held liable.[40]

There is no stipulation that the practice of medicine needed permission.

In the UK the current Medical Act 1983, states,"The legislation does not prevent a person from practising medicine if his name is not in the medical register, but he cannot hold himself out as being a registered medical practitioner... which bars him from (1) recovery of fees...(2) holding certain appointments: i. National Health Service, ii. Army, Navy, and Air Force, iii. any hospital...(3) certain work: i. not to attend midwifery cases, ii. not to treat sexually transmitted diseases..."[41] This reiterates a principle which goes back to the Medical Act of 1858.

This is a point for comparison in legal theory. The stand of the Medical Act is fair and practical, and it is, undoubtedly, commendable to have controls, registers, and licensing bodies to administer the profession.

Muslim fuqaha are agreed that,"The competent practitioner, who performs his duty within the prescribed professional code, and is duly authorised, is not liable; because he is required to perform a duty."[42]

One can infer that, in this particular circumstance, there is no provision for no-fault compensation or strict liability. This applies even if the practitioner chooses a method of treatment contrary to the views of some in the profession, and his patient succumbs.

Faqih Shams al-A'imma al-Hulwani was asked about a girl who fell off a roof and injured her head. Many attending surgeons said: if you allow her head to be opened she will die. One of them said,"If you do not open her head, she will die today. I will do that and cure her." He opened her head. She died a day later. Is he liable? Hulwani said,"No." He was asked,"What if he had promised to cure her?" He replied,"even though.."[43]

Two issues feature in this event: first, Faqih al-Halawani chose a case in which an unusual, novel and dangerous procedure was used; and second, a cure was promised, but it was not fulfilled. Yet there was no liability because there was no fault. Notwithstanding that strictly it might have been; because she was going to die anyway even a risky procedure was sanctioned.

Compare this with modern day practice. As to the first issue of innovative practice, Montgomery has said:

> This does not mean that innovative practice is negligent merely because it is unusual. Professionals will be called upon to justify novel therapies or procedures, but seeking to improve on normal standards is the opposite of negligence provided that it is done properly.[44]

Taking the second issue, 'promise of a cure,' I quote Montgomery again:

> In theory it is possible for a health professional to contract to provide a standard of care that is higher than that required in negligence. However, the courts have shown themselves very reluctant to accept that they have done so. They have refused to accept that surgeons have agreed to exercise closer personal supervision than is normal or to guarantee success.[45]

It is also interesting to note that Faqih Najm ad-Din, quoted by Sarakhsi (d. 349/961) dealt, in one discourse, with similar ideas to these which fashioned the Bolam rule through its stages: of the Bolam test (common practice) in *Bolam v. Friern HMC* [1957]; and the Bolam principle laid down by Lord Scarman, in *Sidaway v. Bethlem Royal Hospital Governors* [1985] (practice contrary to some views); which complemented the Bolam test, more than twenty five years later.

These quotations from Western jurists are similar to the viewpoint of Muslim fuqaha. There is however increasing clamour for no-fault compensation, in Western societies. Sir John Donaldson MR, states:

> The author...draws attention to the continuing 'clamour for no-fault compensation'...However, it is worth pointing to a feature which is unique to medical accidents. That is that in many and perhaps the majority of cases, the same medical or physical disability can result from natural infirmity or from accident in the course of skilled and careful treatment just as well as from medical negligence.[46]

And The Rt. Hon Lord Jusice Otton has said:

> He grapples with the big issue: should the present method of securing compensation of victims of medical mishap continue or should we be moving towards a no-fault or limit of liability or other arrangement? [He] perhaps underestimates the strength of feelings and arguments of those (including some senior judges) who feel that the present system should be re-examined in depth...The status quo is unsatisfactory (to put it mildly)[47]

Some modern day laws which refer to circumstances where there could be damage or complications without the physician necessarily

Muslim fuqaha's classification of liability of medical practitioners 137

having done any wrong, may find the practitioner liable or opt for no-fault compensation.

Lewis discusses 'the philosophy of compensation,' as follows:

It may be that the fault-based system is a hangover from the Victorian ideals of self-help and has no place in a modern welfare state but it is not philosophically, even if it is politically, indefensible…

But if he suffers one of the multifarious misfortunes that the vicissitudes of life are ever dealing us he has no right to demand that his fellows compensate him for that. He can always arrange his own insurance against such events…

I maintain that a decision to permit no-fault recovery for medical misfortunes only has no philosophical justification…[48]

There is *definitely* no strict liability in Islamic fiqh when living creatures are involved. There is no liability if the act was duly permitted and was conducted according to the accepted proscriptions. I refer again to the observation of Ian Edge, "In fact, it is controversial whether Islamic law accepted the idea of strict liability at all."[49]

But I am putting forward an explanation that divides this area into two zones. There is no strict liability where one is dealing with the living, people or animals, because living creatures have their own response to stimuli. Dealing with objects may be different, it can be governed by contract not tort. But there are some minority views to the contrary in Islamic fiqh.

There is no compensation *(daman)* for loss of life, part, or function following permitted acts, performed in an accepted manner. Ibn Rushd said that Qadi Abu Muhammad 'Abd al-Wahhab, of the Maliki school, said: "that in his opinion such a practitioner is responsible for the *diya*, as death has ensued by way of error *(khatta')*."

Should the practitioner be found to be: ignorant, or to have transgressed the limits of permission, or negligent, in all such cases the practitioner is liable." Ibn 'Abd as-Salam said, "The ignorant one is, further, singled out for *adab* (disciplinary action), but error is not punished (though it may be compensated); as to the one who acted without permission, punishment remains an open question."[50]

This rare viewpoint, of Qadi Abu Muhammad 'Abd al-Wahhab, may be a source of reference for those who want to support a 'no-fault compensation' claim in Islamic medical fiqh.

A no-fault scheme would relieve doctors considerably, and be of advantage to the patient from the strictly legal point of view that he would not have to prove that he received negligent care; but he would still have the difficult task of proving causation,...[51]

The legal system may be content not to examine other ideas. It may be a pragmatic approach. But it is of dubious morality. There is no accountability, and one urge to improvement in the medical field is removed. The state may find itself spending money, which might have been better spent for communal welfare on persons who could have insured themselves as for any other mishap.

The British state, (the NHS included), is awarding vast amounts of money for some, whose major reason in getting the awards is to be cared for medically and socially. Some of that money, if diverted, could be spent on public facilities, hospitals and nursing homes included, to care for them and others. Besides, litigation can take years and many opportunities of limiting the damage, teaching and training are lost to the victim.

The British state should also concentrate on preventing mishaps by improving training, supervision, and facilities. It is beyond reason for a profession that knows that prevention is better – and much cheaper – than cure, not to practice the cardinal essence of its role. Its main message is to tell people to eat, rest, exercise, and play reasonably; yet many of its workers are in for long hours of tedious chores. More money should be spent on improving the health services provided, than spending on giving compensation in every case, in order to reduce those cases of compensation.

3. The authorised and competent practitioner who errs

In Islamic medical fiqh at the time of the great fuqaha most of the cases of liability revolved around circumcision or prescribing a drug containing poison. Circumcision was the commonest surgical procedure, hence the richest source of complications and litigation. Circumcision involves physical intervention on the part of the practitioner, and expects him to be in control of the situation all the time. That is the presumption.

Prescribing drugs is an integral part of the practice of medicine, and drugs, sometimes, use poisons as a base. But in prescribing and ingesting a drug other parties may be involved: the patient, his relatives, friends, and other attendants. There are several facets to be explored here: a mere mistake in prescribing or, at the other end of the spectrum, the criminal use of poisons.

Using references to these cases this subsection is devoted to the important category of the 'competent and authorised practitioner who errs.'

Modern day laws do not make a distinction between error and negligence or the implications thereof. That is the whole point of the debate. In Islamic fiqh there is a distinction with applicable legal consequences.

Salmond, explains that,"mistake cannot be a defence in civil law."[52] However Islamic fiqh discusses the mistake *(tajawuz al-hadd)* of a competent practitioner in a separate context from negligence and arranges due compensation, *diya,* for the injured party.

English law has dicta however which indicate this distinction is not entirely unknown. Taylor, says:

> It has been said many times by many judges that negligence should be distinguished from 'a mere error of judgement,' but the line is a very fine one and very difficult to draw.[53]

And Lord Denning, stated in *Hatcher* v *Black* in 1954 that:

> the uncertainties inherent in the practice of medicine were such that a doctor, aware of a law which regards errors of clinical judgement as negligent, would sense this as 'a dagger at his back' when undertaking treatment."[54]

The views of Muslim fuqaha in this respect will be examined. Although they have made an academic distinction between negligence and error, even for them the line is a very fine one and very difficult to draw. It rests on intent, which is not always discernible. Malik said,"It is difficult to assume that the medical practitioner will not do the best for his patient."[55] Shafi'i said,"No restitution *('aql)* is due from a medical practitioner, nor is there any blame if his intentions are good, Allah permitting [sic]."[56]

The patient can be compensated fully without the practitioner being branded negligent. Muslim fuqaha separated error from negligence. There is provision for that in the Qur'an and Sunnah:

> **You are not to blame for any honest mistake you make but only for what your hearts premeditate:**

And,

> **Our Lord, do not take us to task if we forget or make a mistake!**[57]

The Prophet ﷺ said,

My people were excused: error, forgetting things, and what they were forced or compelled to do.[58]

But loss due to error is subject to restitution. Restitution is borne by the *'aqila*. The situation for error is detailed below.

3.1 Error

(a) The Hanafi school

Sarakhsi, (d. 483/1090), gives an example in circumcision. If the guardian of a child asks for him to be circumcised and the practitioner's hand slips and cuts off the *'glans penis'* instead of the prepuce, then the practitioner is liable, and the indemnity *(diya)* is payable by the 'relatives' *('aqila)* of the practitioner.[59]

But, an interesting feature of *diya* compensation is postulated by the fuqaha.

Compensation is computed on the scheme of *diya*. Loss of life (the whole body) is compensated for by the full value of *diya*, one hundred camels. Limbs and organs are computed with reference to the whole body. Since a person has two arms then each arm is worth fifty camels if it is lost; fifty camels compensate for loss of an eye, being one of a pair as well. Ten fingers are worth the full *diya*; each finger is worth ten camels. Single organs deserve the full value of the *diya* when lost, e.g. the nose and the tongue.

The glans penis is a single organ so the compensation is one hundred camels. But that is not the whole story, for if the child bleeds to death or dies of shock at the severance of the glans, the *diya* due is halved, it becomes fifty camels. The reason being that the practitioner was authorised by the guardian of the child, to remove the prepuce; but he erred and removed the glans as well, without permission. The cause of death was 'half-authorised,' or shared or contributed to by the guardian. So only half the *diya* is due, fifty camels.

"This is the strangest and most bizarre of tales: to pay more compensation if the child lives than is due if he dies!" exclaimed Faqih Muhammad.[60]

(b) The Maliki school,

The Malikis have a direct and simple approach. Malik, (d. 179/795), said:

Compensation, *diya*, is due in (non-intentional) mistakes. All the *diya* is the responsibility of the relatives *('aqila)*. Retribution *(qisas)* is the punishment for intentional transgressions; and it rests solely on the transgressor.[61]

Ibn Rushd, (d. 595/1198), said:

If the medical practitioner is competent yet he commits a mistake then he is only liable for what is less than a third of the value of *diya*. More than one third of the full *diya*, should be met by his relatives *('aqila)*. But if he is not knowledgeable, then he is lashed and imprisoned. As regards *diya*, some would say that it is his obligation, others have saddled the *'aqila* with it...

It is attributed to Malik that he said, "A qualified and competent medical practitioner is absolved of all liability, even if he errs. Whereas an impostor is fully and personally liable."[62]

Malik's views may be compared to the quote of Lewis:

An English judge [sic.] in 1953 said:

'It is the duty of a doctor to exercise reasonable skill and care, but a simple mistake in diagnosis or treatment is not of itself negligence. The court is not bound to shut its eyes to the fact that there are quite a few cases at the present time in which doctors are sued for negligence. That may arise from the changing relationship between doctor and patient, but it matters not. There is a *considerable onus on the court to see that persons do not easily obtain damages simply because there is some medical or surgical mistake made* [our italics].

'But the court will not shrink from facing the issue if it finds that the doctor has failed to give to a case the proper skill and care which patients have a right to expect.' (per Finnemore J. in *Elder v. Greenwich Hospital Management Committee, The Times*, 7 March 1953)[63]

The general view in the Maliki school is that, the error of a competent practitioner is compensated for by *diya*: if it is less than one third of the full value of *diya* then it is borne by him, if it is more than that then it is borne by his relatives *('aqila)*.[64] However, the competent practitioner can, on occasions, be totally absolved of any liability.[65]

(c) Shafi'i school

Ash-Shafi'i states that a competent practitioner who errs and causes damage, or practises without permission is liable; *diya* is payable but it is shouldered by his relatives *('aqila)*.

But if the patient dies, although the *diya* is still borne by the *'aqila*, the practitioner has to make a personal expiation *(kaffara)*. He is to fast for two consecutive months, but if sickness prevents that he is to feed sixty of the poor with two fulfilling meals for that day, or permutations of that. This is a purely religious and personal obligation *(wajib)*. That added to the month of fasting *(Ramadan)* for that year comes to three months of fasting. It is a sign of admitting that a wrong was done and of repentance. That is "when the error is of a kind that can happen from his likes; but if the error is gross and not expected to happen, like removing the penis in circumcision, then the responsibility is his own."[66]

Ibn Hajar al-Haithami (d. 974/1566), says that the *diya* should be paid by the *'aqila*, but if that is not possible, the *bayt al-mal* should bear it. If that is not possible, then it becomes a debt of the practitioner.[67]

The summary of the views in the Shafi'i school is that a competent practitioner who errs in his practice is liable. But it is his relatives, *('aqila)* who will bear the cost. A second feature in the school is that the practitioner, and he alone, must carry out the expiation *(kaffara)*, which is mandatory in all cases where there is loss of life.

(d) The Hanbali school

Ibn Qudamah said that:

> a competent practitioner who transgresses is liable: transgression can take the form of an error in performance or lack of responsible consent.[68]

He narrated that, "when a girl died after being circumcised by a woman, 'Umar ibn al-Khattab made the relatives *('aqila)* of the woman pay the *diya*."[69] And he advanced the general Islamic rule:

> *'Aqila* does not bear the restitution of intentional harmful acts, or whatever is less than the value of one third of *diya* in consequences of error *(khatta')*.[70]

Some of the fuqaha in the Hanbali school are not averse to treatment without consent on occasions. Ibn Muflih said:

> It is related in *al-Huda*, that if a competent practitioner undertakes treatment successfully, with no resulting harm, but without consent then he is not liable, because he was lending a helping hand and doing a favour out of his own goodness. The Qur'an says, **"There is no way open against good-doers, Allah is Ever-Forgiving, Most Merciful. Most merciful."**[71]

Ibn al-Qayyim sums up most of the views in the Hanbali school. At times it may seem that there is differing emphasis on the different aspects of the case.

He once unequivocally stated that:

The consequences of the (incompetent) practitioner's felony – according to the opinion of most fuqaha – falls upon his clan *('aqila)*.[72]

And:

An authorised, competent practitioner, who has given the job its due, yet his hand slips and causes damage, is liable for the damage caused as it was by mistake. He is personally responsible for the payment if the damage is valued at less than one third of *diya*; otherwise it is to be born by his *'aqila*.

But what if the practitioner does not have any *'aqila*? Should he be responsible for all of *diya* or should it be the *bayt al-mal*? The two possibilities were both entertained by Ahmad (ibn Hanbal).

It was said [sic] that in case of a of a *dhimmi* practitioner, then it is to be borne by him. But if it is a Muslim practitioner, then the payment should be effected either by himself or the *bayt al-mal*. And what if there are no funds in the *bayt al-mal* in the case of a Muslim tortfeasor? Should *diya* be dropped? or should he bear it? the two possibilities were entertained; with a leaning towards dropping the diya.[73]

These are useful questions to ask because it moves the issue from statements and debate to the making of laws.

3.2 Non-Muslims

At this juncture the situation of a *dhimmi* (non-Muslim) requires elucidation. *Dhimmi* is not a derogatory term. On the contrary, it means somebody in the protection of Allah. Everyone wishes to be so, 'in *dhimmati'llah.*' A Muslim believes that he is in the protection of Allah because he binds himself by Islam or surrenders himself to Allah. A non-Muslim who wants to live, in peace, within a Muslim community has the 'contract' of trust *('aqd adh-dhimma)*, the protection of Allah and His Messenger *(dhimmatu'llahi wa dhimmatu Rasulihi)*. The Prophet ﷺ said, "I am the adversary of anyone who is an enemy of a *dhimmi*."[74] The *dhimmi* status secures the right to, inter alia, organise one's affairs within one's own circle, including making arrangements to have an *'aqila* (relatives) or *ahl ad-diwan* (a guild).

The Prophet ﷺ said, "Each clan, or group, arranges how to cater for indemnification." *('ala kulli batnin 'uquluhum)*[75]

In summary the consensus of Muslim fuqaha is that the practitioner who errs is liable though he is not branded as negligent. The patient who suffers the damage is to be compensated. The compensation is to be borne by the practitioner personally, in values which are less than one third of the full *diya*.

The value of full *diya* in modern day moneys is about £33,000 or $50,000.[76] Thus the amounts involved are in the region of £10,000 for one third of the *diya*.

Values above one third of *diya* are met by the community, be it the close relatives *('aqila)* of the tortfeasor, or members of his guild *(ahl ad-diwan)*, or the *bayt al-mal*. In modern parlance this could possibly translate into the NHS or co-operative and non-commercial insurance bodies[77] to which the practitioner has subscribed.

The Prophet ﷺ said that in case of error or mistake, *diya* is the obligation of the *'aqila* and that the *bayt al-mal* stands in for the one who has no *'aqila.'*[78]

In serious errors resulting in death, ash-Shafi'i required more than the mere compensation of relatives. He demanded expiation of fasting two months. It is not to be converted into monetary terms unless the health of the tortfeasor prevents fasting. It is an indication that more than money is involved.[79]

A mistake or an error can materialise from a competent, attentive, and conscientious practitioner. It should not necessarily be classified as negligence but that should not bar the aggrieved party from being compensated.

3.3 Compensation *(diya)*

Islamic fiqh puts a cap on compensation for loss due to error or mistake *(khatta')*, Q.4: 92 *(wa diyatun musallamatun...)*. In cases of intentional transgression, although it is the right of the aggrieved party to insist on a similar hurt to be inflicted upon the offender to ensure justice, forgiveness is recommended, even for a consideration. The mere fact that the aggrieved party accepts compensation and doesn't insist on retaliatory measures is a kindness that should be appreciated, Q. 2:178 *(fa man 'ufiya lahu min akhihi shay'un fa'ttiba'un bi'l-ma'rufi wa ada'un ilayhi bi ihsan."* All of this is to foster good will, and curb damaging litigation.

Common law reforms consider placing a cap as well:

A significant feature of any discussion of tort reform is an effort to place a cap on monetary awards. There are two varieties of caps - a cap on noneconomic [sic.] damages and a cap on the total award…These caps on total awards vary from a high of $1,000,000… to a low of $250,000… In four states, the total cap is associated with the statutory provision of continued payment for future medical expense as long as the expenses are incurred as a result of the compensable [sic] event.[80]

In Islamic fiqh, values of less than one third of the *diya* are payable by the tortfeasor.[81] That rule could be made into a general rule, and it could even anticipate or pre-empt events by rendering these moneys into a form of co-operative insurance.

Islamic fiqh puts forward *diya* as a scheme of compensation; but is the monetary value valid in modern times? Is it, also, valid if the 'funds' are to be moved from the country where the injury took place to the country of permanent domicile of the injured or the successors?

The value of *diya*

Some have argued that the original value of *diya* was set in *dirhams* and *dinars* (silver and gold). This argument is against the very origin of *diya*.

Islam adopted *diya* from the pre-Islamic customs, and it was one hundred camels.

The Prophet detailed the giving of *diya*: the numbers of camels in each age group, the period in which it was to be paid, with a shorter period for graver transgressions. But even during his time he put other alternatives to camels: 2,000 sheep and goats, 200 cattle, 200 two-piece sets of clothes, 12,000 *dirhams* of silver.[82]

There are several hadith about *diya*, two of them describe different modes of paying *diya* in: gold, silver, cattle, sheep and goats apart from camels.[83]

"First hadith, "The Prophet ﷺ made *diya* 12,000," meaning dirhams of silver.

Second hadith, "The Prophet ﷺ, though he prescribed camels for *diya*, made it 400 (gold dinars) for 'towns people' (*ahl al-Qura*), or the equivalent in silver.

He also varied the price of a hundred camels according to differing values with time, 400-800 gold dinars or the equivalent in silver 8000 dirhams. He also adjudicated that it is 200 of cattle, and 2000 of sheep or goats."

The second Caliph 'Umar ibn al-Khattab, with the spread of Islam, adopted gold and silver moneys as alternative methods of settling *diya*, "as camels were not a feasible proposition for 'towns' people.'"[84]

Sudan is a camel-rearing country. A camel is worth approximately £300. The value of one hundred camels would be £30,000, which is worth Sudanese 120,000,000 *dinars*. A middle class family of five persons can live on 100,000 Sudanese *dinars* a month. The full value of *diya* supports such a family for about 10-15 years. It is argued that this should be the standard adopted. That is money enough to support a family for about 12 years wherever the *loss* has its effect. This transferred to England should translate into an equivalent sum of approximately, £1,000 per month, £12,000 per year, a total of about £144,000 at today's values.[85]

'Umar ibn al-Khattab awarded one person who survived an attack four full *diyas* (400 camels); for the loss of his mental capacity, hearing and eyesight, and because he became impotent as well, thus loosing the function of an organ.[86]

Ibn 'Abidin quoted another example of payment of twice the *diya* for the loss of two testicles (each 50 camels), and the loss of penile copulative function.[87]

It may be argued that this did not occur. But this is not the issue. The issue is that serious Muslim fuqaha have entertained higher values of *diya* for certain catastrophic injuries.

Furthermore, the *diya* in cases of murder, when accepted, is subject to whatever the parties may agree to; they are not bound by any limits. Ibn Rushd said, "Abu Hanifah did not set a value for *diya* in murder: it is whatever the parties agree to *(laysa 'indahu diya fi al-'amad; ma astalaha 'alaihi)*."[88] In reference to what the Prophet ﷺ said, "Cases of murder may be settled by whatever the parties may agree to"*(Ma sulihu 'alaihi fa huwa lahum)*.[89] On one occasion there was a settlement for the value of two *diyas*. The Prophet ﷺ blessed the agreement.[90]

Taking the views of fuqaha into consideration, the *diya* may be set at the value of 400 camels or more, according to the narrative ascribed to Caliph 'Umar ibn al-Khattab. Also the fact that murder cases may be settled for more than the *diya*, all of these open up avenues which may be used to review the values of *diya*.

4. The medical practitioner and criminal negligence

Islamic law punishes crimes by: *Hadd, ta'zir,* or *qisas*.[91]

4.1 Hadd

Hadd is a fixed punishment for specific and named crimes:

Murder and bodily injuries, adultery and fornication, slander - particularly concerning sexual honour *(qadhf)*, theft, highway robbery, intoxication, acts of rebellion, and apostasy. The punishment does not vary with the character of the criminal, nor does it vary with the circumstance of the crime. Proof must be beyond any doubt. Punishment is not to be made if there is any doubt *(idra'u al-hudud bi shubuhat)*.[92]

Once one of these crimes has been brought before the authorities and proven, then the specified punishment must be meted out; but the Prophet ﷺ encouraged people to forgive *hudud* crimes amongst themselves and not to report them should they see them being committed *(ta'afu al-hudud fi ma baynakum, fama balaghani min hadd faqad wajab)*.[93] He told Hizal, the one who sent Ma'iz to admit his adultery,

> It would have been better for you, if you covered him with your clothes, instead of sending him to admit his adultery.[94]

4.2 Ta'zir

Ta'zir is a discretionary punishment, which is left to the authorities, for a range of crimes against law and order in the society. It ranges from a simple summons, or a warning, to the penalty of death: in some cases for the very same transgression. It takes into consideration the character of the offender and the circumstance of the crime. Hadith, *"Aqilu dhawi al-haya'at 'atharatahum"* (Be kind to honourable people (lift them up) when they stumble (blunder)).[95]

It is not necessary for its initiation to prove a crime beyond all doubt as in *hadd*. It includes fines, imprisonment, and lashing. The Prophet ﷺ said, "One should not prescribe more than ten lashes as a punishment except for *hadd*." *(La yajlid ahadun fawqa 'ashrat aswat, illa fi hadd)*.[96] Some are of the view that *ta'zir* lashings should not exceed thirty-nine lashes: since forty lashes are 'the *hadd*' for drinking. Caliph 'Umar ibn 'Abdal-'Aziz recommended that the number of lashes, in *ta'zir* punishment should not exceed ten.

Imprisonment is greatly abhorred in Islam. It usually means changing the usual domicile, or deportation/exile for a year *(taghrib)*. It does not mean incarceration necessarily; so that the offender can still earn his own living. It is not recommended for women. Fines can be a part of *ta'zir* punishment.[97]

4.3 Qisas

Qisas is a punishment, which in its essence is totally left to the jurisdiction of the wronged party or the relatives of the deceased; but its execution is the function of the authorities. It is a punishment which involves retribution, the punishment exacted is exactly similar to the offence, **"free man for free man, slave for slave, female for female"** (Q. 2:177); **"So if anyone oversteps the limits against you, overstep against him the same as he did to you"** (Q. 2:193); **"We prescribed for them in it: a life for a life, an eye for an eye, a nose for a nose, an ear for an ear, a tooth for a tooth, and retaliation for wounds."** (Q. 5:45) It is sometimes difficult to match the offence. *Qisas* is used for murder and bodily injury.

As always, Allah recommends forgiveness. But even if a life is exacted in retribution, then that in itself is saving other lives as far as Islam is concerned (Q. 2:179), meaning that it is a stabilising factor in the society, and it is for community welfare. It will establish law and order, and further on peace. Furthermore, it is an expiation for the person against whom retribution is exacted for the harm he has done.

4.4 Criminal Negligence

Gross negligence or criminal negligence, is considered an intentional crime in Islamic fiqh. Generally the majority of fuqaha are of the opinion that criminal negligence should be penalised by retaliation *(qisas)*.[98]

So if a case involves the death of a patient then the practitioner will lose his life, unless the relatives forgive him for free or for a settlement. Because the practitioner either by intentional commission, or omission, as in refusing to help or rescue a patient, has caused the death of the patient, "if he cuts a blood vessel of someone whom he found asleep and leaves him to bleed to death, then *qisas* is due."[99] For intentional transgression the penalty is stipulated in the Qur'an, **"a life for a life,…and retaliation for wounds."**[100]

But the Hanafis made it almost impossible to accuse a medical practitioner of murder. Murder in the Hanafi school, generally, must be the direct result of injury, using an instrument, which is made for that purpose, like a sword, a knife or an arrow. Even when a medical practitioner actually and forcibly makes a patient ingest poison, it is still not murder to Abu Hanifah, as death was caused by an intermediary and not directly by the action of the practitioner. Stifling with a pillow is not murder to Abu Hanifah. For Abu Hanifah such cases warrant *diya* only.[101]

The Malikis also qualified the actions in which *qisas* is due by saying:

> Although *qisas* is due in case of loss of life, it is impossible to be certain that the crime was intended as this is not what is expected of medical practitioners nor is it the known behaviour amongst physicians; besides, it is impossible to prove beyond reasonable doubt. Therefore it should not be treated as murder.[102]

The Shafi'i fuqaha advocate that:

> Criminal negligence is an intentional crime. The punishment is either *qisas* or *diya*, which are on offer up front.

> In cases of circumcision if the practitioner removes the whole penis, an act which is unacceptable by the standards of his colleagues, then he is kept in custody until the youngster becomes of age. It is up to the youngster then to choose between retribution and the full *diya*. On the other hand if the youngster dies after the injury, then it is up to the heirs to choose between retribution and the full *diya*.[103]

Shafi'i's understanding that in intentional crimes the response is either *qisas* or *diya* has its significance when the deceased has no family. The ruler may always decide to accept *diya* instead of retribution.

The Prophet ﷺ implored someone:

> "Take the *diya* instead [of retaliation], may Allah bless you" *(khudh ad-diya barak'Allahu laka fiha).*[104]

The Hanbalis say that:

> If the practitioner removes a part (organ) without permission, and causes death, then he is liable for retribution *(qisas or qawad).*[105]

It may be opportune to give examples of what was considered criminal negligence, or intentional criminal acts in the views of some fuqaha:

The Hanafi school gave an example of someone who cuts a vein in a person who is asleep (without consent), and lets him die. *Qisas* is the penalty for such an act.[106]

This is not as farfetched as it seems. A practitioner may have consented for a limited or a simple procedure to be conducted under general anaesthesia, then he goes beyond the limits of consent and 'cuts a vessel' or commits a mishap which causes death.[107]

The Maliki school take their example from the implementation of *hudud* punishment. If a practitioner is asked to do an amputation for a *hadd*, and he intentionally transgresses, then *qisas* (retaliation) is due.[108]

Az-Zurqani said:

> An intentional criminal act committed by a medical practitioner is punishable by *qisas*, but in practice it is difficult to ascertain the intentions in such situations, so *diya* is due instead.[109]

The Shafi'i school: Ash-Shafi'i gives an example of gross negligence, which may be equated with malicious intent, in circumcision cases:

> If the practitioner cuts the glans with the prepuce then that is the sort of error that can happen with undue care. But if the practitioner cuts the whole penis, an action the like of which cannot be committed by his peers, then this can only be counted as a maliciously intended crime.

> The penalty is to keep the offender under surveillance until the child comes of age: then he is given the choice of either retaliation *(qisas)* by amputating the practitioner's penis or else opting for the full value of *diya*: one hundred camels. If the child dies at any stage then the one who inherits him, inherits the right of *qisas* or *diya*.[110]

The Hanbali school says:

> If the practitioner operates without permission and death ensues, then retaliation *(qawad)* is due.[111]

And:

> If someone and an accomplice operate without permission on another and cause his death then both are for retaliation *(qawad* or *qisas)*.[112]

The yardstick for gross negligence, which was laid down by ash-Shafi'i (d. 820 CE) is comparable to that of Lord Denning. Ash-Shafi'i said:

> An authorised physician who commits an error, the like of which can be committed by another of his peers is only liable for damages; but should the error be gross and is not expected from one in his position then it is considered as an intentional crime. The punishment is retaliation *(qisas)*; or *diya* if the aggrieved party is agreeable.[113]

Compare this to what Lord Denning said:

> To test it, I would suggest that you ask the average competent and careful practitioner:'Is this the sort of mistake you yourself might have made?'[114]

Muslim fuqaha consider that operating without permission is a crime for which retaliation is due. This assumes great importance with the advent of organ transplantation and the possibility of illicit removal of parts of the bodies of non-donors.

5. Summary

The summary of opinion in Islamic fiqh is that gross negligence, irresponsible and reckless behaviour are considered as intended crimes, and are punished accordingly. The viewpoint of English law may be gleaned from the following captions, and further developments:

> [i]n England and Wales, at least, the advent of the Crown Prosecution Service has done something to counterbalance the inherent reluctance of the police to prosecute doctors and dentists; moreover there is an increasing tendency to apply the criminal law in cases where loss of life follows upon negligence,…instances of a manifestly inexcusable lack of care…in one case; the patient became disconnected from her oxygen supply while the anaesthetist left the operating theatre for a drink of milk.[115]

Montgomery, observes:

> In most circumstances, malpractice is only the concern of the civil law. However, in extreme cases, there may also be criminal implications…it is possible that the health professional could be prosecuted for manslaughter.
>
> For this to happen, there must have been not merely negligence, but gross negligence.[116]

In March 1998 the Guardian newspaper reported the case of consultant cardiologist Dr. James Taylor, of Great Ormond Street Hospital - London:

> …who attempted to dilate an artery in an anaesthetized girl of six (Debbie Jerkins) without the parents' full consent. The child died of brain damage the next day, due to obstruction of blood flow. The doctor is facing charges of serious professional misconduct before the GMC. The St. Pancreas coroner, Stephen Can recorded a verdict of misadventure. He described Dr. Taylor's actions as "erroneous and unwise,…but not grossly negligent…"

The case continues.[117]

One case is already on record where a medical practitioner went to jail for gross negligence.

Anaesthetist jailed (yesterday) for fatal blunder…

> Bradley Miller, 14, died after he was given nitrous oxide gas instead of oxygen to help him recover from the anaesthetic…Sheffield Crown Court was told that the operation should not have been carried out in a dental surgery…

Mr. Justice Poole sentenced (Prabhakar) Gadgil, 65, to six months in prison and ordered him to pay £12,500 towards the costs of the manslaughter hearing....

although Bradley suffered from Goldenhar's syndrome, a rare bone condition, (associated with craniofacial anomalies)…no medical history was taken.

Jailing Gadgil, the judge said: "It is clear this was not a single error. There was a whole catalogue of errors… This was a case of gross negligence."[118]

Islamic law and English law agree on the main theme of duty of care, what constitutes a breach of that duty, and the compensation for the harm, which is caused, by that breach. Both laws have accepted that if there was no negligence there is no liability.

But Islamic law went further to compensate harm that ensues from error, mistake and misadventure without invoking negligence. English law is yet to accept that. But at the same time English law accepts the Bolam test, which, many assume, is weighed against and loses the victim redress for obvious harm if he cannot prove negligence. There may be a point for Islamic law in separating mistake, error, and misadventure from negligence, and 'English law' may find a way for that in the principle of *res ipsa loquitur*.

Notes

1. Examples are: *Hashiyat Ibn 'Abdin: Radd al-Muhtar 'ala* Ad-*Durr al-Mukhtar Sharh Tanwir al-Absar*. Ibn 'Abidin (d. 1252/1834), the *Hashiya (Radd al-Muhtar)*, is his commentary on the explanation *(Sharh)* of al-Haskafi, (d. 1088 AH) to the original text of *Tanwir al-Absar fi Fiqh Abi Hanifa an-Nu'man*, which was written by Muhammad ibn 'Abdullah at-Timurtash (d. 1004 AH). *Fath al-Qadir*, and *al-Mabsut* are others.
2. See pp. 129-131 above, for mistake, error, and misadventure in Islamic Medical Fiqh.
3. Hanafi school: Sarakhsi, *al-Mabsut*, 1958, vol. 16:10-11, and 13-14; Maliki school: Kandhloy, *Awjaz al-Masalik ila Muwatta' Malik*, 1989, vol. 13:27; Shafi'i school: *al-Umm*, 1993, vol. 6:244; and Hanbali school: Ibn Qudama, *Al-Mughni wa al-Khirqi*, 1981, vol. 5:538-9; and Ibn Qudama, *al-Muqni'a*, 1980, vol. 2:217.
4. Ibn al-Qayyim, *Zad al-Ma'ad*, 1979, vol. 4:139.
5. Sarakhsi, (also known as Sarkhasi), *al-Mabsut*, 1958, vol. 16:10-14, and vol. 26:147.
6. Sarakhsi, *al-Mabsut*, 1958, vol. 16:10-11, vol. 26:147; Mirghinani, *al-Hidaya*, 1936, vol. 3:179; compare the following: "The judge [in *Bolam* v. *Friern HMC* [1957] 2 All ER 118] clearly directed the jury to treat the test of negligence which he formulated as exclusively applicable in medical cases." Lord Scarman: *Sidaway* v. *Bethlem RHG* [1985] I All ER 643, [1985] 1 AC 871, [1985] 2 WLR 480, 1 BMLR 132, see
   Mc Hale, fox, and Murphy, *Health Care Law*, 1997:341.
7. Sarakhsi, *al-Mabsut*, 1958, vol. 16:10-11; and vol. 26:147.
8. Sarakhsi, *al-Mabsut*, 1958, vol. 13-14.
9. Sarakhsi, *al-Mabsut*, 1958, vol. 26:147; and Mirghinani, *al-Hidaya*, 1936,, vol. 3:179.
10. Ibn al-Human, *Fath al-Qadir Sharh al-Hidaya*, (1299 AH), vol. 7:206-207.
11. Ibn Qudama, *al-Mughni 'ala al-Khirqi*, 1981, vol. 5:538-539; Ibn Qudama, *al-Muqni'a*, 1980, vol. 2:217.
12. Cane, *Atiah's Accidents*, 1997, pp. 72-75: Nervous shock, mental injury, or psychological damage.
13. Malawi, *as-Sira an-Nabawia*, 1399/1979, pp. 376-377. (That event led the man to embrace Islam, in al-Baihaqi and Ibn Hibban). [*'Ishrin* is twenty; and *sa'*=4 handfuls, usually of grain].
14. Ibn Hazm adh-Dhahiri, *al-Muhalla*, al-Maktab al-Tijari, Beirut,? 1969, vol. 11:24; Ibn Qudama, *al-Kafi*, 1982, vol. 4:60; see also Madkour, *al-Madkhal*, 1966:311.

15. Ibn Rushd, *Bidayat, al-Kulliyat*, vol. 2:255.
16. Ibn Rushd, *Bidayat, al-Kulliyat*, vol. 2:454-455.
17. Baji, *al-Muntaqa Sharh al-Muwatta,'* Dar al-Fikr al-Arabi, vol. 7:77.
18. Muwaq, *al-Taj wa al-Iklil li Mukhtasar Khalil*, vol. 6:321, with Hattab, *Mawahib al-Jalil li Sharh Mukhtasar Khail*, (1329 AH), vol. 5:430-443.
19. Shafi'i, *al-Umm*, 1993, vol. 6:186-187. C.f. *Bolam* test, and *Bolam* rule (*Bolam* v. *Friern HMC* [1957] 2 All ER 118 "the test...as exclusively applicable in medical cases"; *per* Lord Scarman in *Sidaway* v. *Bethlem RHG* [1985] 1 All ER 643 (Bolam Rule: see above p. 147, 164), and Mc Hale, Fox, and Murphy, *Health Care Law*, 1997:341.
20. Ibn Qudama, *al-Mughni*, 1981, vol. 5:538-543; Ibn Muflih, *al-Furu'*, 1962, vol. 4:451-452; Bahwati, *Kashf al-Qina'a*, (1319 AH), vol. 4:34-35; Najdi, *al-Rawd al-Muraba'a*, (1405 AH), vol. 5:337-339.
21. Ibn al-Qayyim, *Zad al-Ma'ad*, 1979, vol. 4:139.
22. Sarakhsi, *al-Mabsut*, 1958, vol. 16:10-11; and vol. 26:147.
23. Ibn al-Humam, *Fath al-Qadir*, (1299 AH), vol. 7:206-207.
24. Ibn Rushd, *Bidayat, al-Kulliyat*, vol. 2:255.
25. Ash-Shafi'i, *al-Umm*, 1993, vol. 6:239.
26. Ibn al-Qayyim, *Zad al-Ma'ad*, 1979, vol. 4:139.
27. Hanafi school: Sarakhsi, *al-Mabsut*, 1958, vol. 26:147, and Ibn 'Abidin, *Hashiya*, 1966, vol. 6:565; Maliki school: Kandhloi, *Muwatta' Malik*, 1989, vol. 13:27; Shafi'i school, ash-Shafi'i, *al-Umm*, 1993, vol. 6:244; Hanbali school: Ibn Qudama, *al-Mughni*, 1981, vol. 5:538-539.
28. (85/374/EEC), see Lewis, *Medical Negligence*, 1998:423-424.
29. Consumer Protection Act 1987 (39 *Statutes*).
30. Lewis, *Medical Negligence*, 1998:430.
31. Jarrahi, *Kashf al-Khafa*, Maktabat al-Turath, Halab, Syria, vol. 1:285, analysis of *hadith* No. 747.
32. Malik, *al-Muwatta,'* (ed.), Saad, 1983:812, *hadith, (ayokuma atab?).*
33. Consent was, mostly, dealt with in Ch. 4.3 pp. 140, 152: *ta'adi* and *tajawz al-hadd* (definition: failure to secure consent or acting beyond the limits of consent), 153 the views of the schools, 160 (negligence).
34. Ash-Shafi'i (d. 204/817), *al-Umm*, 1993, vol. 6:239-240.
35. Sharawani, *Hawashi ash-Sharawani...'ala Tuhfat al-Muhtaj Sharh al-Minhaj,* vol. 9:197;
36. Najdi, *al-Rawd al-Muraba'a*, (1405 AH), vol. 5:337-339.
37. Ibn al-Humam, *Fath al-Qadir*, (1299 AH), vol. 7:206 (Hanafi school); see also Ibn Hajar, *Tuhfat al-Muhtaj*, Dar Sadir, Beirut, vol. 9:197 (Shafi'i school). "Warning against defensive medicine."
38. 'Ulish, *Sharh Minah al-Jalil*, 1984, vol. 3:790 (Maliki school).
39. Ibn Nujaim, *al-Bahr ar-Rai'q*, (1311 AH), vol. 8:33; and in *Hashiyat Ibn Abidin*, 1966, vol. 6:565.

Muslim fuqaha's classification of liability of medical practitioners 155

[40] Hindi, *Kanz al-'Ummal* 1971, vol. 10:32.
[41] Medical Act (1983), Kennedy, and Grubb, *Medical Law*:1994:36-37; see also The Medical Act [1983].
[42] Kandhloy, *Awjaz al-Masalik...Muwatta' Malik,* 1989, vol. 13:27.
[43] Ibn Qadi Samawa, *Jami' al-Fasilin,* (1300 AH), vol 2:186; also attributed to Faqih Najm al-A'imma al-Halimi by Tarabulsi, *Mu'in al-Hukkam,* 1973:204. See also p. 138 above with fn. 488, and p. 142 above with fn. 505. (There is, necessarily, a paucity of examples of 'cases,' hence the repetition).
[44] Montgomery, *Health Care Law,* 1997:170 (*Waters v. W. Sussex Health Authority* [1995] 6 Med. LR 362, *Wilsher v. Essex Area Health Authority* [1986] 3 All ER 801, 812).
[45] Montgomery, *Health Care Law,* 1997:166. Closer than normal supervision, in (*Morris v. Winsbury-White* [1937] 4 All ER 494); guarantee success, in (*Thake v. Maurice* [1986] 1 All ER 497).
[46] In Lewis, *Medical Negligence,* 2nd. ed., 1992:ix. (Foreword).
[47] In Lewis, *Medical Negligence,* 4th. ed., 1998:v. (Foreword).
[48] Lewis, *Medical Negligence,* 4th. ed., 1998:428, and 429.
[49] Edge, Ian, 'The Development of Decennial Liability in Egypt' in *Islamic Law and Jurisprudence,* (ed.), Heer, Nicholas, 1990:173.
[50] 'Illish, *Fath al-'Ali al-Malik,* 1958, vol. 2:348, with *Tabsarat al-Hukkam,* by Ibn Farhun, vol. 2:348.
[51] Lewis, *Medical Negligence,* 1998:427.
[52] Salmond, *Jurisprudence,* 1924:429.
[53] Taylor, *Doctors and the Law,* 1976:80.
[54] *The Times,* 2 July 1954, and in [1980] 1 All ER 650 at p. 658 (his own previous pronouncements).
[55] Zurqani, *Sharh 'ala Mukhtasar Khalil,* Matba'at Mustafa Muhammad, Cairo, vol. 8:117.
[56] Ash-Shafi'i, *al-Umm,* 1993, vol. 6:244.
[57] Q. 33:5, and Q. 2:285; (both verses tr. Bewley).
[58] *Sunan Ibn Majah,* 1952, vol. 1:658-659.
[59] Sarakhsi, *al-Mabsut,* 1958, vol. 16:13-14.
[60] Ibid.; and in Ibn 'Abidin, *Hashiyat,* 1966, vol. 6:69, and 624, where it is also rendered, by at-Tusi, into a verse of poetry in wonderment!
[61] Malik, *al-Muwatta,'* (ed.) Sa'd, 1983:740; see Kandhloy, *Awjaz al-Masalik,* 1989, vol. 13:27.
[62] Ibn Rushd, *Bidayat, al-Kulliyat,* vol. 2:255, and 454-455.
[63] Lewis, *Medical Negligence,* 1998:12-13.
[64] Dardir, *Ash-Sharh al-Kabir,* Dar Ihya' al-Kutub al-Arabia, al-Halabi, Cairo, [n.d], vol. 4:335.
[65] Ibn Rushd, *Bidayat, al-Kulliyat,* vol. 2:454-455.
[66] Ash-Shafi'i, *Kitab al-Umm,* 1993, vol. 6:81-82.

[67] Ibn Hajar, *Tuhfat al-Muhtaj,* (1304 AH), vol. 9:197.
[68] Ibn Qudamah, *al-Mughni,* 1981, vol. 5:538-539.
[69] Ibn Qudamah, al-*Muqni'a,* 1980, vol. 2:217.
[70] Ibn Qudama, *al-Kafi,* 1982, vol. 4:121.
[71] Ibn Muflih, *al-Furu',* 1962, vol. 4:451-452. The Qur'anic quote, *(ma 'ala al-muhsinin min sabil w'Allahu ghafurun rahim),* is in Q. 9:91, (tr. Bewley).
[72] *Medicine of the Prophet,* Johnstone, 1998:105; Ibn al-Qayyim, *Zad al-Ma'ad,* 1979, vol. 4:139.
[73] Ibn al-Qayyim, *Zad al-Ma'ad,* 1979, vol. 4:140-141.
[74] *Sunan Ibn Majah,* 1953, vol. 2:896-897, four *hadith;* see also Sabiq, *Fiqh as-Sunnah,* 1995:49-56 *('aqdu adh-adhimma).* (See f.n. 578 and text for 'Non-Muslim medical practitioner is treated as a Muslim').
[75] Baihaqi, *Al-Sunan al-Kubra,* (1354 AH), vol. 8:107.
[76] Full *diya* =100 camels, less than a third is 33 camels."*Diya* in UA Emirates is over $41,000." Al-Quds al-Arabi, 9 March 1998, p. 18, now it is 150,000 dirhams UAE/6= £25,000 on 23rd January 1999. *Diya* in Saudi Arabia is 100,000 Riyals, about £16,500, reference: Ash-Sheikh Dr. Salih bin Abdul Rahman bin Suliman al-Muhimeed, Chief of Law Courts, al-Madina al-Munawara Region. (Personal communication, March 1999).
[77] The generally agreed on position with respect to insurance is that commercial insurance is not acceptable, but that under certain conditions, co-operative insurance or insurance arranged by the imam can be acceptable [Ed.]
[78] *Sunan Ibn Majah,* 1953, vol. 2:879-880.
[79] Ash-Shafi'i, *al-Umm,* 1993, vol. 6:52-53; Shirbini. *Mughni al-Muhtaj,* (1377 AH), vol. 4:108; Sabiq, *Fiqh,* 1995:348-349.
[80] Kridelbaugh, William W., and Palmisano, Donald J., "Compensation caps for medical malpractice," *American College of Surgeons Bulletin,* vol. 78, number 4, April 1993, pp. 27-30, p. 27.
[81] Ibn Qudama, *al-Kafi,* 1982, vol. 4:121.
[82] Malik, *al-Muwatta,'* (ed.), Sa'd, 1983:737.
[83] *Sunan Ibn Majah,* 1953, vol. 2:878-879.
[84] Malik, *al-Muwatta,'* (ed.), Sa'd, 1983:737. (See also Chapter Three: *diya).*
[85] *Article 293* of the Dutch Criminal Code, considers euthanasia at the express wish of the deceased a serious offense which punishment may not exceed 12 years imprisonment or a fine of the fifth category…and *Article 23* of the Dutch Criminal Code defines, Fifth category fine = ƒ100,000. That, also, may be a yardstick in the assessment of *diya* compensation.
[86] Sarakhsi, *al-Mabsut,* 1958, vol. 26:69; and Ibn 'Abidin, *Hashiyat,* 1966, vol. 6:576, (substituting speech for impotence for the loss compensated for by the fourth diya).
[87] Ibn 'Abidin, *Hashiya,* 1966, vol. 6:577.

88 Ibn Rushd, *Bidayat*, 1935, vol. 2:402; see Ibn 'Abidin, *Hashiya*, 1966, vol. 6:529.
89 *Sunan Ibn Majah*, 1953, vol. 2:877.
90 Sarakhsi, *al-Mabsut*, 1958, vol. 21:9.
91 Qadri, *Islamic Jurisprudence*, 1973:290-291; (1st. ed., 1963); Sabiq, *Fiqh as-Sunnah*, 1995, vol. 2:237-395; (in almost every *Fiqh* book).
92 *Hadith* in *Sunan Ibn Majah*, 1953, vol.2:850.
93 *Sunan Abi Dawud*, 1973, vol. 4:540.
94 *Sunan Abi Dawud*, 1973, vol. 4:541; and *Sahih Muslim*, 1983, vol. 3:1322.
95 *Sunan Abi Dawud*, 1973, vol. 4:540.
96 *Sahih al-Bukhari*, (tr. Khan), 1994:1010; *Sahih Muslim*, 1987, vol. 3:1333; and *Sunan Ibn Majah*, 1953, vol. 2:867.
97 *Sunan Ibn Majah*, 1953, vol. 2:781-782; and Sabiq, *Fiqh as-Sunnah*, 1995, vol. 3:393-395; and Madkour, *al-Madkhal*, 1966:739-740 for a general reference of the contents including fines.
98 Alamgir, *Al-Fatawa al-Hindiya*, Bulaq, (1310 AH), vol. 6:34, (Hanafi)); Ibn Farhun, *Tabsirat al-Hukkam*, 1958, vol. 2:243, (Maliki); Ramli, *Nihayat al-Muhtaj*, 1938, vol. 7:262 and 276, (Shafi'i); and Ibn Qudama, *al-Mughni*, 1981, vol. 7:706, (Hanbali).
99 Damad, (Sheikhi Zada), *Majma'a*, (1327 AH), vol. 2:392-393; Ibn 'Abidin, *Hashiyat*, 1966, vol. 6:68-69.
100 Q. 5:45.
101 Ibn 'Abidin, *Hashiyat*, 1966, vol. 6:543.
102 Zurqani, *Sharh 'ala Mukhtasar Khalil*, Matba'at Mustafa Muhammad, Cairo, vol. 8:117.
103 Ash-Shafi'i, *al-Umm*, 1993, vol. 6:82.
104 *Sunan Ibn Majah*, 1953, vol. 2:880.
105 Ibn Qudama, *al-Muqni'a*, 1980, vol. 3:331-332. *(Qisas=qawad)*
106 Damad, (Sheikhi Zada), *Majma'a al-Anhur*, ([1327 AH), vol. 2:392-393.
107 Case of consultant cardiologist Dr. James Taylor, *The Guardian* 16 March 1998, see below p.197.
108 Dardir, *ash-Sharh al-Kabir*, Dar Ihya' al-Kutub al-Arabia, al-Halabi, Cairo, vol. 4:29, and 4:252.
109 Zurqani, *Sharh 'ala Mukhtasar Khalil*, al-Maktaba al-Tijaria, Mustafa Muhammad, Cairo,, vol. 8:117.
110 Ash-Shafi'i, (d. 820 CE), *al-Umm*, 1993, vol. 6:82.
111 Ibn Qudama, *al-Muqni,'* 1980, vol. 3:331-332.
112 Ibn Qudama, *al-Mughni*, 1981, vol. 9:382; and Bahwati, *Kashaf*, (1319 AH), vol. 5:506.
113 Ash-Shafi'i, *al-Umm*, 1993, vol. 6:82.
114 Davies, *Medical Law*, 1996:87.
115 *R* v *Adomako* [1994] 2 All ER 79; Mason & McCall Smith, *Law and Medical*

Ethics, 1994:214-215.
[116] Montgomery, *Health Care Law*, 1997:187-188.
[117] *The Guardian Newspaper* Monday 16th. March 1998, p. 6 columns 1 and 2 (upper part of page).
[118] *The Times* July 30 1999, p. 4 columns 7 and 8 (mid page), by Paul Wilkinson. (Case started 27 Oct. 1997).

Chapter Six
Euthanasia

1. Introduction and definition
Euthanasia is a combination of two Greek words, 'Eu' and 'Thanatos' meaning a gentle and easy death. As such it has no untoward ethical or religious implications.

"All the major religious traditions take a positive stand against termination of human life. Judaic, Christian, and Islamic teaching, and other religious attitudes have a convergence that earthly or bodily life embody a significance which goes beyond the bodily condition of the individual. Death remains essentially a surrender, something experienced rather than something done, something accepted rather than something chosen..."[1]

Muslims often, in their prayers, ask for a gentle and easy death when the time comes.[2] It is also expressed in the hadith, "Lord! May I live if that is for my good, and take my life if that is better for me."[3]

It is the meaning, which the word has acquired as 'mercy killing' that needs to be considered.

The term euthanasia is used loosely, as a form of shorthand, to describe the whole subject area for this report...

Although focused on 'mercy killing,' debate about euthanasia ... has been qualified with the terms 'active' and 'passive', 'voluntary', 'involuntary' and 'nonvoluntary.' These terms do not lead to precision in argument.[4]

Mason and McCall Smith observe that:

The subject of euthanasia is, in our opinion, clouded by uncertainties of definition. Stedman's Medical Dictionary has two citations - a quiet, painless death and the intentional putting to death by artificial means of persons with incurable or painful disease...Collins English Dictionary confines itself to 'the act of killing someone painlessly, especially to relieve suffering from an incurable illness'...Any useful discussion of euthanasia must accept the - admittedly unpalatable - fact that it involves some form of active killing;[5]

In Holland,[6] Article 293 of the Dutch Criminal Code provided that:

"A person who takes the life of another person at that other person's express and earnest request" is guilty of a serious offence. This is what is considered 'euthanasia' in the Netherlands. 'Euthanasia' is thus on its face illegal, but,…it can under specific conditions be legally justifiable [sic]."

But finally the Dutch Parliament in the Hague legalised 'Euthanasia.'

2. Types of euthanasia

The types described in the 'Report of the Working Party to review the British Medical Association's guidance on euthanasia,'[7] will be adopted as a point of reference:

(1) Active euthanasia

Active euthanasia is usually taken to be an action performed within a medical setting, which is done with the intention of terminating a human life:

'an active intervention by a doctor to end life.'

(2) Passive euthanasia

Passive euthanasia tends to be used to describe the withdrawal or withholding of some necessary treatment for the maintenance of human life:

'a decision not to prolong life' or 'a non-treatment decision.'

(3) Triad of terms: voluntary, involuntary, and nonvoluntary euthanasia.

i. 'Voluntary' euthanasia is a death brought about by an agent *at the request of the person* who dies.

ii. 'Involuntary' euthanasia is the killing of someone who could consent but does not. Such an action is indistinguishable from criminal homicide and the claim that the motive for the killing is in 'the best interests' of the victim is irrelevant.

iii. 'Nonvoluntary' euthanasia is the killing of an individual who has no capacity to understand what is involved, again out of kindness or a paternal consideration of the patient's 'best interests.'

'Active,' and 'passive' may be looked upon as the means to achieve the result. All three may be brought about actively or passively. It is difficult to separate passive killing from active killing when the result is the same. But such a differential requires consideration in Islamic fiqh as well; especially in the doctrine of causation in the Hanafi school, and particularly as regards Abu Hanifah's individualistic views on 'killing by poisoning.'[8]

3. Involuntary euthanasia

Involuntary euthanasia will be examined under four subheadings: (a) relation to homicide, (b) the definition of homicide, (c) the Western view of involuntary euthanasia, and (d) the Islamic view of involuntary euthanasia

(a) Relation to homicide

Involuntary euthanasia is the killing of someone who could consent but does not. Such an action is indistinguishable from criminal homicide and the claim that the motive for the killing is 'the best interests' of the victim is irrelevant."[9]

(b) Definition of homicide

Homicide is lawful if it is committed:
1. In the execution or advancement of justice;
2. In reasonable self-defence of person or property or in order to prevent the commission of an atrocious crime;
3. By misadventure. This is where someone is doing a lawful act without negligence. An obvious instance is afforded by the case of death resulting from a lawful operation carried out with due care by a doctor.

In all other cases homicide is unlawful (murder).[10]

"Murder is unlawful homicide with 'malice aforethought.'

"Malice aforethought consists of an intention on the part of the accused: to kill any human being..., to do grievous bodily harm to any human being..., to do an act which the accused knows, or must, as a reasonable man, be taken to know is likely to kill or do grievous bodily harm to any human being...

"Murder is a felony for which punishment fixed by law is normally imprisonment for life, but it is capital in the five cases specified in s. 5 of the Homicide Act, 1957,...."[11]

(c) Western view of involuntary euthanasia

Montgomery points out:

> Any person who intentionally kills another may be prosecuted for murder or manslaughter. There are no special rules for health professionals permitting them to kill their patients. Murder will be appropriate where the killer acted intending to kill or do serious harm…Manslaughter will be the charge where the intention of the killer is less specific. Consequently, anyone who deliberately ends the life of another, as in active euthanasia, is guilty of murder.[12]

In practice, cases which come to light are rare as Mason and McCall Smith have observed.[13]

In the United Kingdom one of the first cases was that of *R v Adams* [1957] in which Delvin J summed up as follows:

> If the acts done are intended to kill and do, in fact, kill, it did not matter if a life were cut short by weeks or months, it is just as much murder as if it were cut short by years…
>
> But it remains the fact, and it remains the law, that no doctor, nor any man, no more in the case of a dying man than a healthy, has the right deliberately to cut the thread of life.[14]

In *R v Arthur* (1981) Dr. Arthur was acquitted of a charge of murder when he instructed his staff not to feed a newborn, unwanted, baby with apparently uncomplicated Down's syndrome. The infant died sixty-nine hours later.[15]

In *R v Carr* [1986], Dr. Carr was accused of attempted murder, by injecting a massive dose of phenobarbitone into a patient whose lung cancer was declared inoperable. He was acquitted of the charge but, in the course of summing-up, Mars-Jones J had this to say:

> However gravely ill a man may be …he is entitled in our law to every hour…that God has granted him. That hour or hours may be the most precious and most important hours of a man's life. There may be business to transact, gifts to be given, forgivenesses to be made, 101 bits of unfinished business which have to be concluded.[16]

In another case, concerning the injection of potassium chloride and lignocaine, *R v Lodwig* (1990), the case was aborted when the prosecution offered no evidence.[17]

In *R v Cox* (1992) however, Dr. Cox was successfully prosecuted for the attempted murder of Mrs Lilian Boyes. Ognall J set out the issue for the jury as follows:

It was plainly Dr Cox's duty to do all that was medically possible to alleviate her pain and suffering...There can be no doubt that the use of drugs to reduce pain and suffering will often be fully justified notwithstanding that it will, in fact, hasten the moment of death, but...what can never be lawful is the use of drugs with the primary purpose of hastening the moment of death.[18]

Criminal law considers involuntary euthanasia as murder or attempted murder. Involuntary euthanasia may be caused actively or passively. But is passive involuntary euthanasia a crime always? This is often debated as 'killing or allowing the patient to die.' Lord Goff of Chieveley in *Airedale NHS Trust v Bland* [1993] commented that:

> It is true that the drawing of this distinction may lead to a charge of hypocrisy; because it can be asked why, if the doctor, by discontinuing treatment, is entitled in consequence to let his patient die, it should not be lawful to put him out of his misery straight away, in a more humane manner, by a lethal injection, rather than let him linger on in pain until he dies. But the law does not feel able to authorise euthanasia, even in circumstances such as these; for once euthanasia is recognised as lawful in these circumstances, it is difficult to see any logical basis for excluding it in others.[19]

In the House of Lords, it was proposed "that the doctors in withdrawing the feeding tube after which Anthony Bland dies, will nevertheless be guilty of no offence" Lord Mustill pointed out:

> I am bound to say that the argument seems to me to require not manipulation of the law so much as its application in an entirely new and illogical way.[20]

Passive euthanasia is not just 'failing to act' in a general sense as with:

> Is a doctor under a duty to treat when the man next to him in the theatre is taken ill? (An English court would say not). [21]

Montgomery explains:[22]

The usual distinction does not apply when the relationship between the parties obliges them to look after the patient. It is clear that health professionals have such a duty,[23] and are at risk of being prosecuted for manslaughter if their patients die after a negligent failure to treat them.[24] Non-professionals have been found guilty of manslaughter for failing to look after relatives for whose care they have taken responsibility.[25] The real issue in law, therefore, is not whether the euthanasia is active or passive. Passive euthanasia will be treated in the same way as active euthanasia if it happens in breach of a duty to take steps to care for patients.[26]

Mason and McCall Smith mention:

One of the more astonishing examples to have come to light concerns the death of King George V which was, on admission, due to a drug overdose administered by his physician; at least a part motivation for this was that the doctor thought that the news of his death would be better reported in *The Times* than in *The Evening News*! It is perfectly true that the King's life was shortened by only a few hours; nevertheless, the incident is something of a warning to those who would invest the medical profession with yet more powers over life and death.[27]

(d) Islamic view of involuntary euthanasia

Sanctity of life is supreme. The Qur'an points out that:

...if someone kills another person – unless it is in retaliation for someone else or for causing corruption in the earth – it is as if he had murdered all mankind. And if anyone gives life to another person, it is as if he had given life to all mankind.[28]

Homicide is lawful, in Islam, if it is committed in these circumstances:

(i) In the execution or advancement of justice for three crimes only: murder, adultery, and apostasy.[29]

In the case of murder there must be provision, and encouragement, for forgiveness. In the case of adultery, there must be the strict observance of the requirement of a voluntary actual confession upon which the adulterer insists or the evidence of four men who must have unequivocally witnessed actual penetration. In the case of apostasy, there must be a relinquishing of the community *(al-jama'a)*. Apostasy is a crime because it is liable to stir up the community *(fitna)*.

(ii) In reasonable self-defence of person or property or in order to prevent the commission of an atrocious crime.

The Qur'an says, **"Permission to fight is given to those who are fought against because they have been wronged,"** And **"How could we not fight in the way of Allah when we have been driven from our homes and children?"**[30] The Prophet ﷺ said, "If one dies defending himself, his property, his faith, or his people; he is a *shaheed* (deserving immediate entrance to the eternal Garden)."[31]

(iii) By misadventure.

This is where someone is doing a lawful act without negligence. An obvious instance is afforded by the case of death resulting from a lawful operation carried out with due care by a doctor.

In all other cases homicide is unlawful.

Unlawful homicide is the worst crime against another human being in Islam. It is vilified in the Qur'an:

> As for anyone who kills a mumin deliberately, his repayment is Hell, remaining in it timelessly, for ever. Allah is angry with him and has cursed him, and has prepared for him a terrible punishment.[32]

The Prophet ﷺ said:

> There is always a leeway for a person to escape blame for all crimes he might have committed, except for when there is blood on his hands.[33]

And, "The first issue addressed on Judgement day is homicide."[34]

Ash-Shafi'i narrates, that there was found within the Prophet's sword holder, a document that read, "The worst of Allah's enemies is the murderer…"[35]

The recompense of murder in the Hereafter is to abide in the Fire forever, and the wrath, and the curse of Allah.[36] The crime can be forgiven in this life, and the culprit may not be punished at all:

> Do not kill any person Allah has made inviolate, except with the right to do so. If someone is wrongly killed We have given authority to his next of kin…[37]

The penalty for murder in this life may be *qisas* or the culprit may be forgiven or he may be required to furnish the *diya* or settle for more or less than its value.[38] But he may still be subject to *ta'zir*. All fuqaha, including Abu Hanifah, accept that the penalty of *ta'zir* can be meted out whenever deemed necessary. *Ta'zir* includes imprisonment and even the death penalty for repeat offenders or serial killers.[39] Intent is all-important.[40]

The acquired present day meaning of euthanasia (mercy killing: 'involuntary, nonvoluntary, and voluntary euthanasia'), "terms [which] do not lead to precision in argument,"[41] is matched against the views of Muslim fuqaha, as to what constitutes murder.

This lack of precision in argument is also reflected in the views of Muslim fuqaha. Mercy and the care for others are built-in Islamic values. But killing on the pretext of mercy per se is not catered for in Islamic fiqh.

This lack of precision in argument is further compounded by Muslim fuqaha constructing lurid situations where persons are tied up amongst poisonous snakes or in the company of wild animals: lions and wolves. Some are tied up without food or water, and others are given poisons to ingest and in some it is forced down their throats. In some of these situations the perpetrator escapes punishment altogether.[42]

The reasoning behind some of their views is difficult to follow, but that is not the point. The point is that no one said that what is being said is not Islamic fiqh, and no one doubted the piety or the sincerity of the fuqaha involved. This is very important for this work, as it shows that legislation is possible, and is subject to amendments. But, as is often reiterated, there should be no violation of the Qur'an and Sunnah.

What constitutes murder in the different schools of Muslim fuqaha?

(a) The Hanafi school

This is one of the areas where differences within the Hanafi school itself are more pronounced than between the school and the others. It lends weight to the idea that this concept of the schools was not intended by the great fuqaha themselves; rather it was a later development - the work of their students.

The Hanafi fuqaha attribute the causes of loss of life to one of five ways:

(i) an intended act to kill

(ii) an intended act to hurt, that was not intended to kill

(iii) the act was not intended (mistake), but the tortfeasor was conscious

(iv) an act which is (similar to a mistake): as when someone who is asleep rolls over another and suffocates that person (e.g. mother and child)

(v) causing death: but not directly, e.g. by poisoning.[43]

Some examples of Abu Hanifah's thinking are rendered below:

(i) Murder must be caused by an instrument, which is made from 'the likes of iron or copper' for the specific purpose of cutting and wounding, e.g. a sword, or a knife, or a spear etc. Fire and boiling water are considered agents of murder as well...The penalty for death caused by these agents is *qisas*.[44]

Euthanasia

If someone hits another with a heavy object and that person dies, it is not murder, as the heavy object was not specifically designed to kill.

(ii) There is no *qisas* (life for life) for killing by choking, drowning, or throwing off heights. But according to others in the school, Abu Yusuf and Shaybani, *qisas* is due.

(iii) If 'he bricks him in' (locks him up), and the subject dies of thirst and hunger, the tortfeasor is not liable according to Abu Hanifah; because the subject did not die of the cause 'bricking in' but he died of hunger and thirst.[45]

The others in the school hold the tortfeasor liable for *diya* (manslaughter): not for *qisas* (murder).

(iv) If he feeds someone poison, and the other ingests it and dies, then the tortfeasor is not liable for *qisas* nor *diya*, because the actual ingestion of the food was by the option of the deceased. But the tortfeasor is to be lashed and disciplined *(ta'zir)* because he committed an act of deception *(ghurur)* for which there is no *hadd* penalty.

But if he forces poison down the throat of someone who dies as a result, then *diya* is due according to all in the Hanafi group. Whereas ash-Shafi'i considers it murder for which *qisas* (retaliation) is due.

(v) If he drowns someone and kills him, or if he terrifies him until he dies then for us [Hanafis] *diya* is due (manslaughter) but with ash-Shafi'i *qisas* is due (murder).[46]

Abu Yusuf and Muhammad al-Hassan ash-Shaybani, Abu Hanifah's disciples, are opposed to his views as regards death resulting from beating by a heavy object, drowning, suffocation, smothering, strangulation, pushing from great heights. They consider death resulting from such acts as murder.[47] In this they are in line with the fuqaha of other schools.[48]

But, it is the view of Abu Hanifah that if the actor makes a habit *(takarrar)* of strangulating, suffocating, or drowning others, then he may be executed, by way of the policy *(siyasa)* of maintaining law and order *(ta'zir)*.[49]

Killing a patient by: withholding food and water or by any poison, and without the patient's knowledge, is manslaughter to all Hanafi fuqaha. It is not murder. But more interesting are Abu Hanifah's highly individualistic views as regards poisoning, and others. If someone forcibly makes another swallow a poisonous concoction, *diya* is due; there is no *qisas*. But if he mixes the poison with his food and the other one eats the food and dies, then even *diya* is not due; that is so even if the one who succumbed did not know that his food was poisoned. The tortfeasor is subject to *ta'zir* for deception *(gharar)*.[50]

There is also no *qisas* (for murder) nor *diya* (for manslaughter) in: drowning someone in shallow water until death occurs; or restraining someone until death occurs of hunger and thirst.[51]

Taking the views of Abu Hanifah himself, involuntary euthanasia can never be more than manslaughter and the case of poisoning not even that.

According to him it is impossible to construct a case for murder, unless the medical practitioner literally cuts the patient's throat or stabs him to death.

b. The Maliki school

The Maliki school admits of only two causes of loss of life:[52]

(i) by an intentional act, the penalty for which is *qisas* (that is retaliation resulting in death); or:

(ii) by a mistaken act, the penalty for which is *diya* (that is compensation for death). They quote the Qur'an:

> A mumin (believer) should never kill another mumin unless it is by mistake. Anyone who kills a mumin by mistake {khata'}, (compensation is due)…to his family *(diya)*…Anyone who cannot find the means should fast two consecutive months [sic]. This is a concession from Allah…

> As for anyone who kills a mumin deliberately, his repayment is Hell, remaining in it timelessly, for ever. Allah is angry with him and has cursed him, and has prepared for him a terrible punishment.[53]

They argue that no one can infer the intention to kill or not; suffice it that the act itself was intentional and death has resulted from it. Death that ensues from intentional physical violence, which includes wounding, letting one die of haemorrhage are taken as murder (withholding help or denying rescue).[54]

But they are ambivalent as regards poisoning (it is not treated as murder).[55]

They do not recognise quasi-intentional murder, where the assault is intended, but the resultant death might not have been. Although this category is mentioned in a hadith of the Prophet ﷺ:

> In cases of quasi-intentional murder, as in the case of one who is killed by being beaten with a stick or a whip, there is the higher diya.[56]

Euthanasia

The Prophet specified a separate penalty for it. This was neither *qisas* as for intentional murder, nor was it ordinary *diya* as in the case of mistake. The *higher diya* was due, i.e. a more expensive quality of camels and a shorter period of delivery (immediately). Ordinary *diya* for mistake *(khata'a)* could be settled over three years."[57]

They also make the punishment for a certain type of murder mandatory capital punishment as in the case of someone who is killed (especially if it is for his money) where treachery was involved or breach of trust *(qatl al-ghila)*. In that particular situation it is not up to the relatives to take the *diya* instead of *qisas* or to forgive the culprit. The state takes over. The offender is to be killed as a matter of the law of *hadd*, comparable to the ruling in *haraba* (being in rebellion).[58] But all the fuqaha in the other schools are opposed to classifying it as *haraba* and to attaching any significance to a particular type of killing as it all comes to a loss of life for an illegitimate cause. They quote the Qur'an, and in particular,

> **And slay not the life that Allah has forbidden save with right. Whoso is slain wrongfully, We have given power unto his heir....**[59]

They also quote the Prophet's saying: "An heir is free to demand *qisas* or *diya* in case of the murder of his relative."[60] There is neither specification nor qualification in either the Qur'an or the Sunnah for how or why the act was committed apart from the fact that it was not "with right."[61]

The Maliki school has some constructs, which could apply to situations in involuntary euthanasia:

> If someone offers another, what he knows to be poisonous: be it food or drink or an article which can be worn, and the subject doesn't know of the poisoned state of the article, then that is murder for which *qisas* is due.
>
> But if he tells the subject that it is poisoned, and the subject, an adult of full capacity, takes the poison then it may be that the perpetrator is not liable, but if the subject were a child or mentally deranged then *diya* is due.[62]

The Maliki school rulings are not complicated as is usual within the school. Intent is the whole mark. It is inferred from the act itself. If an intended act causes death, then it is murder; providing it was not during games or to discipline those in one's care. Death due to denial of water is murder.[63]

c. The Shafi'i school

Murder in the Shafi'i school is death due to intentionally inflicted injury (the act is intended, and the person is intended) with any means that can usually cause death:

> If it is a weapon that everyone knows that it can kill, sword, knife, dagger, spear, big stone, or a metal bar; then *qisas* is due (murder);[64]
>
> ...in being thrown or restrained in a place from which it is not possible to be free, and the person is drowned; *qisas* is due (murder), but if he throws him in the sea and a fish swallows him then *diya* is due (manslaughter);[65]
>
> ...if someone suffocates another until the subject dies, then *qisas* is due (murder), but if the subject was left alive then he later died then there is no *qisas* unless he was left dying.[66]

To sum up, one is to examine the implement or method used to affect the killing. If it usually kills the likes of the deceased, in age, state of health, and strength; then *qisas* is due. But if the usual outcome is surviving the event, then there is no *qisas*...

Also attention must be paid to the circumstances in which the act was committed. If in such circumstances the outcome is death, then *qisas* is due; if not then there is no *qisas*.[67]

The salient feature in the Shafi'i school is to measure against the 'norms.' Involuntary euthanasia would either be murder or manslaughter depending on the circumstances.

d. The Hanbali school

Murder in the Hanbali school is to intend to kill with a weapon that can, usually cause death; directly or indirectly.[68]

Death following throttling, drowning, and stifling the breath by a pillow is murder and *qisas* is due.[69] Poisoning with a potent poison, or leaving him tied up with a poisonous snake or a wild animal, all these actions if they cause death then it is murder.[70]

> If one mixes, what he knows to be a poison and makes another who does not know, eat it or drink it, then this is murder and *qisas* is due.[71]
>
> If one is denied food and water for a period that is usually followed by death then *qisas* is due (murder); but if not then *diya* is due (manslaughter).[72]
>
> If he exposes one to extremes of heat and cold the likes of which cause

death in the majority of people then *qisas* is due if the subject dies; if the majority would have survived, then *diya* is due.[73]

The Hanbali school is very similar to the Maliki School, in many of their rules. The only difference is that, in the Maliki school any intended act which causes death is murder, whilst the Hanbali's make a proviso, "the act must be one that causes death usually": in this they are closer to ash-Shafi'i.

This shows that schools, in reality, are not set apart in their inception, as the major figures of the schools studied under one another. Members of one school may be closer to others in other schools than to one another or even to their mentor as with the students of Abu Hanifah. Ash-Shafi'i applied his encyclopaedic knowledge according to the problems of the period, locale, and circumstances in which he found himself; sometimes he came up with different views on the same matter in Iraq and in Egypt.

Muslim fuqaha gave examples of being, 'tied up' or 'bricked in' without food and water;[74] these situations are not far removed from what may be the situation of a patient who is being considered for involuntary euthanasia. The patient is literally physically restrained by connections to equipment; paralysed by muscle relaxants; rendered speechless by gags; incapacitated by mind clouding drugs. This is not an unfair presentation of what is involved in involuntary euthanasia. The discussion is not about the well-intentioned practitioners who err, or about transgressions in medical practice. It is not even about criminal negligence. It is about, we have been warned, an:

> admittedly, unpalatable fact that [euthanasia] involves some form of active killing; it is only by so doing that the moral and legal implications can be reviewed in a clear light. To hide behind semantics is obfuscatory.[75]

It may be remembered that:

> Involuntary euthanasia is the killing of someone who could consent but does not. It is indistinguishable from criminal homicide.[76]

I summarise the views of Muslim fuqaha on situations akin to involuntary euthanasia:

(1) "If he throttles or smothers him," and the subject dies, then that is murder and *qisas* is due, in the Maliki, Shafi'i, and Hanbali schools;[77] in the Hanafi school for all these actions *diya* is due.[78]

(2) "If he drowns him," the offence is murder according to fuqaha

of all schools except for the Hanafis.[79] In the Hanafi school the consensus is that *diya* is due.[80] But Abu Hanifah said,"If the water is shallow and he is drowned and dies, neither *qisas* nor *diya* are due."[81]

It is to be noted that in medical practice a patient can be drowned in his own secretions, if not attended to; or by intravenous infusions.

(3) Killing using a poison generally constitutes murder in all schools, and *qisas* is due,[82] except for the Hanafi school in which "only *diya* is due."[83]

So killing using a poison, which is the commonest implement in hospital practice, is never murder in the Hanafi school, the crime is manslaughter. Compare this with *R* v *Cox* [1992] where Dr. Cox was successfully prosecuted for the attempted murder of Mrs Lillian Boyes: not for murder, although he injected a poison intentionally not for the purpose of treatment nor alleviation of pain.[84]

(4) If nourishment, food and water, is withheld until the person dies then according to Abu Hanifah, neither *qisas* nor *diya* is due. Abu Yusuf and ash-Shaybani of the Hanafi school consider that *diya* is due.[85]

The Maliki school considers the act as murder and *qisas* is due.[86] Ash-Shafi'i said:

…if death occurred in a period long enough so that the majority of people would have died then *qisas* is due; otherwise *diya* is due.[87]

The Hanbali school has a similar view to ash-Shafi'i.[88]

To conclude this subsection, involuntary euthanasia, however achieved, is homicide in the thinking of the majority of Muslim fuqaha; with some exceptions in the Hanafi school. But to Abu Hanifah himself it is never homicide, and on occasions it is not even manslaughter.[89]

4. Nonvoluntary euthanasia

Nonvoluntary euthanasia is the killing of an individual who has no capacity to understand what is involved, again out of kindness or a paternal consideration of the patient's 'best interests.'[90]

There are quite a few issues to be considered in this situation:

First, is the loss of capacity to understand what is involved reversible?

If it is, then killing such persons will be in the category of the previously discussed involuntary euthanasia.

Second, if the loss of consciousness is permanent then the person is either brain dead, or in the permanent (persistent) vegetative state, or dying.

Third, cases of 'coma' include these situations and situations where the coma may be reversible, so they must be differentiated from one another.

4.1 Brain-stem dead

The brain can be represented as a three-tiered (layered) structure, with intricate and innumerable interconnections and connections with the rest of the body. The brain-stem, the base, has command of the vital functions like respiration, swallowing etc. Without these functions no form of life is tenable. But organs like the heart have their own rhythmicity and would function if they receive oxygen and nourishment through machines. Ventilators and respirators are variants of such machines. When they are stopped the heartbeat will cease as soon as the oxygen, which was supplied by the machine, is exhausted and so the heart joins the body in its death. The brain-stem dead person is a person fulfilling the criteria of loss of brain-stem functions; thus the person is respirator-dependent and there is no question here that we are dealing with a living being. Although there are emotional problems involved in switching off the respiratory machine, the fact of the matter is that the person is already dead. Switching off the machine is not the cause of death. This was accepted in *Re A* where the judge determined that where the accepted tests established brain-stem death, then for legal purposes death was established.[91]

Kennedy has argued [92] that the vast majority, perhaps all, of living patients with severe brain damage must be offered mechanical ventilation when they present at hospital for the purpose of facilitating diagnosis and assessment. If a diagnosis of irretrievable functional brain loss is made, there is no legal or ethical objection to dispensing with the ventilator with the other tools used for the diagnosis. There is support for this in the Conference of the Royal Medical Colleges and their Faculties,[93] and legislation to this effect is almost universal in the English-speaking world.

The 'brain-stem dead' are persons who have died – but still some issues have to be dealt with:

(i) How to switch off the machines? Sometimes a court ruling is necessary.

(ii) Can such persons be left on the machines for a suitable time for the removal of their organs? Mason and McCall Smith allow that in cases of beating heart organ donation or, conceivably, of post-mortem parturition.[94]
(iii) If such persons left a living will to donate organs, can that be proceeded with?
(iv) If such persons left no will nor expressed any views on organ donation, can the relatives 'donate' their organs?
(v) If there are no relatives, could the 'state' authorise removal of their organs?

These questions and others are dealt with in Chapter Nine (Transplantation)

4.2 Patients in the permanent vegetative state (PVS).

These patients are in a coma and cannot interact with relatives or staff providing care. The brain death criteria are not fulfilled and the patient is not respirator-dependent as breathing is maintained normally. The patient, however, remains in a deep coma with no hope of recovery and without meaningful response to any stimuli. The permanent vegetative state occurs after a prolonged period of cerebral hypoxia (when the brain is deprived from oxygen carried by the blood from the lungs). This happens most frequently after a cardiac arrest (heart stoppage) when the cerebral perfusion of oxygenated blood is interrupted for some time. However these patients can, and do, live for years providing they are cared for and fed. This care involves medical personnel and at times relatives. It can be very expensive and it is emotionally draining; the more so because there is no hope of recovery.

4.3 Coma

There are occasions when people who are in a coma for a long period regain consciousness. These are coma cases in which the traumatised cells of the brain have had the opportunity to recover. This is a function of the state of our medical expertise in diagnosis and management. With advances in knowledge, more of the cases in this pool may recover. Others would be diagnosed as brain-dead or in the permanent vegetative state sooner. Some will die. But the pool will remain as a source of perplexity, doubt and perhaps some confusion, about the classification of the coma.

Euthanasia 175

The main problem will remain with patients in the permanent vegetative state. Should persons in the permanent vegetative state be fed?

This issue will be analysed according to Western, and Islamic views.

4.4 Should persons in the permanent vegetative state and other mentally incompetents be fed?

This is discussed under (a) Western views, and (b) Islamic views.

(a) Western views

This is a most contentious issue in the euthanasia debate. There are uncertainties in the courts. In *R v Arthur* (1981),[95] the case in question was in relation to withholding food and nourishment from a neonate until death occurred. In this way it deals with persons unable to express their wish. The baby was born with apparently uncomplicated Down's syndrome. Dr Arthur wrote in the notes 'Parents do not wish it to survive. Nursing care only'; the baby died sixty-nine hours later. Dr Arthur was charged with murder. During the trial, the charge was reduced to one of attempted murder; Dr Arthur was acquitted. But the reaction in the aftermath of the trial was such that it is doubtful that instructions are now likely to be given not to feed a baby simply because it is likely to be mentally retarded. This is frankly illegal in the United States, Canada, and Australia.[96] Farquharson J stated, "however much the disadvantage of a mongol [sic.] or, indeed, any other handicapped child, no doctor has the right to kill it."[97]

Does this unequivocally establish that it is illegal to withhold food and nourishment from the mentally incompetent?

Consider another example from the meagre supply of case law in terminating the treatment of the incompetent patient is the Bland case,[98] which highlights the nature of the ethical and legal debate in Britain.

Anthony Bland suffered in the crush that took place in the Hillsborough football stadium in April 1989. After emergency treatment it was found that Bland was in a persistent (now called permanent) vegetative state.

The treating doctors were unanimous that the condition would never improve but might persist for a considerable time.[99] The NHS Trust applied to the court for declarations that such withdrawals would not be unlawful in September 1992. Hoffmann LJ in supporting the proposed withdrawal of treatment said:

To argue from moral rather than from purely legal principles is somewhat unusual enterprise for a judge to undertake...that there might well be respect for the sanctity of life combined with a respect for the dignity of that life, which is expressed in the idea of autonomy ... sanctity and autonomy, are not always complementary, and can indeed conflict."[100]

Montgomery commenting on this case said:

Once again the law is not clear. The implications of the law governing euthanasia suggest that life support may be ended in accordance with a responsible decision by the professionals involved that this is the best way forward. They are obliged to act in the patient's best interests, but it has been shown that this does not mean that life should be preserved at all costs...in the case of Airedale *NHS Trust* v *Bland*.[101]

The House of Lords rejected any distinction between the provision of food and water and other aspects of care. They upheld a declaration that it would be lawful to discontinue all life-sustaining treatment for Tony Bland, and to refrain from further treatment except for the sole purpose of enabling him to die peacefully in dignity.[102]

Mason & McCall Smith noted:

'Irreversible loss of consciousness' may, indeed, 'one day become the mark of death' but that day is not here yet - certainly not in a legal sense.[103]

(b) Islamic views

The views in Islamic fiqh for situations akin to nonvoluntary euthanasia can only be inferred from an amalgam of laws, rulings, and hypothetical cases, where life of an incompetent is terminated. Islam considers human life as of the same consequence from the moment of birth. All human beings have the right to live, not to be harmed, to inherit, and to be inherited from irrespective of capacity. The current situation of nonvoluntary euthanasia, will be discussed under three categories for the sake of clarity:

i.　infanticide
ii.　killing of minors and those under care
iii.　killing, or terminating the life, of the unconscious.

(i) Infanticide

The Qur'an orders that infanticide should never be committed, no matter for what reason.[104] Infanticide is homicide in Islam.[105] The state of the deceased, mentally, physically, or health-wise, is of no consideration: what matters is life.[106] Crying, breathing, and kicking or limb movements are accepted signs of life. Refusing to suckle or care for the newborn incriminates the mother, but only if there was nobody else to do the job.[107]

Considering the case of *R v Arthur* (1981), where Dr Arthur ordered nourishment to be withheld from a Down's syndrome new-born on the request of the parents, until the infant died sixty nine hours later,[108] there would have been a conviction of homicide on the part of fuqaha in the Maliki, Shafi'i, and Hanbali schools. The Hanafi school would have considered it manslaughter, as death ensued by causation and not by a direct active act. Abu Hanifah's personal view would have absolved the doctor from both *qisas* (murder) and *diya* (manslaughter).[109]

(ii) Killing of minors and those under care

Islam protects the material and social rights of minors entrusted to one either because of parenthood or duty of care. Depriving them of their rights and their moneys,[110] or marrying them to acquire their property,[111] is a great wrong action.

Killing them is murder. The Maliki fuqaha put it under a special category, *qatl al-ghila*, where the punishment is more severe as the murderer is killed by law *(hadd)* and it is not for the relatives to forgive the crime: even a parent may be killed for that.[112] This is despite the Prophetic hadith to the effect that a parent should never be killed because he/she killed his/her child *(la yuqad walidun bi waladihi)*.[113]

The Qur'an says:

Do not kill your children out of fear of being poor. We will provide for them and you. Killing them is a terrible mistake.[114]

The Prophet ﷺ said:

The gravest of all wrong actions is not to believe in Allah: next to that is to kill your child so that you do not have to feed him.[115]

(iii) Killing, or terminating the life, of the unconscious

Muslim fuqaha gave an example of, "someone who severs a vein in a person who is asleep and lets him die of the haemorrhage, such an act is murder and *qisas* is due."[116] This quotation is from the Hanafi school, the mildest of schools, yet they attached the crime of murder to an act committed on someone who is asleep (unconscious). The Hanafi school is also in agreement with all other schools that the state of health, physical or mental, and the constitution of the body complete or incomplete are of no consequence in attributing quality to life. Life is sacred always:

> As the Qur'an and the Prophet ﷺ have said 'blood is the same'; it follows that those with complete limbs are the same as those without or amputees, those with complete senses are the same as those with no senses, the learned are the same as the ignorant, those in higher classes of society are the same as those in lower ones, the sane and the insane the adult and the child are all the same as far as the quality of life is concerned. *Qisas* is due for the murder of any.[117]

Islamic fiqh would have held other members of the hospital staff to be liable for prosecution along with Dr Arthur, as accomplices:

> If people will stand by and allow bad deeds *(munkar)* to occur; then Allah will punish everyone.[118]

Ibn Rushd said that all schools are agreed that several persons can be subjected to *qisas* if they murder a single person, even if that person is a child.[119] A case supporting this took place in Yemen at the time of Caliph 'Umar ibn al-Khattab. A woman who was in charge of her absent-husband's son (stepson) took a lover. Fearful of the disclosure of her affair, she herself, the lover, his friend, and her servant killed the child. Qadi Ya'ali, wrote to Caliph 'Umar for his opinion. Caliph 'Umar, after conferring with 'Ali ibn Abi Talib, replied that:

> all should be killed: if all the people of San'a killed him then all the people of San'a should be killed, otherwise this will become a device to escape punishment, by collectively engaging in crimes.[120]

Furthermore, there is scope in Islamic fiqh, to enact laws that make people who consort with one in the professional field *(ahl ad-diwan)*, or in the tribe *(qasama)*, responsible for the harm that may befall some, or where a person entrusted to the care of others meets his death without any particular person being charged.

The reason for involving relatives and kinship in the professions or trades in the payment of *diya* is to raise their awareness, so that their wayward ones do not ramble unbridled, and to cultivate togetherness to ward off harm.[121]

5. Voluntary euthanasia

Voluntary euthanasia is a death brought about by an agent *at the request of the person* who dies.[122]

Muslim fuqaha have discussed this issue in great detail and at length, under the titles of "he who asks someone to kill him," and "permission to kill."[123]

5.1 Western views

The Western view is examined from numerous sources: the laws and their modifications; the views of some informed members of the community; assisted suicide by word or actions (including Kevorkian's suicide machine); and the hospice alternative of care for those in need of help to continue living.

The attitude of English law towards a positive act of euthanasia is summed up in the words of Delvin J:

> If the acts done intended to kill and did, in fact, kill, it did not matter if a life were cut short by weeks or months; it was just as much murder as if it were cut short by years.[124]

Glanville Williams wrote:

> The law does not leave the issue in the hands of doctors; it treats euthanasia as murder.[125]

Montgomery points out:

> When people bring a patient's life to an end because they believe it to be the kindest thing to do, their actions are considered by the law to be homicide.[126]

As regards the situation of euthanasia and assisted suicide in Europe, some references are quoted to show the shifting emphasis. The BMA Report takes note of society and the formulation of the rules that govern it:

> An important part of our society and its fabric are the religious traditions that exist within it.
>
> All the major religious traditions take a positive stand against the active termination of human life. The Christian view is well expressed by the Archbishop of York…
>
> The same points are stressed by the Guild of Catholic Doctors (in their submission to the BMA Working Party on Euthanasia)…The Christian view is, in fact, very close to that taken in Judaic and Islamic teaching (as might be expected in that all three are monotheistic and have developed from the Mosaic tradition). There is an even wider convergence in religious attitudes when one considers those of the East. It is invidious to refer to some of these religions and not others.[127]

Professor Margaret Brazier's views are a reflection of the community's interest in mercy killing:

> In Britain today the numbers of people practising any religious faith are in a minority…Thriving communities of Jews and Muslims remain committed to their traditions. But Britain is overwhelmingly a secular society…If life is not bestowed by God, on what grounds is it sacred?
>
> There can be no doubt that belief in the sanctity of life does survive the death or absence of religious belief. Taking life is as reprehensible to many agnostics and atheists as it is to the Christian or Jew…The move away from a concept of life as God-given, however, has certain consequences. If the basis of belief in the sanctity of life is a perception of the freedom of the individual, of the joy that life can bring, then the quality of life comes into account…When pain and handicap cause an individual to cease to wish to live, then he may be free to end that life. It is his to do with as he wishes…People have an intrinsic right to life. Life is sacred, but not 'absolutely inviolable.' This is the view occupying the 'middle ground.'[128]

There are reports from European countries:

> Anyone working in medicine knows that euthanasia is practised even though it is prohibited in all European countries…The practice is publicly acknowledged in Netherlands, although it is not legal…
>
> The legislation of euthanasia has been rejected by the Standing Committee of Doctors of the EC in its declaration on euthanasia adopted in 1987 and by the World Medical Association in its declaration adopted at the 39th world medical assembly in Madrid in 1987.[129]

The Netherlands

Griffiths, Bood, and Weyers state that,

> The Netherlands is presently the only country in the world in which euthanasia, under specific circumstances, is legally permissible.[130]

But even there, some ambivalence still existed as:

> Article 293 of the Dutch Criminal Code provides that a "person who takes the life of another person at that person's express and earnest request" is guilty of a serious offence. This is what is considered 'euthanasia' in the Netherlands.
>
> 'Euthanasia' is thus on its face illegal, but,…it can under specific conditions be legally justifiable [sic.].[131]

Until finally 'Euthanasia' was legalised by the Dutch Parliament in The Hague on 29th. November 2000.[132]

Euthanasia 181

Suicide and assisted suicide at common law

i. The Suicide Act 1961 s. 1 decriminalised suicide and attempted suicide; but s. 2 (1) states:

A person, who aids, abets, counsels or procures the suicide of another, or an attempt by another to commit suicide, shall be liable on conviction on indictment to imprisonment for a term not exceeding 14 years.

Section two may seem a simple statement of law, but it is not as simple to apply. This was evident in *A. G. v. Able* [1984],[133] when the Attorney General contended that a publication by the Voluntary Euthanasia Society was associated with at least fifteen cases of suicide within eighteen months of its appearance. There was no conviction, as the court held that, in order to prove the allegations, three things had to be shown: (a) that the accused knew that suicide was contemplated, (b) that he or she assented to it, and (c) that he or she encouraged the suicide attempt. In the case itself, publishing the booklet was not necessarily illegal because the third requirement was not made out in relation to any specific death."[134]

Assisted suicide and Jack Kervorkian's (Kevorkian) suicide machine

Since 1990 Jack Kevorkian has been assisting suicide in Michigan. As a result of his activities the state enacted a criminal prohibition on assisting suicide. [135]

Once, in a world wide transmitted interview, Dr. Kevorkian said, "The American Supreme Court has nothing to do with what I am doing."[136]

There are many in the medical field in the West who would not like to see doctors as executioners;[137] and many more who do not approve of Jack Kervorkian's approach to euthanasia.[138]

In March 1999, Julie Grace wrote in Time magazine:

It's Curtains For Dr. Death
After assisting 130 suicides since 1990, Jack Kevorkian is found guilty of a murder.

Jack Kevorkian had been warned that acting as his own attorney might have dire consequences."You realize that being convicted of first-degree, premeditated murder means you could spend the rest of your life in prison?" Judge Jessica Cooper asked sternly at the beginning of his trial in Pontiac, Michigan. Four times in the past, Kevorkian's lawyer …had beaten assisted-suicide charges by arguing that…the patients administered their own suicides. This time was different, Cooper said: Kevorkian had done the deed himself, and the crime was murder. Last September, Youk, who was suffering from Lou Gehrig's disease (a motor-neurone disease), received the deadly mixture of drugs from Kevorkian as the procedure was recorded on videotape. It was later broadcast on CBS's 60 minutes...

Thirteen hours of deliberation found him guilty of second-degree murder, rather than the first-degree charge...(demanded by the prosecution), which would have put Kevorkian in line for a mandatory life sentence.[139]

The case against Kervorkian, this time, is not different from that of *R v Cox* [1992],[140] an attempted-murder trial in which Dr. Cox administered a lethal dose of potassium chloride (not a pain killer) to Mrs. Lillian Boyes who was suffering from an incurable and increasingly distressing form of arthritis, so that Mrs. Boyes died within minutes.

On 13th. April 1999 Jack Kervorkian was sentenced to between 10 and 25 years in prison for the charge of second-degree murder of patient Thomas Youk, and 3-7 years for injecting a controlled substance. His license to practise had been rescinded for the last six years. Bail was refused.

In passing sentence in Pontiac, Michigan, the judge, Jessica Cooper, told Kevorkian:

"This trial was not about the political or moral correctness of euthanasia.

It was about lawlessness. It was about disrespect for a society that exists because of the strength of the legal system. No one, Sir, is above the law.

You had the audacity to go on national TV and show the world what you did and dared the legal system to stop you. Well Sir, consider yourself stopped."[141]

In my view the patient-doctor relationship should not be rocked by controversy or clouded by suspicion. There is no scientific challenge in ending life (or killing people): lethal injections can be mastered by others. The medical profession should face up to relief of pain and suffering through research and application of advancements of knowledge. The hospice system is more in line with the concerns of the medical profession. It is in total harmony with Islamic teachings.

The Hospice system of care for the terminally ill

The medical practitioner is expected to act as a member of a team of doctors, nurses, technicians, social workers, counsellors and others in his circle, together with the patient and his relatives to alleviate pain, anxiety, and fear.

Hospices are a particularly British system of care for the terminally ill.

> Hospices, resting places for travellers, including the sick and wounded, have been in existence for centuries. But in the 1950s, with the introduction of psychotropic drugs, pain killers, pain relief techniques, and increased insight into problems of families and bereavement by such centres as the Tavistock Clinic, that the way was open for Dame Cicely Saunders, nurse, social worker and doctor, to found St. Christopher's Hospice in 1967. It was committed not only to care for dying patients and their families at home as well as in its wards, but also to teaching and research.
>
> Symptom control, communication, comfort, counselling, family support, are some of the methods which are practiced, and refined.[142]

It may be added that:

> The hospice movement in the Netherlands is quite unlike that which exists in Britain and the development of palliative care is not as advanced...
>
> It is still a crime for a doctor to kill a patient in the Netherlands and a doctor who does so even at the patient's express or written request is liable to prosecution for murder. In practice such prosecutions are not pursued provided that certain clearly circumscribed guidelines are followed. In these circumstances the doctor is reckoned to be acting under a conflict of duties in which he submits to 'force majeure' created by the merciful moral compulsion to relieve his patient of unmitigated suffering.[143]

5.2 Islamic views

The directives in the Qur'an and Sunnah, not to kill a human being were discussed above. But there are also specific orders not to kill oneself.

Do not cast yourselves into destruction.

And,

And do not kill yourselves. Allah is Most Merciful to you.[144]

The Prophet ﷺ warned sternly against suicide,

> He, who uses a weapon or poison to kill himself, will remain eternally

and perpetually, in the Hereafter, stabbing himself: or swallowing the poison.[145]

Fuqaha are not agreed as to the responsibility of the one who takes the life of another who has permitted the act. Al-Bahwati (d. 1051/ 1664), summarises the views in his Hanbali school and compares them with views in other schools,[146]

> There is no retribution *(qisas)* when one kills another, who has permitted him to do so; but those in the Maliki school, and Zufar from the Hanafi school think that *qisas* is due.
>
> The consensus is that *qisas* is out of the question because of the permission given; as it constitutes a *shubhah* (doubt) as to the sanctity of the blood of the one who has allowed himself to be killed.
>
> As regards whether *diya* is due or not; there are two views: one is that it is not due, the more popular one is that it is due. The reason being that doubt can negate the death penalty but it does not negate pecuniary penalties for which the proof need not be 'beyond any reasonable doubt.'

The views of the fuqaha on this matter are examined in detail below.

"Death brought about by an agent at the request of a person who dies," may go unpunished in Islamic fiqh according to most fuqaha,[147] except for those in the Maliki school. The fuqaha, in the Maliki school, differentiate between a situation when a person asks another to kill him (I will forgive you if you kill me) where after the act is done either *qisas* is due,[148] or the killer may be lashed with one hundred strokes and deported for a year;[149] and a situation when the tortfeasor is actually forgiven by the fatally injured person *after* injury but whereas death is imminent. In this latter situation the killer may escape all punishment.[150]

Compare this with common law. Under the title of 'Advance declarations' one finds:

> It is clear that an advance declaration or 'living will' does not solve all the problems and could not be expected to, no matter how carefully it was framed. There are difficulties in interpretation and in assessment of a range of hypothetical states, which the patient has not experienced at the time, the declaration is framed...
>
> Many US doctors find advance declarations elusive, indefinite and of dubious legality...

Such wishes may change when the patient realises the number of positive things that are left even with a supposedly intolerable disability.[151]

Montgomery said:

The problem with advance statements of intent is created by the fact that the patient may very well have lost the capacity to revoke an earlier decision.[152]

And there is a similarity between the Maliki insistence that the subject's forgiving must be after the fatal act and 'dying declarations.'

Dying declarations may only be proved at trials for murder or manslaughter. The deceased must have made them, they must relate to the cause of his death, he must have been someone who would have been a competent witness, and he must have been under a settled hopeless expectation of death. He need not have expected to die immediately, but if he says that "at present" he has no hope of survival, this implies a belief in the possibility that he will survive, and the statement will be inadmissible.[153]

Detailed examination and analysis of the Muslim fuqaha's views, in this matter of great controversy, are as follows:

(a) The Hanafi school

As-Sarakhsi said:

If someone asks another to amputate his diseased finger, and consequently the injured party dies; then there is no blame attached to that. As it was legal to ask on one side, and legal to act on the other. There is no *diya* to pay. But Abu Hanifah said, "*diya* is due, just as it is due in the case of one who asks another to kill him."

Although it is not allowed to give permission to kill oneself, still the penalty can never be *qisas*; because there was permission, albeit faulty. This is the doctrine of *shubhah*; i.e. doubt that the deceased does not possess the right to dispose of his own life (autonomy). So, reasonable doubt precludes retaliatory punishment *(qisas)* but it does not absolve the tortfeasor from paying *(diya)* for his transgression.

But one cannot ask another to kill his minor son. The tortfeasor is subjected to *qisas*. The parent, himself, cannot be the subject of *qisas*.[154]

Al-Kasani said:

If someone asks another to kill him, and he does: then there is no qisas, as held by Abu Hanifah, Abu Yusuf, and Muhammad ibn al-Hasan Ash-Shaybani. But should there be *diya*? There are two views attributed to Abu Hanifah on the issue: one view is that it is due; the other view is that nothing is due. The latter view is forwarded by Qadouri and he says that, 'it is the reliable saying of Abu Hanifah, and it is also the view of Abu Yusuf and Muhammad.'

But I (Kasani) think that *diya* should be due; as life remains sacrosanct, permission to dispose of it is not acceptable, but it constitutes doubt *(shubhah)* which although it prevents *qisas* (the taking of the life of the tortfeasor) it does not preclude *diya*. Zufar, the fourth of Abu Hanifah's companions, is for *qisas* as life remains sacred, there is no qualification for that, and hence there is no exemption to the rules of *qisas*.[155]

Ibn 'Abidin explained:

If someone asks another to kill him, and the other does so using a sword (the unequivocal sign of murder in the Hanafi school), then *diya* is due and the tortfeasor pays it from his own funds. There is no *qisas* because there was permission. Although the permission is invalid, it does prevent *qisas*, defective as it is, because there is doubt about its validity. But if he says "kill my minor son", then the tortfeasor is subject to *qisas*. *Qisas* is also due if he says, 'I have sold you my blood for so much.'[156]

The conclusion in this school is that someone may forgive acts against his own blood, but cannot sell it. Also a man cannot forgive acts against the blood of the minors in his care.

(b) The Maliki school

Al-Baji said:

If a person says, "I wish someone would kill me"; and another answers, "If you say that you have given me your 'blood' (life) and forgive me, then I will kill you." The first one says, "That is so." The other one kills him.

This situation has led to different responses from our fuqaha. The most acceptable one is that the tortfeasor is subject to *qisas*, because the deceased has forgiven something that did not happen. The consequence of his death is the concern of his inheriting relatives, who are the ones who can forgive the perpetrator or insist on taking his life.

The situation would have been different if the deceased had forgiven the tortfeasor after he was fatally interfered with, and he knew that his death was imminent as a result of that act. Because he is forgiving an action that, he knows, has terminated his life. Consequently there is no *qisas*.[157]

Al-Hattab said:

If someone says, "If you kill me, then I would have forgiven you," or, "I have given you my blood (life)," and the other person executes him, then there are two viewpoints on the matter: the better one of the two, as Ibn al-Qasim says, is that *qisas* is due. The case would have been different had he been forgiven after the act was committed and death was imminent as its result. *Qisas* is out of the question because there is doubt *(shubhah)* whether one has the right to forgive an act, which he has engineered to terminate his life, or not. But the tortfeasor is liable for *diya* from his own moneys, as doubt does not preclude financial settlements.[158]

Ad-Dardir said:

If someone says to another 'If you kill me, I would have forgiven you,' the perpetrator is subject to *qisas*, because what was forgiven did not happen then. Whereas if he was forgiven after a fatal act and death was imminent as its result, then he bears no consequences.

But if the subject survives an act which was forgiven and was meant to kill him, then *qisas* for that injury is due because the relatives reappear in the picture.[159]

Ad-Dasuqi said:

If someone kills another in response to, 'If you kill me then you are not responsible.' That is not enough to ward off *qisas*, which may be demanded by the relatives. But if after the fatal assault the subject forgives the assailant, then there is no *qisas*.[160]

An-Nafrawi said:

If someone promises another, "If you kill me you are forgiven." The promise and the forgiveness should be ignored. *Qisas* is the penalty for the act. Because the subject cannot forgive what has not happened yet. That is the prerogative of the relatives. But should he declare his wish of forgiving the totrtfeasor after he has been fatally assaulted, and death was eminent, then that is acceptable. It is comparable to when one asks another to amputate his hand or burn his clothes, and the other one does so. There is nothing to the act and no blame rests on the perpetrator.[161]

'Illish said:

If someone says to another, "Kill me and you have one thousand *dirhams*." And the other one kills him; there is no *qisas*. But the propitiator is to receive one hundred lashes, and he is to be imprisoned for one year.[162]

The summary of the views of the Maliki fuqaha is that, "Death brought about by an agent at the request of a person who dies," can be forgiven after the fatal act has been committed. There is unanimity among the fuqaha that no *qisas* is due. Some fuqaha have suggested *diya* is payable by the tortfeasor personally. But the relatives of the deceased can forgive that.

In the event of someone being hired by a person to kill him; the punishment is one hundred lashes and imprisonment for one year.

(c) The Shafi'i school

An-Nawawi said:

If someone asks another to amputate his hand, and it is done; then there is neither *qisas* nor *diya*: because it is just like asking a person to destroy one's own property. By the same token if one asks another person to kill him or to amputate his hand and he bleeds to death, then there is no *qisas*.

As to the question of *diya*, it can be examined in two ways: is it due towards the end of life, whereupon it is forgiven by the deceased-to-be, or is it due after death when it becomes the right of the relatives to claim? Ibn as-Sabbagh says, 'as far as the second view is concerned, I am in total disagreement with it. The issue is not that the deceased has forgiven the *diya*, as though it was the compensation for the destruction of property; the issue is that he has willingly allowed for his life to be taken. We are dealing with licence to kill. Hence there is no *diya* without a shred of doubt.[163]

Ar-Ramli said:

If someone kills another who has permitted him to do so, the *madhhab* is that there is no *qisas*. Out of the *diya* all his debts and what he had bequeathed should be deducted. There is also the view that permission to kill is not valid and is of no consequence, hence *qisas* is due.

But the most dominant of all views is that neither *qisas* nor *diya* is due.

It is a fact that the tortfeasor has committed a wrong action and he should fast for two consecutive months as expiation.[164]

Ash-Sharawani and Ibn al-Qasim[165] are of the same opinion of Ar-Ramli, mentioned above.

So the consensus in the Shafi'i school is that, "death brought by an agent at the request of a person who dies," may go unpunished, although the tortfeasor has undoubtedly done wrong and he should offer expiation for that.

(d) The Hanbali school

Ibn Qudama said:

If someone, in full command of his senses, asks another to kill him, or to wound him; then that act demands no action *(hadar)*.[166]

And,

If someone should ask another to kill or injure him, and that is done; then neither act demands action according to the best in the *madhhab*: but it is also said that *diya* is due.[167]

Ibn Muflih said:

It is stated in the *madhhab*, that if someone asks to be killed or wounded and his request is carried out; then there is no case for action *(hadar)*. But it is also mentioned that Ahmad ibn Hanbal said that *diya* is due.

But I (the author) have found that, the act is without consequence *(hadar)*, and there is a narrative related from Ahmad, that *diya* is due, and there is a saying attributed to Ahmad that even *qisas* is a possibility.[168]

I have examined in detail the views of Muslim fuqaha, which are expressed on this issue. Because of the great controversy which surrounds euthanasia at all times, special care was exercised not to miss any reference of note in the field. The summary of their aforementioned views on "death brought about by an agent at the request of a person who dies," can be classified into four categories:

First, some fuqaha think that the penalty is retribution *(qisas)*; which could be capital punishment if the relatives of the deceased wished it. Zufar holds this view from the Hanafi school, at variance with Imam Abu Hanifah himself and the other two pillars of the school, namely Qadi Abu Yusuf and Muhammad ibn al-Hassan ash-Shaybani.[169] It is the view of the Maliki school, if the permission was given before the subject was fatally interfered with. According to them the act can only be forgiven after it has been committed and the subject was certain of his impending death. Even then *diya* is due unless the relatives opt not to collect it.[170] Some in the Hanbali school also hold this same view.[171]

Second, there are those who think that, *qisas* is out of the question and it is only *diya* which is due.

This view is held by some Hanafi fuqaha,[172] some Shafi'i fuqaha,[173] and it is one of the views attributed to Ibn Hanbal.[174]

Third, there are those who think that neither *qisas* nor *diya* is due.

This view is attributed to Abu Hanifah, and his two companions, namely Abu Yusuf and ash-Shaybani. Al-Qaduri submits that it is the most acceptable view in the Hanafi school.[175] The majority of the Shafi'i school holds this same view,[176] and it is the most accepted one amongst the Hanbali school.[177]

Fourth, some Shafi'i fuqaha think that what is necessary is expiation only; to mend one's ways with Allah.[178] This is a most interesting view, simple though it may appear.

Expiation *(kaffara)* is an offering of repentance in the form of freeing a slave, fasting sixty consecutive days or feeding sixty poor people. It is purely a religious cleansing act. But if the punishment of murder in the Hereafter is eternal banishment in Hell, the wrath of Allah, and His curse,[179] even if one had been punished or forgiven in this life, what is the point of expiation then? Could it be that some Shafi'i fuqaha think that murder can even be forgiven in the Hereafter as well?

These are the views of notable, pious, and very knowledgeable men of Islamic fiqh. Most of the situations are hypothetical and contrived. There was no reference to actual cases even by Imam Abu Hanifa. But that is no reason to assume that there were not such cases. The subject discussed by them was a part of fiqh (jurisprudence), which was not interested in reporting and documenting real cases.

6. Conclusions

(1) Killing within the medical field, for any motive, is homicide. It is not allowed *(haram)* in any religion.

> All the major religious traditions take a positive stand against the active termination of human life…The Christian view is, in fact, very close to that taken in Judaic and Islamic teaching.[180]

It is also illegal in the overwhelming majority of laws. But in the Netherlands the situation was:

> 'Euthanasia' is thus on its face illegal, but…it can under specific conditions be legally justifiable [sic.].[181]

> Article 293 (of the Dutch Criminal Code) prohibits killing a person at his request…Article 294 prohibits assisting a suicide (suicide itself is not a crime in the Dutch law)…

> Despite the apparently forbidding text of these provisions, the courts have held that Article 40 of the Criminal Code makes a defence of justification available to a doctor charged under Articles 293 or 294…

Shoonheim case in 1984…defence of justification due to necessity…[182]

Until it was legalised on 29th. November 2000.[183]

In Britain:

> there is an innate reluctance on the part of the courts to convict the genuine 'mercy-killer'…the prosecutor may well exercise his discretion and accept the plea of manslaughter;[184]

(2) Consent of the subject ('voluntary' euthanasia)[185] may be a mitigating factor, in the punishment for the crime of 'mercy killing,' which is murder. The expected punishment being *qisas*,[186] but the one meted out by many fuqaha is *diya* for manslaughter, because of the doubt involved in the validity of the consent of the subject.[187] The Prophet ﷺ is narrated to have said: "Ward off the penalty of *hudud*, if there is any doubt."[188]

That is in the case of *hadd*, which is Allah's stipulated penalty for a specific crime. It is more applicable to *qisas*, which may be forgiven by the relatives anyway. The Qur'an encourages forgiveness in this respect.[189] The Prophet ﷺ always implored the relatives for it.[190]

Someone brought another to the Messenger of Allah ﷺ saying that the man had killed his brother with an axe, and that he would like *qisas* (retribution). The Prophet said, " That is for you; but if you kill him you are no better than him." The man forgave the one who had killed his brother.[191]

That should not be taken as lightening the gravity of the crime, as it is still punishable in the Hereafter even when it is forgiven.[192]

(3) Few of the Muslim fuqaha ascribe no worldly penalty, no *qisas* nor *diya*, to "death brought by an agent at the request of a person who dies."[193]

(4) As regards euthanasia and assisted suicide

> Many of the Prophet's companions were fatally injured in battles, and they remained for several days in agony and torment. They never entertained killing themselves to relieve their suffering, nor did the other companions.[194]

The hospice concept of caring for the terminally ill is in line with the concepts of Islam. A Muslim should not engineer his own death.

(5) The British Medical Association (BMA) 'guidelines on curtailing life' were released in June 1999. They still generate debate:

> …particularly in relation to the requirement to seek a court order before withdrawing nutrition and hydration by tube and wish to allow doctors to seek a second opinion in order to authorise the withdrawal

of food and fluids in cases such as those involving stroke patients or the confused elderly, even when the patient is not terminally ill...the guidance claims for doctors the right to overrule the wishes of the patient's family in this matter...[195]

The BMA began an Internet debate on 5 July 1999, on euthanasia.

Michael Wilks, chairman of the BMA's ethics committee, explained that the aim...was to find...a consensus that doctors might follow, and to identify precisely the meaning of terms and expressions. For example, 'respect for human life' may mean that there should be no intentional interference to bring it to a conclusion; or it might also mean that an individual may decide whether or not to be treated."[196]

The Prophet ﷺ said, "Do not force food and drink on your patients, as Allah provides for them."[197] But that is when they can fend for themselves.

Although it is the right of the mother to opt out of suckling her newborn, or ask to be paid for that; a mother who does not suckle her infant when there is no provision for a wet-nurse is guilty of murder should that infant die.[198] Compare this with what has been put forward by Montgomery, when he said that health professionals are obliged to look after the patient at the risk of being prosecuted for manslaughter for failure to do so. And that non-professionals have been found guilty of manslaughter for failing to look after relatives for whose care they have taken responsibility.[199]

The Prophet said: O Lord! Please let me live if that is for my good; and please let me die if that is better for me.[200]

It is inherent in this prayer that termination of life is not in any person's hands. Islamic fiqh does not allow 'euthanasia'; so is the case with common law and civil law in the overwhelming majority of countries. Holland is the exception so far.

Notes

1. *Euthanasia, Report of the Working Party to review the British Medical Association's guidance on euthanasia*, BMA 5 May 1988, p. 60. (Henceafter"BMA Report").
2. Suyuti, *Sahih al-Jami'i as-Saghir wa ziyadatuh*, 1969, vol. 1:398-399.
3. Suyuti, *Sahih al-Jami'i as-Saghir wa ziyadatuh*, 1969, vol. 1:411; and *Sunan Ibn Majah*, 1953, vol. 2:1443.
4. *Euthanasia*, BMA Report, p. 3.
5. Mason and McCall Smith, *Law and Medical Ethics*, 1994:316, and 1999:414.
6. Griffiths, Bood, and Weyers, *Euthanasia And Law In The Netherlands*, Amsterdam, 1998: 98. But on 29th. November 2000 the Dutch Parliament in The Hague legalised 'Euthanasia,' with 104 members for the motion and 40 members opposed. (BBC World Service, 18 hrs. GMT, and CNN).
7. *Euthanasia*, BMA Report, p. 3. 'The Working Party' included representatives of many of the concerned circles with the issue and from several European countries.
8. Kasani, *Bada'i* 1910, vol. 7:235; see also: Colin Imber, "Why you should poison your husband: a note on liability in Hanafi law in the Ottoman period" in *Islamic Law and Society* 1,2 pp. 206-216, © E.J. Brill, Leiden, 1994.
9. *Euthanasia*, BMA Report, 1988:3.
10. Cross, and Jones, *An Introduction to Criminal Law*, 1959:122, (an old reference has been chosen in order to match Islamic definitions; see below p. 203. Some states in the USA still retain the death penalty).
11. Cross, and Jones, *Criminal Law*, 1959:125-126, (see fn. 590 at p. 199).
12. Montgomery, *Health Care Law*, 1997:439.
13. Mason & Smith, *Law and Medical Ethics*, 1994:317. (Examples given: R v. Adams [1957]; R v. Arthur, 1981, (1993) 12 BMLR 1; R v. Carr, 1986, (aborted); R v. Lodwig (1990), R v. Cox (1992) 12 BMLR 38).
14. *R v Adams* [1957] Crim. LR 365 was a case of trial for murder in which it was alleged that Dr. Adams injected an incurably (not terminally) ill patient with increasing doses of opiates.
15. (1981) 12 BMLR 1, *The Times*, 6 November 1981, pp. 1, 12, Mason and Smith, 1994:150. See f.n.791.
16. Mason and McCall Smith, *Law and Medical Ethics*, 1994:316-317, citing R v Carr, (1986), *The Sunday Times*, 30 November 1986, p. 1.
17. *R v Lodwig* (1990) The Times, 16 March, p 3, see f.n. 594, and C Dyer 'SHO Has Murder Charge Dropped' (1990) 300 *Brit Med J* 768.

194   The Fiqh of Medicine

18 *R v Cox* [1992] 12 BMLR 38 was an attempted murder trial in which Dr. Cox administered a lethal dose of potassium chloride (not a pain killer) to Mrs. Lilian Boyes who was suffering from an incurable and increasingly distressing form of arthritis: Mrs. Boyes died within minutes of the act. Mason et, al., 1994:317.
19 [1993] AC 789 at p. 865; and see Davies, *Medical Law*, 1996:314, and.
20 [1993] AC. 789 at p. 895.
21 Lewis, *Medical Negligence*, 1998:158.
22 Montgomery, *Health Care Law*, 1997:437.
23 *Barnet v. Chelsea & Kensington HMC* [1968] 1 All ER 1068.
24 *R v. Bourne* [1983] 3 All ER 615,618.
25 *R v. Instan* [1893] 1 QB 450; *R v. Stone* [1977] 2 All ER 341.
26 *Airedale NHS Trust v. Bland* [1993] 1 All ER 821, 880-3.
27 'The King's Peace?' (1986) *The Times*, 28 November, p. 17; Mason & McCall Smith, *Law and Medical Ethics*, 3rd. ed., 1991:320). (This does not appear in the 4th. ed., 1994:316).
28 Q. 5:32.
29 *Sunan Ibn Majah*, 1953, vol. 2:847.
30 Q. 22:37, (tr. Bewley); and Q. 2:244, (tr. Bewley).
31 *Sunan al-Tirmidhi* 1983, vol. 2:435-436, three *hadith*; see *Sahih Muslim*, 1987, vol. 1:170; and *Sunan Ibn Majah*, 1953, vol. 2:861-862.
32 Q. 4:92, Q. 17:33, **"Do not kill any person Allah has made inviolate, except with the right to do so."** (tr. Bewley).
33 *Sunan Ibn Majah*, 1953, vol. 2:873; *Sahih al-Bukhari*, (tr.), Khan, 1994:1011
34 *Sunan Ibn Majah*, 1953, vol. 2:873; Jakni, *Bukhari and Muslim*, 1967, vol. 1:118.
35 Ash-Shafi'i, *al-Umm*, 1993, vol. 6:7.
36 Q. 4:93.
37 Q. 17:32; also Q. 2:178, and Q. 5:45.
38 *Sunan Ibn Majah*, 1953, vol. 2:876-977; see Ibn Rushd, *Bidayat* 1935, vol. 2:402"Abu Hanifah has no *diya* as such for murder, when the relatives opt for other than *qisas*: they can agree on any sum, and though the payment should be immediate, that also is left to the parties," and Ibn 'Abidin, *Hashiya*, 1966, vol. 6:529.
39 Ash-Shafi'i, *al-Umm*, 1993, vol. 6:543.
40 Jakni, *Bukhari and Muslim*, 1967, vol. 1:7. hadith"*innama'l-a'malu bi'n-niyat."* (Ash-Shafi'i said,"it embodies one third of the whole of Islam."). Also in *Sahih al-Bukhari*, (tr.), Khan, 1994:49, and 79.
41 *Euthanasia*, BMA Report, 1988, p. 3.
42 Ash-Shafi'i, *al-Umm*, 1993, vol. 6:62-64; Ibn 'Abidin, *Hashiya*, 1966, vol. 6:543.
43 Kasani, *Badi'a* 1910, vol. 7:235

Euthanasia 195

[44] Ibn'Abidin, *Hashiya*, 1966, vol. 6:527-531; Kasani, *Badi'a* 1910, vol. 7:234.

[45] Ibn'Abidin, *Hashiya*, 1966, vol. 6:527-531; Kasani, *Badi'a* 1910, vol. 7:234. (Abu Hanifah's [causation] logic, calls for Lord Mustill's comment in *Airedale NHS Trust* v. *Bland* [1993] AC 789, p. 895,"I am bound to say that the argument seems to me to require not manipulation of the law so much as its application in an entirely new and illogical way." Bland, "the comatose patient was not fed and was left to die: there was no action as it was done for the patient's good").

[46] Kasani, *Badai'a* 1910, vol. 7:234-235; Ibn'Abidin, *Hashiya*, 1966, vol. 6:529.

[47] Kasani, *Badai'a* 1910, vol. 7:234-235, (note the vacillation and change of ruling for drowning: dependent on many variables); Ibn'Abidin, *Hashiya*, 1966, vol.6:528-531.

[48] Dasuqi, *Hashiyah 'ala ash-Sharh al-Kabir*, Matba'at Mustafa Muhammad vol. 4:317, (Maliki); *Takmilat al-Majmu'a*, vol. 17:260, (Ash-Shafi'i); Bahwati, *Kashf al-Qina'a*, (1319 AH), vol. 5:592, (Hanbali).

[49] Ibn'Abidin, *Hashiya*, 1966, vol. 6:530.

[50] Kasani, *Badi'a,* 1910, vol. 7:235.

[51] Kasani, *Badi'a,* 1910, vol. 7:234-235, (bricking in: restraining); Ibn'Abidin, *Hashiya*, 1966, vol. 6:529 (drowning); and p. 543 (restraining).

[52] Sahnun, *al-Mudawanah*, (1323 AH) vol. 4:432; Ibn Rushd, *Bidayat*, 1935, vol. 2:390.

[53] Q. 4:91-92, (tr. Bewley).

[54] Dasuqi, *Hashiya 'ala al-Sharh al-Kabir,* Matba'at Mustafa Muhammad, vol. 4:215,and 252.

[55] Ibn Rushd, *Bidayat,* 1935, vol. 2:397. See *hadith* in *Sunan Abi Dawud*, 1973, vol. 4:647-652.

[56] *Sunan Ibn Majah*, 1953, vol. 2:878-9; *Sunan Abi Dawud*, 1973, vol. 4:683.

[57] Ibn Rushd, *Bidayat* 1935, vol. 2:401-402, and 405; Saraskhi, *al-Mabsut*, 1958, 26:65; and Ibn'Abidin, *Hashiya*, 1966, vol. 6:530; in all of these references it is stated that, "Higher *diya (mughaladhah)* is due on the spot for intentional murder, unless the parties agree to a grace period; whereas *diya al-khata'* (mistake) is due over three years." See also Sabiq, *Fiqh as-Sunnah*, 1995, vol. 2:371-372.

[58] Ibn Rushd, *Bidayat,* 1935, vol. 2:235; Sahnun, *al-Mudawwanah*, (1323 AH), vol. 6:427; and 'Asqalani, *Fath al-Bari...al-Bukhari*, al-Matba'a al-Bahiya, vol. 12:261. (This has bearing when a doctor'kills' to collect bequeathed moneys from his patient).

[59] Q. 17:33; also Q. 2:178; and Q. 5:45.

[60] *Sunan Ibn Majah*, 1953, vol. 2:876.

[61] Sabiq, *Fiqh as-Sunnah*, 1995, vol. 2:355; Hanafi school: Ibn Nujaim, *al-Bahr ar-Ra'iq*, 1980, vol. 8:337; Kasani, *Badi'a*, 1910, vol. 7:237; Shafi'i school: *al-Umm*, 1993, vol. 6:16-17, and *Mawsu'at al-Imam ash-Shafi'i*, 1996, vol.

12:34; Hanbali school: Ibn Qudama, *al-Mughni*, 1981, vol. 7:648.
62 Dasuqi, *Hashiyah ' ala ash-Sharh al-Kabir*, Matba'at Mustafa, vol. 4:317.
63 Sahnun through Ibn al-Qasim to Malik, *al-Mudawwanah*, 1323 AH, vol. 4:433; Ibn Rushd, *Bidayat al-Mujtahid*, 1935, vol. 2:390.
64 Ash-Shafi'i, *al-Umm*, 1993, vol. 6:10.
65 Ash-Shafi'i, *al-Umm*, 1993, vol. 6:11.
66 Ash-Shafi'i, *al-Umm*, 1993, vol. 6:12.
67 Ash-Shafi'i, *al-Umm*, 1993, vol. 6:12-13, all in *al-Umm: Mawsu'at al-Imam ash-Shafi'i*, 1996, vol. 12:20-26.
68 Ibn Qudama, *al-Mughni*, 1981, vol. 7:642; and in Ibn Qudama, *al-Kafi*, 1982, vol. 4:3 and 4:12.
69 Ibn Qudama, *al-Mughni*, 1981, vol. 7:627; and *al-Kafi*, 1982, 4:13. .
70 Ibn Qudama, *al-Mughni*, 1981, vol. 7:642; and *al-Kafi*, 1982, 4:14-15.
71 Ibn Qudama, *al-Kafi*, 1982, vol. 4:15; and Bahwati, *Kashf*, (1319 AH), vol. 5:592 (Hanbali school). The Maliki school, has the same ruling over this issue, giving the same example, see Dasuqi, *Hashiyah 'ala ash-Sharh al Kabir*, vol. 4:317. The two schools are similar, and rely heavily on *hadith* (*ahl al-hadith*).
72 Ibn Qudama, *al-Kafi*, 1982, vol. 4:16.
73 Ibn Qudama, *al-Mughni*, 1981, vol. 7:643; and Bahwati, *Kashf*, (1319 AH), vol. 5:591.
74 Ash-Shafi'i, *al-Umm*, 1993, vol. 6:12-13, "if the person dies within a period in which most people would have died, it is murder; otherwise it is manslaughter."
75 Mason & McCall Smith, *Law and Medical Ethics*, 1994:316.
76 *Euthanasia*, BMA Report, 1988:3.
77 Maliki school: Sawi, *Balghat al-Salik*, vol. 2:383; Shafi'i school: *al-Umm*, 1993, vol. 6:12; Ibn Qudama, *al-Mughni*, 1981, vol. 7:617.
78 Hanafi school: Ibn 'Abidin, *Hashiyah*, 1966, vol. 6:543.
79 Maliki school: Dasuqi, *Hashiyah 'ala al-Sharh al-Kabir*, Matba'at Mustafa, vol. 4:215; Ash-Shafi'i, *al-Umm*, 1993, vol. 6:12 " if he throws him in deep water, and he dies, then that is murder where *qisas* is due; but if he throws him close to the shore and he is a good swimmer and there were no currents yet he died then there is no *qisas*; and if he throws him in water which is no challenge to his ability as a swimmer but a great fish takes him away, then there is no *qisas*, but *diya* is due."
80 Ibn 'Abidin, *Hashiyah*, 1966, vol. 6:544, (for Abu Hanifah to be paid by *'aqila*).
81 Ibn 'Abidin, *Hashiyah*, 1966, vol. 6:529.
82 Maliki school: Dasuqi, *Hashiyah 'ala ash-Sharh al-Kabir*, Matba'at Mustafa, vol. 4:317, but Ibn Rushd, *Bidayat*, 1935, vol. 2:397 said "No retaliation in poisoning *(la yuqad min sim)*"; Shafi'i school: Shirazi, *al-Muhadhab*, vol.

17:260; Hanbali school: Bahwati, *Kashf al-Qina'a*, 1319 AH, vol. 5:592.
83 Kasani, *Badi'a*, 1910, vol. 7:235, (he mentions that with ash-Shafi'i *qisas* is due).
84 R v *Cox* [1992] 12 BMLR 38 was an attempted murder trial in which Dr. Cox administered a lethal dose of potassium chloride (not a pain killer) to Mrs. Lillian Boyes who was suffering from an incurable and increasingly distressing form of arthritis, and Mrs. Boyes died within minutes.
85 Kasani, *Badi'a*, 1910, vol. 7:234-235; and Ibn 'Abidin, *Hashiyah*, 1966, vol. 6:543. *C.f* R v *Arthur* (1981) 12 BMLR 1, Dr. Arthur went on trial because he instructed his staff not to feed a newborn, unwanted, baby,...The infant died sixty-nine hours later.
86 Dasuqi, *Hashiyah 'ala ash-Sharh al-Kabir*, Mutba'at Mustafa, vol. 4:214-215.
87 Ash-Shafi'i, *al-Umm*, 1993, vol. 6:12.
88 Ibn Qudama, *al-Kafi*, 1982, vol. 4:16.
89 Ibn 'Abidin, *Hashiyah*, 1966, vol. 6:543
90 *Euthanasia*, BMA Report, 1988:3.
91 *Re A* [1992] 3 Med. LR 303, also in Montgomery, *Health Care Law*, 1997:449.
92 Kennedy, I. M., 'Switching off Life Support Machines: the Legal Implications' [1977] Crim LR 443.
93 'Diagnosis of Death' (1979) 1 Brit Med J 332.
94 Mason and McCall Smith, *Law and Medical Ethics*, 1994:336.
95 R v *Arthur* (1981) 12 BMLR 1.
96 Mason & McCall Smith, *Law and Medical Ethics*, 1994:339.
97 Davies, *Medical Law*, 1996:292.
98 *Airedale NHS Trust* v *Bland* [1993] AC 789.
99 *The Times* Wednesday June 17 1998 p. 7 column 8 **'Mother wins legal right to let son die'**. A mother's request for treatment to be withdrawn from her son so that he could die with dignity after seven years in a "persistent vegetative state" after he was hit by a car, was granted by Sir Stephen Brown, President of the High Court Family Division. Another example: Karen Quinlan survived for more than eight years in that state, before it was ruled that artificial respiration should be stopped. She lived for eight more years after the respirator was disconnected. *Quinlan* 70 NJ 10, 355 A 2d. 664 (1976), per Hughes CJ.
100 *Airdale NHS Trust* v *Bland* [1993] AC 780 at p.825.
101 *Airedale NHS Trust* v *Bland* [1993] 1 All ER 821, 866, 880-3.
102 Montgomery, *Health Care Law*, 1997:450-451.
103 Mason & McCall Smith, *Law and Medical Ethics*, 1994:334.
104 Q. 6:137; 6:140; 6:153; 17:31; 60:12; 81:8.
105 *Sunan Ibn Majah*, 1953:895-897, seven *hadith*: "all lives (blood) are the same and equal in sanctity; be it: Muslim, *dhimmi*, mu'ahid, those in your care,

and anybody who trusts you."
[106] Kasani, *Badi'a*, 1910, vol. 7:237 (Hanafi); Ibn Rushd, *Bidayat, al-Kulliyat*, vol. 2:433 (Maliki); Shirbini, *Mughni al-Muhtaj*, (1377 AH), vol. 4:16 (Shafi'i); Ibn Qudama, *al-Mughni*, 1981, vol. 7:648 (Hanbali).
[107] *Qisas* is due in killing by exposure to the cold: Bahwati, *Kashf al-Qina'a*, (1319 AH), vol. 5:591; Ibn Qudama, *al-Mughni*, 1981, vol. 7:643; or when the mother refuses to suckle the newborn with the intention of terminating life: Dasuqi, *Hashiyah 'ala ash-Sharh al-Kabir*, Matba'at Mustafa, vol. 4:215.
[108] (1992) 12 BMLR 1 Farquharson J said that Dr. Arthur has, 'Set into train the course of events which could only have resulted in the child's death.' In summing up, Farquharson J informed the jury that the case 'really revolves round the question of what is the duty of the doctor....' Some criticised Farquharson J's summing up as the 'duty of a doctor' is a matter of law not a matter of fact. Hence perceived the acquittal as "a perverse jury verdict." Davies, *Medical Law*, 1996:287-292.
[109] Ibn 'Abidin, *Hashiyah*, 1966, vol. 6:543
[110] Q. 4:127; 93:9; 2:83; 2:220 et al.
[111] Q. 4:3; 4:6; 4:127 et al.
[112] Ibn Rushd, *Bidayat, al-Kulliyat*, vol. 2:436, and 473; see also *Ashal al-Madarik...Malik*, vol. 3:118.
[113] *Musnad Ibn Hanbal*, 1993, vol. 1:292; Ibn Rushd, *Bidayat, al-Kulliyat*, vol. 2:433 and 436; Ash-Shafi'i, *al-Umm*, 1993, vol. 6:50; As-Suyuti, *Tanwir al-Hawalik*, vol. 3:70; Ibn Qudama, *Al-Mughni*, 1981, vol. 7:666.
[114] Q. 17:31, and 6:151; (tr. Bewley).
[115] Baihaqi, *al-Sunan al-Kubra*, (1354 AH), vol. 8:15 and 18, citing al-Bukhari.
[116] Damad, (Sheikhi Zada), *Majma'a*, (1327 AH), vol. 2:393; and Ibn 'Abidin, *Hashiyat*, 1966, vol. 6:69.
[117] Kasani, *Badi'a* 1910, vol. 7:237-238; Baihqi, *al-Sunan al-Kubra*, (1354 AH), vol. 8:28; Ibn Qudama, *al-Mughni*, 1981, 7:648.
[118] *Musnad Ahmad Ibn Hanbal*, 1993, p. 178.
[119] Maliki school: Ibn Rushd, *Bidayat*, 1935, vol. 2:392, and *al-Kuliyat* edition, vol. 2:435; Hanafi school: Kasani, *Badi'a*, vol. 7:238; Shafi'i school: Shirazi, *al-Muhadhab*, vol. 17:231; Hanbali school: Ibn Qudama, *al-Mughni*, 1981, vol. 7:671).
[120] Sabiq, *Fiqh as-Sunnah*, 1995, vol. 2:356.
See also Malik, *al-Muwatta*, (ed.), Sa'd, 1983:756, ('Umar ibn al-Khattab killed five or seven persons for the treacherous slaying (*ghilah*) of one man and he said, "If all the people of San'a were the plotters I would have killed them all").
[121] Sarakhsi, *al-Mabsut*, 1958, vol. 26:66.
[122] *Euthanasia*, BMA Report, 1988 p. 3.

Euthanasia 199

[123] Hanafi: Sarakhsi, *al-Mabsut*, 1958, vol. 16:14; Kasani, *Badi'a* 1910, vol. 7:236; and Ibn 'Abidin, *Hashiyah*, 1966, vol. 6:547; Maliki: Baji, *al-Muntaqa*, vol. 7:75; Hattab, *Mawahib*, (1329 AH), vol. 5:253; Dardir, *al-Sharh al-Saghir*, vol. 6:16; Shafi'i: Nawawi, *al-Majmu'a*, vol. 17:275; al-Ramli, *Nihayat al-Muhtaj*, (1357 AH), vol. 7:260; Hanbali: Ibn Qudama, *al-Mughni*, 1981, vol. 9:342.

[124] Palmer, H., 'Dr. Adam's Trial for Murder' [1957] Crim LR 365.

[125] Williams, *Textbook of Criminal Law*, 1983:580.

[126] Montgomery, *Health Care Law*, 1997:441, (*Airedale NHS Trust v. Bland* [1993] 1 All ER 890).

[127] *Euthanasia*, BMA Report, 1988 pp. 59-60.

[128] Brazier, Margaret, *Medicine, Patients and the Law*, 1992 pp. 30-31.

[129] *Medicine in Europe*, edited by Tessa Richards, BMJ., 1992 pp. 121-122.

[130] Griffiths, Bood, Weyers, *Euthanasia and Law in the Netherlands*, 1998:15.

[131] Griffiths et. al., *Euthanasia...in the Netherlands*, 1998:98; "Article 293 states that, A person who takes the life of another person at that other person's express and earnest request is liable to a term of imprisonment of: not more than twelve years or a fine of the fifth category" (Griffiths et. al., 1998:308). Fifth category fine = f 100,000 (Criminal Code Article 23). (In Griffiths et. al., 1998:307).

[132] On 29th November 2000 the Dutch Parliament legalised 'Euthanasia.' (See fn. 570 at p. 196 above).

[133] [1984] 1 All ER 277.

[134] Montgomery, *Health Care Law*, 1997:442-443.

[135] Blacki, Meredith, "Physician Assisted Suicide: A Criminal Offence or a Patient's Right," *Med. L. Rev.*, vol. 5, n. 3, Autumn, 1997, pp. 294-316 at p. 295.

[136] CNN interview with Larry King, on 15 January 1997, 22 hours GMT.

[137] Mason and McCall Smith, *Law and Medical Ethics*, 1994:337.

[138] Keon, John, (ed.), *Euthanasia Examined*, CUP, 1995 p. 2 "Jack Kervorkian's [sic] suicide machine was not helpful to the cause of euthanasia." (spelt as Kevorkian in many American references).

[139] *Saudi Gazette*, (Time magazine weekly selection), Jeddah, Saudi Arabia, Tuesday 30 March 1999, p. 10, columns 1,2, and 3.

[140] [1992] 12 BMLR 38.

[141] CNN, April 13 1999, 23 hours GMT; and The *Times* April 14 1999, p. 14, top of column 8.

[142] *Euthanasia*, 'BMA Report,' 1988:43 (abridged).

[143] *Euthanasia* 'BMA Report,' 1988:49.

[144] Q. 2:194, and Q. 4:29; (tr. Bewley).

[145] *Sahih Muslim*, 1987, vol. 1:144; Baihaqi, *al-Sunan al-Kubra*, (1354 AH), vol. 8:24.

146. Bahwati, *Kashf,* (1319 AH), vol. 5:602.
147. Kasani, *Badi'a* 1910, vol. 7:236, (Hanafi school); Ramli, *Nihayat al-Muhtaj,* (1357 AH), vol. 7:260-261, (Shafi'i school); Ibn Qudama, *al-Mughni,* 1981, vol. 9:342, (Hanbali school).
148. Baji, *al-Muntaqa...al-Muwatta,'* vol. 7:75.
149. 'Illish, *Sharh Minah* 1984, vol. 4:347.
150. Dardir, *Al-Sharh al-Saghir,* vol. 6:16.
151. *Euthanasia,* 'BMA Report,' 1988:57-58.
152. Montgomery, *Health Care Law,* 1997:446.
153. Cross, and Jones, *An Introduction To Criminal Law,* 1959:454.
154. Sarakhsi, *al-Mabsut,* 1958, vol. 16:14.
155. Kasani, *Badai'a,* 1910, vol. 7:236.
156. Ibn 'Abidin, *Hashiya,* 1966, vol. 6:547.
157. Baji, *al-Muntaqa...al-Muwatta,'* vol. 7:75.
158. Hattab, *Mawahib* 1329 AH, vol. 5:235-236.
159. Dardir, *Al-Sharh al-Saghir,* vol. 6:16.
160. Dasuqi, *Hashiyah 'ala al-Sharh al-Kabir,* vol. 4:245.
161. Nafrawi, *al-Fawakih* (1332 AH), vol. 2:201.
162. 'Illish, *Sharh Minah* 1984, vol. 4:347.
163. An-Nawawi, *al-Majmou'a,* Dar al-Fikr, vol. 17:275.
164. Ramli, *Nihayat,* (1357 AH) vol. 7:260-261.
165. Ibn Hajar, (1304 AH), vol. 8:391, *Hawashi ash-Sharawani wa Ibn al-Qasim 'ala Tuhfat al-Muhtaj bi Sharh al-Minhaj.*
166. Ibn Qudama, *al-Mughni,* 1981, vol. 9:342.
167. Ibn Qudama, *al-Muqnia,* 1981, vol. 3:341.
168. Ibn Muflih, *al-Furu',* 1963, vol. 5:623.
169. Kasani, *Badi'a* 1910, vol. 7:236.
170. Hattab, *Mawahib* (1329 AH), vol. 6:236.
171. Ibn Muflih, *al-Furou'a,* 1962, vol. 5:633.
172. Kasani, *Badi'a* 1910, vol. 7:236; and Sarakhsi, *al-Mabsut,* 1958, vol. 16:14.
173. Ramli, *Nihayat,* (1357 AH.), vol. 7:260-261.
174. Bahwati, *Kashaf,* (1319 AH.), vol. 5:524; Ibn Muflih, *al-Furu',* 1962, vol. 5:623.
175. Kasani, *Badi'a* 1910, vol. 7:236.
176. Ramli, *Nihayat al-Muhtaj,* (1357 AH.), vol. 7:260-261.
177. Ibn Qudama, *al-Mughni,* 1981, vol. 9:342.
178. Ibn Hajar, *Tuhfa* (1304 AH), vol. 8:391.
179. Q. 4:93.
180. *Euthanasia,* 'BMA Report,' 1988 pp. 59-60.
181. Griffiths et. al., *Euthanasia and Law in the Netherlands,* 1998:98. [Article 293 states that, "A person who takes the life of another person at that other person's express and earnest request is liable to a term of imprisonment

of not more than twelve years or a fine of the fifth category,…]

[182] Griffiths, et. al., *Euthanasia and Law in the Netherlands,* 1998:18.

[183] On 29th November 2000 the Dutch Parliament legalised 'Euthanasia.' (See fn. 686 and fn. 815).

[184] Mason & McCall Smith, Law and Medical Ethics, 1994 p. 317.

[185] *Euthanasia,* 'BMA Report,' 1988:3 "death brought about by an agent at the request of a person who dies."

[186] Kasani, *Badi'a*, 1910, vol. 7:236; Ibn Muflih, *al-Furu'a*, 1962, vol. 5:633; Hattab, *Mawahib,* (1329 AH), vol. 6:236.

[187] Kasani, *al-Badi'a*, 1910, vol. 7:236; Ramli, *Nihayat,* (1357 AH), vol. 7:260-261; Ibn Muflih. *al-Furu',* 1962, vol. 5:623.

[188] *Sunan Ibn Majah*, 1953, vol. 1:850. "*idra'u al-hudud bi'sh-shubuhat.*"

[189] Q. 2:178 and Q. 5:45.

[190] Four *hadith* in *Sunan Ibn Majah,* 1953, vol. 2:897-898.

[191] Hadith, *"in qatalahu fa huwa mithluhu"* in *Sunan Ibn Majah*, 1953, vol. 2:897.

[192] Q. 4:93.

[193] Kasani, *al-Badi'a*, 1910, vol. 7:236; Ramli, *Nihayat*, (1357 AH), vol. 7:260-261; Ibn Qudama, *al-Mughni* 1981, vol. 9:342.

[194] *Sahih Muslim*, 1987, vol. 1:146; Ibn Hazm adh-Dhahiri, *al-Muhalla,* (1347 AH), vol. 7:418 and vol. 10:518.

[195] *The Times* June 28 1999 Letters to the Editor: BMA guidelines on curtailing life p. 21, column 3. signed, P. Howard, (Dr.), G. Wright (QC, Barrister), et. al., June 24 1999.

[196] *The Times* July 5 1999, p. 2, columns 5, 6, and 7 (middle of page).

[197] *Sunan Ibn Majah,* 1953, vol. 2:1139-1140; Hakim, *al-Mustadrak,* (1334 AH), vol. 4:410; and al-Baihaqi, *al-Sunan al-Kubra,* (1356 AH), vol. 9:347 (al-Baihaqi says it is a weak hadith).

[198] Kasani, *Badi'a*, 1910, vol. 7:235, (Hanafi school, but the mother is not subject to retaliation per se because it is manslaughter); but Dasuqi, *Hashiyah 'ala ash-Sharh al-Kabir*, vol. 4:214-215 (Maliki school); ash-Shafi'i, *al-Umm,* vol. 6:6; and Ibn Qudama, *al-Kafi,* 1982, vol. 4:16 (Hanbali school), though they consider it as murder, only *diya* is due because no parent is killed for murdering his offspring, (hadith in: *Musnad Ahmad,* 1993, vol. 1:292-293).

[199] Montgomery, *Health Care Law,* 1997:437, see page 203, and footnotes 701-705.

[200] *Sunan Ibn Majah,* 1953, vol. 2:1425.

Chapter Seven
The Prevention and Termination of Pregnancy

1. Introduction
This chapter deals with the prevention of pregnancy, and the termination of unwanted ones. Prevention includes both contraception and birth control measures. 'Termination of pregnancy' may be more encompassing than 'abortion,' which is, in the medical sense, limited to the first three months (trimester) of gestation. But abortion, etymologically, can mean failure of, or stopping, the process in any of its stages.

Muslim fuqaha have linguistic, technical, and legal *(fiqh)* definitions of these terms. The counterpart of abortion in its widest sense (linguistic) is *ijhad* which has the same meaning of aborting a process or making it impossible to carry on with, or hurrying up things leading to miscarriage; technically it means 'slipping of the contents of a womb';[1] legally it refers to a transgression that results in a woman losing the contents of her womb.

In the Hanafi school:

Ijhad is transgression *(jinaya)* upon what is 'person' *(nafs)* on one count and a 'non-person' on another: person because it is human, and non-person because it has no separate existence from the mother.

For such a transgression to have occurred on the foetus *(janin)*, it is enough to recognise any parts in the dropped 'slipped' material.

The causative agent could be physical or mental: hitting, using a drug, shouting at, or terrifying a woman.[2]

The Maliki school defined it as:

This is when a foetus is dropped by: (hitting) a woman, which was intentional in the case of the mother but the foetus was not intended; or terrifying her for no legal reason; or making her smell vapours. The transgression is proved once the product does not dissolve on pouring hot water on it (to ascertain that it is an *'alaqa* and not a blood clot).[3]

The Shafi'i school defined the transgression as:

Hitting a woman or releasing vapours that will cause a pregnant woman to miscarry.⁴

The Hanbali school define it as:

Hitting the abdomen of a woman, resulting in her dropping a foetus.⁵

The important realm of the fate of fertilised ova outside the womb was also analysed. Although technically it may not be considered as abortion, it is of great legal concern.

2. Children within Marriage

Islam encourages marriage and having children; no offspring should be procured outside this relationship.⁶

The Prophet ﷺ said:

Marry, and beget children; for I would be proud of your large numbers amongst other peoples;⁷

and,

Whoever can support a family should marry;.⁸

and,

If a decent person comes for marriage, marry him off; riches are not important: if you do not do so, there will be unrest in the community.⁹

The Prophet ﷺ was asked by someone, whether he could marry a beautiful and rich woman who was barren; the Prophet said no three times adding,

marry the pleasant and fertile woman for I would be proud of your large numbers amongst other peoples.¹⁰

Since Islam favours marriage and having children, are there any occasions when it is allowed to have fewer children in the families?

This issue will be discussed under the following headings:

(1) Is it allowed to have fewer children in the family?
(2) Is it allowed to have smaller families by preventing pregnancy?
(3) Whether pregnancies can be terminated lawfully by induced abortion, in accordance with Islamic fiqh. This will be dealt with separately in section three as it involves the actual termination of existing pregnancy.

2.1 Is it allowed to have fewer children in the family?

The Qur'an considers having wealth and children as the adornment of life.¹¹ Having many children is coveted,¹² and perhaps enviable as revealed in the story of Israel and his sons.¹³ The Prophet ﷺ expressed this in several *hadith*, and he was full of praise for the fertile wife.[14]

But all of this is against a backdrop of bringing them up well, and looking after them even after one's death by leaving them 'wealthy.'[15]

According to the general rules in Islam of striking a balance between too much and too little,[16] that one should shoulder what is possible,[17] and that Allah wants things to be easy for people,[18] it can be inferred that it is allowed to have fewer members in one's family to avoid hardship.

Islam (similar to the action of Ibrahim (AS), the father of the Prophets) accepts the legal notion of polygyny. But it is regulated: Q. 4: 3, **"But if you are afraid of not treating them equally, then only one, ..."** Another reasons given is, *(dhalika adna alla ta'ulu* – **"That makes it more likely that you will not be unfair"***)*, which is explained and translated by some fuqaha as **"So that you may not have too many children to support."**[19]

The Prophet ﷺ expressly said, "It is a great misery to have too many children without the means to support them."[20] He also said, "Too many children are the other face of poverty, and fewer children are the other face of comfort."[21]

2.2 Is it allowed to have smaller families by preventing pregnancy?

There is no worse wrong action than killing one's own children (infanticide) except perhaps not believing in Allah or associating partners with Him.[22] But there is nothing in the Qur'an or the Sunnah against devising means to have fewer children, providing that it is done with the agreement of the couple.

These devices include: (i) coitus interruptus *('azl)*, (ii) blocking the neck of the womb, and (iii) other means.

(i) *'Azl*

'Azl, coitus interruptus, can prevent pregnancy if the sperm do not reach the birth canal. The Prophet ﷺ attached no blame to coitus interruptus *('azl)* as a means of contraception. "There is nothing in that; whatever is destined will occur",[23] he said when he was asked about it. Jabir, a companion of the Prophet ﷺ, says that coitus interruptus was practised with the knowledge of the Prophet and he did not object to it. Jabir went on to say, "this happened at the time when the Qur'an was still being revealed; had it been *haram* (prohibited) the

Qur'an would have forbidden it."[24]

Judge Abu Ya'ali said that:

> Obeid ibn Rofa'a al-Ansari told them that his father said that, Caliph 'Umar ibn al-Khattab, 'Ali ibn Abi Talib, az-Zubayr ibn al 'Awwam, Sa'd ibn Abi Waqqas, and others were all gathered when the subject of *'azl* came up. Someone said that it is 'minor infanticide,' 'Umar said that, "there is nothing wrong with it" and turned to 'Ali. 'Ali said, "It can never be so, because it had not passed through the seven stages of development which are mentioned in the Qur'an (Q. 23:12, 13, and 14) which are: a progression of products of earth and water (the elements) *(sulalatin min tin)*, then there is the stage of the *nutfa* (a drop of sperm) which becomes mixed *(nutfatin amshaj)* in *Surah* 76 verse 2, then an *'alaqa* (a product that clings), then *mudgha* (a chewed up flesh-like material, differentiated and un-differentiated), then bones appear, then they become coated with flesh, finally it is given a soul and becomes 'another creation' *(khalqan akhar).*"'Umar, was well pleased with him and said, "you are so right, may Allah reward you, and may you have a long life."[25]

It may be noted that 'Umar, 'Ali, az-Zubayr, and Sa'd, were very close to the Prophet ﷺ. They were amongst ten to whom the Prophet promised the Garden while he was living. The subject of *'azl* was an important and subject often discussed in detail. A most learned Judge, Abu Ya'ali, narrates this event and it was authenticated by al-Baihaqi and an-Nasa'i.

Al-Ghazali (1058-1111) said:

> This, [*'azl*], is neither like abortion nor it is like infanticide, because the latter two involve acts against existing beings *(mawjud hasil)*. Existence has stages; and the wrong committed against each stage is graded. The first stages of existence are the settling of the semen *(nutfa)* in the womb and mixing with the woman's secretions. The mere disturbance of this is wrong and that progresses through the stages of *'alaqa* and *mudgha*. But when it reaches infanticide (after separation of the foetus from the mother alive) that is the ultimate of crimes.[26]

'Azl being a male practice must be subject to the agreement of the wife.

Abu Hurairah, quoting 'Umar ibn al-Khattab, said that the Prophet ﷺ said, "*'azl* is not allowed without the consent of...the wife."[27]

Most Muslim fuqaha accept that *'azl* is allowed, and that it should be done with the consent of the wife; but they made an exception for that consent in case of, "bad times, and the fear of delinquency in the children *(fasad az-zaman, wa walad as-su')*."[28]

The whole debate rests on the meanings of the Prophet's *hadith* in this respect, which are:

(i) "There is nothing in that (coitus interruptus), whatever had been ordained will take place (creation of a soul)."
(ii) "Do you really do that?" (which he repeated three times).
(iii) "That (coitus interruptus) is hidden infanticide *(dhalika al-wa'd al-khafi)*."
(iv) "Not every emission of semen results in offspring *(ma min kulli ma'in yakunu al-walad)*."[29]

This must be put against the unequivocal impermissibility of infanticide.

The Qur'an says:

Do not kill your children out of fear of being poor. We will provide for them and you. Killing them is a terrible mistake.[30]

The Prophet ﷺ said:

The gravest of all wrong actions is not to believe in Allah: next to that is to kill your child so that you do not have to feed him ...[31]

"All Muslim fuqaha are agreed that in coitus interruptus, no conception has taken place, and no soul is created. The inquiry of the Prophet ﷺ in the second hadith, and his saying that, 'it is hidden infanticide' in the third one, are but mannerisms of speech common in Arabic, denoting in this instance 'it is not very nice to do.' An example of that is a hadith, which says, 'not being truthful or genuine is hidden disbelief in Allah *(ar-riya'u ash-shirk al-khafi)*'; *shirk* the ultimate unforgivable wrong action. But in this context it was not meant literally. So is the case when it was said that, *"dhalika ['azl] al-wa'd al-khafi."* It is not meant literally."[32]

It is only the literalist Ibn Hazm adh-Dhahiri (994-1063), (from the school of Dawud adh-Dhahiri, (d. 883)), who took the *hadith* of coitus interruptus being hidden infanticide literally to mean so.[33] The fact of the matter is that, no fertilisation took place, and no infant was created.

Musallam has written:

There was a remarkable unanimity among Muslim jurisprudents concerning this technique (coitus interruptus). Apart from Ibn Hazm..., I have searched in vain for opposition to the basic permission of contraception among the writings of Muslim jurisprudents of all ...Sunni and Shi'i schools of law...[34]

A summary of the views of Muslim fuqaha incorporating what was gleaned from al-Bukhari and Muslim (al-Jakni), Musallam, and Omran is given below:[35]

Hanafi school

Coitus interruptus is licit, but with the consent of the wife as she had a right to her own progeny. That right may be rescinded in 'bad times.'[36]

Maliki school

Some in the Maliki school have given the wife the right to be compensated financially in lieu of her consent.[37]

Shafi'i school

The Shafi'is permitted coitus inturruptus without any conditions. A few considered it licit only with the woman's consent. Although the Shafi'is considers a woman's right to intercourse as irrefutable, some have wavered about her right to insist that ejaculation should take place inside her.[38]

Hanbali school

In contrast to the Shafi'is, the Hanbali school insisted on the woman's permission, because of her right to progeny and her right to undiminished pleasure in intercourse. That right may be forfeited in certain circumstances as in war.[39]

Shi'ite Zaydi school

This is similar to the views in the Shafi'i school but on balance, it is allowed with the wife's permission.

Twelvers (Imamia) Shi'ite school, and the Ja'afari

'Azl is allowed, but the majority would seek the wife's permission.

Isma'aili Shi'ite school

'Azl is allowed with the permission of the wife.

Ibadia (Kharijite) school

In the Ibadia school, *'azl* is allowed with the permission of the wife.

Zahiri school, of Dawud adh-Dhahiri (d. 883 CE)

This is the only school, which prohibited coitus inturruptus *('azl)*. Ibn Hazm adh-Dhahiri maintained that the questionable license was definitely abrogated by the Prophet's *hadith*, "*dhalika ['azl] al-wa'd al-khafi* (that *['azl]* is hidden infanticide)." Judama bint Wahab al-Asadia (half-sister of Akasha ibn Muhsin) said that she heard the Prophet ﷺ say it.[40]

Although '*azl* is still practised, a more certain way of contraception, is the use of the condom. There is no Islamic reason why it should not be used.[41]

(ii) Blocking the neck of the womb, as a method of contraception

This practice is aimed at preventing sperm, which are in the vagina, from navigating up the birth canal through the neck of the womb. The woman used to introduce a rag, sometimes immersed in concoctions, as a barrier.

Ibn Taymiyya (d. 728/1328), the grand Hanbali faqih, acknowledged the fact that women do insert material to stop semen from entering the 'channels of conception' *(majari al-habal)*.[42]

Ibn Nujaim (d. 968/1562) the Hanafi faqih said:

> women can block the mouth of the uterus, in order for them not to beget children. This practise is permissible, so long as it is done with the husband's consent.[43]

Ibn 'Abidin (d. 1252/1836), the Hanafi faqih said that blocking the neck of the womb was permissible, even without the permission of the husband.[44]

The modern variety is the diaphragm, Dutch cap, or female condom.

(iii) Other means

a. Hormonal methods to prevent ovulation in the female or formation of sperm in the male (spermatogenesis). They can be used orally, by injection, or by applying medicated adhesive pads to the skin. No conception takes place.

b. Chemical spermicidal agents, gel or foam which can be introduced into the vagina. The sperm is killed before it can reach the ovum in the fimbrianated end of the Fallopian tube. Again there is no conception. In essence the practice is not different from the rag (sometimes immersed in concoctions usually vinegar or tar), which was used to block the neck of the womb and was authorised by Ibn Nujaim. Omran considered such practices permissible.[45]

c. Surgical interruption (vasectomy) of the passage that conveys the sperm from the testes to the seminal vesicles and the prostate in the male (to be discharged later through the urethra). No castration is involved. The same principal is applied in the case of the female by ligation, clamping, or severance of the tubes, which allow the passage of the sperm to the end of the tube where fertilisation of ova, from the ovary, takes place. There is no fertilisation or conception with such procedures.

But are such procedures allowed in themselves? They are allowed for medical reasons, which can be: physical, psychiatric, psychological, or mental. But can family planning be counted as one? The general state of well being, freedom from worry, stress, or want, are elements of mental and physical health. Islam does stress that the five essential things in life (indispensable necessities) are: "deen, life (*nafs* or self), consciousness ('*aql* or intellect), lineage, and property" [and some add honour ('*ird*)] are to be guarded, preserved, defended and even fought for.[46]

Recently Muslim fuqaha have discussed sterilisation at length.

Dr Madkour told the Rabat Conference in 1971 that, "We have found no text in the Qur'an or *Sunnah* that prohibits permanent sterilisation without acceptable justification."

The Grand Mufti of Egypt, Sheikh Jad al-Haq stated in December 1980 that, "If we examine the Qur'an or the Sunnah, we find *no text* prohibiting sterilization, i.e. rendering a man or a woman unable to procreate totally and permanently by surgery or chemical or other means."

The two theologians were, however, opposed to permanent sterilisation... Sheikh Shaltout had similar views of disallowing permanent sterilisation except for serious reasons of hereditary or transmissible diseases...

The High Council of Research ruled in 1965 that the use of means, which lead to infertility, is forbidden. Similar prohibition was made by *fiqh* [sic] Council in Saudi Arabia.

...Many participants [Rabat Conference on Islam and family planning] were opposed, but a *minority* group expressed support for sterilisation [sic], since they found no text in the Qur'an or Sunnah prohibiting it...Physicians were afraid that sterilisation was confused with castration in the minds of non-medical scholars...

The Imamis sanction permanent sterilisation. Sheikh M. Shamsuddin (of the Imami Shi'ites) expressed his sanction...'on examining our legal sources on the subject, we have found that there is nothing preventing the husband or the wife from undergoing such operations' ...Sheikh Sayyid Sabiq provided a statement that sterilisation may be allowed by those who allow *al-'azl*...Sheikh Ahmad Ibrahim ...a leading theologian...The Sheikh declared, 'I do not see any religious objection to sterilisation...This is not a crime against any being already in existence; nor, a crime against a living child. The matter is crystal clear. There should be no hesitation in sanctioning it and blessing it with approval.[47]

d. The placement of intrauterine devices to prevent the fertilised ovum or ova from clinging to the uterine wall to affect further growth and development.

Is this a form of abortion? Fertilisation did take place at the tubal end, and the embryo has taken about nine days to arrive to the uterine cavity where it was denied implantation and further development. Some such devices are said to contain spermicidal agents, but the validity of such claims cannot be ascertained in every case. I prefer to deal with this differently, from the cases in which no fertilisation took place at all, as in all the previously mentioned cases. It is dealt with below, and in discussing reproduction and 'the fate of surplus fertilised ova.'

e. 'Abortifacient' hormonal intervention

These include:

(i) RU 486 (anti-progestan), a hormone based, oral, or gel application, which induces abortion in the early stages of pregnancy (12 weeks).

(ii) Morning-after pill (4 pills: taken two at a time every 12 hours within 72 hours after exposure). *If* fertilisation had occurred, it is denied further development than the stage reached within the 72 hours frame. This will also be dealt with under the heading 'termination of pregnancy'.

3. Can pregnancies be terminated lawfully, in accordance with Islamic fiqh?

Muslim fuqaha have discussed this as early as the time of the companions of the Prophet ﷺ. The seminal guidelines were ayat from the Qur'an:

> We created man from the purest kind of clay; then made him a drop (*nutfa*) in a secure receptacle; then formed the drop into a clot (*'alaqa*) and formed the clot into a lump (*mudgha*) and formed the lump into bones and clothed the bones in flesh; and then brought him into being as another creature (*khalqan aakhar*).
>
> Blessed be Allah, the Best of Creators![48]

And the Prophetic *hadith*:

> The creation of any one of you is gathered in the belly of his mother for forty days as a drop (*nutfa*), then later a blood clot (*'alaqa*) for the like of that, then later a morsel of flesh (*mudgha*) for the like of that. Then the angel is sent to him and breathes the *ruh* into him.[49]

They attached especial importance to,"'another creation' at the end of the third phase," mentioned in the Qur'an; and similar importance

The Prevention and Termination of Pregnancy 211

to the 'breathing the ruh into him' mentioned by the Prophet ﷺ at the end of the same third stage, but this time the Prophet had detailed the time involved in each of the three phases, 40 days in each: a total of 120 days. So at the end of 120 days, there comes into being 'a different, and another creation with a *ruh* (spirit).'

The views of the fuqaha are examined: first, as to the permissibility (legality) of induced abortion; secondly, the consequences of termination of pregnancy in Islamic fiqh; and thirdly legislation and induced abortion in the light of Islamic fiqh, and common law.

3.1 The views of Muslim fuqaha regarding permissibility of induced abortion

The following commentaries are found:

(a) The Hanafi school

Al-Fatawa al-Hindiya

A breast-feeding woman became pregnant and consequently her milk dried up; the father could not afford a wet nurse...

{Fatwa}: She is allowed to procure an abortion so long as the pregnancy is in one of the stages of *nutfa*, or *mudgha*, or *'alaqa*; with no defined limbs.[50]

Badai'a as-Sanai'a

If a woman procures an abortion and the product cannot be identified as male or female then the product is in the stage of *mudgha*; it is not a *janin* (foetus) yet, therefore there is nothing to that.[51]

Ad-Durr al-Mukhtar

It is said that, 'it is up to the wife to procure an abortion before four months have elapsed since the beginning of the pregnancy.[52]

Al-Ikhtiyar

A woman procured an abortion; she is not culpable unless the discarded product had been differentiated into recognisable parts.[53]

(b) The Maliki school

Ad-Dardir said:

The dislodging of semen that has developed within the womb, even before forty days have elapsed, is not to be done *(la yajuz)*. As to dislodging the products of conception after the breathing of the *ruh* into it, that is *haram* (forbidden) in the view of everyone *(ijma')*.[54]

Many other references in the school may be quoted to the same effect; they immediately prescribe the punishment for such an act, of the value of five camels, if the mother was alive at the end of the termination of pregnancy; but if she died during the procedure and before the conception material has separated then the matter is dropped and the issue becomes the death of the mother.[55]

(c) The Shafi'i school

Ash-Shafi'i said:

If in the material that descended something beyond the stage of *mudgha* or *'alaqa*, a finger or a nail or an eye, could be discerned then *ghurrah* is due (the value of five camels).[56]

Ar-Ramli said:

The learned people were divided in their opinion about the *nutfa*, before the completion of forty days of pregnancy, one group said that it is not like an induced abortion nor infanticide; the other group thought that whatever has settled in the womb should not be disturbed, it has sanctity and it is not to be removed *(la yajuz)*.[57]

...al-Karabisi asked Abu Bakr ibn Sa'id al-'Iraqi, about someone who gave his wife some medicine and caused her to abort; al-Iraqi said, 'so long as it is *nutfa* there is nothing to it: the balance is in favour of disallowing it *(haram)* after the breathing of the *ruh* into it (120 days) and allowing it before then *(ja'iz)*.[58]

(d) The Hanbali school

There are two diametrically opposed views within the school. Ibn Qudama said:

In the case of someone who hits a pregnant woman causing her to abort; and in the case of the woman who aborts herself: in either case *ghurrah* (five camels) and *kaffara* (expiation) are due.[59]

This is remarkable in that, although the Hanbali are usually close to the Maliki, Ibn Qudama in this case meted out the maximum penalty for the act, but he went further and coupled it with expiation which is a particularly Shafi'i stance.

Al-Bahwati says, "Aborting a pregnancy, so long as the *ruh* has not been breathed into it, is allowed *(mubah)*."[60]

3.2 Some special issues on terminations

The previous subsection considered the views of the Muslim fuqaha, as they were given in their basically unqualified form. It may be opportune to examine some of the special issues alluded to by Muslim fuqaha.

Termination of pregnancy, is a situation where the lives, interests, and rights of more than one person are intricately entangled: (i) the mother, in health, sickness, and in rape cases; (ii) the embryo, when it is healthy or defective; (iii) the husband's options, consent, and permission.

(i) Pregnancy and the 'mother' in health, sickness and in rape cases

a. Pregnancy and the well mother

Pregnancy and the well mother were considered in the general basic view of Muslim fuqaha in the subsection above. It basically involves situations where a woman may not want the pregnancy to continue for reasons not directly connected with an illness of hers, but concerning her well-being or that of her children. This situation may be encountered when she is fearful that a child, she is still suckling, may not find milk when she continues with the pregnancy. If the father cannot pay for a wet-nurse or for milk, then the child will suffer from malnourishment and could die.

"In such circumstances she may terminate the pregnancy."[61]

b. Pregnancy and ill health in the mother

All fuqaha allow therapeutic abortion. The Qur'an says:

And do not kill yourselves.[62]

Do not cast yourselves into destruction.[63]

No mother should be put under pressure in respect of her child nor any father in respect of his child.[64]

The welfare of the child is never advanced before that of the parents, especially the mother. The Prophet ﷺ said, "Paradise is at the feet of the mother." When someone asked the Prophet about which of his parents he should care for? The Prophet ﷺ said, "Your mother," three times and then mentioned the father.[65]

Someone complained to the Messenger of Allah ﷺ that his father took his money. After listening to both sides the Prophet said to the son, "Yourself and your wealth are your father's."[66] He ﷺ also revoked *qisas* in cases where a parent kills his own child, *(la yuqad walidun bi waladihi).* [67]

This is the case with living children. It should be more applicable in the case of the unborn. The mother's health and welfare should, unquestionably, be given priority over a pregnancy.

The nearest reference to this is in *al-Fatawa al-Hindiya*, over 300 years ago, where a breast-feeding mother is allowed to procure an abortion, so long as it is within the first 120 days of pregnancy, if she feared for the health of the breast-fed child.[68]

If the health of a breast-fed child is an indication for an abortion, the health of a pregnant woman herself may be so. If the mother's health is threatened by a pregnancy, that pregnancy may be terminated. This may be inferred from the general rules in Islamic fiqh, which I tried to build from the Qur'an and Sunnah, and from the doctrines of Muslim fuqaha:[69]

No harm and no harassment
Harm must be removed
Harm must not be removed by a greater harm
Where it is inevitable, the lesser of the two harms should be implemented
Removing the harm comes before realising the benefit.
More recently, Omran said:

> The mother's life takes precedence over the child's life on the juristic [sic.] principle 'the root is more valuable than the branch.'[70]

The High Council for Islamic Legal Opinions in Kuwait issued a declaration on 29th September 1984, which says:

> After 40 days and before 120, abortion may not be done except in the following two circumstances:
> (i) If the continuation of pregnancy would cause...harm to the woman...and
> (ii) If it is certain that the foetus will be born with severe deformation, or
> physical or mental deficiency, neither of which can be cured.[71]

The Council of Grand Jurists in the Kingdom of Saudi Arabia had particularly proclaimed a *fatwa* in 1976,[72] in this concern, it says:

> There is no objection to prevent pregnancy if there is need for that, as in the case of a Caesarean section being necessary for delivery, or if delaying the pregnancy for a period suits the welfare *(maslaha)* of the married couple, there is no objection, then, to prevent pregnancy or delay it; enacting what is in the *Sahih al-Hadith* (Prophetic sayings) and what is related from a multitude of *sahaba* (companions of the Prophet) as to the permissibility of *'azl* (coitus interruptus), and in accordance with the sayings of some *fuqaha* as to the permissibility of taking medicines which will lead to abortion, providing that it is within the first forty days of pregnancy, it may be mandatory to prevent pregnancy in case of a virtual necessity.

The Prevention and Termination of Pregnancy   215

And the decision of *Majam'a al-Fiqh al-Islami*, in Makkah al-Mukarramah, 10-17 February 1990, regarding termination of pregnancy for malformation of the foetus, is that:

> if the pregnancy is earlier than 120 days, and the foetus or embryo is deemed grossly malformed and that if born at term then its life will be miserable and will cause misery to its people, the pregnancy may be terminated. But if the pregnancy is beyond 120 days then it is impermissible to terminate the pregnancy whatever the condition of the foetus: termination of pregnancy to preserve the life of the mother is permissible irrespective of the condition of the foetus.[73]

c. Pregnancy following rape

Health includes mental health. Rape complicated by pregnancy can be extremely distressing to the victim. It is of dire consequences to both the mother and child in most cases. Could the woman have an abortion?

> and in accordance with the sayings of some *fuqaha* as to the permissibility of taking medicines which will lead to abortion, providing that it is within the first forty days of pregnancy it may be mandatory to prevent pregnancy in case of a virtual necessity.[74]

And what about the 'morning-after' pill? It is taken within 72 hours after exposure. *If* fertilisation has taken place, the product of fertilisation would still be navigating within the Fallopian tube and would not have implanted itself in the wall of the uterus. There is absolutely no difference between this situation and the intrauterine mechanical devices (the loop), which are used in family planning with the permission of Muslim fuqaha:

> Sheikh M. S. Madkour, a contemporary faqih, used analogous reasoning to demonstrate the permissibility of the use of the modern mechanical and chemical methods of contraception as follows:
>
> ...The third instance corresponds, as I see it, to the plastic filament known as the coil (IUD), for it definitely is a foreign body inserted into the uterus, which, by causing contractions, prevents the fertilised egg [sic] from attaching itself to the uterine wall, and thus the uterus expels it instead.[75]

If the coil (IUD) is permissible, according to Islamic fiqh, then the morning-after pill should be permissible according to the medical facts, which are common to both situations. This is the basis of *qiyas* (analogy) in Islamic fiqh.

Thus, the issue may be: would it be permissible to give victims of rape this treatment should they want it?

Victims of rape may be subject to the problems of an unwanted pregnancy, on top of the grievous harm they have suffered; they may also be saddled with the task of bringing up a child not in the best circumstances. These victims are usually poor or of limited resources; simply because the rich are not the majority in the world. "Bad times and fear of begetting delinquent children" were reasons given by Muslim fuqaha for not having children *(fasad az-zaman; wa al walad as-su')*.[76] Since there is a chance that rape may result in pregnancy, could that be considered as a factor for sanctioning the morning-after pill? The Qur'an states that:

Allah desires ease for you; He does not desire difficulty for you.[77]

Allah does not impose on any self any more than it can stand.[78]

Allah desires to make things lighter for you. Man was created weak.[79]

He has selected you and not placed any constraint upon you in the deen.[80]

The Prophet said:

No harm and no harassment[81]

Religion is free from hardship *(ad-din yusr)*[82]

Islam requires the community, which makes its own regulations, to be caring for one another, and compensates the victims of crimes.[83] The first step in compensation is to stop the escalation of complications.

When the question of termination of pregnancy is addressed in its abstract, or hypothetical form almost all fuqaha mention the 40 days as the watershed between the permissible and the impermissible. Many of them opt for the 120 days (when the *ruh* is breathed in) landmark. They even quote with great relish 'Ali ibn Abi Talib's admirable thesis about the seven stages of development, before the completion of which, getting rid of the products of conception are almost equated with *'azl*.

As to abortion, az-Zurqani quoted Ibn Hajar's *al-Fath ar-Rabani* that the position on expelling the *nutfa* before 'the breathing in of the *ruh*' parallels that on *'azl*; whoever sanctions *'azl* sanctions that too.[84]

Accommodating as that may be, medically (factually) *'azl* is not abortion. But Muslim fuqaha made allowances for a woman to have an abortion just because she wants to.

It was asked, in *Al-Nahr* and in *Al-Fath*, 'is it allowed to procure an abortion? Yes, so long as no definition or differentiation has been created, and that takes place after 120 days of gestation. This entails that 'creation' should be taken to mean the breathing in of the *ruh*. Because literally speaking creation is taking place all the time through all stages.[85]

(ii) The embryo (foetus) and abortion

The embryo is the next consideration. With advances and developments in medical science, it is increasingly possible to know the physical condition of the foetus. This knowledge is expanding not only in its scope, but it is rendered earlier and earlier during the pregnancy.

If the condition of the foetus is so diseased as to cause unnecessary suffering to the foetus later when it is delivered and during its life, would that be an indication to terminate the pregnancy?

Islamic fiqh dealt with termination of pregnancy before 40 days and up to 120 days. What about the welfare or even the mere survival of other members of the family which was considered and accommodated by Muslim fuqaha of the past,[86] balanced against the 'rights' of a foetus to be born severely handicapped and defective?

The High Council for Islamic Legal Opinions in Kuwait issued a declaration on 29th September 1984 which allows abortion to take place if continuation of the pregnancy "would cause harm to the woman or if it is certain that the foetus will be born with severe deformation, or physical or mental deficiency, neither of which can be cured."[87]

(iii) The husband's options, consent, and permission

'Azl, as a method of contraception was discussed above.

It should be performed with the consent of the wife.[88] The wife may ask for financial compensation in lieu of her consent.[89] But, sometimes her consent may not be necessary, as in cases of war, or long journeys or trips, and also when it is feared that the future may be unpredictable, and the offspring may become delinquent.[90] The wife should not use a shield against pregnancy except for when permission of the husband is secured, but this is not unanimous.[91] All of these situations concern conception, and they were discussed before.

But as for aborting a pregnancy, Muslim fuqaha held that this is a matter purely left to the wife. She can herself abort without the consent or permission of the husband. Ibn 'Abidin said:

> It was asked, in *Al-Nahr* and in *Al-Fath* 'is it allowed to procure an abortion?' 'Yes, so long as no definition or differentiation has been created, and that takes place after 120 days of gestation.' This entails that 'creation' should be taken to mean the breathing in of the *ruh* (spirit). Be-

cause literally speaking creation is taking place all the time through all stages.[92]

4. Treatment of Abortion in the UK

Other countries have also had problems with the bounds and limitations of abortion. It took many years to change the law of abortion in Great Britain.

It can be surmised from Mason and McCall Smith that:[93]

> The fundamental law in England and Wales lies in the Offences Against the Person Act 1861, sections 58 and 59. The Act proscribes procuring the miscarriage of a woman by a third party, self-induced miscarriage, attempted procurement of miscarriage and supplying the means to do so. The Act makes no distinction between criminal and therapeutic activity and has not been repealed.
>
> In addition to being punished by the courts, a doctor involved in an abortion was extremely likely to have his name erased from the Medical Register.
>
> The first statutory break is to be found in the Infant Life (Preservation) Act 1929 which introduced the offence of child destruction or causing the death of a child capable of being born alive before it has an existence independent of its mother. The offence was not committed, however, if the act was done in good faith for the purpose only of preserving the mother's life.
>
> It was left to the case of *R v Bourne* [94] to temper the legal influence on medical practice in the field. Mr Bourne performed an abortion, with no attempt at secrecy, on a 15-year-old girl who was pregnant following a particularly unpleasant rape. Although he was indicted under the Offences Against the Person Act 1861, the trial judge, Mc Naghten J, took the opportunity to link the 1861 and 1929 statutes and ruled that, in a case brought under the 1861 Act, the burden rested on the Crown to satisfy the jury that the defendant did not procure the miscarriage of the girl in good faith for the purpose only of preserving her life: the word 'unlawful' in the 1861 Act 'imports the meaning expressed by the proviso in section 1(1) of the Infant Life (Preservation) Act of 1929.'[95] Mr Bourne was acquitted, the summing-up essentially recognising that a woman's life depended upon her physical and mental health and that an abortion was not illegal if it was performed because these were in jeopardy.
>
> But there was still no authority on the validity of abortion in the event of probable deformation or other handicap of the foetus when

born – a proposition which many would regard as being of first importance. The situation was resolved when the Abortion Act, which started out (perhaps more aptly) as the Medical Termination of Pregnancy Bill, was put into law in 1967. This remained the law until it was significantly amended by s 37 of the Human Fertilisation and Embryology Act in 1990.

In summary, it now states that a person shall not be guilty of an offence under the law of abortion when termination is performed by a registered medical practitioner and two registered medical practitioners have formed the opinion in good faith that the continuance of the pregnancy would involve risk, greater than if the pregnancy was terminated, of injury to the physical or mental health of the pregnant woman or any existing children of her family (section 1(1)(a)). These therapeutic and social conditions are subject to the pregnancy not having exceeded its 24th week. The remaining justifications are now free of gestational restrictions. These are, firstly, that there is a risk of grave permanent injury to the physical or mental health of the pregnant woman (section 1(1)(b)); that continuance of the pregnancy would involve risk to the life of the pregnant woman (section 1(1)(c)); and, finally, that there is a substantial risk that, if the child were born, it would suffer from such physical or mental abnormalities as to be severely handicapped (section 1(1)(d)). Subsections (b) and (c) are not subject to the opinion of two registered medical practitioners; single persons may operate on their own initiative in such circumstances. Termination under the Act may be carried out in National Health Service hospitals or in places approved for the purpose by the Minister or the Secretary of State (section 1(3)).

5. Comparison of Islamic law and UK law on Abortion

5.1. The welfare of other siblings as a reason to procure an abortion

Muslim fuqaha took into consideration the welfare of other siblings to procure an abortion in an otherwise 'healthy pregnancy,' which may compromise the milk supply of a suckling sibling.[96] This may be compared with section 1(1)(a) of the 1967 Act, by which a person shall not be guilty of an offence when termination is performed to offset the risk of injury to the physical or mental health of the pregnant woman or "any existing children of her family."

5.2. A time limit was set before which abortion could be performed

Muslim fuqaha set 120 days as a date before which termination of pregnancy is 'allowed,'[97] which compares favourably with, "these therapeutic and social conditions are subject to the pregnancy not having exceeded its 24th week," in the same section of the 1967 Act.

5.3. The welfare of the mother

In section 1 (1)(c) of the 1967 Act allowance was made for termination of the pregnancy when the life of the mother was threatened.

Islamic fiqh prevents one causing injury or death to oneself **"do not cast yourselves into destruction."** *(wala tulqu bi aydikum ila at-tahluka)*, (Q. 2:194).

5.4 Severe deformation of the foetus

The High Council for Islamic Legal Opinions in Kuwait issued a declaration on 29th September 1984, which says:

> After 40 days and before 120, abortion may not be done except in the following two circumstances:
>
> (i) If the continuation of pregnancy would cause…harm to the woman…
>
> (ii) If it is certain that the foetus will be born with severe deformation, or physical or mental deficiency, neither of which can be cured.[98]

Compare this with the United Kingdom Human Fertilisation and Embryology Act 1990, s. 37, which mentions as indications to procuring an abortion:

> the physical or mental or mental health of the pregnant woman or any existing children of her family (section 1(1)(a), (b), (c), and finally, that there is a substantial risk that, if the child were born, it would suffer from such physical or mental abnormalities as to be severely handicapped (section 1(1)(d)).

5.5 Is the husband's consent or permission necessary?

Muslim fuqaha said, "No.."[99] This may be contrasted with a Scottish case where the estranged husband blocked the abortion procedure by a court order in Scotland. The wife came down to England where the

Scottish court order would not have applied and she could have had the abortion, a situation in the English law comparable to the views of Muslim fuqaha who think that the husband's permission for the termination of pregnancy is not necessary, before 120 days have elapsed.

The case was the subject of debate in the House of Lords, in May 1997.[100]

6. The consequences of termination of pregnancy in Islamic fiqh

The views in Islamic fiqh are determined by: the stage at which the pregnancy is terminated; and who has caused it.

This calls for recapitulation of certain definitions and the stages of pregnancy.

The embryo, or foetus, is called *janin* (hidden) or cloaked in darkness, the word is often used to describe the night; and the meaning is also given to the creations 'we cannot see' *(jinn, jinni)*. *Majnun* (mad person) is the one whose mind is clouded 'cloaked, or veiled in darkness.'

For legal purposes Muslim fuqaha have determined that the *janin* (foetus) can be considered 'person' on the one hand, because it is a human creation, and 'non-person' on the other, because it is living within the mother and from her.[101] If that embryo is separated from her, then the consequences will depend on the stage of development, and how it was terminated.

The stages of development (Q. 23:12, 13, and 14) go through: 'origins from water and earth' *(sulalah min tin)*; a 'sperm' *(nutfa)*, which becomes mixed up with elements from the female *(nutfatin amshaj)* Q. 76:2; 'something that clings' *('alaqa)*; 'something that resembles a chewed up lump, differentiated and undifferentiated' *(mudgha, mukhalaqa wa ghaira mukhalaqa)*; 'bones appear'; 'the bones become coated with flesh'; 'then it becomes another creation' *(khalqan akhar)*. The Prophet ﷺ said that, "That takes place at the end of 120 days, when the *ruh* is breathed into it."[102]

6.1 Termination of pregnancy with the consent of the woman in question

(i) If the termination of pregnancy was committed voluntarily by the woman, or with her consent, and within the 120 days: then there is nothing to answer for, even if it were done without the husband's permission.[103]

(ii) If it was committed voluntarily or by her consent, after 120 days of pregnancy but there was no life in it when it was expelled, then she is culpable *(haram)* according to all fuqaha.[104] A crime has been committed against a creation, which is past the stages where no penalty would have been meted out. The husband, the government, and the heirs can take up the case. The penalty for that is *ghurrah*, the value of five camels, no matter what the sex of the embryo had been. It is payable by the *'aqila* of the woman in question. Any of her accomplices are to pay *diya* from their personal funds.

(iii) If she had produced a living foetus, that died consequently, then *qisas* or the full *diya* (as for an adult person) is due. The signs of life are: crying, coughing, breathing, suckling, or movements. Attendant women are accepted as witnesses. Even one woman is enough, as in this respect and 'other respects pertaining to women' the evidence of a single woman is accepted.[105]

The mother herself is not subject to *qisas*, as no parent's life should be forfeited for killing their offspring.[106] But she is liable for *diya* and her associates are liable for *qisas* or *diya* (with *qasama*).[107] *Qisas* is the penalty only in the Maliki school, in all the others only *diya* is due.[108]

6.2. Termination of pregnancy at the hands of a tortfeasor

The outcome could be a dead foetus, a living foetus that dies, or a dead foetus that is miscarried after the mother has died.

(i) Miscarriage of a dead foetus

The fuqaha are agreed that if a miscarriage had occurred, *diya* is payable which is called *ghurrah*, the value of five camels, whether the aborted material was male or female, and whether the causative factor was intentional or not.[109] The *ghurrah* is payable immediately if the act was intentional, which is the assumption of the Maliki school (in the Maliki school, if the act was intended, then the consequences are treated as though they were intended as well) and it should be paid by the tortfeasor himself.[110] The other schools treat the result as not intended. So payment of *ghurrah* is in instalments, payable by the tortfeasor unless it is in excess of one third of the diya where the *'aqila* pays it.[111]

Expiation *(kaffara)* is not required in the Hanafi school, it is recommended with the Malikis, and it is mandatory in the Shafi'i and Hanbali schools.[112]

(ii) Miscarriage of a living foetus, that dies

The Maliki consider *qisas* (retribution) if the assault was on the abdomen, or on the back behind the womb, but if the assault was on an arm or a leg then *diya* (compensation) is due. In either situation *qasama* (compurgation) may be called for.[113]

The Hanafi, Shafi'i, and the Hanbali consider it a case for full *diya* (one hundred camels); on top of that *kaffara* is mandatory in the Shafi'i and in the Hanbali schools, but to the Maliki it is recommended *(mustahabb)*.[114]

(iii) Death of the mother due to assault, followed by expulsion of a dead foetus

The Hanafi and the Maliki schools disregard what happened to the foetus, as they consider it as a result of the death of the mother.

The Shafi'i and the Hanbali schools consider it as a separate crime, which entails *ghurrah* whether it occurred before or after the death of the mother. That is on top of the crime committed against the mother.[115]

(iv) What if a pregnant woman is killed and nothing is expelled

The Hanafi, the Maliki, and the Shafi'i, consider the crime against the mother only, but the Hanbali will consider two crimes: one against the mother and *ghurrah* for the pregnancy.[116]

(v) General considerations

a. From which stage in conception is compensation *(ghurrah)* due?

The Maliki school and al-Ghazali from the Shafi'i school do not allow abortion from the time the *nutfa* reaches the womb. So *ghurrah* is due from the earliest stage of *nutfa*.[117]

The Hanafi, the majority in the Shafi'i school, and the Hanbali have determined that *ghurrah* is due from the time some form of development can be ascertained *(tabayana khalquhu)*.[118]

b. Who should pay the *ghurrah*?

The Maliki school determined that it is payable by the tortfeasor himself, as the miscarriage was a result of an intentional unlawful act.[119]

Abu Hanifah and ash-Shafi'i have determined that the ghurrah is the responsibility of the *'aqila*.[120] The Prophet ﷺ made the relatives *('aqila)* pay the *ghurrah* in such a situatiuon.[121]

c. What is the rule if the woman gave birth to a living foetus that died immediately?

All fuqaha are agreed that a full *diya* (100 camels) is due, but Ahmad ibn Hanbal, and al-Muzni were of the opinion that there is a period of gestation short of which life is untenable, that period is six months pregnancy (24 weeks), which they deduced, like many others, from the Qur'an.[122]

d. Is it essential to expiate on top of paying the *ghurrah* or the *diya*? Abu Hanifah said, "It is not the rule."[123]

Malik said that if it was an intentional act of assault, then there is no place for *kaffara* in intentional murder, but if the death is by mistake there is place for *kaffara* as in Qur'an, 4:92. But since it is not clear that an intentional act against the mother would necessarily be an intended act against the foetus, it is acceptable to recommend *kaffara* (expiation).[124]

Ash-Shafi'i, and Ahmad ibn Hanbal said that expiation is mandatory *(al-kaffara wajib fi al-janin)*.[125]

7. Legislation and induced abortion, in the light of Islamic fiqh and common law.

Abortion is one of the subjects that generates a lot of debate. The debate is very old and continues, in Muslim communities and others.

Induced abortion remains a great concern for many, as evidenced in pressure groups, and campaigners.

The British Pregnancy Advisory Service (BPAS) announced its scheme, (on July 2 1999), aimed at helping women to "be prepared for the unexpected"; (by making the 'morning-after pill' available before sex). The pill must be prescribed by a doctor and until now has been available only to women who attend the clinics or go to their GP within three days of unprotected sex…The BPAS, which has 40 clinics nationwide, will offer one dose consisting of four pills for a payment of £10…Last year there were 170,000 abortions in England and Wales. The number of women using the morning-after pill rose from 400,000 in 1993 to 700,000 in 1997.

The decision to open the new service was attacked by family and pro-life groups who said it would encourage teenagers to have casual sex.[126]

This reflects changes in some attitudes in some communities; but Islamic fiqh accepts no sexual relations at any age outside 'the marriage contract' (*'aqd*). The use of the morning-after pill in this (new) manner and within the marriage bond may be acceptable even in the Maliki school where there is a guide that no abortion is allowed after 40 days. There would be a chance that fertilisation did not take place, let alone being of few hours duration if they were taken within the former 72 hours time limit; which would have been covered any way but grudgingly by some. But the important application of this 'law' would be the ready availability of the pill at some legal outlets without visits to clinics or GP practices in cases of rape.

Although there is a wealth of material regarding termination of pregnancy in the writings of Muslim fuqaha, attempts to codify these views into laws according to Islamic jurisprudential concepts remain tentative and perhaps furtive. There are different situations to be considered, many issues to be argued, and many questions to be answered. These questions must be answered in a manner that ensures a consensus, in freely elected or delegated bodies of the qualified, taking into consideration material and findings such as has transpired in my research, in this area of Islamic fiqh, with the findings of others.

Should there be need to legislate for an issue on the subject matter of termination of pregnancy, Islamic fiqh can be tapped to enact laws, which will be compatible with the accepted norms of practice, determined by international bodies of the profession and governed by its codes of ethics.

Notes

1. Fairouzabadi, *al-Qamus al-Muhit*, 1987, vol. 1:469, Arabic dictionary *(Qamus)*.
2. Ibn Nujaim, *al-Bahr ar-Ra'iq*, 1980, vol. 8:389.
3. Dardir, *al-Sharh al-Saghir*, vol. 4:377. (*'Alaqa* is an early stage of pregnancy up to the first 40 days).
4. Ansari, (d. 925 AH), *Tuhfat al-Tullab*, (1360 AH), vol. 2:380.
5. Hijawi, *al-Iqna'a ma'a Kashaf al-Qina'*, (1319 AH), vol. 4:209.
6. Q. 30:21 "Among His Signs is that He created spouses for you of your own kind so that you might find tranquillity in them. And He has placed affection and compassion between you."(tr. Bewley); Q. 2:186 "They are clothing for you and you for them" (tr. Bewley); Q. 16:72 "Allah has given you wives from among yourselves, and given you children and grandchildren" (tr. Bewley); Q. 4:24, 25, and Q. 5:5 "in the sacred relation of marriage" (tr. Y. 'Ali).
   Q. 18:46 "Wealth and sons are the embellishment of the life of the dunya." (tr. Bewley).
7. *Sunan Ibn Majah*, 1952, vol. 1:599, *(inkahu fa inni mukathirun bikum)*.
8. *Sunan Ibn Majah*, 1952, vol. 1:592; *Sunan at-Tirmidhi*, (ed.),'Awad, vol. 3:392
9. *Sunan Ibn Majah*, 1952, vol. 1:633; *Sunan at-Tirmidhi*, (ed.),'Awad, vol. 3:394-395.
10. Hakim, *al-Mustadrak*, (1340 AH), vol. 2:162.
11. Q. 18:46; 3:14; 23:55; et al.
12. Q. 68:14; 71:12; et al.
13. 'He asked 10 of them to walk in through separate entrances on their visit to Egypt...' a commentary on the ayah Q. 12:67.
14. *Sunan Ibn Majah*, 1952, vol. 1:592, and 599 "for I would be proud of your large numbers – *mukathirun bikum"*; and in p. 593 (the Prophet ﷺ did not like his people to be hermits).
15. *hadith:* (the best gift for a person is good upbringing) *(al-khuluq al-hasan)* in Hakim, *al-Mustadrak*, (1342 AH), vol. 4:199 and 399; (to leave your heirs rich, is better than leaving them dependent upon peoples' charity), in *Sunan Ibn Majah*, 1953, vol. 2:904. See Omran, *Family Planning*, 1992:34-36, for "The right of a child on his parents is to be given a decent family background, the choice of a good name, good breeding, education, and training in sports..." citing *hadith* in al-Baihaqi and at-Tabarani, "and if possible wealthy" citing one *hadith*, narrated by Sa'd ibn Abi Waqqas, in al-Bukhari.

[16] Q. 25:67 etc. "those who, when they spend, are neither extravagant nor mean, but take a stance mid way between the two" (tr. Bewley).

[17] Q. 2:286. "Allah does not impose on any self any more than it can stand" (tr. Bewley).

[18] Q. 2:185; 18:88; 94:6 et al. "Allah desires ease for you; He does not desire difficulty for you" (tr. Bewley).

[19] Q. 4:3; (Ibn al-Qayyim in, *Tuhfat al-Wadoud bi Ahkam al-Mawlud*, said that, "This ayah was explained to mean 'fewer children if the means dictate' by ash-Shafi'i. And in, *Sunan ad-Daraqutni*, it is said that, 'this is the view of Zayd ibn Aslam and Jabir ibn Zayd, two notable imams, who preceded ash-Shafi'i'"). Cited by Omran, *Family Planning in the Legacy of Islam*, 1992:106-107.

[20] Omran, *Family Planning*, 1992:106, citing al-Hakim, on the authority of Abdullah ibn 'Umar.

[21] Omran, *Family Planning*, 1992:106, citing al-Quda'i, *Musnad ash-Shihab*.

[22] Q. 6:152, "**that you do not kill your children because of poverty – We will provide for you and them;**"; and Q. 81:8 and 9, Remonstrate, "**When the baby girl buried alive is asked for what crime she was killed.**" And Prophetic *hadith*, "killing your child lest it shares (eats) with you" in al-Baihaqi, *Al-Sunan al-Kubra*, (1354 AH), vol. 8:15 and 18.

[23] Jakni, *Bukhari wa Muslim*, 1967, vol. 2:274-278; *Sunan Ibn Majah*, 1952, vol. 1:620; *Sahih Al-Bukhari* (tr. Khan), 1994:773. See also Musallam, *Sex and Society in Islam*, 1983:15.

[24] Jakni, *Bukhari wa Muslim*, 1967, vol. 2:275; *Sunan Ibn Majah*, 1953, vol. 1:620.

[25] Omran, *Family Planning*, 1992:132-133.

[26] Al-Ghazali, *Ihya,'* vol. 2:58.

[27] *Sunan Ibn Majah*, 1953, vol. 1:620; and Omran, *Family Planning*, 1992:125.

[28] Omran, *Family Planning*, 1992:153-155. Also see Jakni, *Bukhari wa Muslim*, 1967, vol. 2:276, "The Malikis, Hanafis, and the Hanbalis are all agreed that 'azl should be done with the consent of the wife."

[29] Jakni, *Bukhari wa Muslim*, 1967, vol. 2:274-275, the four *hadith* were debated in detail at the footnotes.

[30] Q. 17:31, and 6:151; (tr. Bewley).

[31] Al-Baihaqi, *Al-Sunan al-Kubra*, (1354 AH), vol. 8:15 and vol. 8 18.

[32] Jakni, *Bukhari wa Muslim*, 1967, vol. 2:275-276 (a summary: particularly of the footnotes).

[33] Musallam, *Sex and Society in Islam*, 1983:28; "The Dhahiri school fuqaha do not allow coitus inturruptus ('azl), likening it to 'minor infanticide.'" In Ibn Hazm adh-Dhahiri, *al-Muhalla*, (1352 AH), vol. 10:70-71; ash-Shawkani, *Nayl al-Awtar*, (1357 AH), vol. 6:221. See also Omran, *Family Planning*, 1992:136.

[34] Musallam, *Sex and Society in Islam,* 1983:28.
[35] Jakni, *Bukhari wa Muslim,* 1967, vol. 2:274-276; Musallam, *Sex and Society in Islam,* 1983:31-33; Omran, *Family Planning,* 1992: 137-139, (for arguments of fuqaha for *'azl*).
[36] Kasani, (d. 587/1191), *Bada'a,* 1910, vol. 2:334; Ibn'Abidin, (d. 1252/1836), *Hashiyat,* 1966, vol. 3:176, *(fasad uz zamani wa walad as-su')*.
[37] Musallam, *Sex and Society in Islam,* 1983:32, citing ad-Dardir, (d. 1786) *Al-Sharh al-Kabir 'ala Mukhtasar Khalil,* printed with *Hashiyat al-Dasuqi* (d. 1815), Cairo, (1373 AH), vol. 2:266.
[38] Al-Ghazali, *Ihya'* vol. 2:57-60.
[39] Ibn Qudama, *Muqni'a,* al-Matba'a as-Salafiyya, Cairo, vol. 3:103; Ibn Qudama, *al-Mughni,* (1348 AH), vol. 8:133-4.
[40] Ibn Hazm, *al-Muhalla,* Cairo, (1352 A. H.), vol. 10:70-71. See also Musallam, *Sex and Society in Islam,* 1983:18-19; and Omran, *Family Planning,* 1992:130.
[41] Madkour, Sheikh M.S., "Be it a Dutch cap for the female or a condom *(kabut)* for the male," cited by Omran, *Family Planning,* 1992:80.
[42] Ibn Taymiyyah, *Fatawa,* Dar al-Kutub al-Haditha, Cairo, 1966, vol. 1:71 *(Fatwa* no. 36).
[43] Ibn Nujaim, *al-Bahr ar-Ra'iq,* 1937; vol. 3:215; Musallam, *Sex and Society in Islam,* 1983:37; and Omran, *Family Planning,* 1992:154.
[44] Ibn'Abidin, *Hashiya,* 1966, vol. 3:176.
[45] Omran, *Family Planning,* 1992:81.
[46] (Preservation of deen) Q. 2:190; Q. 3:4; 3:56; 3:157; 8:12; 60:9; 88:23 et al.): (permission to fight back) Q. 2:190-191; 22:39: (self preservation) Q. 4:229: (honour) Q. 4:75; 7:141; 9:36: (children) Q. 6:140; Q. 6:151; 17:31;(property) Q. 2:246: Prophet's *hadith,*"He who dies defending his property is a shaheed." In Jakni, *Bukhari and Muslim,* (1967 vol. 3:227).
[47] Omran, *Family Planning,* 1992:188-190.
[48] Q. 23:12,13, and 14. Also in Q. 22:5 **"know that We created you from dust then from a drop of sperm then from a clot of blood then from a lump of flesh, formed yet unformed, so We may make things clear to you. We make whatever We want stay in the womb..."**; Q. 39:6 **"He creates you stage by stage in your mothers' wombs in a threefold darkness"**; and, Q. 71:14 **"...when He created you by successive stages."**
[49] Jakni, *Bukhari wa Muslim,* 1967, vol. 1:69; also in *Sunan Ibn Majah,* 1952, vol. 1:29. Translation from *The Complete Forty Hadith,* by Imam an-Nawawi, translated by Abdassamad Clarke, (Ta-Ha Publishing Ltd., London).
[50] Alamgir, *al-Fatawa al-Hindiya,* (1310 AH), vol. 5:356.
[51] Kasani, *Bada'i,* 1910, vol. 7:325.
[52] Haskafi, (d. 1774), *ad-Durr,* in *Hashiyat Ibn 'Abidin,* 1979, vol. 3:176.

53. Musali, *al-Ikhtiyar* 1356 AH, vol. 4:168.
54. Dardir, *al-Sharh al-Kabir*, Dar Ihya' al-Kutub, vol. 2:266.
55. Ibn Rushd, *Bidayat, al-Kulliyat*, vol. 2:451-453; Baji, *al-Muntaqa...Muwatta,'* vol. 7:89; Khirshi, *Sharh 'ala Mukhtasar Khalil*, (1317 AH), vol. 8:32.
56. Ash-Shafi'i, *al-Umm*, 1993, vol. 6:107.
57. Ramli, *Nihayat al-Muhtaj*, (1357 AH), vol. 7:379-380.
58. Ibid. vol. 7:442-443.
59. Ibn Qudama, *al-Mughni*, 1981, vol. 8:815.
60. Bahwati, *Sharh Muntaha al-Iradat*, Beirut, vol. 1:115.
61. Alamgir, *al-Fatawa al-Hindiya*, (1310 AH), vol. 5:356.
62. Q. 4:29.
63. Q. 2:194
64. Q. 2:231
65. *Sunan Ibn Majah*, 1953, vol. 2:903.
66. *Sunan Ibn Majah*, 1953. Vol. 2:769.
67. *Sunan Ibn Majah*, 1953. Vol. 2:888; and *Musnad Ahmad Ibn Hanbal*, (1413/1993), pp. 292-293, hadith, *"la yuqad walidun min waladin,"* and *"la yuqadu li waladin min walidih"* Narrated by 'Umar ibn al-Khattab.
68. Alamgir, a*l-Fatawa al-Hindiya*, (1310 AH), vol. 5:356.
69. *Sunan Ibn Majah*, 1953, vol. 2:784, hadith, (la darara wa la dirar). This *hadith* and the corollary fiqh doctrines are found in: Borno, *al-Wajiz*, 1998, pp. 251-257, 258, 259, 260-264, and 265-269; the *hadith* was adopted in *Majallat al-Ahkam al-'Adlia (Al-Majalla)*, Article 19.
70. Omran. *Family Planning*, 1992:9.
71. al-'Awadi, A. A., (ed.), Human Life, its Beginning and End in Islamic Law (in Arabic), *Kuwait: Islamic Organization of Medical Sciences*, 1985:128-129.
72. *Fatwa* No. 42 Dated 13 / 4 / 1396 AH. (1976). Abdel Wahab Ibrahim Abu Suliman.
73. *Majallat al-Buhuth al-Fiqhiyya* (*Contemporary Jurisprudence Research Journal*), No. 8, Second Year: January February March 1991, Riyadh, Saudi Arabia, p. 105: signed Abdel Aziz bin Baz, President, et. al.
74. *Majallat al-Buhuth*, 1991:105, Re/ *Fatwa* No. 42 Dated 13 / 4 / 1396 AH, (1976). See also above fn. 952
75. Omran, *Family Planning*, 1992:80-81.
76. Omran, *Family Planning*, 1992:153-154. Omran cites the views of all Fiqh schools at pp. 152-167. See also Omran, *Family Planning*, 1992:9, for *Fatwa*: "Prevention of pregnancy, and abortion before 120 days are not killing a 'person'," source *Al-Fatawa al-Islamiyyah*, Cairo (1983), vol. 9, pp. 3087-92, pp. 3110-13, and pp. 3093-3193.
77. Q. 2:184.
78. Q. 2:285.
79. Q. 4:28.

[80] Q. 22:76.
[81] Malik, *al-Muwatta,'* (ed.), Sa'd, 1983:638; and *Sunan Ibn Majah,* 1953, vol. 2:784.
[82] *Sahih al-Bukhari,* 1981, vol. 1:25; and *Sahih al-Bukhari,* (tr.) Khan, 1994:86.
[83] Sarakhsi, *al-Mabsut,* 1958, vol. 26:65-66.
[84] Omran, *Family Planning,* 1992:158.
[85] Ibn'Abidin, *Hashiyat,* 1966, vol. 3:176.
[86] Alamgir, *Al-Fatawa al-Hindiya,* (1310 AH), vol. 5:356; *Hashiyat Ibn Abidin,* 1966, vol. 3:176.
[87] Abdel Haleem, 'Medical ethics in Islam' *Choices and Decisions in Health Care,* 1993:14, see appendix H.
[88] *Sunan Ibn Majah,* 1952, vol.1:620; see also Omran, *Family Planning,* 1992:153-154.
[89] Omran, *Family Planning,* 1992:158, citing ad-Dardir, *Al-Sharh al-Kabir,* vol. 2:266.
[90] Omran, *Family Planning,* 1992:153 *(fasad az-zaman)* (bad times), *(al-walad as-su')* (delinquent children).
[91] Ibn Nujaim, *al-Bahr ar-Ra'iq,* 1937, vol. 3:215, is for husband's permission; while Ibn 'Abidin is not: Ibn 'Abidin, *Minhat al-Khaliq,* vol. 3:215, and *Hashiya,* 1966, vol. 3:176.
[92] Ibn'Abidin, *Hashiyat,* 1966, vol. 3:176.
[93] Mason and McCall Smith, *Law and Medical Ethics,* 1994:98-100.
[94] [1938] 3 All ER 615, [1939] 1 KB 687.
[95] [1939] 1 KB at 691; the summing up [1938] 3 All ER at 619.
[96] Alamgir, *al-Fatawa al-Hindiya,* (1310 AH), vol. 5:356; Ibn'Abidin, *Hashiya,* 1966, vol. 3:176.
[97] Hanafi school, Ibn al-Humam, *Fath al-Qadir,* (1299 AH), vol. 2:495, *al-Fatawa al-Hindiya,* (1310 AH), vol. 5:365-7, *Hashiyat Ibn Abidin,* 1966, vol. 3:176; Shafi'i school, Ibn Hajar, *Tuhfat al-Muhtaj,* (1304 AH), vol. 8:241, and *Nihayat al-Muhtaj,* (1357 AH), vol. 8:239); Hanbali school, *al-Mughni,* 1981, 7:816, and Ibn Muflih, *al-Furu',* 1962, vol. 1:281, all generally allow it before 120 days. The Malikis do not allow it, but some allow it if the pregnancy is 40 days or less; *Dasuqi m'a al-Sharh al-Kabir,* vol. 2:266.
[98] See Appendix H; also in Abdel Haleem, 'Medical ethics,' *Choices and Decisions in Health Care,* 1993:14
[99] Haskafi, (d. 1088/1678), in *Al-Durr, Hashiyat Ibn 'Abidin,* 1966, vol. 3:176.
[100] Lynne & James Kelly case, May 1997, HL.
[101] Ibn Nujaim, (d. 970 /1558), *al-Bahr ar-Ra'iq,* 1980, vol. 8:289, (Hanafi school).
[102] Jakni, *Bukhari wa Muslim,* 1967, vol. 1:69; and in *Sunan Ibn Majah,* 1952, vol. 1:29.
[103] Ibn'Abidin, *Hashiyat,* 1966, vol. 3:176.

The Prevention and Termination of Pregnancy 231

[104] Ibn 'Abidin, *Hashiyat,* 1966, vol. 3:176 (Hanafi); Dasuqi, *Hashiyat 'ala al-Sharh,* Matba'at Mustafa, vol. 2:266 (Maliki); Nawawi, *al-Majmu'a,* Dar al-Fikr, vol. 5:301 (Shafi'i); Ibn Muflih, *al-Furu',* 1962, vol. 1:281 (Hanbali).

[105] Sabiq, *Fiqh as-Sunnah,* 1995, vol. 3:244." The Prophet ﷺ accepted the evidence of a single midwife, narrated by Hudhaiyfah; Ibn Abbas accepted the evidence of one woman in live birth. Ash-Sha'bi, an-Nakha'i,'Ali, and Shurayh accepted it. Malik says two are necessary, ash-Shafi'i, required four women. It can be of immense consequence as in cases of legitimacy, inheritance, infanticide, rape, etc.

[106] Ibn Qudama, *al-Kafi,* 1982, vol. 4:7, citing Ibn Majah, an-Nasa'i, at-Tirmidhi, and al-Baihaqi.

[107] Dasuqi, *Hashiyat,* Matba'at Mustafa, vol. 4:269 (Maliki school).

[108] Ibn Rushd, *Bidayat, al-Kulliyat,* vol. 2:408.

[109] Kasani, (Hanafi), *Bada'i,* 1910, vol. 7:325; Ibn Rushd, (Maliki), *Bidayat, al-Kulliyat,* vol. 2:407; Shirbini, (Shafi'i), *Mughni al-Muhtaj,* (1377 AH). vol. 4:103; Ibn Qudama, (Hanbali), *al-Mughni,* 1981, vol. 7:799.

[110] Ibn Rushd, (Maliki), *Bidayat, al-Kulliyat,* vol. 2:408.

[111] Ibn 'Abidin, (Hanafi), *Hashiyat,* 1966, vol. 6:588-9); Shirbini, (Shafi'i), *Mughni al-Muhtaj,* (1377 AH), vol. 4:108; Bahwati, (Hanbali), *Kashaf al-Qina'a,* (1319 AH), vol. 6:160.

[112] Zaila'i, (Hanafi), *Tabyin al-Haqa'iq,* (1313 AH), vol. 6:141; Dasuqi, (Maliki), *Hashiyat,* Matba'at Mustafa, 4:268; Shirbini, (Shafi'i), *Mughni al-Muhtaj,* (1377 AH), vol. 4:108; Bahwati, (Hanbali), *Kashaf al-Qina'a,* (1319 AH), vol. 6:65.

[113] Baji, *al-Muntaqa...al-Muwatta,'* Sa'ada, vol. 7:89.

[114] Kasani, *Bada'i,* 1910, vol. 7:326 (Hanafi); Dasuqi, *Hashiya,* Matba'at Mustafa, 4:269 (Maliki); Shirbini, *Mughni al-Muhtaj,* (1377 AH), vol. 4:105 (Shafi'i); Ibn Qudama, *al-Mughni,* 1981, vol. 8:811 (Hanbali).

[115] Kasani, *Bada'i,* 1910, 7:326; Dasuqi, *'ala al-Sharh al-Kabir,* Matba'at Mustafa, 4:269; Shirbini, *Mughni al-Muhtaj,* (1377 AH), vol. 4:105; Ibn Qudama, *al-Mughni,* 1981, vol. 8:811.

[116] Ibn 'Abidin, *Hashiyat,* 1966, vol. 6:589 (Hanafi); Dasuqi, *'ala al-Sharh al-Kabir,* Matba'at Mustafa, vol. 4:268-269 (Maliki); Ramli, *Nihayat al-Muhtaj,* (1357 AH), vol. 7:362 (Shafi'i); Ibn Qudama, *Mughni,* 1981, vol. 7:802 (Hanbali).

[117] Dasuqi, *'ala al-Sharh,* Matba'at Mustafa, vol. 2:266 (Maliki); Al-Ghazali, *Ihya'* vol. 2:47 (Shafi'i).

[118] Alamgir, *al-Fatawa al-Hindiya,* (1310 AH), vol. 5:365-367 (Hanafi school); Ramli, *Nihayat al-Muhtaj,* (1357 AH), vol. 8:239 (Shafi'i); Ibn Qudama, *al-Mughni,* 1981, vol. 7:816 (Hanbali).

[119] Ibn Rushd, *Bidayat, al-Kulliyat,* vol. 2:408.

[120] *Hashiyat Ibn 'Abidin,* 1966, vol. 6:589; Ramli, *Nihayat al-Muhtaj,* (1357 AH), vol.8:416.

[121] *Al-Muwatta,'* (ed.) Sa'd, 1983:742. The case of a pregnant woman who was hit by a solid object that led to her death. The Prophet ﷺ ordered a *diya* on account of the deceased, and a *ghurrah* on account of the foetus to be paid by the *'aqila* of the offending woman, despite the rhymed protestations of one of her relatives "have we to pay for something that did not drink or eat, nor did it speak or cry; such a loss should not matter."

[122] Ibn Qudama, *al-Mughni*, 1981, vol. 7:816. (Q. 46:15 says 'pregnancy and lactation (breast-feeding and weaning) are for thirty months'; and Q. 2:233 says 'Mothers should nurse their children for two full years – those who wish to complete the full term of nursing': so they deduced that pregnancy that ends in a viable being cannot be less than six months).

[123] Ibn Nujaim, *al-Bahr* 1980, vol. 6:139; and Ibn al-Humam, *Fath al-Qadir*, (1299 AH), vol. 8:329.

[124] Ibn Rushd, *Bidayat, al-Kulliyat,* vol. 2:408; and Dasuqi, *Hashiya,* Matba'at Mustafa, vol. 4:287.

[125] Shirbini, *Mughni* (1377 AH), vol.4:108; Bahwati, *Kashaf al-Qina'a,* (1319 AH), vol. 6:65.

[126] *The Times* 3 July 1999, p. 4, column 1-4, (mid page). "The sale (over the counter) of the morning-after pill (s) to those over 18 years has been legalised in the UK; effective as from January 2001."

Chapter Eight
Reproduction and cloning

1 Reproduction

Reproduction, subject to Islamic fiqh, should only take place within marriage. Marriage in Islam, can take place between a husband and more than one wife. The maximum number of wives is four; but Islam discourages being married to more than one wife,[1] in the case where the man fears that he may not be able to be just to his wives:

> ...then marry other permissible women, two, three or four. But if you are afraid of not treating them equally, then only one, ,...
>
> You will not be able to be completely fair between your wives, however hard you try.

Islam did not introduce polygyny (polygamy); it has always existed in tribes across the world throughout history, and in other faiths [and can arguably be said to exist widely today in covert forms even in societies which do not permit it such as Europe and America – Ed]. Islam regulated what was already there. The main reasons for having more than one wife are: sickness or infertility of the first wife, the great number of widowed or orphaned women due to the death of men in battle or other causes, etc.[2]

This chapter is intended mainly to examine the issues linked with the management of infertility, and the methods of facilitating procreation in the light of Islamic fiqh.

1.1 Infertility

Infertility can be primary, where the couple have never had any offspring; or secondary where there has been a previous pregnancy, but no present possibility. Both may be due to any of a number of afflictions.

(i) Primary infertility

Primary infertility means that a spermatozoon of the male does not fertilise an ovum of the female, hence there are no products of conception to be dealt with. The causes can be that:

(a) There are no spermatozoa, or there are too few of them, or that they are in a very early stage of development which has not allowed their migration to suitable sites from whence they would have been available for the process of fertilisation. The male is responsible for 40% of the causes of primary infertility because of this.

(b) There are no ova, available for fertilisation, either because they are not there at all, or because they are there but cannot be released from the ovary. The female is responsible for 50% of the cases of primary infertility because of this.

(c) Other causes, most of them unknown so far, cause the remaining 10% of the cases of primary infertility, including the very rare cases of congenital unavailability of parts of the birth canal.

Primary infertility is not an uncommon occurrence between couples that have been living together for more than two years; a figure of 10-20% worldwide has been given.[3]

(ii) Secondary infertility

Secondary infertility is present when a woman who has conceived before, is unable to become pregnant. There can be many causes for that, the commonest being:

(a) Infection and consequent blockage of the passages that convey the ovum, or the fertilised egg in the female or the sperm in the male.

(b) Non-production of ova or spermatozoa because the organs that produce them have been destroyed by disease, cancer, or have been removed.

(c) Removal of the womb, or the tubes in the woman.

(d) The exhaustion of the supply of ova in the female, menopause (more of a 'primary' concept of a cause).

A fertilised ovum is known as an embryo up to eight weeks of gestation; after that and until delivery it is a foetus.

The success rate in those who attempt management of infertility is about 10-17%, and up to 24-35% with IVF (in vitro fertilisation).[4] Higher claims were made for 'nonsurgical embryonic selective thinning and transfer' (NEST).[5]

The crux of the matter is for a sperm from the husband to fertilise an ovum, or ova from his wife, and for the product to remain in the mother's womb until it reaches a stage compatible with extra-uterine life.

Islam allows the treatment of ailments, encourages marriage and begetting children, within the framework of the family (see chapter three).

2. How does Islamic fiqh impinge on reproduction?

The methods of overcoming primary and secondary infertility will now be examined, as to their permissibility in Islamic fiqh.

According to the fuqaha, any form or description of donated sperm from a person other than the husband is ruled out. Also, ova in any situation must have come from the wife of that husband. The basic rule is that the procreation of children should be within the bond of marriage between a man and a woman. This limits the methods of treatment that are permissible. The following examples, however, are cleared:

(i) Infertility could be due to the fact that healthy spermatozoa are too few in numbers to effect fertilisation. The semen is collected from the husband at intervals and it is cooled and pooled, until enough spermatozoa are collected to effect fertilisation. Then that seminal pool is applied to suitable parts of the wife's birth canal to ensure fertilisation of her ovum or ova (*in vivo fertilisation*).

(ii) A second approach would be to fertilise the ovum of the wife with her husband's spermatozoa under less wasteful and more favourable laboratory conditions of incubation in a Petri dish (*in vitro fertilisation*), or what is commonly called a 'test tube baby.'

(iii) The aforementioned technique can be further refined by actually 'injecting' or impregnating an ovum from the wife with a spermatozoa of the husband (a microscopic technique), and rearing the product in a Petri dish, then implanting it at a suitable stage of division of the cells into the wife's womb.

(iv) In cases where the availability of ova is the problem, ova are harvested after suitable hormonal preparation, from the wife and are fertilised by the sperm of the husband, then returned to the womb, which would have been prepared for implantation of the fertilised ova (usually three).

All the above procedures are suitable for cases where the tubes, which convey the fertilised ovum to the uterus, are blocked or have been removed, as in secondary infertility cases in the female (the commonest cause).

All of these techniques are acceptable in Islamic fiqh.[6]

3. What happens to surplus embryos in modern infertility techniques?

Fertilisation of an ovum by a spermatozoon is the essence of the procedure in the management of infertility. But to achieve the result of having an embryo implanted in the womb and proceeding to term, more than one fertilised product is necessary to be put in the prepared womb: the optimum number being three or four. To achieve this about nine to ten fertilised ova have to be available in the laboratory Petri dish (usually more than fifteen). After selecting three of them a surplus of about six to seven fertilised ova (usually more) remain. They are saved for other attempts in other cycles of the female in case the first attempt fails which is more often than not. But generally there will be some fertilised ova as a surplus.

What happens to them? Are they human beings? 'My babies': as they are called in some of the litigation cases, or 'orphans' as they are called by 'pro-life' campaigners and pressure groups, who are opposed to their destruction. Laboratories do accumulate some embryos as they can be kept in cold storage for years.

> The destruction of embryos conceived in vitro is an act of abortion in so far as the process of cell division and organisation is 'aborted' but this is not the definition of abortion intended in the criminal law. The Offences Against the Person Act 1861 (section 58) defines abortion as procuring a miscarriage, while the Abortion Act 1967 refers to terminating pregnancy. The process of disposal is, thus, clearly not abortion, and equally clearly, it is not murder since the embryo can in no way be considered to have achieved a separate existence in a legal sense...
>
> That being so, the problem is purely ethical and devolves on the nature of the embryo...either the embryo is a full human being within the rigid theological, perhaps mainly Roman Catholic, doctrine or it is a laboratory artefact...
>
> In our view, ensoulment and humanity are inseparable; humanity, in its turn, depends on a natural human environment. It seems reasonable to regard the embryo as deriving its humanity only after having established normal unity with its human mother; prior to such an 'infusion of humanity,' it appears both kinder and more practical to look upon the embryo as a laboratory artefact. This view is criticised on the grounds that it does not define a soul and that is clearly so; our thesis is simply that there is no way in which the in-vitro embryo can possess that indefinable soul.[7]

In accordance with Islamic fiqh, a legal case may be made for the view that the gravity of responsibility for destruction of such fertilised ova is related to the stage of development reached. There is the very early stage before implantation in a *qararin makin*[8] (in a deep and secure place within the mother), which does not possess an 'infusion of humanity'[9]; but after implantation there are stages of development through 120 days, at the end of which, the embryo can possess that 'indefinable *ruh* (spirit).'

They will ask you about the Ruh.

Say: 'The Ruh is my Lord's concern.

You have only been given a little knowledge.'[10]

The Qur'an mentions different stages of development: *sulalah min tin* (purest kind of clay), *nutfa* (a drop 'of seed'), *'alaqa* ('clot' that clings), *mudgha* (like a lump), then bones appear, and become clothed with flesh, "and then brought him into being as another creature. Blessed be Allah, the Best of Creators!"[11]

The Prophet ﷺ said: -

The creation of any one of you is gathered in the womb of his mother for forty days as a *nutfa* (drop), then later an *'alaqa* (blood clot) for the like of that, then later a *mudgha* (morsel of flesh) for the like of that. Then the angel is sent to him and breathes the *ruh* into him.[12]

Similar suggestions of stages, or landmarks, of development of the embryo and foetus have always existed in other literature as well. A summary of which draws on what Michael Davies discussed in this regard:

A simple preliminary question to consider: Is the fertilised egg and sperm in a Petri dish 'human'?

To many…the key issue is when human life comes into existence.

Legally, birth itself has been regarded as important…

The time of *quickening*. In England, before 1861, there was a more serious offence of abortion when the woman was 'quick with child' than earlier in the pregnancy. Ethically the link was with Aristotle's theory of a sudden 'ensoulment' that takes place, therefore morally animating the unborn.

Conception or *fertilisation* has great significance ethically, and is one of the main features of the opposition to embryo research and abortion. The Roman Catholic Church, in particular, maintains that a human 'person' comes into existence at the moment of fertilisation…

Implantation of the embryo in the womb has been argued as having importance too…

certain proponents of this phase of development argue that legislation could be interpreted with implantation in mind as a cut-off point for certain procedures under the abortion regulatory mechanism.[13]

The debate continues, the issues in question are not purely scientific; or cannot be determined as of now on a purely 'scientific' basis. It is essentially to determine the undeterminable: when does *life* start? The difficulty is reflected in the way each viewpoint coins its own definition to exclude or to include certain stages of existence in the argument. Thus we have: fertilisation, pre-embryos, embryos, and human 'persons.' Those who support embryo research make a distinction between the point at which human life starts (fertilisation) and that at which a human 'person' comes into existence, and therefore deserving of protection.

In the United Kingdom, the "*Report of the Committee of Inquiry into Human Fertilisation and Embryology* (Cmnd 9314) (the Warnock Report) of 1984, reflects the difficulties and the problems encountered in dealing with the issues involved.

Davies analyses the Committee's report:

The general remit of the committee was described as being:

"To consider recent and potential developments in medicine and science related to human fertilisation and embryology; to consider what policies and safeguards should be applied, including considerations of the social, ethical and legal implications of these developments; and to make recommendations."

At the start of the report's consideration of the issue of embryo research (para. 11.9) it appears that the specifics of the debate on the status of the embryo are ignored and the conclusion enunciated:

"Although the questions of when life or personhood begin appear to be questions of fact susceptible to straightforward answers, we hold that the answers to such questions in fact are complex amalgams of factual and moral judgements. Instead of trying to answer these questions directly we have therefore gone straight to the question of *how it is right to treat the human embryo.*"

The report confirmed that the human embryo per se did not have any legal status. This was the position at common law...(para. 11.17)...

The report stated that once fertilisation has occurred, there is no particular point of development that is more important than another; all are parts of a continuous process (para. 11.19). Nevertheless the report went on to set a 14-day limit on experimentation on embryo.[14]

The 14-day limit was chosen because no neural tissue has been differentiated until then (no nerves nor brain tissue are present), so there is no possibility of feeling pain or discomfort.

The report pleased neither those who support embryo research, nor the Life organisation that deemed it 'a betrayal of human life at its earliest stages.' But both groups accused the report of 'fudging the issues.' Many regard it as having failed to answer Professor Margaret Brazier's two questions: of "the position one should take on the embryo in pure theory and whether one can create effective and enforceable legal rules on the same ethical basis."[15]

But these are difficult questions. Mores and norms change. The target itself moves in two parameters: much research can now be conducted within the very first five days of *life* of the human organism (which may alleviate some of the discomfort or anxiety attached to the procedures) but at the same time scientists are becoming more 'ambitious.' Cloning and transplantation of embryonic tissue to cure diseases is becoming a possibility, as envisaged by Professor Ian Wilmut:[16]

> On a simpler level, there has been the argument that it is simply unrealistic to expect society to accept that a microscopic conglomeration of cells is a human being…
>
> It has already been seen that some theological theories hold that the relevant criterion is ensoulment…
>
> A significant ethical argument in favour of destructive embryo research is the utilitarian argument… "it is for the greater good of society."[17]

An example of the change in attitudes is reflected in the recommendation of the National Bioethics Advisory Commission of the USA Congress, 1999 that the federal government begin funding some research on human embryos, saying 'the moral cost of destroying in research is outweighed by the social good that could come from the work.'

Citing recent evidence that some human embryo cells have the potential to grow into replacement tissues to treat a wide variety of chronic diseases, … 'that it is essentially unfair to millions of patients for Congress to continue its broad, four-year-old funding ban on human embryo research.'[18]

Muslim fuqaha covered the same ground: the 'removal or aborting,' the sperm-ovum union stage *(nutfa amshaj)* or the semen that is being formed within the uterus *(al-maniyyu al-mutakawwin fi'r-rahim)*, through the different stages of development of the fertilisation product (mentioned several times) when it may or may not be removed, and the ensoulment at 120 days (corresponding to the clinically recognised quickening of the foetus at 17th week), beyond which point all fuqaha are agreed that it is not permissible to destroy the foetus, mulling over the 'aborted' foetus, which though it might have had movement yet in reality was incompatible with extra-uterine life.[19] A fertilised ovum in a Petri dish is not a 'baby' in Islamic fiqh. It has not reached the preserve of the womb *(qararin makin)*. Yet, profound respect is accorded to it, as it is the precursor of life. Jurists in the Maliki school do not permit *(la yajuz)* the removal of the semen once it has reached the uterus *(al-mutakawwin fi'r-rahim)*.[20] All other fuqaha do not approve of interference with the products of conception at any stage *(makruh)*, although it does not become a culpable offence until it has reached forty days for some[21] and 120 days for others.[22]

Surplus embryos may be disposed of according to Islamic fiqh after they have been used for begetting offspring for the married couple during that cycle or any others. Moreover a *fatwa* in 1989 said that, "Under certain circumstances, and under the supervision of a committee set up for the purpose, tissues from embryos can be used for organ transplantation."[23]

But in November 1998, it became possible to isolate stem cells from embryos and foetal tissue - cells that could be used to treat conditions such as Alzheimer's and Parkinson's disease.

Thomas Murray, chairman of the National Bioethics Advisory Commission's genetics advisory subcommittee (USA) said:

There is a consensus forming that it is permissible to conduct this type of research on embryos left over from in-vitro fertilization procedures (test tube) where they would have been discarded in any event.

Do you thaw and throw them away or use them as a source of stem cells?"[24]

Stem cells have possibilities of replacing cells ravaged by chronic diseases such as Alzheimer and Parkinson's disease, spinal cord injury, diabetes, stroke and congestive heart failure. "Within five years humans could be cloning themselves and obtaining stem cells from their own pre-embryos to replace diseased cells in a wide range of disorders."[25]

4. Can a widow use stored fertilised ova of her late husband?

...and it is not lawful for them to conceal what Allah has created in their wombs if they have iman in Allah and the Last Day.[26]

Although the ayah concerns divorced women, the purpose of the ruling is applicable in our case as death is more terminal than divorce. Once a relation has ended, all matters concerning it should be drawn to a close. Rights and obligations are attended to. Debts, legacies, bequests, inheritance, and all other estate matters are settled.[27] The widow is not to marry for four months and ten days following the loss of her husband, so as, inter alia, to ensure whether she is pregnant or not. Islam is a whole. Children should be born within the marriage framework of the family unit: "...**so that you might find tranquillity in them. And He has placed affection and compassion between you.**"[28] No tranquillity, love or mercy can be expected in the cantankerous arguments that will follow a new birth that will upset the determinate shares in the inheritance defined in the Qur'an:

Men receive a share...and women receive a share of what their parents and relatives leave, a fixed share, no matter whether it is a little or a lot.[29]

This is not a simplistic attitude towards the issue; because the more it is delved into the more intricate it becomes, to no end.

The Rios case has shown that serious problems can result when there are no legal provisions to cover such problems as the right of the frozen embryo to be born and, in case the parents die, the rights of someone other than the parents to adopt the embryo and inherit from its estate (Ozar, 1985)...

While these legal provisions specify certain things, they bypass serious philosophical and ethical issues. Does the frozen embryo have a serious right to life? ...Do even married couples have a right to have children by any means?[30]

Mason and McCall Smith point out that:

The 1990 Act, section 13(5) tends to emphasise the importance of the need of the child for a 'father' as one of the welfare principles to be satisfied before treatment is given.[31]

And:

It follows that whether or not an embryo can be used for treatment or research or whether it is to be destroyed...depends upon the agreed consent of two persons (1990 Act, Schedule 3, para 6).[32]

In these cases the father's consent may be absent altogether, but supposing he left a will, would it hold in an Islamic legal context?

Living wills exonerating the dying person's killer were discussed with euthanasia in chapter four. Muslim fuqaha have argued that such a will is invalid; for such a will to be valid it must have been made after the subject had been mortally assaulted and death became inevitable; only then can it be considered that the tortfeasor has been forgiven.[33] By analogy, the permission in the living will sanctioning the implantation of the embryo may not be valid unless it was given in the last moments of life and complied with forthwith. This is a situation hard to construct in real life. If such is the case, then it is against Shari'ah to construct imaginary set-ups and engage in the futility of solving them. Several hadith point this out.[34]

Even then, it may be weighed against the right of the frozen embryo to be born or not to be born; or against the right of the 'mother' to give birth to a child after the marriage had ended, and the right of the embryo to have a father. English law emphasises 'the need of the child for a father' as in the 1990 Act, section 13(5).

Recently the case of the widow who insisted on having herself impregnated by the sperm of her dead 'husband' stirred several issues.

'Diane Blood pregnant after 3-year battle' the *Sunday Times* announced:[35]

> Diane Blood, the widow who fought a prolonged legal battle for the right to use her dead husband's sperm without his consent, has become pregnant by him more than three years after his death...
>
> Blood,...was forced to go abroad to be impregnated, after the regulatory authorities and the courts refused to let her be treated in Britain.... the British courts ruled that although it would be illegal to use the sperm here it could be exported.

It was continued as, 'Birth of hope for widow who fought law and won':[36]

> The action by the medical team - arguably an assault in common law - paved the way for a protracted legal battle and, eventually, a historic ruling by the Court of Appeal.

But the main issue was avoided: Is it 'legal' or right to remove spermatozoa from a man without his permission, and even more pressing from a dead person, who did not leave a will, by an interested party?

I have argued that Islam accepts having children only in a married relation, and during the life of the father. Once death occurs, the estate has to be divided according to determinate shares: for that to occur it cannot be linked to an indeterminate factor of the possibility of more children on the way for up to ten years who may argue for a share. This comes in Islamic fiqh under *gharar* (transactions involving an undetermined, or an unknown factor, which are absolutely forbidden).[37]

5. Surrogate wives and polygamy

Can the fertilised ovum of 'one wife and her husband' be implanted into the uterus of the other wife of the same husband?

This was first considered to be blameless.[38] But the *fatwa* was later rescinded to concur with a previous *fatwa* of al-Azhar.[39] I have examined the Azhar *Fatwa* in this concern [1980].[40] It points out that all fertilisation of ova must be from the sperm of 'her husband only', not adulterated by or mixed with semen from another person or animal. When the product of this *in vitro* fertilisation is returned to the womb of that wife, this is permissible in Shari'ah.

But incubating the product of such fertilisation in the womb of an animal (not human [sic]) for some time then returning it to the womb of the woman in question is corrupting Allah's creation and is not permissible. There is no mention of 'another wife of that husband.' This was also referred to by Abu us Sorour, and Omran, (1992:186), when he was discussing the same *fatwa*:

> The question was put to Sheikh Jadel Haq [sic] (Jad al-Haq) in 1980, when he was Mufti of Egypt,…His response is summarized below:
>
> Insemination of a wife (*in vivo*) with semen taken from her husband…is allowed…Artificial insemination *in vitro* (test-tube babies) using the husband's semen only is allowed…Mixing the wife's ovum with her husband's sperms, and transferring the fertilised ovum to the uterus of an animal (for whatever reason) for a period, then returning it to the wife's uterus is forbidden…
>
> Note: although surrogate motherhood was not specifically mentioned in the *fatwa*, it is understood from other evidence that it is forbidden.[41]

The issue of surrogate incubation by humans was not addressed by the *fatwa* of Sheikh Jad al-Haq [1980]: he spoke of animals only. Surrogate humans are an important issue, the more so in Islamic fiqh as of the practical fact that there can be another wife of the same husband at the same time. Its importance was highlighted by the *fatwa* of

Majlis al-Fiqh al-Islami (7th.), [1984] Makkah, Saudi Arabia, allowing it; then rescinding it. Twelve years later Omran (1992) quoted the 1980 *fatwa* of Sheikh Jad al Haq of incubation in animals and noted that, "although surrogate motherhood was not specifically mentioned in the *fatwa*, it is understood from other evidence that it is forbidden."[42]

I still think that the original *fatwa Majlis al-Fiqh al-Islami* was not in violation of any rules of the Qur'an, Sunnah, or the views of the learned Muslim fuqaha, and that there may be room for more detailed analysis of the situation. The question resurfaces from time to time. Al-Qaradawi (1987),[43] spoke of the possibility of hired wombs, but was opposed to the idea, and suggested womb transplants as a possible solution.

Majma' al-Fiqh al-Islami in its third congressional meeting 11-16 October 1986, in Omman, Jordan decided that it was impermissible to implant the fertilised ovum (by the sperm of her husband) into the womb of the other wife of that husband.[44]

In 1999 it is thought that it is possible to use the shell of the ovum of the donor after removing its nucleus to harbour a nucleus from a cell of the recipient. Thus a cell is cloned which has the genetic material of the recipient (nuclear transfer technology).[45] Is that comparable to a transplanted uterus?

But recently, (on Sunday 6th May 2001), Sky News at 20.07 said that scientists in the USA proved that a baby was born with genetic material from three parents, one male and two females. So the ovum of the other female does contribute genetic material. Will this technology be acceptable in Islamic fiqh, even if there was a marriage bond between the husband and his two wives?

6. Cloning

6.1 Cloning and the laws

(i) Preamble

The purpose of this section is not to extol Islamic fiqh as having solutions for the dilemma of cloning in humans: 'for every complex problem there is a solution that is neat, plausible and wrong.'[46] The purpose is more to stop the passing of blanket judgements on such intricate procedures before their details are known. In Islam, there is no crime worse than making the impermissible permissible, or vice versa.[47]

Also, it is forbidden to dig into events that have not yet happened.

You who have iman! do not ask about matters which, if they were made known to you, would make things difficult for you. (tasu'kum).[48]

Sayed Sabiq, the late Professor of Shari'ah, Cairo University said, "There is a *hadith* in which the Prophet prohibited the discussion of events that have not yet occurred (*al-ughlutat*), which literally means 'things which have not yet been clarified.'"[49]

Robert Edwards, the IVF pioneer, thinks that the big questions, about the possible wider implications of cloning, are premature:

But I think asking all these questions at the present time is misleading, because you are forced into making decisions on things you don't know, and I think it's wise to keep well within the bounds that you're reasonably certain about."[50]

But cloning is linked with reproduction, surplus embryos, and experimentation with such and other human embryos, which may be bred specifically for that purpose. Thus it becomes imperative to examine the areas in cloning which are inseparable from fertilisation, and experimentation. Such examination must depend on transparency, shared information, and (to discover the responses in Islamic fiqh) shared platforms of making recommendations for laws as well.

(ii) The existing 'laws' and the expected changes

The "Opinion of The Group of Advisors on the Ethical Implications of Biotechnology to the European Commission" as it deals, inter alia, with 'informing about cloning, and its human implications,' "the Resolution on Cloning of the European Parliament 1997-1998," and the Progression in Cloning with its *defacto* 'laws' are chosen as references:

(a) Opinion of The Group of Advisors on the Ethical Implications of Biotechnology to the European Commission

Cloning occurs commonly in nature in plants and some invertebrate animals (worms and insects). It also occurs at the hands of plant and animal breeders. Monozygotic 'identical twins' occur in humans naturally.

But the Group submitted that "(reproductive cloning) in humans should be prohibited."[51]

(b) Resolution on cloning of the "European Parliament 1997-1998"

Minutes of the sitting of Wednesday 12 March 1997

9. Cloning animals and human beings

...

I. 3."Urges the member states to ban the cloning of human beings at all stages of formation and development, regardless of the method used, and to provide for penal sanctions to deal with any violation."[52]

(c) Progression in Cloning and the changes in laws

The first successful cloning in vertebrate animals was reported in 1952, in frogs, from the nuclei of early embryos.

Dolly's uniqueness comes from being cloned from an adult cell, taken from the mammary gland of a ewe. This raised for the first time the possibility of making identical copies of adult humans.

Other centres succeeded in repeating the procedure. Steve Farrer writes,

> First Dolly, now Mickey: scientists clone mouse...Scientists are expected to reveal that they have succeeded in creating the first animal cloned from the cells of an adult since the birth of Dolly two years ago.[53]

Furthermore, Nigel Hawkes writes about successful cloning in five cows, by Japanese scientists.[54]

The USA is a leader amongst countries, which can enforce "penal sanctions to deal with any violation." But attitudes change. An example of the change in attitudes is reflected in the recommendation of the National Bioethics Advisory Commission of the USA Congress, 1999

> ...that the federal government begin funding some research on human embryos, saying 'the moral cost of destroying in research is outweighed by the social good that could come from the work.'[55]

Recently, Aileen Ballantyne published an article in reference to the work of Professor Ian Wilmut of the Roslin Institute (near Edinburgh) where Dolly the sheep was cloned.

> "'Dr Dolly plans the clones that will save lives'...

> He believes that, within the next five years, a loving daughter will consider donating her eggs to create an embryonic copy of her mother or father. From such a creature - the world's first human clone - will come life-saving tissue transplants, perfectly matched to their recipients. They will be used to treat a wide range of crippling diseases, including the diabetes that...

The clone would never be more than a five-day embryo, but it could produce the cells that manufacture the human body's insulin."[56]

The isolation of stem cells took place in Geron Corporation of Menlo Park, California – which recently (May 1999) has acquired the company created by Scotland's Roslin Institute, which cloned Dolly the sheep.[57]

> "It has been reported in *Nature Genetics* that scientists Teruhiko Wakayama and Ryuzo Yanagimachi of the University of Hawaii have succeeded in cloning the first male animal. A male mouse cloned from cells of the tail of another male mouse, shows that males too can be cloned and that cells from the reproductive system are not essential. The nucleus of eggs of female mice was removed and replaced with the nucleus of cells from the tail tip of a male mouse. The 'developed' eggs were placed in the wombs of female mice. This makes it possible to store animals as frozen cells rather than eggs or embryos."[58]

6.2 Implications for Human Cloning

"The world's 'first cloned human embryo' was created in November 1998 at the Advanced Cell Technology Firm, Massachusetts, USA.

Cloning of human embryos for research is illegal in Britain under the 1990 Human Fertilisation and Embryology Act. But at the end of 1998 a Government watchdog group called for changes in the law to allow cloning for medical research, as long as the embryos were destroyed before 14 days. Despite months of internal debate, the Government has not yet reached a decision.

> "…The world's 'first cloned human embryo' has been created…in the 'Advanced Cell Technology Firm,' USA, and Dr. Robert Lanza, the director of tissue engineering at the firm, says the embryo cannot be seen as a person because it is less than 14 days old, the age at which a human embryo implants itself into the wall of the womb and starts to develop a nervous system. The techniques were similar to those, which produced Dolly the sheep at the Roslyn Institute in Edinburgh. The DNA-loaded nucleus of a human cell, part of a skin sample from a man's leg, was inserted into the 'shell' of a cow's ovum, from which, the nucleus and all DNA material was removed. In a process identical to natural conception the cell repeatedly doubled itself and could, theoretically, develop into a recognisable human foetus. But in the first 14 days all cells are stem cells, each of which has the potential to develop into nerves, blood, skin or bone, but has not begun to do so."[59]

The BBC, Channel One TV, on 20 June 1999 at 5 am announced that Parliament was expected to pass the recommendation of the 'Government watchdog group' that day: 'to allow cloning for medical research, as long as the embryos were destroyed before 14 days.' There was no further news. But on 19th December 2000 the House of Commons passed the motion.[60]

6.3 Islamic fiqh and the new challenges

It may be opportune to conclude this section by a general overview of what Muslim fuqaha call "Rulings as regards to what Shari'ah was silent about" *(hukm al-maskuti 'anhu)*.

As a forward-looking plan and an ongoing process it becomes necessary to analyse the idea that, "if something is not expressly forbidden, then it is permissible." Muslim fuqaha have addressed the question:

Hal al-aslu fi al-ashya'i al-ibaha aw al-hurma...? (Is it the basic rule that, "Everything is allowed unless it was specifically forbidden, or is it that, everything is not permitted except for what Allah has ordained for us?").

Advocates of each viewpoint quoted the Qur'an, the *hadith*, and reasoning *(al-'aql)*. There was the third group who said, "we do not know." The majority of fuqaha *(al-jamhur)* are of the first viewpoint.[61]

I have gone into great detail over this debate, because the essence of Islamic fiqh is the knowledge of what is permissible and what is not:

> so they could increase their knowledge of the deen *(yatafaqqahu)* they would be able to notify their people when they returned to them so that hopefully they would take warning![62]

Muslim fuqaha have stressed that. Ash-Shafi'i said:

> The rule of Allah *(al-ahkam)* based on Qur'an and *Sunnah* never escaped the mass of fuqaha at any time; as ignorance of it is inconceivable.[63]

It is of particular importance in uncharted domains. There are certain observations, which must be reiterated to make the debate purposeful and relevant:

(1) Islam is for everyone, everywhere, and for all times. (2) Islam must govern all aspects of life. (3) The rules are concerned basically with: *'ibadat* (faith and worship), and *mu'amalat* (transactions and dealings).

As far as matters of faith and worship are concerned, everything is detailed. There must be scrupulous adherence to the letter and spirit of the rules. Nothing should be added or removed.

But transactions and dealings (in life) vary with circumstances. As-Sarakhsi said, "Rules in the texts are limited whereas events are unlimited." *(an-nususu ma'duda wa al-hawadithu mamduda)*.[64] Shahrastani, said:

> Rules must be found to the innumerable events in the multifarious avenues of endeavour and change. These rules must never transgress the Qur'an and *Sunnah*, but it is not expected that every rule would have been spelt out in them.[65]

It is best to avoid passing blanket judgements on 'things, which have not yet been clarified' *(al-ughlutat)*.[66]

Notes

1. Q. 4:3 and 128 (Chapter 4 *Surat an-Nisa'* 'Women'). [Translation of Bewley]. [These two ayat taken together are wrongly interpreted by modernist muslims to imply a discouragement of polygyny, which is not the correct understanding. Rather, the second ayah is an acknowledgement that humanly it is almost impossible to be completely fair. The first ayat is the command (in the sense of permission or recommendation) to marry more than one wife with the concession that it is permitted to marry only one wife, and there are many textual sources in the Sunnah also recommending it; the status of plygyny is a recommended Sunnah, and it is certainly not discouraged – Ed.]
2. Polygyny = multiple wives, polyandry = multiple husbands (a form of it was practiced by the Arabs in *al-jahiliyya*); polygamy includes both, but has come to mean polygyny by popular use. Polygyny in Islam is a 'conditional permission,' and though abused at times, its occurrence is no more than 3%. (Omran, *Family Planning*, 1992:19.
3. Omran, *Family Planning*, 1992:184.
4. MacNaughton, Malcolm, "Assisted fertilisation and embryo research" *Proceedings:* (ed.), Jamal Abu us-Sorour, Azhar University, 1992, pp. 209-213, at p. 213, and others.
5. (NEST) *Ash-Sharq Al-Awsat*, 6 June 1999 "Science & Technology" p. 19, columns 1-5.
6. Abu us-Sorour, "Assisted Fertilisation and Islam" *Proceedings of the First International Congress on Controls and Ethics of Reproduction in the Islamic World,* Cairo, 1992:217-220; also Omran, 1992 :185-186.
7. Mason and McCall Smith, *Law and Medical Ethics*, 1994:62.
8. Q. 23:13, and 77:21.
9. Q. 31:14 (**Bearing him caused his mother great debility**) (tr. Bewley).
10. Q. 17:85 (Bewley).
11. Q. 23:12-14, (mostly Bewley's translation).
12. Jakni, *Bukhari and Muslim*, 1967, vol. 1:66-67. Translation by Abdassamad Clarke mostly from *The Complete Forty Hadith* (Ta-Ha Publishing, London.)
13. Davies, *Medical Law*, 1997:201-202.
14. Davies, *Medical Law*, 1997:207.
15. Brazier, M., 'Embryos'"Rights": Abortion and Research' in Freeman (ed.), *Medicine etc* 1988.
16. Ballantyne, Aileen, "Dr Dolly plans the clones that will save lives," The Sunday Times 16 May 1999, 5.6 News Review (top of page), columns 4, and 5.

17. Davies, *Medical Law*, 1997:204-206.
18. Weis, Rick, "Federal Embryo Research Is Backed: Ethicists See Benefits Overriding Qualms" *The Washington Post*, May 23, 1999, p. 1 column 1.
19. Ibn Qudama, *Al-Mughni*, 1981, vol. 7:816 (both al-Muzni and Ahmad ibn Hanbal have mentioned this point, which may be compared with modern medical views on viability of the foetus).
20. Dardir, *Al-Sharh al-Kabir*, vol. 2:266.
21. Ibn Hajar, *Tuhfat al-Muhtaj*, (1304 AH), vol.8:241.
22. Ibn Qudama, *Al-Mughni*, 1981, vol. 7:816, and Muflih, *Al-Forou'a*, 1962, Vol. 1:281.
23. *Fatawa al-Majma' al-Fiqhiyya*, Jedda, Saudi Arabia, 14-20 March, 1990, Decision No. (58/7/6), concerning the use of embryos for transplantation: recommendation of the meeting in Kuwait 23-26 October, 1989; in *Majalat al-Buhuth al-Fiqhiyya al-Mu'asara* (Contemporary Jurisprudence Research Journal), second year, No. 6, August September October 1990, Riad, Saudi Arabia, pp. 144-145.
24. Friend, Tim, "OK to foetal tissue research may ignite ethical firestorm" in *USA Today*, May 24, 1999, p. 1, columns 3, 4, and 5, centre.
    In the U.K. there are more than 250,000 IVF out of which less than 50,000 are implanted every year. On 19th December 2000 the House of Commons allowed for research in embryonic stem cells. (See fn.1069).
25. Friend, Tim, "Report: Medical potential is huge" in *USA Today*, May 24, 1999, p. 2, columns 1-4.
26. Q. 2:226 (tr. Bewley).
27. Q. 5:1 **"You who have iman! fulfil your contracts."** (tr. Bewley).
28. Q 30:20 (tr. Bewley).
29. Q. 4:7 (tr. Bewley).
30. Garrett, Thomas M., Baillie, Harold W., and Garrette, Roisellen M., *Health Care Ethics*, 2nd. ed., Prentice Hall, New Jersey, 1993:189-190.
31. Mason & McCall Smith, *Law and Medical Ethics*, 1994:54.
32. Mason & McCall Smith, *Law and Medical Ethics*, 1994:64.
33. Dasuqi, *Hashiyah 'ala ash-Sharh al-Kabir*, Matba'at Mustafa, vol. 4:245; and Nafarawi, *al-Fawakih al-Dawani*, (1332 AH), vol. 2:201.
34. *hadith*: (i)."Lost are those who split hairs" in *Sahih Muslim*, 1978, vol. 5:223"; (ii)"Allah protect us from useless knowledge, futile labour, and unanswered prayers" in as-Suyuti, *al-Jami' as-Saghir*, 1969, vol. 1:409; (iii) Sabiq said, "The Prophet ﷺ said, 'keep away from imaginary problems'," *Fiqh as-Sunnah*, American Trust Publications, (1406 AH), vol. 1:ix, (English) and in, 1995, vol. 1:7, (Arabic).
35. *The Sunday Times* 28 June 1998 p. 1 (middle of the page) columns 2-6 by Lois Rogers.
36. *The Sunday Times* 28 June 1998 p. 8 (upper half) columns 1-5.

[37] Darir, as-Siddiq Muhammad al-Amin ad-Darir, *al-Gharar wa Athuruhu fi'l-'Uqud,* Dar al-Jeel, Beirut, 1990, pp. 47, 51, 58. (Darir is Professor of Law, University of Khartoum).

[38] *Majlis al-Fiqh al-Islami as-Sabi'a* (7th.), [1984] Makkah, Saudi Arabia, published in *Jaridat as-Siyasa al-Kuwaitia* March 1984 (22), *fatwa* allowing the transfer of a fertilised ova of one wife to the uterus of another wife of the same husband. But *Majlis al-Fiqh al-Islami* rescinded this *Fatwa.* See Abu us-Surour, 'Assisted Reproduction (Islamic viewpoint)' 1992, pp. 214-220 at p. 218, Abu us-Sorour, *"Proceedings"* Cairo, 1992

[39] Abu as-Surour, 'Assisted Reproduction (Islamic viewpoint), 1992:218.

[40] Ibid. p. 217. (*Fatwa*: Sheikh Jad al-Haq, Sheikh al-Azhar and the Mufti of Egypt (then), issued 6 *Jumada al-Awal* 1400 AH. 23rd March 1980 Re/'Artificial Fertilisation in Humans' *(At-Talqih as-Sinna'i fi'l-Insan)*; and in Omran, *Family Planning,* 1992, pp. 6-10, 186, and 228.

[41] Ibid. p. 217; and Omran, *Family Planning,* 1992:186, and 228. Re/ *Fatwa al-Azhar*: 1980 *"At-Talqih as-Sinna'i fi'l-Insan."* (Artificial Fertilisation in Humans). (See above f.n. 1029).

[42] See p. 299 with its fn. No 1031

[43] Qaradawi, Dr. Yusuf al-Qaradawi, of al-Azhar University, Cairo, and Shari'ah College, University of Qatar, 'Shatl al-janin,' in *al-Fatawa al-Mu'asirah,* 3rd ed., Kuwait 1987 pp. 562-563.

[44] Decision No. (4) D 3 /07/86, *Majallat al-Buhuth al-Fiqhiyya al-Mu'asira* 1st. year, No. 3, 1410 AH, pp. 213-214; and *Majallat Majma' al-Fiqh al-Islami,* No. 3 and 4, 1408 AH.

[45] *USA Today*, "Out of one cell, many" May 24, 1999, p. 2A columns 5-7 (top of page).

[46] Davies, *Medical Law,* 1996:200.

[47] Q. 16:116 "Do not say about what your lying tongues describe: 'This is halal and this is haram,' inventing lies against Allah. Those who invent lies against Allah are not successful" (nothing can be more reprehensible) (tr. Bewley, and Y. Ali's note in brackets). *Hadith,* "what Allah has allowed is allowed, and what He has forbidden is forbidden: lost are those who engage in hair-splitting" in as-Suyuti, *Sahih al-Jami'i al-Saghir,* 1969, vol. 1:417.

[48] Q. 5:101, (tr. Bewley).

[49] Sabiq, *Fiqh as-Sunnah,* (English text), 1985, vol. 1 p. ix; and in Arabic text, 1995, vol. 1:7. (1st. ed., 1947).
hadith in Ibn Qutaiba al-Dinuri, *'Uyun al-Akhbar,* 1925, vol. 2:117.

[50] Challoner, *The Baby Makers,* 1999:151-152.

[51] McLaren, (Rapporteur), No. 9 28 May 1997, pp. 1-7, at 2.6, see Appendix E for a summary on cloning.

[52] European Parliament 1997-1998. See Appendix F. for the full text of the document.

Reproduction and cloning 253

[53] *The Sunday Times* 5 July 1998 p.1.1 column 8 (By Professor Ryuzo Yanganagimachi, University of Hawaii, winner of the International Prize for Biology in 1996).
[54] *The Times* 7 July 1998 p.1.12 columns 7-8 (middle of page).
[55] Weis, Rick, "Federal Embryo Research Is Backed: Ethicists See Benefits Overriding Qualms", *The Washington Post*, May 23, 1999, p. 1 column 1.
[56] *The Sunday Times,* 16 May 1999, 5. **6** News Review, top page, columns 4, and 5.
[57] Friend, Tim, "Report: Medical potential is huge" in *USA Today*, May 24, 1999, p. 2, columns 1-2.
[58] Hawkes, Nigel, "Mouse tail produces first male clone," *The Times* June 1 1999, p. 6 News columns 4-6.
[59] Cobain, Ian, New York, *Daily Mail*, London, June 17 1999, p. 1, all columns, and p. 4, all columns.
[60] BBC TV, Parliament (live) at 19 hrs. There were 366 votes for the motion and 174 were opposed.
[61] Borno, *al-Wajiz fi Eidah Qawa'id al- Fiqh al-Kulliyya*, 1998:191-198; see Appendix G.
[62] Q. 9:123, (tr. Bewley).
[63] Ash-Shafi'i, *al-Umm*, 1993, vol. 7:494; see also Madkour, *al-Madkhal*, 1966:35-37; and Qadri, *Islamic Jurisprudence*, 1973:241.
[64] Sarakhsi, (d. 483/1090), *al-Mabsut*, 1958, vol. 16:62.
[65] Shahrastani, (d. 548/1153), *al-Milal wa 'n-Nihal*, 1968, vol. 2:4.
[66] *hadith*. See f.n. 1056; and Edwards, in Challoner, 1999:151-152, see f.n. 1057 and text.

Chapter Nine
Transplantation

1. Introduction
An unknown Arab poet, in an old poem, said,
> I would like to barter my ulcer-ridden liver,
> for one which is not so afflicted;
> but none was on offer!

Ibrahim al-Musali (d. 128/746) sang it to Caliph Harun ar-Rasheed.[1]

The Prophet ﷺ allowed 'Arfaja ibn Sa'd, to have a nose made of gold when he lost his nose on *Yawm al-Kilab* (a battle which took place between Kufa and Basra).[2]

The Messenger of Allah ﷺ replaced the dangling eye of a warrior, which healed; and it became the source of fame and pride for the tribe of that warrior.[3]

The Prophet ﷺ said, "Two are priceless gifts: health and leisure."[4] He advised, that there should be an attempt to treat all ailments, and by all means, except for *haram* methods.[5]

2. The Modern History of Transplantation
Medical science in its search for cures looked for replacement of lost parts or functions. The idea became feasible with technical advances in different loci, which seemed unrelated but converged to give the twentieth century one of its outstanding medical achievements.

One area, the technique of joining blood vessels (vascular anastomosis), was pioneered by Dr. Alexis Carrel in 1905-1906 in Chicago, IL. His technique is still used today. He transplanted kidneys from one dog to another and from one cat to the other.

> ...he postulated that the cessation of function was not a result of infection or infarction [reaction to cessation of blood flow], but something different [later to be known as rejection]. He was even so imaginative as to put a second head on a dog, and for about six or eight days, that head was viable.[6]

But the roots of these speculations go back to the 18th century. The great John Hunter (1728-1793), in London, studied 'freemartins,' which are cattle twins of different sexes - one is male and always normal, while the female is almost always sterile. It was left to F. R. Lillie in 1916 to discover the 'intermingling of the blood vasculature' in their placentae,

> and he surmised that this probably accounted for the sterility of the female...Another 30 years elapsed until Ray Owen...published his paper in *Science*. He pointed out the immunological consequences of these vascular anastomoses...These observations were expanded 10 years later by... Billingham, Brent, and Medwar in their classic paper...in *Nature*...[7]

Another area was in the field of plastic surgery and skin grafting, as it interwove with "Sir Peter Medwar's new science of immunogenetics, elucidated in the treatment of burned aviators from the Battle of Britain, beginning in 1943."[8]

But going back to grafts, Parrott said:

> Dr. Yu Voronoy in Russia is credited with the first technically successful human renal transplant in April 1933. The recipient survived four days before dying of uraemia.[9]

A third area was the development of haemodialysis (kidney-machine), by the Dutch scientist Willem Kolff in 1943, which he and Carl Walter improved at Peter Bent Brigham Hospital.

It was first used in haemodialysis at the Brigham in about 1947. This development was an absolute prerequisite for the study of transplantation:[10]

> On 23rd December 1954, a team headed by Drs. George Thorn and Francis Moore of Harvard Medical School performed the first successful human renal transplant. They had overcome the rejection barrier because the transplant took place between identical twins (monozygotic twins - isograft). The donor was Roland Herrick, and the recipient was Richard[11].

This brings into consideration the important area of immunosuppression, which has enabled transplants to be carried out between parties who are not identical twins.

Agents which would suppress the immunological reaction were sought and found: radiation, steroids, 6-Mercaptopurine and its imidazole derivative Imuran (1960), cyclosporine (1965), and in 1998, anti-interleukin-2 receptor agents (a chimeric murine/human monoclonal antibody).[12]

Kidney transplants (1954), were followed by liver (1960), heart (1967), combined heart-and-lungs (1986), triple: liver, pancreas, and bowel (1996), and combined kidney-pancreas (1998) to scan some. The sources were animal and human: dead and living.[13]

3. Evidence of permissibility of transplants in Islamic fiqh

Life, the gift of Allah, is so sacred that, if one saves one single life, it is as though that person has saved the whole of the human race.[14] Praised be the ones who give others, what they themselves are in need of.[15]

Transplantation was not known at the time of the Prophet ﷺ. But, Islam is always for the good of the people *(maslahah)*.

Maslahah means preserving what is the purpose of Shari'ah: and the purpose of Shari'ah that is required from people; is to preserve the deen, their lives, their consciousnesses and intellects, their offspring, and their wealth, and some say their honour: anything that preserves these fundamentals is *maslahah*, and any thing that threatens them is *mafsadah*, and warding it off is *maslahas*.[16]

Ash-Shatibi said:

The purpose of all the rules of Shari'ah *(takalif)* is to preserve what it is intended for, which can be summed up in three groups of things:

essentials, necessities, and complimentary pursuits

Essentials: are mandatory for the welfare of deen and society; if lost there will be chaos, loss of life, and disappearance of security and safety. Essentials can be preserved in two ways, one way is to secure its existence, and the other way is to ward off all threats present or expected.

The essentials are five: preservation of deen (law), life *(nafs* – self), offspring, wealth, and the mind (intellect).

Necessities must be taken care of as their existence eases the stresses of life, and removes hardship whether that be in worship, as with *rukhas* (concessionary licences) such as not fasting when sick or travelling; in customs, such as enjoying oneself with allowed pleasures; in transactions, such as allowing borrowing and agreements on irrigation questions; in transgressions, such as accepting *qasama*, that the *diya* should be paid by the *'aqila*, and making labourers liable.

Complimentary pursuits, such as decency in behaviour, elegance in appearance, table manners, and coming closer to Allah by doing more of the good deeds than *al-wajib*, (what is mandatory).[17]

The Islamic concept of caring for welfare *(maslaha)*, the doctrines of preservation of the 'essentials,' and catering for necessity *(daroura)*, can be invoked in the acceptance of transplantation within the methods of treatment of disease. This is accepted amongst Muslim fuqaha with some controls and regulations: *Majma' al-Fiqh al-Islami* (Makkah al-Mukarramah, 19-28 January 1985) and that of The Committee of the Grand Jurors *('Ulama)* in the Kingdom of Saudi Arabia (Decision No. 99, dated 6/11/1402 A.H. (1988)), it is allowed to transplant organs from the dead; and that the living can donate organs or parts thereof to others.[18]

These views are summarised below as put forward by Al-Qattan:[19]

(i) Necessity, renders the forbidden permissible *(ad-darurat tubihu al-mahdhurat)*. This is derived from many ayat in the Qur'an e.g.

...when He has made clear to you what He has made haram for you except when you are forced to eat it.[20]

An example of necessity is when a person would die of hunger if he does not eat carrion, or he would be killed by food stuck in the throat if he does not drink the thenavailable wine.[21] Need is of a lesser degree.

(ii) Harm or hurt should be removed. This is a Prophetic *hadith (la darara wa la dirar)*.[22] Fuqaha deduced corollaries to it: (a) harm should not be removed by a similar harm, (b) greater harm should be removed by a lesser harm, and (c) the lesser of the two harms should be chosen, if there is no other way.[23]

(iii) Need can be equated to necessity sometimes: if it involves many of the community, or if the hardship becomes prolonged, or if the situation becomes critical.[24]

(iv) Warding off harm is advanced to acquiring gain *(maslahah)*: when two gains compete, the greater one should be preferred, and if a gain clashes with a harm the more pressing and urgent one should be dealt with; many questions revolve around these variations of the theme [warding off harm is advanced to acquiring gain] for example if a woman at term dies and the foetus within is still alive, and then the dead woman's belly is slit to remove the baby. Slitting the abdomen of the dead is a grave deed and violates both the dignity of the woman as such, and the respect for the dead, but saving the life of the child is a gain that outweighs that.[25]

Al-Bahwati was opposed to this argument:[26]

It is said that if a pregnant woman dies, and it is thought that the foetus is alive, still it is not allowed *(hurrima)* to slit her abdomen to let out the foetus. Because there is a certainty that such an act is disallowed according to the Prophet's *hadith*, 'breaking the bone of the dead is as wrong *(ithm)* as breaking the bone of the living,'[27] whereas the life of the foetus is not certain.

However, it is surely essential to interpose in the issue of the 'pregnant dead woman.' While the *hadith* concerning 'breaking the bones of the dead is as wrong as breaking the bones of the living' is correct, it is irrelevant to quote it in this context. It is meant to be respectful to the dead. There is no disrespect involved in trying to save another life. One can counter argue, quoting the Qur'an, that, **"And if anyone gives life to another person, it is as if he had given life to all mankind."**[28] Besides, technological advances make it possible to ascertain whether the foetus is alive or not, which makes the interposition more likely to succeed.[29]

The views of Muslim fuqaha will be analysed below under three headings:
(1) Transplants from animals, dead and living
(2) Transplants from humans, the living, the dead, and the 'brain-dead'

(1) Foetal Tissue Transplants and Genetically engineered organs

3.1 Transplants from animals, dead and living

(i) Transplants from dead animals

Treated bone from animals can be used as a bridge or scaffolding so that new bone can grow and effect healing. Treated skin from animals has been used in cases of burns. However the results were not impressive.

But the issues of interest, for our purpose, are legal. I have advanced a contemporary Islamic view on this subject because transplants are contemporary. The Prophet ﷺ, in his day, said that one should not pass judgement on events that have not occurred, nor keep on asking question after question about them.[30] The views of Muslim fuqaha on matters relevant to this subject have been examined. But the limitations set by the state of science at the time they were written must be taken in consideration. Even then, and within the same school, there were opponents and proponents. Using parts of dead animals was discussed by them and was clearly a controversial topic. Some said:

> There is nothing wrong with treatments employing bones from goats, cow, camel, horse, or any other animal except for swine and that of human beings.[31]

Al-Kasani, in discussing why carcasses are forbidden, said that the reason is not that it is dead, as consumption of dead fish is allowed, "but it is due to the processes that accompany death (with their moisture, [sic.]): that is why the use of tanned skin (leather) is permitted."[32] The Prophet ﷺ stated clearly that, "*Any* skin which has been tanned can be used freely even if it came from carrion; no matter whether the meat of that animal was allowed or not when it was living (as explained in *Sunan Ibn Majah*) *'ayyuma iyhabin dubigha fa qad tahur.'*"[33] The Messenger of Allah ﷺ was passing by a dead goat when he said, "Why don't you tan the skin and use it?" "But it is dead," retorted one. The Prophet ﷺ said, "What has been prohibited is eating it."

Ibn 'Umar was asked about some oil which had a dead rat in it. He said, "You can use it in your lamps, and you can use it as skin ointment."[34] The skin can be a portal of entry for many substances, which get absorbed and affect the body.

Could this understanding be transferred to the use of porcine heart valves, which are harvested from swine? They would have been subject to denaturing processes to prevent rejection and furthermore they would have been rendered sterile to ward off infection. An-Nawawi (d. 676 AH), the Shafi'i Muslim faqih discussed the issue of treatment with 'impermissible' materials; he said:

> When there is compulsion to ingest blood or the likes, except for wine, it is permitted...Using these materials for medical treatment, except for wine, is permitted; though, some have disallowed it. But it has been said (by our companions) that even wine is only prohibited if there is another option (referring to the Prophet's *hadith* that there is no cure in wine).
>
> A single Muslim knowledgeable medical man can take this decision.[35]

Shinqiti, a contemporary Muslim faqih, discussed the issue of medicinal use of swine parts, and quoted an-Nawawi: "it is allowed to use pig's bones if there is need for that, and no alternative is available."[36]

Muslim fuqaha in their quest for solutions rely on the doctrines of necessity, need, and social welfare. The Qur'an says:

> He has only forbidden you carrion, blood and pork and what has been consecrated to other than Allah. But anyone who is forced to eat it – without desiring it or going to excess in it – commits no crime. Allah is Ever-Forgiving, Most Merciful.[37]

Recently in 1999, Dr. Muhammad Sayed Tantawi, Sheikh al-Azhar, allowed the use of porcine (pig) skin in the treatment of burns.[38]

(ii) Transplants from living animals

Heterotransplantation or xenografting or the successful transplantation of organs from one species to another e.g. animal to human, is currently a practical impossibility.[39]

"Transplatation of a chimpanzee heart to a human was tried in 1964, but functioned for only a short time."[40] In 1984[41] a baboon's heart was connected to the circulation of a human neonate who would not have lived on her own for long enough to receive a donor's heart.

Cartwright"raises the real prospect of transplanting pigs' hearts into humans."[42] Muslim fuqaha have often asked the question,"Should all ailments be treated? And to what extent?" Some fuqaha, who concerned themselves with medical matters, included similar procedures, under the title of 'Fearsome, or risky, surgery (*al-jirahat al-mukhawifa*),' which they said should be avoided.[43] It may even not be permissible at all if on balance the outcome was known to result in failure. Baghawi (d. 516 AH) said that if treatment is very dangerous then it becomes impermissible.[44] One is not allowed to harm or kill oneself.[45] Ash-Shafi'i had his rules for such situations

> What do one's peers do? What is the usual, or expected, outcome of the procedure? These should be the guidelines that govern the action; at the pain of the perpetrator being liable.[46]

The question remains, is it allowed to experiment with human life, even if one is sure that death is going to occur either way? As necessity cannot be invoked as an argument in this situation a solution must be looked for in the realm of social welfare (*maslahah*). In Islamic fiqh, welfare has been classified into three categories: two legitimate varieties (*mutayaqqanah* 'certain,' and *mursalah* 'open or neutral'), and a third, illegitimate variety (*maslahah mawhumah* 'figment'); the latter was unacceptable as a legal support.[47]

But the Prophet ﷺ has opened a leeway for medical research:

For every ailment there is a cure. Allah has not created a disease for which He did not create a cure, known to the one who knows it and unknown to the one who does know it; so be treated.[48]

With developments and progress what is not possible today may become possible tomorrow, what is fearsome or risky may become safe and routine.

At the same time Islam must be taken as a whole: honesty, meaning well, doing good by others, justice, are the essence of iman.[49] A balance is the theme in doing things.[50] There must be a reasonable chance of a procedure benefiting someone before it is undertaken. All acts are judged by the intentions of the doer.[51]

3.2 Transplants from humans:

Generally, transplants from one human to another come from one of two categories of organs: regenerative and non-regenerative.

Regenerative 'organs' are capable of replenishing themselves, or regenerating, examples of which are blood and bone marrow. There are no problems in sanctioning the donation of such material in common law or in Islamic fiqh. On the one hand the donation is life-saving to another human being, on the other hand it is soon replenished with little or no discomfort. The procedure poses no danger to the donor.[52]

Non-regenerative 'organs,' are the ones which do not regenerate; once lost they are lost forever. They can be single or paired.

Single organs like the heart, cannot be the subject of donation. It is suicide on the part of the donor, and aiding and abetting suicide on the part of the recipient; he was a participant. Sometimes it is possible to take part of a single organ without any adverse effects on the donor, as with the liver. The kidneys exemplify paired organs, and it is possible to take one. There is the very remote possibility that one who has donated a kidney may be involved in a situation where the function of the remaining kidney may be endangered.

The issues involved will be discussed under transplantation from: (i) the living, (ii) the dead, (iii) the brain-dead, (iv) anencephaly and (v) fetal tissue.

(i) Transplantation from a living donor

The organ donated can be from any of the two categories: regenerative or non-regenerative.

Transplants from a living donor offer the best results, as the procedure can be meticulously and leisurely planned. Sometimes it may be too well planned for comfort, as with the case of getting a new baby to become a bone marrow donor for a sick sibling.[53]

The donor is exposed to the risk of surgery, which may be life threatening, as with kidney donors, and particularly so with 'part-of-liver' donations.

(The recipients are also exposed, but they stand to gain from the procedure).

There are also considerations in the area of consent: adults may be under pressure to oblige, and there are problems in dealing with minors and infants. It can be a sad, yet rewarding, field of practice.

A few points need to be analysed:

(a) It is a principle in common law, that no person is deemed to be capable of consenting to his being killed or seriously injured. This is also reflected in Islamic fiqh. The Qur'an reiterates this on several occasions:

And do not kill yourselves. Allah is Most Merciful to you.[54]

And,

Do not cast yourselves into destruction;[55]

(b) Although Islam encourages beneficence, and although donations of organs for transplantation is appreciated, it is imperative that this should only be motivated by humanitarian considerations and the desire to worship Allah, Who has honoured humanity, **"We have honoured the sons of Adam."**[56]

Human parts are not for sale.[57]

(c) There should be no compulsion. Just as **"There is no compulsion where the deen is concerned"**;[58] so there is no compulsion in all transactions.[59] The donation should have been made voluntarily, and the consent should have been informed. This brings into the debate, the consent of minors.

In Islamic fiqh, if a minor is involved in an agreement or a contract, or an obligation, then there are three possibilities to entertain:[60]

(1) If it is totally beneficial to the minor, it should be *accepted* on his behalf, *immediately*, so that no loss is caused by delay.

(2) If it is totally harmful to the minor, this should be *rejected* on his behalf, *immediately* to ward off any damage.

(3) If it could be beneficial or it could be harmful, this sort of situation is *put on hold* until the minor becomes of age and makes his own choice.

The minor cannot be a donor unless it can be argued that donating one of his kidneys to his/her mother or father will be in his/her interest. If refused, no pressure should be applied. It is even harder to ask for a sibling to donate to the other sibling unless it is argued that the company of the sibling is for the benefit and welfare of the donor.

For regenerative organs, such as blood or bone marrow, the case is much easier; but to become pregnant in order for the coming baby to help a sibling with bone marrow is a hard question. Removal of organs from the mentally retarded must be harder still, even when it is to benefit the carer of the mentally retarded person. Who takes such a decision? If a carer is involved then the donation is most likely not for a parent or a sibling. Could another carer be found or is the subject particularly dependent on that carer? Is it an administrative decision of the authorities?

Al-Fatawa al-Hindiya, discussed the following situation:

> A mad woman had some problem in her scalp, and no one was her guardian: whoever cuts her hair to rid her of the problem is a good-doer *(muhsin)*, providing he leaves some mark to denote that she is a woman.[61]

And Muhammad ibn Muflih from the Hanbali school posed this situation:

> If some one removes a part *(sil'a)* from a person with diminished capacity, and without permission then he is liable, but there is a view expressed in *Kitab al-Huda*, that he is not liable as it was a charitable act. This viewpoint is subject to scrutiny.[62]

(ii) Cadaver donations, and parts from dead persons

The human being is also honoured when dead. The Prophet ﷺ said:

> Breaking the bone of a dead person is as wrong as breaking the bone of the living.[63]

He ﷺ stood up when a funeral passed by him, but his companions said, "He is a Jew!" The Prophet ﷺ said "So! He is human."[64]

But necessity, need, and *maslahah* (welfare), are reasons to use parts of the cadaver. This question is only brought up for remedies of the slips and conflicts in the laws and ordinances that regulate the procedure. The parts must be taken without any unnecessary delay to be useful. Those responsible for allowing the donation may not be accessible physically, or mentally. There may be conflicts even in the cases of card-carrying donors. The laws may not be the best recourse in these situations.

As for the position in England, Michael Davies says:

Cadaver transplantation is governed by the Human Tissue act 1961, which expanded on the obviously limited provisions of the Corneal Grafting Act 1954. It should be evident on any reading of the 1961 Act that it is vague and open to a wide variety of interpretations. In addition, far from facilitating the supply of organs, which the legislation aimed to do while giving the public reassurance, it may have the opposite effect…

The innate vagueness of many of the preconditions for the invocation of s. 1 (1) of the Act is exacerbated by the fact that there is still no directly applicable case law that can be utilised. One has therefore to proceed carefully by way of legal analogy.

The main culprit as far as this vagueness is concerned is also the key concept underlying the legislation, namely, authorisation by a person 'lawfully in possession' of the body… a corpse at law can never be the subject of ownership. An individual cannot decide what shall happen to his or her body after death (although usually as a matter of respect for the deceased the next of kin will comply with any request that had been made during life). This person 'in lawful possession' is therefore an important figure; but who are the available candidates?[65]

Davies, further, explains:

Those are moments of compassion, empathy, understanding, respect, and decorum. The Human Tissue Act 1961 fails to observe the preconditions for the removal of an organ from the deceased…the mother of a child killed in a car crash, informed that the child's organs had been removed without consulting her or considering the child's wishes.[66]

The Qur'an advises on how to manage such situations:

Call to the way of your Lord with wisdom and fair admonition, and argue with them in the kindest way.[67]

Muslim fuqaha have argued using quotes from the Qur'an and *hadith* to arrive at diametrically opposite conclusions. Those who were opposed to using human parts quote from the Qur'an:

[Shaytan says] "I will lead them astray and fill them with false hopes. I will command them and they will cut off cattle's ears. I will command them and they will change Allah's creation."[68]

And:

We have honoured the sons of Adam;[69]

They argue that removing organs from a creature of Allah and putting it into another is defacing the fair nature created by Allah; even if the organ is obtained from a dead person, because Allah has honoured human beings. They quote the Prophet's *hadith*, "Breaking the bones of the dead is as wrong as breaking the bones of the living."[70]

The Prophet ﷺ always told members of his armies to, "Fight for the cause of Allah, do not be cruel, or treacherous, and do not mutilate…"[71]

They also used this latter directive to argue that removing organs from the dead is mutilation. They further put forward the dictum, "What you cannot sell you cannot give away, nor bequeath *(hiba)*."[72]

Although they did not quote the *hadith*, "There should be no sale involving the corpse of a non-believer" *(la bai'a fi jifat mushrik)*.[73] That would be applicable for the corpse of a Muslim as well, and more so for the living.

A fortiori, for them, there should be no organ donations from the living. They added to their arguments that the risk involved in the procedure falls under the commands in the Qur'an: Q. 2:195 **"And do not kill yourselves"**; and Q. 4:29 **"Do not cast yourselves into destruction."**

Among present day fuqaha who subscribe to this view are Professor Abdul Salaam as-Sukkari, and Professor Hassan'Ali ash-Shadhali, who are both professors of Islamic law at Al-Azhar University, in Cairo.[74]

On the other hand those who think that it is permissible to transplant human organs, argue that the Qur'an has been very explicit in exempting cases of necessity from general rules. As in: Q. 2:172, (tr. Bewley),

> He has only forbidden you carrion, blood and pork and what has been consecrated to other than Allah. But anyone who is forced to eat it – without desiring it or going to excess in it – commits no crime. Allah is Ever-Forgiving, Most Merciful.

Other ayat reiterating the same rule are in Q. 5:3; 6:118-119; and 6:154. In all of them, necessity constitutes grounds for exemption from culpability.

I would like to argue that all of these ayat were addressing the ingestion of articles of food, which were forbidden in the first place, and the situations where an exemption was made for them to be taken. Blood was such an article of food that was included in the prohibition. Yet Muslim fuqaha have always allowed blood transfusions to take place.[75] Donor organs are not ingested. They are grafted as a necessity to give a chance of life to others.

Muslim fuqaha who were in favour of organ transplants also argued that the Qur'an says:

that if someone kills another person – unless it is in retaliation for someone else or for causing corruption in the earth – it is as if he had murdered all mankind. And if anyone gives life to another person, it is as if he had given life to all mankind.[76]

So, organ donation may be classified in that category. Helping others, and rescue, are commendable. The hardship involved only augments the value of the acts. The Qur'an praises those who give others, even though they may be in need themselves;[77] and the Prophet ﷺ said, "Allah loves it, when those in need are rescued *(wa Allahu yuhibbu ighathat al-lahfan)*."[78]

Those are some of the arguments and reasons given by those who vouched for the permissibility of organ donation. The majority of Muslim fuqaha are in favour of utilising cadaver parts, and donation of organs from the living.

This was expressed in *fatwas*, recommendations, and decisions of many 'official' Islamic forums:

(1) The International Islamic Congress (Malaysia, April, 1969)

(2) *Majma' al-Fiqh al-Islami* (Makkah al-Mukarramah, 19-28 January 1985)

(3) The Committee of the Grand Jurors *('Ulama)* of Saudi Arabia (Decision No. 99, dated 6/11/1402 A.H. (1988))

(4) *Fatwa* Committee of the Hashmite Jordanian Kingdom: Abdul Salaam al-'Abadi, *Buhuth Majma' al-Fiqh al-Islami*, p. 8

(5) *Fatwa* Committee, Kuwait, No. 97 'aien/84, dated 22 Rabie' al-Akhar 1405 A.H. (1991)

(6) *Fatwa* Committee, al-Azhar, Egypt, No. 491, Dar al-Ifta' al-Misriyya, *musajjal* 88 *musalsal* 212 p. 93

(7) *Fatwa* Committee, al-Majlis al-Islami al-A'ala, Algiers, April 20 1972."[79]

A notable example of individual fuqaha who support transplantation of human parts is the late Sheikh Al-Azhar: Jad al-Haq 'Ali Jad al-Haq.[80]

The present Sheikh Al-Azhar, Dr. Muhammad Sayed Tantawi allows living-donors' transplants and transplants utilising organs from the dead. He went further and said that the permission of the relatives and that of the authorities *(al-Niyaba al-'Amma)* is not required.

The Grand Mufti of Egypt, Dr. Nasr Farid Wasil does not agree. He says that transplants from the dead should only take place if there has been a living will.[81]

Both views need to take in consideration the circumstances of each case and the situation. One has to tread carefully and with sensitivity. Removing organs from the dead without the acceptance of the relatives even if it were 'by the law' is not recommended. Especially when it is realised that all these are stopgap measures, as the practical solution is in finding more readily available sources, be they: mechanical, genetically engineered, animal-harvested or combinations thereof. In the meantime the field should retain the good will of the people including would-be organ donors, and financiers of research. The lesser the unnecessary controversy the better.

Is it allowed to transplant one testicle from a donor?

This is a very complex situation as regards Islamic fiqh. There are those amongst Muslim fuqaha who allow it, and others who do not. Among those who allow it, was the late Professor Sheikh Sayed Sabiq, of Umm al-Qura University, Makkah; and it is the view of *Mashyakhat Al-Azhar*.[82]

Those who were against this procedure, including Shanqiti, quoted all the reasons given above and added that, "just as it should not be allowed to transplant an ovary it is not allowed to transplant a testicle."[83]

Although I am personally of the opinion that Islamic fiqh allows transplantation, I have my reservations about testicular transplantation. Medically viewed, the aim of transplantation of a testicle is to produce spermatozoa. Since successful transplantation precludes rejection: it means that the organ donated is functional. Will the sperms produced be genetically those of the donor? If so then the situation is akin to insemination from a donor. The offspring would be illegitimate if my doubts are correct. But there is no question of *zina* (adultery) at all. *Zina* involves unlawful carnal knowledge, where four men have witnessed actual penetration. Artificial insemination from a donor is not permitted, it may be punished according to the doctrine of *ta'zir* discretionary punishments with the severest of punishments short of a *hudud* punishments; but it is not *zina*.

It is best to reserve judgement until such a birth takes place where there are no reservations about it and the genetics are cleared.

At the same time I do not subscribe to the reasoning that it is similar in every respect to transplantation of an ovary. Because if the transplanted ovary came from another wife of the same husband then, although the ova produced may still be those of the donor, the situation is closer to surrogacy. But for the validity of my argument it must be assumed that the 'family' of the husband and the spouses involved must remain in the bond of marriage, at least to the time of menopause of the transplanted ovary. [See p. 244 above].

The Prophet ﷺ warned against idle speculation. He said, "Lost are those who are engaged in 'hair-splitting' *(halaka al-mutanat'un)*."[84] Caliph Abu Ja'far al-Mansur al-'Abbasi (d. 158/775), addressing Malik ibn Anas, said:

> Compile *hadith* and *fiqh*. Make your treatise approachable to people *(tawatta'hu li'n-nas:* hence the name of the book *(al-Muwatta'))*. Avoid the toughness, or hardness *(shada'id),* of 'Abdullah ibn 'Umar (ibn al-Khattab); the licenses – 'easy ways' *(rukhas)* – of Ibn 'Abbas; and the strange matters, or rarities *(shawadhdh)* of Ibn Mas'ud.[85]

But such dissection may be the call of the 'making of laws.' Developments in the field necessitate responding to the problems as they surface. They have surfaced. They have been asked of prestigious bodies such as *Mashyakhat al-Azhar ash-Sharif,* and learned fuqaha, the likes of Professor Sheikh Sayed Sabiq, of Umm al-Qura University, Makkah al-Mukarramah.[86]

(iii) Transplantation from the brain dead

Brain death is a fairly new definition, which may need some explanation.

A 1980 'Panorama' program, entitled:

'Organ Transplants: Are the Donors Really Dead?'

> Public anxiety after the program was such that there was evidence of a 65 per cent reduction in the number of donors within that frame of time.[87]

The brain initiates, controls, and regulates all functions. It can be imagined as a three tier complex. The foundation, the mezzanine, and the higher.

The foundation has the primary functions of life: heartbeat, breathing, swallowing, cough-reflex, and other vital autonomic (automatic) functions.

The mezzanine has the basic instincts and desires: sleep and waking, hunger, fear, rage, and others.

The higher centres refine the accomplishment of the basic instincts; and in the human being are bestowed with intellect.

The brain, as all other parts of the body, needs nourishment to survive. Nourishment is composed of numerous components, carried by the blood, the most important of which is oxygen, without which the brain can only survive for a few minutes (about three minutes at a temperature of 37 degrees centigrade, the time increasing with lower temperatures).

Various parts of the brain have different requirements: the higher centres require much more nourishment than the lower centres, particularly oxygen. So when the brain is depleted of oxygen, its functions are curtailed accordingly. The brain stem, (the base, the foundation, the 'lowest' part) is the toughest part and the least differentiated. If it is dead all other parts of the brain are dead. A corollary to that is: other parts of the brain can 'die' while the brain stem can still survive. Death is expressed in loss of function, the finer before the cruder. So, due to injury or other causes of oxygen depletion, other parts of the brain might have died leading to deep coma, while the brain stem, or base continues its function of basically maintaining the heartbeat and respiration. That state is the persistent (now called permanent) vegetative state (PVS), where no mechanical ventilation is required to maintain the heart and lung functions. Our case is a step further down the ladder of 'lost functions.' It concerns the function of the base, entrusted with breathing and heartbeat. If that part of the brain is dead then there is no heartbeat and no respiration. The person is dead.

But, how does the problem arise then? It arises when the brain stem has died, but modern methods and technology come into play at that particular moment, when the brain stem has died, but the heart has not yet 'shut off,' as it takes a few more moments for it to do so (and even more time for the nails and hair to stop growing), the heart is supplied by oxygen by establishing mechanical breathing. In its turn the heart continues its innate function of just contracting and relaxing thus maintaining the circulation to the lungs and the body. This, theoretically, can last as long as the machines last. When the machines are stopped, the lungs do not move and do not ventilate, the heart stops after a time lapse for it to use up the oxygen that was pumped in it.

I have tried to explain that brain death is real death, and is very different from the persistent (permanent) vegetative state, and deep coma cases.

In practice: how do we have the situation on our hands? That is mainly because resuscitation must be started in every case (because it cannot be inferred from the beginning, without examination and without conducting some investigations, whether the injury is fatal or not), the body is supplied with oxygen through mechanical ventilators, until the person under treatment is assessed and managed. Some cases would have been in this category.

If brain death is accepted as death, then this dead 'person' is a better donor than a cadaver, because: the tissues continue to be oxygenated until the optimum time for the procedure is chosen. The organs to be removed would be in prime condition as they are no different from the organs of the living. They would have deteriorated if they were not mechanically perfused.

But persons in deep coma are alive; they may come out of the coma, whereas persons in permanent vegetative state (PVS), though alive, never regain consciousness. The difference between them and the brain dead is in the fact that their lower centres, which maintain breathing and heartbeat, were spared. So they do not need mechanical ventilation. They can live for years if fed and cared for. The question is should they be fed by naso-gastric tube or gastrostomy? and for how long?

Roman Catholic opinion, traditionally a strongly pro-life group with a closely reasoned moral perspective, has affirmed that in the case of artificial feeding regimes:

'To persist in indiscriminately using such gestures can convey stupidity and cruelty, not compassion and love.'[88]

The Prophet ﷺ said,

Our Lord! Please keep me alive if that is for my good; and please let me die if it is better for me to die.

He prayed for death with dignity and integrity *(meetatan sawiya, wa maradan ghir fadih)*.[89]

Persons in the PVS are not dead; and they are also not in the category of the brain-dead. My personal opinion is that persons in the PVS should never be considered as donors even if they have had a living will, or a donor card. Because the situation (of perhaps not feeding them and letting them die) is so complex and heart rending, that it will be insensitive to introduce yet another unpleasant twist to it, by asking for a 'donation' for a transplant. The decision will always be suspect *(shubha)*.

Shubha precludes inheriting from the wealth of the deceased, even if it was proved that manslaughter was by mistake *(khatta')*.[90]

(iv) Anencephalic Infants as Organ Donors[91]

Although anencephalic infants are not dead, they may be confused with brain-dead situations. They do not have a cerebral cortex (so they do not have measurable electroencephalographic activity; they do not have cerebral circulation; and they cannot demonstrate seizure activity). In simple but accurate terms they are born without that part of the brain, which can be tested to determine that they are 'brain dead.' But they have the mid-brain that maintains respiration and heartbeat: without any possibility of ever becoming conscious, as the organ for that function is not there: the cerebral cortex (anencephalic = without cerebral cortex).

A few hundred anencephalics are born alive each year in the USA. (Population 250 million). 90% of them die within 7 days, and survival beyond 14 days is rare. Only one case on record lived for 2.5 years. But they constitute a great medico-legal dilemma. They will never become conscious. But they do not satisfy the criteria of death.

The situation has led to the suggestion that current laws may be modified in one of three ways. Anencephalic infants could be declared legally dead as soon as their medical diagnosis is established beyond doubt (as in Germany). Or, the present standard of whole brain death could be changed to make permanent loss of consciousness the critical brain function defining life and death (higher-brain criterion for death). Or, the law could be modified to permit donation of organs from anencephalic newborns while they are still living (as the only exception to the dead-donor rule).[92]

Muslim fuqaha have come very close to this 'contemporary' debate.[93] Ghazali (d. 505/1111) contemplated the meaning of 'the soul leaving the body.' He surmised that the limbs, and other parts, are instruments of the soul: to move, to hear, and to see, to comprehend. The *conscious soul*, which imparts function to these parts: *is life*. If all the parts (the instruments or tools) are not responsive then there is no life, as death is when there is no emotive force to all parts of the body *(al-mawt* (death) *zamantun mutlaqa* (is total loss) *fi al-a'adi kulliha* (of control over all parts)).[94]

His philosophy about 'the *conscious soul*, which imparts function *is life*' almost coincides with the concepts of brain death, and the call of redefining death taking into consideration consciousness.

'Irreversible loss of consciousness' may, indeed, 'one day become the mark of death' but that day is not here yet - certainly not in a legal sense.[95]

Some contemporary Muslim fuqaha utilised his concept to accept brain death as death, notwithstanding even the involuntary twitches that may occur. They further supported their argument by the Islamic viewpoint that if someone is fatally injured, or wounded by a beast or a person *(nafaz al-maqatil)*, and another person kills him: then that second person is not culpable for murder *(qisas)*. They quote Zarkashi (745-794 AH):

> Life is present when the body is under the control of the soul, which also entails voluntary movement. If someone is fatally wounded, by the removal of his vital organs *(akhraja hashwatahu wa 'abanaha)* he is considered dead. A third person who finishes him off is not culpable for *qisas*, even if the would-be deceased was involuntarily twitching, because he was already counted as dead *(fi hukm al-mayyit)*.[96]

3.3 Foetal tissue transplants and genetically engineered organ donation

The subject matter of this subsection is intricately linked with reproduction, experimentation on embryos, and cloning.

Transplantation therapy using foetal neural tissue has been tried for Parkinson's disease:

> Normal adult nerve cells cannot replicate whereas foetal cells are actively growing and multiplying; theoretically, therefore, an implanted foetal cell will grow and provide a source of important cellular metabolites that are often deficient in the aged...foetal brain cells must be immature and are ideally harvested at 10-14 weeks' gestation. Thus...excluding some very rare opportunities derived from natural spontaneous miscarriage, the process is inextricably linked with abortion...the individual brain cells must be viable in themselves; can it then be said that the foetus is dead when subjected to surgery? Here, we must rely to an extent on semantic and pragmatic arguments. A 10-14 week-old foetus is not viable - it has no organised heart beat, its lungs cannot conceivably function as oxygenators...

> But,...it is still very difficult to answer the question: 'Is it brain dead?' in the affirmative.[97]

Some Muslim fuqaha have made viability as a condition for liability as, Ahmad ibn Hanbal and al-Muzani:

There must be a time set before which the foetus is considered not viable *(la yuta sawaru baqa'uhu)*.[98]

The views of Muslim fuqaha which have a particular bearing on this chapter concern the period of gestation, before 120 days. Abortion in that period is penalty free, though not blameless, unless there is a reason for it. This period, if accepted, allows for a lot of research. But is research allowed during these weeks? What happens to surplus embryos in infertility clinics in the Muslim world today? Experimentation is an integral part of infertility treatments. The use of intra-uterine devices (loop) for family planning are essentially preventing the *embryo* from clinging to the uterine wall, and thus leading to its expulsion during its first week or so.

The majority of Muslim fuqaha have:

(a) Allowed the use of the loop as a 'contraceptive' device, whereas in actual fact a fertilised ovum (or ova), five days old, might have been denied further development; by making the uterus uninhabitable.

(b) They have accepted fertilisation of the ova of a wife by her husband's sperm, in the treatment of 'infertility'; which inevitably leads to the existence of surplus embryos (up to ten), a fact well known to contemporary Muslim fuqaha. None of them is in favour of implanting all the ten or so embryos in the wife's uterus, although that is possible as the embryos can be kept in deep freeze and used at intervals. So it means that they have tacitly accepted the 'legality' of their destruction.

(c) If it is accepted that surplus embryos can be destroyed in principal, what is the time limit set for that?

(d) Since their fate is destruction: can they be used in fertility research within that time limit?

This type of research has enabled the couple in question to have their offspring in the first place. But in 1990 there was a decision by *Majma'a al-Fiqh al-Islami*, that embryonic foetal tissue could be used with certain provisos.[99]

4. Conclusion

Recently, 'transgenic' transplantation is being discussed. Developments in genetic engineering have resulted in the development of mammals particularly pigs that can be harvested for major organs to transplant into human beings.[100] The field is advancing so rapidly that the lay press, the Internet, and the rest of the media are all engaged in the finer details of the most recent developments.

It is understood that Yanagimachi (University of Hawaii) was able to clone the mouse using a technique slightly different from that employed by scientists at the Roslin Institute (where Dolly the sheep was cloned)...

Scientists hope cloning, once perfected, will enable revolutions in transplant surgery, allowing skin and organs to be grown to order without fear of patient rejection. It will also be a powerful tool in finding cures for genetic diseases.

But fears that cloning techniques could eventually be used in the creation of carbon-copy humans have prompted western governments, including Britain, to ban such research.[101]

Furthermore, artificial-kidney machines are now being laced with genetically modified (engineered), living pigs' cells; which make them more efficient and effective in haemodialysis.[102] Can such machines be used in accordance with Islamic fiqh? Again, the general rule is that swine parts are not to be used; but there is an exemption for cases of necessity or need, providing that there was no other alternative, as advanced by Imam an-Nawawi (d. 676 AH) the Shafi'i faqih.[103]

Islamic fiqh is there to legislate for different peoples at different times. So long as rulings do not permit the impermissible, or prohibit what was allowed, people can seek what is best for them.[104]

Queen Rania of Jordan, Patron of 'The National Society of Organ Donation and Transplantation' attended its first meeting held in July 1999; in which Imam Dr. Ahmad Halil stated that, "according to Islamic fiqh it is permissible to donate and transplant human organs."[105]

In Saudi Arabia, organs from two brain-dead 'persons' were used for transplantation for six needy patients, between 10 and 15 July 1999.[106]

These events are very important. The decision to accept brain death as an end to life is particularly significant. Both usher the transition from academic debate into formulation of general rules of law in two of the most contentious areas of medical jurisprudence. They are especially *"avant guarde."*

Notes

1. Asfahani, *Kitab al-Aghani*, 1983, vol. 5:211.
2. *Sunan Abi Dawud*, 1973, vol. 4:434.
3. 'Ayad, al-Qadi'Ayad, *Sharh ash-Shifa' wa Sharh al-'Ala 'ala al-Qari,*'Dar al-Kutub al-'Ilmia, Beirut, (n.d.), vol. 1:65," Qatada ibn an-Nu'man was injured in the battle of Uhud, his eye was dislocated until it dangled on his cheek. The Prophet ﷺ replaced it and it healed. His great grandson, later, introduced himself to Caliph 'Umar ibn 'Abd al-'Aziz by the poem, 'I am the son of the one whose eye ran (dangled) on his cheek, to be re-set in its place by the Prophet.' (*Ana ibn man salat 'ala al-khadi 'aynuhu: faruddat bi kafi al-Mustafa ayyama raddu*).
4. *Sunan Ibn Majah*, 1953, vol. 2:1396.
5. 'Asqalani, *Fath al-Bari: al-Bukhari*, 1988, vol. 10:110; and *Sunan Abi Dawud*, 1973, vol. 10:315.
6. Murray,"The Origins and Consequences of Organ Transplantation,"*Bulletin of the American College of Surgeons (ACS)*, vol. 80,1995, p. 16.
7. Ibid., pp.15-16. (Billingham, Brent, and Medwar,"Activity acquired tolerance to foreign cells"*Nature*, 172:603, 1953.
8. Moore,"Origins...of Organ Transplantation: Introduction" *Bulletin ACS*, 1995:13.
9. Parrott,"Transplantation" in *International Journal of Intensive Care*, London, 1996 Vol. 3 No. 4, p.126.
10. Murray,"The Origins ...of Organ Transplantation," *Bulletin* ACS, vol. 80, no. 8, 1995:15.
11. Ibid. p.17-18.
12. Murray,"The Origins ...of Organ Transplantation,"*Bulletin American College of Surgeons*, vol. 80, no. 8, 1995:19; Medwar,"Transplantation of tissues and organs: Introduction," *Brit Med J*, 21:97, 1965; and Teperman, "Transplantation,"*Journal American College of Surgeons*, vol. 188, no. 2, 1999:186.
13. Murray,"The Origins ...of Organ Transplantation," *Bulletin ACS*, vol. 80, no. 8, 1995:20-21; Cartwright,"The Pig, The Transplant Surgeon, and the Nuffield Council,"*Med. L. Rev.*,4, Autumn 1996:250, (the real prospect of the transplantation of pig's heart into humans); and Teperman, "Transplantation,"*Journal ACS*, vol. 188, no. 2, February 1999:184-190.
14. Q. 5:32.
15. Q. 59:9.

16. Ghazali, (d. 505/1111), *al-Mustasfa*, 1935, vol. 1:139.
17. Shatibi, (d. 790 AH.), *al-Muwafaqat*, 1975, vol. 2:8-11.
18. Jamal,"Human Organs Transplants," *Contemporary Jurisprudence J.*, 1990:21. Also see appendices.
19. Qattan, "Islamic viewpoint on Human Organ Transplantation," *Majallat al-Azhar*, No. 50, 1997:763.
20. Q. 6:120 (tr. Bewley); Q. 2:173, and Q. 16:115 (**But if someone is forced ...without desiring to or going to excess in it, your Lord is Ever-Forgiving, Most Merciful.**).
21. As-Suyuti, *al-Ashbah wa n'-Nadha'ir*, Dar Ihya' al-Kutub al-Arabia, Cairo, p. 93; and Ibn Nujaim, *al-Ashbah wa n'-Nadha'ir*, Dar al-Kutub al-Ilmia, Beirut, p. 85, cited by Quttan.
22. Malik, *al-Muwatta,'* (ed.), Sa'd, 1983:638; and *Sunan Ibn Majah*, 1953, vol. 2:784.
23. As-Suyuti, *al-Ashbah wa n'-Nadha'ir*, pp. 3-7, 92, 95, and Ibn Nujaim, *al-Ashbah wa n'-Nadha'ir*, p. 89.
24. As-Suyuti, *al-Ashbah*, p. 97; and Ibn Nujaim, *al-Ashbah*, p. 91.
25. As-Suyuti, *al-Ashbah*, p. 97; and Ibn Nujaim, *al-Ashbah*, p. 90.
26. Bahwati, *Kashaf al-Qina'a*, (1319 AH), vol. 2:146.
27. *Sunan Ibn Majah*, 1952, vol. 1:516.
28. Q. 5:32 (author's introduction of the opposing argument in *Kashaf al-Qina'a* and the author's rebuttal).
29. *hadith*, "Deeds are judged according to intentions" in Jakni, *Bukhari and Muslim*, 1967, vol. 1:7.
30. Jakni, *Bukhari and Muslim*, 1967, vol. 1:193, *hadith*, "*da 'uni ma taraktukum fa inna ahlaka man kan qablakum su'aluhum*"; and in *Sahih Muslim*, 1987, Vol. 4:509; and *Majmu 'at al-hadith an-Najdia*, (ed.) Rashid Rida, (1383 AH), p. 235 "*kuriha lakum kathrat as-su'al, wa qeela wa qal*'" ("it is disliked for you to pose incessant questions about things that did not happen") "*amma lam yaqa'a min al-ahdath*".
31. Alamgir, *al-Fatwa al-Hindiya*, (1310 AH), vol. 5:354, Damad, (Sheikhi Zada), *Majma'a al-Anhur*, Al-Tiba'a al-'Amira, vol. 2:525; Ibn al-Humam, *Sharh Fath al-Qadir*, (1299 AH), vol. 2:65.
32. Kasani, *Bada'i*, 1910, vol. 5:142-143.
33. *Sunan Ibn Majah*, 1953, vol. 2:1193-1194, four *hadith* allowing its use, and a fifth *hadith* disallowing it: *hadith* 3609-3613. (There is an error in the index of *Sunan Ibn Majah* p. 1472, *hadith* referred to as 3906).
34. Sabiq, *Fiqh as-Sunnah*, 1995, vol. 3:96. (1st.ed., 1947).
35. An-Nawawi, *al-Majmu'a Sharh al-Muhadhdhab*, Dar al-Fikr li't-Taba'a wa'n-Nashr, vol. 9:48.
36. Shinqiti, *Ahkam al-Jiraha*, 1997:401-402; citing an-Nawawi, *al-Majmu'a*, Taba'a al-Muniriyya, Cairo, vol. 3:138.

[37] Q. 2:173, and Q. 16:115. (tr. Bewley).
[38] Muhammad Khalil, Cairo, in *Ash-Sharq Al-Awsat*, London 14 November 1999, p. 1, col. 3-4, bottom page.
[39] Mason and McCall Smith, *Law and Medical Ethics*, 1994:291.
[40] Ryan, Kenneth J., "Ethics and the transplant surgeon," Bulletin *ACS*, vol. 80, June 1995:12.
[41] Hubbard, L, 'The Baby Fae Case' (1987) 6 Med Law 385.
[42] Carwright, Will, "The Pig, The Transplant Surgeon, and the Nuffield Council," *Med. L. Rev.*, 4, Autumn 1996, pp. 250-269, at p. 250.
[43] *Sunan Abi Dawud*, 1973:197, hadith "Do not use cauterisation," Jurist Khattabi interpreted it as: "treatment is impermissible *(mahdhur)* if it involves fearsome danger *(al-mukhawaf minhu)*."
[44] Baghawi, al-Hussein ibn Mas'ud, *Sharh as-Sunnah*, vol. 12:147; cited by Shinqiti, *Ahkam*, 1997:119.
[45] Ghazali, *Ihya,'* vol. 4:283-286; and Ibn Taymiyya, *Majmu'a al-Fatawa*, vol. 18:12.
[46] Ash-Shafi'i, *al-Umm*, 1993, vol. 6:239, and 244
[47] Ghazali, *Ihya'*, Misriya-Lubnania, vols. 2:114, and 4:300; Ibn 'Abidin, *Hashiyat*, 1966, vol. 6:69; and Mubarak, *At-Tadawi wa al-Mas'uliyya at-Tibbiyya*, 1991:175.
[48] 'Asqalani, *Fath al-Bari al-Bukhari*, 1988, vol. 10:110, "Allah has not created a disease for which He did not create a cure."
[49] Q. 16:90; 4:135; 5:8; 7:181; 5:8; 4:58; 16:76.
[50] Q. 26:182; 55:9; 6:152; 7:185; 11:85; 42:17; 57:24 (in this last the Book i.e. 'law,' the balance i.e. 'justice,' are mentioned along with the might vested in iron).
[51] Jakni, *Bukhari and Muslim*, 1967, vol. 1: 7; *Sahih al-Bukhari*, (tr. Khan), 1994, pp. 49 and 79; and in *Sunan Ibn Majah*, 1953, vol. 2:1413. (hadith, narrated by 'Umar ibn al-Khattab).
[52] It can actually diminish the risk of heart attacks (by removing some of the iron ions from the donor's blood: one of the reasons why menstruating females, have fewer heart attacks than males); there are other benefits: as for people with excess of red blood cells, and it may lessen the risk of stroke. [This is one possible explanation for the benefits of old treatments such as blood-letting and cupping-Ed.]
[53] *Evening Standard* 3 October 2000, p.1 "Ethical controversy as doctors custom-design a life. A test-tube baby custom designed to save the life of his six-year-old sister has been created by doctors using controversial genetic screening," and at the bottom of p.2 columns 2,3, and 4, "Baby born to be a bone marrow donor."
[54] Q. 4:29; (tr. Bewley)
[55] Q. 2:194; (tr. Bewley).

278   The Fiqh of Medicine

56 Q. 17:70; (tr. Bewley).
57 Ibn'Abidin, *Hashiyat*, 1966, vol. 5:58, and 6:385; "a sale {transaction} must fulfill three requirements: (1) Free will (mutual consent); (2) Object (place) must be permissible, e.g. land, a house, it cannot be *any* human being or part of; and (3) Reason for the transaction must be legal (cannot rent a house for gambling)."
58 Q. 2:255. (tr. Bewley).
59 Q. 4:29, **"You who have iman! do not consume one another's property by false means, but only by means of mutually agreed trade."** (tr. Bewley).
60 Q. 4:6 **"Keep a close check on orphans until they reach a marriageable age, then if you perceive that they have sound judgement hand over their property to them. Do not consume it extravagantly and precipitately before they come of age."** (Tr. Bewley). See Ibn'Abidin, *Hashiya*, 1966, vol. 6:390, and Sabiq, *Fiqh as-Sunnah*, 1995, vol. 3:294.
61 Alamgir, *Al-Fatawa al-Hindiya*, (1310 AH), vol. 5:358.
62 Ibn Muflih, *Kitab al-Furu'*, 1962, vol. 4:451-452.
63 *Sunan Ibn Majah*, 1952, vol. 1:516 (narrated by Umm Salama).
64 *hadith*, *Sahih al-Bukhari*, (Khan) Kazi Publications, 1986 vol. 2 p. 24; and three *hadith* in *Sahih Muslim*, 1987, vol. 2:353-354.
65 Davies, *Medical Law*, 1996:354-5.
66 Davies, *Medical Law*, 1996:357-358.
67 Q. 16:125, (tr. Bewley); Pickthall translates it as **"Call unto the way of thy Lord with wisdom and fair exhortation, and reason with them in the better way,"** and Y.'Ali as, **"Invite (all) to the way of thy Lord with wisdom and beautiful preaching; and argue with them in ways that are best."**
68 Q. 4:118, (tr. Bewley).
69 Q. 17:70, (tr. Bewley).
70 *Sunan Ibn Majah*, 1952, vol. 1:516.
71 *Sunan Ibn Majah*, 1953, vol. 2:953.
72 Zarkashi, (d. 794 AH), *al-Manthur*, (1402 AH), vol. 3:238. ("Human parts, irrespective of creed, are precluded from the contract of sale" in Ibn'Abidin, *Hashiyat*, 1966, vol. 5:58, and 6:385."
73 Baihaqi, *al-Sunan al-Kubra*, (1344 AH). vol. 9:133.
74 Shinqiti, *Ahkam al-Jiraha*, 1997:354-355.
75 Decission of 'Fatwa Committee,' Al-Azhar, 5th. December 1979: in *Majalla al-Buhuth al-Fiqhiyya al-Mu'asira* (Contemporary Jurisprudence Research Journal), No. 18, July - August - September 1993, Riyadh, Saudi Arabia, p. 66.
76 Q. 5:32 (tr. Bewley).
77 Q. 59:9.

[78] Hindi, *Kanz al-'Ummal*, 1971, vol. 10:131.
[79] Shinqiti, *Ahkam al-Jiraha*, 1997:355-356.
[80] Shinqiti, *Ahkam al-Jiraha*, 1997:356; and refers to an article by Sheikh al-Azhar, Sheikh Jad al-Haq, "Human organ transplantation," *Majallat al-Azhar*, vol. 9, Ramadan Issue, 1403 AH.
[81] Muhammad Khalil, Cairo, reported in *Ash-Sharq Al-Awsat*, London, 14 November 1999, p. 1 columns 3-4, bottom of page and in p. 16 columns 1-6, top of the page.
[82] Shinqiti, *Ahkam al-Jiraha*, 1997:393.
[83] Shinqiti, *Ahkam al-Jiraha*, 1997:394, and 395.
[84] *Sahih Muslim*, 1987, vol. 5:223.
[85] Madkour, *al-Madkhal*, 1966:107-108; and Abu Zahra, *Malik*, 1963-1964, p. 210.
[86] Shinqiti, *Ahkam al-Jiraha*, 1997:393-394.
[87] Davies, *Textbook on Medical Law*, 1996:354.
[88] *Euthanasia*, BMA, 1988:23; see (*Airedale NHS Trust v Bland* [1993] 1 All ER 821, **866**, 880-3)
[89] *Sunan Ibn Majah*, 1953, vol. 2: 1425; also in as-Suyuti, *Sahih al-Jami' as-Saghir wa Ziyadatuh*, 1969, vol. 1:398-399, and 411.
[90] hadith, "*al-qatil la yarith*" in *Sunan Ibn Majah*, 1953, vol. 2:883-884.
[91] Lafreniere, Rene, "End-of-Life Issues: Anencephalic Infants as Organ Donors," *Journal of the American College of Surgeons*, vol. 187, no. 4, October 1998, pp. 443-447.
[92] Ibid. p. 444, (Lafreniere, 1998:444); see also Holgrewe, W., Beller, F. K., Buchholz B., et al., "Kidney transplantation from anencephalic donors," *N Engl J Med.*, 1987, 316, 1069-1070.
[93] Shinqiti, *Ahkam al-Jiraha*, 1997:342-354. But Shinqiti equates brain death with anencephaly for his 'legal' debate (p. 353). In fact medically they are different. In brain death we are dealing with death, in anencephaly there is human life. For anencephaly see text above.
[94] Ghazali, *Ihya,'* vol. 4:525, Dar al-Misriya al-Lubnania, Cairo, and Ilmiya, Beirut.
[95] Mason & McCall Smith, *Law and Medical Ethics*, 1994:334.
[96] Shinqiti, *Ahkam al-Jiraha*, 1997:352; citing Zarkashi, *Al-Manthur*, (1402 AH), vol. 2:105.
[97] Mason and McCall Smith, *Law and Medical Ethics*, 1994:310-311.
[98] Ibn Qudama (d, 620 AH), *al-Mughni*, 1981, vol. 7:816.
[99] (1990) Decision (58/7/6), in the Meeting of 14-20 March 1990 Jeddah; see Appendix H and *Contemporary Jurisprudence Research J.*, 2nd. Year, No. 6, Aug.-Sept.-Oct. 1990:144, Riyadh, Saudi Arabia.
[100] Cartwright, Will, "The Pig, The Transplant Surgeon, and the Nuffield Council" *Med. L. Rev.*, 4, Autumn, 1996, pp. 250-269.

[101] *The Sunday Times* 5 July 1998 p. 1.1 column 8, and back page columns 4-6.

[102] *The Times* 29 April 1999, p. 4, column, 3.

[103] Shinqiti, *Ahkam al-Jiraha*, 1997:401-402, cites an-Nawawi, *Al-Majmu'a*, al-Munirya, vol. 3:138.

[104] Q. 88:22 **"You are not in control of them."** (tr. Bewley); and *hadith*, 'If the matter is about your own lives' concerns then it is up to you, and if it concerns your deen it is for myself' in *Sunan Ibn Majah*, 1953, vol. 2:825.

[105] *Ash-Sharq Al-Awsat*, 14 July 1999, p. 16 (upper half), columns 6 and 7. The meeting was presided by Chief Justice Izzed Din al-Khatib at-Tamimi, Consultant to the King for Islamic Affairs.

[106] *Ash-Sharq Al-Awsat*, 26 July 1999, p. 18 (lower half), columns 7 and 8, Muwafaq an-Nuwysir, reporting the work of "The Saudi Centre for Organ Transplantation": Director, Dr. Faysal Shahin.

Chapter Ten
Conclusion

This work examined the compatibility of Islamic fiqh with modern Western world laws. The example of modern law chosen was, mostly, Anglo-American common law. A personal reason for this is its accessibility in more than one sense because English is almost the *lingua franca* in this age of the World Wide Web.

The focus of the analysis has been medical fiqh-jurisprudence as it relates to responsibility and liability and as it impinges on developments in the field.

There is a revival of interest in Islam, in many communities in the post-colonial, and post-cold war era. Social inequalities, political injustices, and lack of development in the economic field have to be addressed.

These communities are looking for solutions to their problems, and laws to govern them. It is natural that they use what they possess: their customs, cultures, traditions, religion, faith, and belief.

Islam has elements of *'demokrat,'* in that the people may not be denied a hearing when they give counsel. The Qur'an describes the Muslim community as one who **"manage their affairs by mutual consultation"** *(wa amruhum shura baynahum)*.[1] Allah requires Muslims to adopt Islam to govern all facets of their lives.[2] Allah also calls upon the people of the Torah,[3] and Injil (the revelation granted 'Isa, peace be upon him),[4] to govern themselves according to the guidelines of their Books.

Allah made provisions for Muslims and non-Muslims to be integrated into one community: the Zoroastrians in their time were treated like people of the Book.[5] The rights of others are fully preserved in Islam. Differences are recognised, yet justice reigns.

> Among His Signs is the creation of the heavens and the earth and the variety of your languages and colours. There are certainly Signs in that for every being.[6]
>
> Mankind! We created you from a male and female, and made you into peoples and tribes so that you might come to know each other.

> The noblest among you in Allah's sight is the one with the most taqwa.[8]

> We have appointed a law and a practice for every one of you. Had Allah willed, He would have made you a single community, but He wanted to test you regarding what has come to you.[8]

Chapter two examined the developments and sources of Islamic fiqh, and the dynamism therein, the schools of thought that came about from these developments, in search for common ground in making laws.

Shari'ah is Allah's given law as revealed in the Qur'an and embodied in the *Sunnah*. Muslims are ordered not to go against Shari'ah, but otherwise they are allowed to find rules to run their life with ease and comfort. Since Shari'ah is for every Muslim, in every place and for all time it becomes mandatory on Muslims to exert themselves to find the necessary rules that would enable them to run their affairs providing that these rules do not violate the Shari'ah.

Muslim fuqaha contributed profusely for this purpose. But none of them formed a school during his lifetime to be followed as such, and least of all to be the base of a sect or a cult.

The Qur'an and Sunnah are the sources of the law. But, as it was succinctly put by Shahrastani:

> Prescriptions and injunctions are limited, but occurrences are unlimited. Since the limited cannot cater for the unlimited, and since the Qur'an and *Sunnah* did not prescribe for every event, nor do we expect them to; it becomes mandatory to exercise our own judgement to find solutions to problems of our times.[9]

Chapter three and the following six chapters focused on the issues of medical fiqh. The issues were examined in the light of Islamic fiqh, compared and contrasted with current Western laws represented mostly by English law.

The Qur'an and *Sunnah* are not medical or science books. They are not compendiums of legal ordinances for the details of life situations. They are:

> a guide, a mercy, and glad tidings, to those who are prepared to think, analyse and deduce.[10]

On balance Islamic fiqh rests on the important maxim, "what is not expressly forbidden is allowed." *(al aslu fi'l-ashya' al-ibaha).*[11]

Some of the more major of my findings, syntheses, analyses, and interpretations are briefly summarised below:

The first finding is the closeness of Islamic fiqh to English law in matters of medical practice and liability. Islamic law and English law agree on the main theme of duty of care, what constitutes a breach of that duty, and the compensation for harm, which is caused by that breach. Both laws have accepted that if there is no negligence there is no liability.

Ash-Shafi'i (d. 820 CE), said:

> In cases of bloodletting, or circumcision, or animal husbandry if the practitioner has done what those who are proficient in that craft usually do to affect a beneficial result, then he is not liable...[12]

This may be compared with the Bolam test. The case held that:

> A doctor is not guilty of negligence if he has acted in accordance with a practice accepted as proper by a responsible body of medical men skilled in that particular art.[13]

But Islamic law goes further to compensate harm that ensues from error, mistake and misadventure without there being negligence. English law is yet to accept that. But at the same time English law accepts the Bolam test, which many assume, is weighed against and loses the victim redress for obvious harm if he cannot prove negligence. There may be a point for Islamic fiqh in separating mistake, error, and misadventure from negligence. This is a point not lost to 'English' jurists.

Whereas "the overwhelming majority of malpractice cases are brought under the law of negligence"[14], Taylor said:

> It has been said many times by many judges that negligence should be distinguished from 'a mere error of judgement,'...[15]

And, Lord Denning summed up:

> the uncertainties inherent in the practice of medicine were such that a doctor, aware of a law which regards errors of clinical judgement as negligent, would sense this as 'a dagger at his back' when undertaking treatment...[16]

The second point is consequent to the assumption of Muslim fuqaha that damage can occur without a wrong. An authorised and competent medical practitioner who performed according to the accepted methods in the profession and was not errant is not liable at all. "Executing one's duty *(wajib)* does not entail a guarantee of safety or success."[17] It may be argued that, "in fact, it is controversial whether Islamic law accepted the idea of strict liability at all,..."[18]

For this debate I have split the issue into two zones: dealing with the living, human or animal, and dealing with solid objects. In dealing with the living there is no strict liability, because living organisms have a reaction of their own to the stimulus applied; whereas objects are devoid of this:

> In all crafts, men are liable for handling objects, be it piercing pearls, engraving stones, making swords, or baking bread. But the physician and the veterinarian are exempt so long as they are qualified, are within the bounds of the permission given, and perform according to the accepted methods.[19]

Sir John Donaldson, comments on, 'the continuing clamour for no-fault compensation,'[20] and Lewis, finds no philosophical justification for it.[21]

Modern laws, accept unforeseeable causes as a defence against awarding damages.[22]

The third point concerns vicarious liability. Many Muslim fuqaha quote:

> **What each self earns is for itself alone. No burden-bearer can bear another's burden.**[23]

"...thus suppressing all vicarious responsibility."[24] But I would argue that, although Allah holds everyone responsible for his own deeds: Islam fosters interdependence, and comradeship in the community for its own welfare. Hence it adopted the system of *'aqila*, where the relatives help pay the *diya*. 'Umar, the second Caliph developed that into *ahl ad-diwan* (those with you in the office) e.g. it is possible that we might equate this with the NHS in the case of medical practitioners. In the doctrine of *qasama*, if a life is lost amongst a clan, fifty able-bodied male, clan-members are required under oath to state that they have not committed the crime nor do they know who did. Despite that, they must pay *diya* (compensation) for that life. This can find a modern application in situations such as when a patient in theatre, or someone in custody, comes to harm.

> The complexity of modern medical procedures means that the patient who wakes up from the anaesthetic with some form of paralysis...
>
> It would be unfair on the patient to have to prove negligence...[25]

The fourth point I find is that Islamic fiqh (1000 years ago), allowed experts to undertake novel and unusual procedures without fear of litigation:

> *Faqih* Shams al-Ai'mma al-Halawani was asked about a girl who fell

off a roof and injured her head. Many attending surgeons said, "If you allow her head to be opened she will die." One of them said, "If you do not open her head, she will die today. I will do that and cure her." He opened her head. She died a day later. Is he liable? Al-Halawani said, "No." He was asked, "What if he had promised to cure her?" He replied, "Even though."[26]

Which is comparable to modern day thinking:

This does not mean that innovative practice is negligent merely because it is unusual,…but seeking to improve on normal standards is the opposite of negligence providing that it is done properly.[27]

The fifth point concerns euthanasia. Euthanasia deals with *termination* of life, which is neither permitted in Islamic law nor in common law. Medical practice should be concerned with research into the relief of pain, including anxiety, fear, phobia and depression. The British hospice concept deals with all aspects of dying with dignity, and is consistent with Islamic values.

Farquharson J stated:

However serious a case may be;… no doctor has the right to kill it.

There is no special law in this country that places doctors in a separate category and gives them extra protection over the rest of us.

…they are given no special power … to commit an act which causes death, which is another way of saying killing.[28]

Glanville Williams said, "The law does not leave the issue in the hands of doctors; it treats euthanasia as murder."[29]

In the Netherlands, the situation changed from:

Euthanasia is explicitly and apparently absolutely [sic.] prohibited by two articles of the Dutch Criminal Code. Article 293 prohibits killing a person at his request…Article 294 prohibits assisting a suicide (suicide itself is not a crime in the Dutch law)…[30]

When it has been legalised by the parliament on 29th November 2000. [Note that during the editing of this book, the Dutch altered this section of their criminal code to permit Euthanasia-Ed.]

Muslim fuqaha, although agreed that permission to kill does not make for any lighter punishment in the Hereafter, have different views as regards what could be the law. There are four points of view: the first, is that it is murder and *qisas* (retaliation) is due; the second, is that it is manslaughter and that only *diya* (compensation) is due; the third, is that there is no punishment since it was permitted; the fourth is the interesting view of the Shafi'i school, where only expiation is necessary. This view goes beyond the law and hopes that even in the Hereafter there may be a chance for forgiveness; as expiation is purely a personal religious matter. [31]

The sixth point I make concerns abortion. All Muslim fuqaha find abortion after 120 days impermissible. The majority see it as a disapproved deed *(makruh)* before then; but a few find it 'impermissible at any time.'

Fuqaha who hold such a viewpoint will have to consider whether an intra-uterine devise (the loop), is a contraceptive procedure, or whether it is, as I think, destruction of an embryo before it fixes itself to the uterus (about nine days of gestation). On the other hand those who tolerate abortion within 120 days of gestation face the challenge of allowing experimentation with the human embryo.

This is closely linked with fertilisation and the treatment of infertility, which deals with the problems of experimentation with embryos and the destruction of surplus ones. These embryos are less than 120 days old which is held by the majority of Muslim fuqaha *(al-jumhur)* as the beginning of human life, and the forty days landmark is held by some Maliki fuqaha, and it is not in utero to qualify for even the strictest of the Malikis who are against disturbing any pregnancy that has 'settled in utero.'

This discourse might have given a positive reply to the question: "Is Islamic fiqh compatible with common law?"

Numerous issues have been examined and many situations have been analysed in the medical field. It is always possible, on almost every issue or count, to find similarities between what is put forward by Muslim fuqaha and Western laws. The aim of this work is not to say that Islamic fiqh had it all. No; rather it is to put forward that Islamic fiqh is compatible with present day views in medical law; and has the ability to move on with time, as Islam itself is not restrictive. There are considerable areas of agreement; and on many occasions Islamic fiqh was more accommodating than 'common law' as it evolves.

Once again this is put forward only to prove that there is nothing in Islam that precludes its communities from joining other communities of the world while being firmly bound by the Qur'an and *Sunnah*.

Laws in the Western world are not identical, nor congruent in every detail; yet they are compatible. There is room to join the international medical forums, the associations, and the leagues that organise the profession. This is not because of a change in Islamic fiqh engineered by myself, but all of it was always there, as referenced.

A corollary to the first question is considered below:

Is it possible to implement Islamic fiqh in these modern times, and to take it as a viable option for the future?

> One of the best-known and most widely held ideas in the social sciences is the secularisation thesis: in industrial and industrializing societies, the influence of religion diminishes. ...
>
> One thing, however, is clear: the secularisation thesis does not apply to Islam. In the course of the last one hundred years, the hold of Islam over the minds and hearts of believers has not diminished and, by some criteria, has probably increased.[32]

'Western' secular laws shun Islamic laws: they do not do so because they are based on Christianity. They have shunned Christianity before. The reason may be cultural.

> The adjective 'Promethean' is often applied to the Renaissance ideal, and the Greek myth of Prometheus has great significance if we wish to understand Western culture. It is a myth that could never conceivably have arisen or been tolerated within the sphere of Islamic thought and Muslim imagination. Prometheus stole the gift of fire from 'the gods.'
>
> The myth of Prometheus dominated the Renaissance mind and, in a sense, dominates Western culture today: God does not give – man takes.
>
> The exclusion of the Divine...gave rise, in due course, to an entirely secular philosophy, and the first of these 'modern' philosophers was Rene Descartes (b. 1596).
>
> It is from Descartes that Western culture, and above all, science, has inherited the dualistic view of the world, which is contrary to Islam in root and in branch.[33]

The idea that Islam poses a threat to Western culture is considered below:

> In the West, the 'challenge' of Islamic movements has been construed, variously, as the rise of a new threat equal to communism, or as part of the 'clash of civilisations'...
>
> The argument,...that 'Islam' constitutes a strategic challenge to the West is nonsense – not least because of the weak economic condition of the supposedly menacing countries. The theory of a clash of civilisations operates with a deterministic concept of 'civilisation,' and understates the degree to which conflict is between people of similar orientation.[34]

These are important reasons for the lack of empathy with Islamic fiqh by modern Western laws. But the main reason lies within Muslim societies. It is basically: ignorance, lack of economic development, and political ineptitude. These factors are intertwined and they interplay as cause-and-effect. Ignorance is predominant in the spheres of science, technology, and culture. Lack of economic development, a consequence of multiple factors: colonisation, international debt, tyranny, corruption, and ignorance, is crippling these societies. Political ineptitude, because of all the aforementioned conditions, makes for poor relations with others.

From time to time there are calls to implement Islam in one place or another. Implementation of Islamic rule should not begin with the implementation of a penal code or *hudud* in a poverty-stricken, disease-ridden, and destitute community.

The Prophet ﷺ spent over ten years in Makkah teaching people the spirit of Islam. The essence of which is, **"enjoin right and forbid wrong."**[35] In the first Islamic government in Madinah the principles of equality before Allah and before the law, justice, and social care ranked supreme. Nobody was above the law nor was anybody beneath it. All rights were unequivocally protected. Education, fair opportunities, the sharing of wealth by a wide range of qualities in the Islamic shari'ah from the pillar of the zakat to the encouragement of personal sadaqah, the application of the laws of inheritance which disperse wealth among heirs rather than concentrating it in a few hands, the preservation of human rights, the election of and allegiance to the ruler on the basis of his capabilities, and the pervasiveness of the practice of mutual consultation are integral parts of a community described as:

> You are the best nation ever to be produced before mankind. You enjoin the right, forbid the wrong and have iman in Allah.[36]

Allah has determined that people "**…manage their affairs by mutual consultation**,"[37] because He [Allah] is the one in command,[38] and He has ordained that man is His viceroy on earth.[39]

"It is He who made the earth submissive to you, so walk its broad trails and eat what it provides."[40] Man is to safeguard, shepherd and utilise what he needs on the whole globe. Islam is for everyone everywhere. Its message of freedom, equality before Allah and before the law, the fraternity of the muminun, and justice is universal.

Ideas of globalisation are not new. All Muslims and those who live under their governance are one people *(umma wahida)*. There would be enough in Islamic political theory for the adoption of genuinely human rights, protection for animal and other species, and care for the environment.

Justice entails that those who exercise power should do so for the furtherance of the shari'ah the essence of which is justice. The ruler of a muslim polity, or his appointed qadis, must make laws within the framework of the fiqh and with consultation with the people of knowledge, both the fuqaha and those with expertise in the relevant area. The polity will naturally interact and communicate with other Muslim polities, in order to reach further consensus on the basics.

The Ayatollah Muhammad 'Ali At-Taskhiery commenting on the debates in the 11th Session of the "International Islamic Fiqh Group" *(Majami'a al-Fiqh al-Islami al-'Aalami)*, a subsidiary of the "Islamic Congress" *(Munazamat al-Mu'tamar al-Islami)*, which was held recently in Bahrain, praised its continuous efforts to establish compatible grounds with *Majami' Ahl al-Bayt* so that the views of all schools *(madhahib)*, be they Hanafi, Maliki, Shafi'i, Hanbali, Imami Shi'ite, and Ibadi are drawn closer together if not united in their *fatwas* as regards contemporary legal issues including concerns in the fields of cloning and genetic engineering.[41]

Muslim polities should be an effective part of the world order.

Mankind! We created you from a male and female, and made you into peoples and tribes so that you might come to know each other.[42]

A ruler and his functionaries should honour treaties, and discharge duties. **"You who have iman! fulfil your contracts."**[43]

For a simpler goal and in order that Islamic fiqh may materialise, it needs to be approachable: it is not now; even to Arabic speaking people. It is a wealth of knowledge, and a mine of information. It is a useful and a rewarding heritage.

Those who feel sore about the way 'their' contribution has been overlooked may not have presented their case well or perhaps not even prepared it. Many developed countries spend money and time on cultural, educational, and vocational matters. Those interested in Islamic fiqh are to do the same. The beautiful and bountiful books of *Fiqh* need to be edited, translated, and made available through modern methods of retrieval and dissemination of information.

Al-Qarafi al-Maliki, said:

> To be fossilised in the past, is straying from the purpose of deen. This is not what was intended by our ancestors, and the learned men of our past.[44]

Islam teaches that truthfulness, honesty, transparency and informing others with tact and sensitivity, are the qualities of the messengers. This may entail the creation of an autonomous body like a UNESCO, which may utilise avenues of first league universities, other academic and professional bodies, and nation-states' councils of *fatwas* to create a consensus on issues, and formulate general rules of law. Thus addressing the chronic problem that has beset Islamic fiqh so far:

> In the main these works discussed questions of law on a case-by-case basis, presenting solutions from the different relevant sources of law and arguments for their application, and then indicating the solution for their particular school.
>
> None of these works attempts analysis of law and legal rules from first principles and few formulate general rules of law from the mass of particular instances.[45]

This was a stage in English Legal History:

> Decisions settled the matter in hand and were not expected to do more; they were not constrained by the past and did not fix rules for the future.[46]

On a closer focus it is suggested that the legal and medical professions should have platforms of contacts and interaction. This may take the form of joint university studies in 'medical law' between law and medical students, which may be structured, and academically rewarded. It should cover areas of common interest and shared responsibility. Such a relationship once established should be continued in postgraduate life.

The medical profession should be aware that the law that governs all other professions, and all other events in life, governs their profession as well. That duty rests, naturally, with the legal profession, just as medicine is the function of the medical profession, with the attendant provision of facts when required.

Finally it is suggested that there should be closer links and consultations between fuqaha and the medical profession in order to anticipate problems and work for a better understanding and solutions.

This is an Islamic duty. *"People of knowledge are the heirs to the Prophets."*[47]

Notes

1. Q. 42:35, (tr. Bewley).
2. Q. 5:48-50.
3. Q. 5:43-45.
4. Q. 5:46-47.
5. Qaradawi, *The Lawful...* 1960:62.
6. Q. 30:21 (tr. Bewley).
7. Q. 49:13 (tr. Bewley).
8. Q. 5:48 (tr. Bewley).
9. Shahrastani, *Al-Milal*, 1968, vol. 2:4.
10. Q. 16:89; and Q. 4:83; 16:43; 29:43; 30:22; and 35:28.
11. Borno, *al-Wajiz*, 1998:191-198; Abu Zahra, *Ibn Hanbal*, 1981:10, and Ramadan, *Islamic Law*, 1970:46.
12. Ash-Shafi'i, *al-Umm*, 1993, vol. 6:239.
13. *Bolam v. Frien HMC* [1957] 2 All ER 118.
14. Montgomery, *Health Care Law*, 1997:166.
15. Taylor, *Doctors and the Law*, 1976:80.
16. *Hatcher v Black* (1954) Davies, *Textbook on Medical Law*, 1996:87, citing [1980] 1All ER 650 at p. 658.
17. Sarakhsi, *al-Mabsut*, vol. 16:13-14.
18. Edge, Ian, 'The Development of Decennial Liability in Egypt' in *Islamic Law* (ed.), Heer, 1990:173.
19. Ibn Rushd, *Bidayat, al-Kulliyat*, vol. 2:255. But at the same time he points out that Abu Muhammad Abdel Wahab, of the Maliki school rejects that, and holds the practitioner liable.
20. Lewis, *Medical Negligence*, 1994:ix.
21. Lewis, *Medical Negligence*, 1994:444.
22. Lewis, *Medical Negligence*, 1994:437-439."The EC Product Liability Directive (85/374/EEC), Art. 7 (e)." UK "The Consumer Protection Act 1987." The Government enacted the 'development risks' defense." The Swedish system does not cover misfortunes which were within the area of forseseeable risk of a medically justified act."
23. Q. 6:166; 17:15; 35:18; 39:7; 53:38.
24. Ramadan, *Islamic Law*, (1970:65).
25. Davies, *Textbook of Medical Law*, 1996:95.
26. *Faqih* al-Halawani (d. 456/1064) Ibn Qadi Samawa, *Jami'a al-Fusilien*, (1300 AH), vol. 2:186.

Conclusion 293

[27] Montgomery, *Health Care Law*, 1997:170. *Waters v. W. Sussex HA* [1995], *Wilsher v. Essex AHA* [1986]

[28] *R v Adams* (1981) 12 BMLR 1, cited Davies, *Textbook on Medical Law*, 1996:292.

[29] Williams, *Textbook of Criminal Law*, 1983:580.

[30] Griffiths, Bood, and Weyers, *Euthanasia and Law in the Netherlands*, 1998:18.

[31] Ibn Hajar, *Tuhfa*, (1304 AH), vol. 8:391.

[32] Gellner, Foreword in *Islam, Globalization and Postmodernity*, (ed.), Ahmed, and Donnan, 1994:xi.

[33] Charles Le Gai Eaton, 'The Roots of Western Culture,' in *Islamica*, 2.4/ 98, pp. 11-18, at pp. 14-15."

[34] Halliday, Fred, "The politics of Islamic fundamentalism Iran, Tunisia and the challenge to the secular state," 91-113, in *Islam, Globalization and Postmodernity*, (ed.), Ahmed, and Donnan, 1994:91 [The clash of civilizations, referred to is the authorship of Samuel Huntington].

[35] Q. 3:110 et. al.

[36] Q. 3:110, (tr. Bewley).

[37] Q. 42:35, (tr. Bewley).

[38] Q. 6:57; 6:62; 12:40; and 12:67

[39] Q. 2:30; 6:165; 10:14; and 38:26.

[40] Q. 67:15, (tr. Bewley).

[41] *Ash-Sharq Al-Awsat*, (Arabic Daily Newspaper, London and Washington D.C), 19 December 1998, p. 16 (upper half), columns 1-5, 'Any Deviation form the Qur'an and the Sunnah is Rejected by All Islamic Schools,' a dialogue conducted by Imam Muhammad Imam with Ayatollah Muhammad'Ali At-Taskhiery. (Author's translation of title and summary).

[42] Q. 49:13, (tr. Bewley).

[43] Q. 5:1, (tr. Bewley).

[44] Cited by Omran, *Family Planning*, 1994:82, see Qarafi, *al-Furuq*, Halabi, Cairo, (1344 AH), vol. 1:3 and p 8 "Happenings never end whilst dicta *(nusus)* are limited, therefore people must find rules).

[45] Edge, Ian, (ed.), *Islamic Law and Legal Theory*, 1996:xxviii.

[46] Baker, *An Introduction to English Legal History*, Reprinted 1998 p. 1.

[47] *Sahih al-Bukhari*, 1981, vol. 1:25; *Sunan Ibn Majah*, 1952, vol. 1:81; Hindi, *Kanz al-'Ummal*, 1971, vol. 10:135; Ghazali, *Ihya*,' vol. 1:16.

Appendices

Appendix A.1
The Hippocratic Oath

I swear by Apollo the god of all gods, by Aesculapius the healer, by Hygiena, by Panacea*, and call to witness all the gods and goddesses that I may keep the Oath and Promise to the best of my ability and judgement.

I will pay the same respect to my master in the Sciences as to my parents and share my life with him and pay all my debts to him. I will regard his sons as my brothers and teach them the Science, if they desire to learn it, without fee or contract. I will hand on Precepts, Lectures and all other learning to my sons, to those of my master, and to those pupils duly apprenticed and sworn and to none other.

I will use my power to help the sick to the best of my ability and judgement; I will abstain from harming or wronging any man by it.

I will not give a fatal draught to any one if I am asked, nor will I suggest any such thing. Neither will I give a woman means to procure an abortion. I will be chaste and religious in my life and practice. I will not cut, even for the stone, but I will leave such procedures to the practitioner of that craft.

Whenever I go into a house, I will go to help the sick and never with the intention of doing harm or injury. I will not abuse my position to indulge in sexual contacts with the bodies of women or men, whether they be freemen or slaves.

Whatever I see or hear, professionally or privately, which ought not to be divulged, I will keep secret and tell no one.

If, therefore, I observe this Oath and do not violate it, may I prosper both in my life and in my profession, earning good repute among all men for all time. If I transgress and forswear this Oath, may my lot be otherwise.

Appendix A.2
International Code of Medical Ethics

One of the first acts of the World Medical Association, when formed in 1947, was to produce a modern restatement of the Hippocratic Oath, known as the Declaration of Geneva, and to base upon it an International Code of Medical Ethics.

International Code of Medical Ethics

Duties of Doctors in General
A DOCTOR MUST always maintain the highest standards of professional conduct.
A DOCTOR MUST practise his profession uninfluenced by motives of profit.
THE FOLLOWING PRACTICES are deemed unethical:
(a) Any self-advertisement except such as is expressly authorised by the national; code of ethics.
(b) Collaboration in any form of medical service in which the doctor does not have professional independence.
(c) Receiving any money in connection with services rendered to a patient other than a proper medical fee, even with the knowledge of the patient.

ANY ACT OR ADVICE which could weaken physical or mental resistance of a human being may be used only in his interest.
A DOCTOR IS ADVISED to use great caution in divulging discoveries or new techniques of treatment.
A DOCTOR SHOULD certify or testify only to that which he has personally verified.

Duties of Doctors to the Sick

A DOCTOR MUST always bear in mind the obligation of preserving human life.

A DOCTOR OWES to his patient complete loyalty and all the resources of his science. Whenever an examination or treatment is beyond his capacity he should summon another doctor who has the necessary ability.

A DOCTOR SHALL preserve absolute secrecy on all he knows about his patients because of the confidence entrusted in him.

A DOCTOR MUST give emergency care as a humanitarian duty unless he is assured that others arte willing and able to give such care.

Duties of Doctors to each other

A DOCTOR OUGHT to behave to his colleague as he would have them behave to him.

A DOCTOR MUST NOT entice patients from his colleagues.

A DOCTOR MUST OBSRVE the principles of the principles of'The Declaration of Geneva' approved by the World Medical Association.

Appendix A.3
Declaration of Geneva
A modern restatement of the Hippocratic Oath 1947

As amended by the 22nd World Medical Assembly, Sydney, Australia, in August 1968 and the 35th World Medical Assembly, Venice, Italy, in October 1983

> At the time of being admitted as a member of the medical profession:
> I will solemnly pledge myself to concentrate my life to the service of humanity;
> I will give to my teachers the respect and gratitude which is their due;
> I will practise my profession with conscience and dignity;
> The health of my patient will be my first consideration;
> I will respect the secrets which are confided in me, even after the patient has died;
> I will maintain by all the means in my power the honour and noble traditions of the medical profession;
> My colleagues will be my brothers;
> I will not permit considerations of religion, nationality, race, party politics, or social standing to intervene between my duty and my patient;
> I will maintain the utmost respect for human life from the time of conception;
> even under threat I will not use my medical knowledge contrary to the laws of humanity.
> I make these promises solemnly, freely and upon my honour.
> ***

for medical oaths, declarations, codes, and guidelines please refer to:
British Medical Association 1993
Medical Ethics Today: Its Practice and Philosophy
London: BMA Publications, Reprinted October 1998 pp. 326-335

British Medical Association.
Rights and Responsibilities of Doctors.
BMJ Publishing Group Tavistock Square London 1992:201-208

Gillon, Raanan :
Philosophical Medical Ethics.
Wiley & Sons Chichester et. al. 1994:9-13
Islamic Code of Medical Ethics.
First International Conference on Islamic Medicine.
Kuwait January 1981. *(Text given in appendix A.4).*

Mason & McCall Smith:
Law and Medical Ethics. 4th ed.
Butterworths London et. al. 1994, (Appendices).

Appendix A.4
Islamic Code of Medical Ethics

Drawn at the First International Conference on Islamic Medicine: Kuwait, January 1981. On the occasion of the beginning of the fifteenth Islamic century.

Doctors' Oath

I swear by Allah, the Almighty, to have regard for Him in exercising my profession.

To protect human life in all its stages, and under all circumstances. That I will do my utmost to save it from death, illness, pain, and anxiety.

To preserve peoples' dignity, protect their privacy, and keep their secrets.

To be, always, an instrument of Allah's mercy, extending my medical care to the near, and to the far; to the virtuous and to the sinner, friend or foe.

To strive in the pursuit of knowledge and to put it to use for the benefit, but not to the harm, of Mankind.

To revere my teacher, teach my junior, and to be a brother to the members of my profession and to co-operate with them in what is good and legitimate.

To live out my life according to my Faith, in private and in public; avoiding anything that might blemish me in the eyes of Allah, His Messenger ﷺ, and my fellows in the Faith.

May Allah be my witness in this oath.

Al-Awadi, A. A. (ed.) [1981], *Islamic Medicine*, Kuwait: p. 700. al-'Awadi, A. A., (ed.), Human Life, its Beginning and End in Islamic Law (in Arabic), *Kuwait: Islamic Organization of Medical Sciences*, 1985

Dr. Abd al-Rahmamn al-Awadi, President,
Islamic Organizain for Medical Sciences (IOMS).

Appendix B
The Declaration of Helsinki
Human experimentation

In 1964, the World Medical Association drew up a code on human experimentation. This code, known as the Declaration of Helsinki, as amended by the 29th World Medical Assembly, Helsinky, Finland, in 1975, and by the 35th, Venice, Italy, in 1983, and the 41st, Hong Kong, in 1989, reads:

Introduction

It is the mission of the medical doctor to safeguard the health of the people. His or her knowledge and conscience are dedicated to the fulfilment of this mission.

The Declaration of Geneva of the World Medical Association binds the physician with the words, "The health of my patient will be my first consideration," and the International Code of Medical Ethics declares that "A physician shall act only in the patient's interest when providing medical care which might have the effect of weakening the physical and mental condition of the patient."

The purpose of biomedical research involving human subjects must be to improve diagnostic, therapeutic and prophylactic procedures and the understanding of the aetiology and pathogenesis of disease.

In current medical practice most diagnostic, therapeutic or prophylactic procedures involve hazards. This applies especially to biomedical research.

Medical progress is based on research which ultimately must rest in part on experimentation involving human subjects.

In the field of biomedical research a fundamental distinction must be recognised between medical research in which the aim is essentially diagnostic or therapeutic for a patient, and medical research, the essential object of which is purely scientific and without implying direct diagnostic or therapeutic value to the person subjected to the research.

Special caution must be exercised in the conduct of research which may affect the environment, and the welfare of animals used for research must be respected.

Because it is essential that the results of laboratory experiments be applied to human beings to further scientific knowledge and to help suffering humanity, the World Medical Association has prepared the following recommendations as a guide to every physician in biomedical research involving human subjects. They should be kept under review in the future. It must be stressed that the standards as drafted are only as guide to physicians all over the world. Physicians are not relieved from criminal, civil and ethical responsibilities under the laws of their own countries.

I. Basic Principles

1. Biomedical research involving human subjects must conform to the generally accepted scientific principles and should be based on adequately performed laboratory and animal experimentation and on a thorough knowledge of the scientific literature.

2. The design and performance of each experimental procedure involving human subjects should be clearly formulated in an experimental protocol which should be transmitted to a specially appointed independent committee for consideration, comment and guidance.

3. Biomedical research involving human subjects should be conducted only by scientifically qualified persons and under the supervision of a clinically competent medical person. The responsibility for the human subject must always rest with the medically qualified person and never rest on the subject of the research, even though the subject has given his or her consent.

4. Biomedical research involving human subjects cannot legitimately be carried out unless the importance of the objective is in proportion to the inherent risk to the subject.

5. Every biomedical research project involving human subjects should be preceded by careful assessment of predictable risks in comparison with foreseeable benefits to the subject or others. Concern for the interests of the subject must always prevail over the interest of science and society.

6. The right of the research subject to safeguard his or her integrity must always be respected. Every precaution should be taken to respect the privacy of the subject and to minimize the impact of the

study on the subject's physical and mental integrity and on the personality of the subject.

7. Physicians should abstain from engaging in research projects involving human subjects unless they are satisfied that the hazards involved are believed to be predictable. Physicians should cease any investigation if the hazards are found to outweigh the potential benefits.

8. In publication of the results of his or her research, the physician is obliged to preserve the accuracy of the results. Reports of experimentation not in accordance with the principles laid down in this Declaration should not be accepted for publication.

9. In any research on human beings, each potential subject must be adequately informed of the aims, methods, anticipated benefits and potential hazards of the study and the discomfort it may entail. He or she should be informed that he or she is at liberty to abstain from participation in the study and that he or she is free to withdraw his or her consent to participation at any time. The physician should then obtain the subject's consent freely-given informed consent, preferably in writing.

10. When obtaining informed consent for the research project the physician should be particularly cautious if the subject is in a dependent relationship to him or her or may consent under duress. In that case the informed consent should be obtained by a physician who is not engaged in the investigation and who is completely independent of this official relationship.

11. In case of legal incompetence, informed consent should be obtained from the legal guardian in accordance with national legislation. Where physical or mental incapacity makes it impossible to obtain informed consent, or when the subject is a minor, permission from the responsible relative replaces that of the subject in accordance with national legislation. Whenever the minor child is in fact able to give a consent, the minor's consent must be obtained in addition to the consent of the minor's legal guardian.

12. The research protocol should always contain a statement of the ethical considerations involved and should indicate that the principles enunciated in the present Declaration are complied with.

II. Medical research combined with professional care (clinical research)

1. In the treatment of the sick person, the physician must be free to use

a new diagnostic and therapeutic measure, if in his or her judgement it offers hope of saving life, re-establishing health or alleviating suffering.

2. The potential benefits, hazards and discomfort of a new method should be weighed against the advantages of the best current diagnostic and therapeutic methods.

3. In any medical study, every patient –including those of a control group, if any – should be assured of the best proven diagnostic and therapeutic method.

4. The refusal of the patient to participate in a study must never interfere with the physician-patient relationship.

5. If the physician considers it essential not to obtain informed consent, the specific reasons for this proposal should be stated in the experimental protocol for transmission to the independent committee (I.2).

6. The physician can combine medical research with professional care, the objective being the acquisition of new medical knowledge, only to the extent that medical research is justified by its potential diagnostic or therapeutic value for the patient.

III Non-therapeutic biomedical research involving human subjects (non-clinical biomedical research)

1. In the purely scientific application of medical research carried out on a human being, it is the duty of the physician to remain the protector of the life and health of that person on whom biomedical research is being carried out.

2. The subjects should be volunteers – either healthy persons or patients for whom the experimental design is not related to the patient's illness.

3. The investigator or the investigating team should discontinue the research if in his or her or their judgement it may, if continued, be harmful to the individual.

4. In research in man, the interest of science and society should never take precedence over considerations related to the well-being of the subject.

*

See "International Ethical Guidelines for Biomedical Research Involving Human Subjects." Prepared by the Council for International Organizations of Medical Sciences, and the WHO, Geneva, 1993:pp. 13-24 for 'Informed Consent,' pp. 25-32 for 'Research involving subjects in underdeveloped countries.'

Appendix C
Declaration of Oslo 1970
Statement on therapeutic abortion

1. The first moral principle imposed upon the doctor is respect for human life as expressed in a clause of the Declaration of Geneva: I will maintain the utmost respect for human life from the time of conception.

2. Circumstances which bring the vital interests of a mother into conflict with the vital interests of her unborn child create a dilemma and raise the question whether or not the pregnancy should be deliberately terminated.

3. Diversity of response to this situation results from the diversity of attitudes towards the life of the unborn child. This is a matter of individual conviction and conscience which must be respected.

4. It is not the role of the medical profession to determine the attitudes and role of any particular state or community in this matter, but it is our duty to attempt both to ensure the protection of our patients and to safeguard the rights of the doctor within society.

5. Therefore, where the law allows therapeutic to be performed, or legislation to that effect is contemplated, and this is not against the policy of the national medical association, and where the legislature desires or will accept the guidance of the medical profession, the following principles are approved:

(a) Abortion should be performed only as a therapeutic measure.

(b) A decision to terminate pregnancy should normally be approved in writing by at least two doctors chosen for their professional competence.

(c) The procedure should be performed by a doctor competent to do so in premises approved by the appropriate authority.

6. If the doctor considers that his convictions do not allow him to advise or perform an abortion, he may withdraw while ensuring the continuity of (medical) care by a qualified colleague.

7. This statement, while it is endorsed by the General Assembly of

the World Medical Association, is not to be regarded as binding on any individual member association unless it is adopted by that member association.

Appendix D
Declaration of Tokyo
Torture and other cruel, inhuman or degrading treatment or punishment

In 1975 the World Medical Association adopted the following guidelines for medical doctors concerning Torture and Other Cruel, Inhuman or Degrading Treatment or Punishment in relation to Detention and Imprisonment (Declaration of Tokyo).

Preamble

It is the privilege of the medical doctor to practise medicine in the service of humanity, to preserve and restore bodily and mental health without distinction as to persons, to comfort and to ease the suffering of his or her patients. The utmost respect for human life is to be maintained even under threat, and no use made of any medical knowledge contrary to the laws of humanity.

For the purpose of this Declaration, torture is defined as the deliberate, systematic or wanton infliction of physical or mental suffering by one or more persons acting alone or on the orders of any authority, to force another person to yield information, to make a confession, or for any other reason.

Declaration

1. The doctor shall not countenance, condone or participate in the practice of torture or other forms of cruel, inhuman or degrading procedures, whatever the offence of which the victim of such procedures is suspected, accused or guilty, and whatever the victim's beliefs or motives, and in all situations, including armed conflict and civil strife.

2. The doctor shall not provide any premises, instruments, substances or knowledge to facilitate the practice of torture or other forms of cruel, inhuman or degrading treatment or to diminish the ability of the victim to resist such treatment.

3. The doctor shall not be present during any procedure during which torture or other forms of cruel, inhuman or degrading treatment is used or threatened.

4. A doctor must have complete clinical independence in deciding upon the care of a person for whom he or she is medically responsible. The doctor's fundamental role is to alleviate the distress of his or her fellow men, and no motive, whether personal, collective or political, shall prevail against this higher purpose.

5. Where a prisoner refuses nourishment and is considered by the doctor as capable of forming an unimpaired and rational judgement concerning the consequences of such a voluntary refusal of nourishment, he or she shall not be fed artificially. The decision as to the capacity of the prisoner to form such a judgement should be confirmed by at least one other independent doctor.

The consequences of the refusal of nourishment shall be explained by the doctor to the prisoner.

6. The World Medical Association will support, and should encourage the international community, the national medical association and fellow doctors, to support the doctor and his or her family in the face of threats or reprisals resulting from a refusal to condone the use of torture or other forms of cruel, inhuman or degrading treatment.

Appendix E
(a) Opinion of the Group of Advisors on the Ethical Implications of Biotechnology to the European Commission 28 May 1997

Ethical Aspects of Cloning Techniques...

1. Whereas

1.1. Cloning is the process of producing "genetically identical" organisms. It may involve division of a single embryo, in which case both the nuclear genes and the small number of mitochondrial genes would be "identical," or it may involve nuclear transfer, in which case only the nuclear genes would be "identical"...

1.2. It is inherent in the process of sexual reproduction that the progeny differ genetically from one another. In contrast, asexual reproduction (cloning) produces genetically identical progeny. This is a common form of reproduction in plants; both in nature and in the hands of plant breeders and horticulturists...Asexual reproduction is also common in some invertebrate animals (worms, insects)...

1.3. The first successful cloning in vertebrate animals was reported in 1952, in frogs...The resulting clones were not reared beyond the tadpole stage. In 1960, clones of adult frogs were produced by transfer of nuclei from early frog embryos; and also by transfer of nuclei from differentiated larval intestinal cells...Nuclear transfer in frogs has not yet generated an adult animal from cells of an adult animal.

1.4. Nuclear transfer can be used for different objectives...

1.5. Nuclear transfer has also been used for cloning in various mammalian species (mice, rabbits, sheep, cattle), but until recently only nuclei taken from very early embryos were effective,

1.6. In contrast, cloning by embryo splitting, from the 2-cell up to the blastocyst stage, has been extensively used in sheep and cattle to increase the yield of progeny from genetically high-grade parents...

1.7. In 1996, a new method of cloning sheep embryos was reported, which involved first establishing cell cultures from single embryos. Nuclei from the cultured cells were transferred to enucleated unfertilised sheep eggs...which were then artificially stimulated to develop. Genetically identical normal lambs were born.

1.8. Cell cultures were then established not only from embryonic and foetal stages, but also from mammary tissue taken from a 6-year old sheep... Nuclear transfer was carried out as before, and in 1997 Dolly [was born](out of 277 attempts) from the adult nuclear transfer.

1.9. From the point of view of basic research, this result is important...Such work may also increase our understanding of cell commitment, the origin of cancer process, and whether it can be reversed, but at present the research is at a very early stage.[1]

Concerning Human Implications

1.14. A clear distinction must be drawn between reproductive cloning aimed at the birth of identical individuals, which in humans has never been performed, and non-reproductive cloning, limited to the in-vitro phase.

1.15. In considering human implications, we must again distinguish between cloning by embryo splitting and cloning by nuclear replacement (see 1.1). We must also distinguish between nuclear replacement as a means of cloning and nuclear replacement as a therapeutic measure.

1.16. Embryo splitting in the human is the event that gives rise to monozygotic (one-egg) twins and higher multiples...

1.17. Monozygotic twins show us that genetically identical individuals are far from identical:

1.18. There is no ethical objection to genetically identical human beings per se existing, since monozygotic twins are not discriminated against. However, the use of embryo splitting, or the use of human embryo cells as nuclear donors, deliberately to produce genetically identical human beings raises serious ethical issues, concerned with human responsibility and instrumentalization, of human beings.

1.19. However, research involving human nuclear transfer could have important therapeutic implications, for example the development of appropriate stem cell cultures for repairing human organs....

2. The Group submits the following opinion to the European Commission...

Concerning Human Implications

2.6. any attempt to produce a genetically identical human individual by nuclear substitution from a human adult or child cell ("reproductive cloning") should be prohibited.

2.7. The ethical objections against cloning also rule out any attempt to make genetically identical embryos for clinical use in assisted reproduction, either by embryo splitting or by nuclear transfer from an existing embryo, however understandable.

2.8. Multiple cloning is *a fortiori* unacceptable. In any case, its demands on egg donors and surrogate mothers would be outwith the realms of practicality at the present time.

2.9. Taking into account the serious ethical controversies surrounding human embryo research: for those countries in which non-therapeutic research on human embryos is allowed under strict license, a research project involving nuclear substitution should have the objective either to throw light on the cause of human disease or to contribute to the alleviation of suffering, and should not include replacement of the manipulated embryo in a uterus.

2.10. The European Community should clearly express its condemnation of human reproductive cloning and should take this into account in the relevant texts and regulations in preparation as the Decision adopting the Vth. Framework Programme for Research and Development (1998-2002) and the proposed Directive on legal protection of biotechnological inventions.[2]

Notes
[1] McLaren, 1997, pp 1-7, at pp. 2-3.
[2] McLaren, 1997, pp 1-7, pp. 4-5.

Appendix F
European Parliament 1997-1998
Minutes of the sitting of Wednesday 12 March 1997

9. Cloning animals and human beings
B4-0209, 0213, 0214, 0225 and 0242/97
Resolution on cloning
The European Parliament
having regard to…
A. whereas cloning breaks new ethical ground and has led to great public concern,
B. in the clear conviction that the cloning of human beings, whether experimentally, in the context of fertility treatment, preimplantation diagnosis, tissue transplantation or for any other purpose whatsoever, cannot under any circumstances be justified or tolerated by any society, because it is a serious violation of fundamental human rights and is contrary to the principal of equality of human beings as it permits a eugenic and racist selection of the human race, it offends against human dignity and it requires experimentation on humans,…
C. whereas there is a need to ensure that the benefits of biotechnology are not lost as a result of sensationalist and alarmist information,
D. whereas adequate methods of regulating and policing developments in the field of genetics must be established,
E. whereas all necessary information must be made available to the public,
F. whereas the Convention on Human Rights and Biomedicine does not expressly ban the cloning of human beings, and in any event is not yet in force in any EU Member State,
G. whereas some Member States have no national legislation prohibiting the cloning of human beings,
H. whereas cloning of humans for all purposes should be banned in the EU,

I. whereas international action is required,

1. Stresses that each individual has a right to his or her own genetic identity and that human cloning is, and must continue to be, prohibited;

2. Calls for an explicit world-wide ban on the cloning of human beings;

3. Urges the Member States to ban the cloning of human beings at all stages of formation and development, regardless of the method used, and to provide for penal sanctions to deal with any violation;[1]

Notes

[1] European Parliament 1997-1998 Minutes of the sitting of Wednesday 12 March 1997 Provisional Edition PE 257.132/52-55 at 53-54.

Appendix G
Hukm al-maskuti 'anhu (Rules when Shari'ah is silent about a matter).

Is it the basic rule that, "Everything is allowed unless it was specifically forbidden, or is it that, everything is not permitted except for what Allah has ordained for us."? (Hal al-aslu fi'l-ashya'i al-ibaha awi'l-hurma?). There are three viewpoints:

The First Viewpoint is that:
"Everything is allowed unless it was specifically forbidden."

This is the view of the majority. They support their argument by quoting: (A) The Qur'an, (B) Prophetic *hadith*, and (C) Reasoning (*al-'aql*).

A. The Qur'an:
(1) **"It is He who created everything on the earth for you"** (Q. 2:28, tr. Bewley). Allah said that He has created *everything* for us.

(2) **"Say: 'Who has forbidden the fine clothing Allah has produced for His slaves and the good kinds of provision?'"** (Q. 7:30, tr. Bewley). This is taken to mean by some that things in their totality (or basically) are allowed.

(3) **"Say: 'I do not find, in what has been revealed to me, any food it is haram to eat except for carrion, flowing blood, and pork – for that is unclean – or some deviance consecrated to other than Allah.'"** (Q. 6:146, tr. Bewley). Which means that everything is allowed except for what was singled out.

(4) **"Say: 'Come and I will recite to you what your Lord has made haram for you': that you do not associate anything with Him; that you are good to your parents; that you do not kill your children because of poverty – We will provide for you and them; that you do not approach indecency – outward or inward; that you do not kill any person Allah has made inviolate – except with the right**

to do so. That is what He instructs you to do so that hopefully you will use your intellect. And that you do not go near the property of orphans before they reach maturity – except in a good way; that you give full measure and full weight with justice – We impose on no self any more than it can bear; that you are equitable when you speak – even if a near relative is concerned; and that you fulfil Allah's contract."(Q. 6:152, tr. Bewley). In these ayat and the ones that follow Allah is explaining what He has forbidden: it means that what He does not mention, here or elsewhere in the Qur'an or in the Sunnah, is allowed.

(5) "Say:'My Lord has forbidden indecency, both open and hidden, and wrong action, and unrightful tyranny, and associating anything with Allah for which He has sent down no authority, and saying things about Allah you do not know.'"(Q.7: 31, tr. Bewley). Allah has specified what He has designated as impermissible: it means that other things are permitted.

B. The Prophetic Sunnah

(1) hadith, "Allah has specified what is permitted *(halal)* and what is impermissible *(haram)*; what He has not mentioned is forgiven *('afu)*: accept that; as Allah is not forgetful." (narrated by Abu'd-Darda'; authenticated by at-Tabarani, al-Bazaz, and al-Hakim).

(2) hadith, "Allah asked for things to be done: do them; He stipulated that others should not be done: do not do them; He marked some limits: do not transgress them; and He kept silent about many things, without being forgetful about them but out of His kindness: accept His kindness and do not probe into them, or do not burden yourselves with them." (narrated by Abu Tha'laba, and authenticated by at-Tabarani).

(3) hadith, "What is permissible and what is not permissible is disclosed in the Book. What was not mentioned was forgiven *('afu)*." In at-Tirmidhi and Ibn Majah.

(4) hadith, "The worst crime is that of the one who asked about something which was not forbidden, which became so on account of him asking about it." Narrated by Sa'd ibn Abi Waqqas; and authenticated by al-Bukhari. (Presumably that meant at the time of revelation *(wahy)*).

C. Reasoning (al-'aql)

(1) Making use of what does not hurt the owner is a reasonable thing to do, like utilising light or standing in the shade of a tree. Allah who owns everything will not begrudge people that.

(2) Allah has created everything; it can not be without reason."We created not the heavens, the earth, and all between them, merely in (idle) sport;" (Q. 44:38, tr. Yusuf 'Ali); and "Did ye then think that We had created you in jest," (Q. 23:115, tr., Yusuf 'Ali). Since He has no need for those things then they may be utilised by the people. This is proof that utility is reason for allowing things.

The Second Viewpoint is that:

'Everything is not permitted except for what Allah has ordained for us.'

As-Suyuti (in *al-Ashbah*) said that, "Everything is allowed unless there is proof that it is not. And with Abu Hanifa everything is forbidden unless there is proof that it is allowed."

Az-Zarkashi (in *al-Ma'thour fi al-Qwa'id*) attributed to Ash-Shafi'i that he said,"If there is no proof that something is forbidden then it is *halal* (allowed). He also attributed to Abu Hanifa that he said, "You need a proof that something is allowed *(halal).*

The Hanafis themselves think that,"The original rule is that everything is allowed with specified exceptions."They argue the point quoting the Qur'an (Q. 2:28, tr. Bewley) **"It is He who created everything on the earth for you."** And it is mentioned in *al-Hidaya*, that "permission is the rule."

So, if the Shafi'is and the Hanafis think that 'permission is the rule,' who is it then who thinks that the original rule is prohibition?

Ibn Nujaim, in his *al-Ashbah,* attributed that to (some of *ahl al-hadith*).

Ibn Qudama (in his *ar-Rawda*), Ibn Hamid al-Baghdadi, al-Qadi Abu Ya'la (all three from the Hanbali school), and some of the *Mu'tazila* subscribe to this view. They quote:

(1) The Qur'an, (Q. 16:116)

"Do not say about what your lying tongues describe: 'This is halal and this is haram,' inventing lies against Allah."; and they conclude that,"It is not up to us to say what is permitted or not permitted; it must all come from Allah."

Their opponents say, "That they have resorted to the Qur'an and Sunnah, to confirm their point of view; and that those who say that 'prohibition is the rule' have done so without proof; and that one should neither make the impermissible permissible nor visa versa."

(2) The Sunnah

"What is permissible is obvious, and what is impermissible is obvious; between them are indeterminate matters *(shubuhat)*: the believers will stop at the indeterminate." This *hadith* was narrated by al-Bukhari and Muslim. Supporters of the first viewpoint argued that the 'indeterminate issues' are those where there is evidence for both sides of the argument; and that such matters are not the subject of their case: their case is about, "what Allah has kept silent about and is *'afu* (forgiven)."

(3) Reasoning (*al-'aql*)

The supporters of the second viewpoint say that, "utilising what is not yours is not correct. Things and affairs belong to Allah. What He has not specifically permitted is out of bounds." Their opponents argued that in their case the owner was Allah who could not be hurt or harmed if His things were utilised: He did not create them in vain or without purpose or for idle jest; and that anyway there was no prohibition by Him.

The Third Viewpoint is that of those who "Do not know"

This view is held by Abu al-Hasan al-Ash'ari al-Bisri (d. 324/884) (Shafi'i school); Abu Bakr as-Sirafi (d. 330/900) (Shafi'i school); and Abu al-Hasan al-Kharazi (Hanbali school). But the supporters of the first viewpoint responded by saying that, "There must be a ruling for all actions: this rule is known to some and unknown to others."

The difference amongst these views becomes apparent when there is no rule as regards an issue (silence). Examples of which are animals, which were not classified, as to whether they are consumable or not, e.g. the giraffe or elephant. In the case of giraffe the probability is that it is allowed. Other examples as regards foods are vegetables and fruits, which are not known to be poisonous, or not; probably it is permissible to consume them. Sometimes it may not be known whether a stream is privately owned or not, so its utilisation is an open question. If stray pigeons become mixed up with ones own, then probably it is allowed to utilise them unless they were marked or trained ones which should be kept for their owner.

This has its application when discussing types of materials, furniture, and the use of new equipment (methods) where there was no prohibition.

It will also have its application in contracts the likes of which were not encountered before; and also in the newer versions of transactions. All of which may be acceptable if they are free of usury, hurt, harm, and ignorance of their outcome *(gharar).*"[1]

Notes

[1] Borno, *al-Wajiz*, 1998, pp. 191-198: Based on, Suyuti, *al-Ashbah*, Dar al-Kutub al-'Ilmia, Beirut, 1st ed., (1399 AH), p. 60 (Shafi'i school); Ibn Nujaim, *al-Ashbah*, Dar al-Kutub al-'Ilmia, Beirut, (1400 AH), p. 66 (Hanafi school); and Zarkashi, Muhammad ibn Bahadir *al-Manthur fi'l-Qawa'id*, Wazarat al-Awqaf, Kuwait, (1404 AH), vol. 1:176, and vol. 2:70.

Appendix H
Some Resolutions of
Al-Majami' al-Fiqhia And Fatwa.

Resolution No. (3) *Al-Ijtihad*
Basically allowed
Majlis al-Majm'a al-Fiqh al-Islami, 18-29 Jan. 1985, in Makkah al-Mukarramah, pp.208-210, and pp. 43-45 English part.

Resolution No.(4) D 3/7/86 Test Tube Babies
Allowed within Shari'ah bounds
Majlis al-Majma' al-Fiqh al-Islami, 11-16 Oct 1986, in Omman, Kingdom of Jordan
pp.213-214, and pp. 48-49 English part

Resolution No. 1 D 4/08/88 Organs Transplant
Basically allowed
Majlis al-Majma' al-Fiqh al-Islami, 6-11 Feb 1988, in Jeddah, Kingdom of Saudi Arabia.
pp. 220-222, and pp. 55-58 English part. All in:
Contemporary Jurisprudence Research Journal, 3rd. Edition First year Nov-Dec 1989 Jan 1990, Riyadh, Kingdom of Saudi Arabia.

Resolution No. (58/76) The Use of Foetal Tissue in Transplantation
Allowed providing it is a spontaneous abortion or therapeutic to save the life of the mother, and that the products cannot lead a separate existence.
Majlis Majma' al-Fiqh al-Islami, 14-20 March 1990, Jeddah, Saudi Arabia, in:
Contemporary Jurisprudence Research Journal, Second year No. 6 Aug Sep Oct 1990, Riyadh, Saudi Arabia, pp. 144-145.

Resolution Number Four: Termination of pregnancy when the foetus is seriously deformed

– if the foetus has reached 120 days, then it is not allowed unless the pregnancy actually endangers the life of the mother,

– before 120 days have elapsed then it is allowed to terminate the pregnancy if the foetus is seriously deformed, if that is the wish of the parents.

Contemporary Jurisprudence Research Journal, Second year No. 8 Jan Feb Mar 1991, Riyadh, Saudi Arabia, pp. 105-106.

Fatwa: Islamic Fiqh on Donating and Receiving Blood

A Muslim may donate and receive blood from any human being, A Muslim can be advised on the matter, and other matters, by non-Muslims as well as by Muslims. pp.45-46

Qattan, Manna' ibn Khalil al-Qattan, *"Al-Ijtihad al-Fiqhi li't-Tabar'i bi d-Dami wa Naqlihi"* Majallat al-Majma' al-Fiqhi al-Islami, No. 3 1409/1989 pp. 40-51.

Al-Qattan, is Professor of Law at Imam Muhammad ibn Sa'ud Islamic University, Riyadh.

Formerly Director of the High Institute of Justice

Bibliography and Bibliographical Abbreviations

European Titles

Abdel Haleem, M. A. S., 'Medical ethics in Islam' *Choices and Decisions in Health Care,* Edited by A. Grubb © 1993 John Wiley & Sons Ltd.
ACS = The American College of Surgeons, *(Bulletin,* and/or *Journal).*
Allott, Antony Nicolas, *The Limits of the Law,* Butterworths, London, 1980.
Anderson, Norman, *Law Reform in the Muslim World,* London, Athlone Press,1976.
Ansari, Zafar Ishaq,"The Contribution of the Qur'an and the Prophet in the Develpopment of Islamic *Fiqh,"Journal of Islamic Studies,* 3:2 (1992).
Asad, Muhammad, *The Principles of State and Government in Islam,* First Published, University of California Press, 1961, new edition 1980, Dar al-Andalus, Gibraltar, Reprinted, 1981, 1985, 1993, Great Britain by Redwood Press, Melksham, Wiltshire.
Atiyah, P. S, *The Damages Lottery,* Hart Publishing, Oxford, 1997.
'Awa, Mohamed S. el-'Awa, *Punishment in Islamic Law: Comparative Study,* American Trust Publications, Indianapolis, 1982.

Baker, J. H., *An Introduction to English Legal History,* 3rd. ed., Butterworths, London, Boston, Dublin, Edinburgh, et. al. 1990; 1st. ed., 1971, 2nd. ed. 1979; Reprinted 1993, 1994, 1995, 1996, 1997, 1998.
Ballantyne, William,"A Reasertion of the Shari'ah: The Jurisprudence of the Gulf States,"in Heer, Nicholas, (Ed.), *Islamic Law and Jurisprudence: Studies in Honor of Farahat J. Ziadah,* London and Seattle, University of Washington Press, 1990:149-159.
Bankowski, Z. and Levine, R. J. (ed). *Ethics and Research on Human Subjects: International Guidelines* (Proceedings of the XXVIth. Conference of the Council for International Organizations of Medical Sciences, Geneva, Switzerland 5-7 February 1992); and its addendum for the International Ethical Guidelines for Biomedical Research Involving Human Subjects, prepared by the Council in collaboration with the WHO, Geneva 1993.
Bewley, *Al-Muwatta',* translated, see Malik below.
BMA. British Medical Association.

BMJ. British Medical Journal, or British Medical Journal Publications, London.

Brahimi, Abdelhaid, "The Origin of Islamic Economics" in *ISLAMICA* vol. 2 No. 3 1996, *Journal of the Islamic Society of the London School of Economics*.

Brazier, M., 'Embryos' "Rights": Abortion and Research' in Freeman (ed.), *Medicine, Ethics and the Law* London: Stevens, 1988.

Brazier, Margaret, *Medicine, Patients, and the Law*, First Published in Pelican Books, 1987, 2nd. ed., Penguin Books, London et. al., 1992.

British Medical Association, *The handbook of medical ethics*, London, BMA 1984.

British Medical Association, *Euthanasia: Report of the Working Party to Review the British Medical Association's guidance on euthanasia*, London: BMA 5 May 1988.

British Medical Association, *Rights and Responsibilities of Doctors*, BMJ Publishing Group Tavistock Square, London, 1992.

British Medical Association, *Medical Ethics Today: Its Practice and Philosophy*, BMJ Publishing Group Tavistock Square, London, 1993, Reprinted 1998.

Bukhari, (d. 256/870):
Sahih al-Bukhari, (ed.), M. Muhsin Khan, Kazi Publications, 6th ed., Lahore, 1986.
Sahih al-Bukhari, (ed.), Siddiqi, A., Islamic Bonds Publications, Kuwait, 1993.
Sahih al-Bukhari, *(Mukhtasar)* Summarised by Ahmad Abdul Latif az-Zubiedi, and Translated by Muhammad Muhsin Khan, Maktabat Dar us-Salam, Riyadh, 1994.

Burton, John, *The Sources of Islamic Law: Islamic Theories of Abrogation*, Edinburgh University Press, Edinburgh, 1990.

Burton, John, *An Introduction to the hadith*, Edinburgh University Press, Edinburgh, 1994.

Cane, Peter, (ed.), *Atiyah's Accidents Compensation and the Law*, First Published 1970, 5th ed., 1993, Reprinted, 1994, 1997, Butterworths, London, Dublin, Edinburgh, 1993.

Cartwright, Will, "The Pig, The Transplant Surgeon, and the Nuffield Council," *Med. L. Rev.* 4 Autumn, 1996, pp. 250-269.

Challoner, Jack, *The Baby Makers*, Channel 4 Books, Macmillan Publishers, London, Basingstoke and Oxford, 1999.

Coker, Christopher, "The United States and the Challenge of Islam" In vol. 2 No. 3 (Summer 1996) *ISLAMICA. Journal of the Islamic Society of the London School of Economics*.

Coulson, N. J. [1994] *A History Of Islamic Law*, Edinburgh University Press (First Published, 1964, Reprinted 1970, Paperback ed., 1978, Reprinted, 1990, 1991, 1994) Redwood Books, Trowbridge, G.B., 1994.

Coulson, N. J., *Conflicts and Tensions in Islamic Jurisprudence*, University of Chicago Press, Chicago and London, 1969.

Crone, Patricia, *Roman, Provincial and Islamic Law: The Origins of Islamic Patronate*, Cambridge University Press, Cambridge, 1987.

Cross, Rupert, and Asterly Jones, P., *An Introduction to Criminal Law*, 4th. ed., Butterworths, London, 1959.

CUP. Cambridge University Press.

Daniel, Norman, *Islam and the West: The Making of an Image*, First Published Edinburgh University Press, 1960, Revised 1993, One World, Oxford, Paperback 1997.

Davies, Michael, *Textbook on Medical Law*, Blackstone Press Ltd., London 1996.

Devereux, John, *Medical Law: Text, Cases, and Materials*, Cavendish Publishing, Sydney, Australia, 1997.

Doi, 'Abdur Rahman I. *Shari'ah: The Islamic Law*, Ta Ha Publishers, London, 1984.

Duff, Antony, (Sterling University), "Inclusion and Exclusion, Citizens, Subjects, and Outlaws."University College, London, Series of Legal Theory at the End of the Millennium Lectures.' Bentham House, London, 26 February 1998.

Dutton, Yasin, *The Origins of Islamic Law: The Qur'an, The Muwatta' and Madinan, 'Amal*, Curzon Press, Richmond, Surrey, 1999.

Edge, Ian, (ed.), *Islamic Law and Legal Theory*, Aldershot, Dartmouth, 1996.

Edge, Ian, "The Development of Decennial Liability in Egypt," in Heer, Nicholas, (ed.), *Islamic Law and Jurisprudence*, University of Washington Press, Seattle and London, 1990, pp. 161-175.

ed., = edition; and (ed.), = edited by

Encyclopaedia of Islam (ed.), Lewis, B., Pellat, Ch., and Schacht, J., Leiden, E. J Brill, London, Luzac and Co., 1965.

EUP. = Edinburgh University Press.

Finnis, John, *Natural law and natural rights*, Clarendon Press, Oxford, 1980.

Friedman, L. M.,"The Concept of Legal Cultures: A Reply,"in Nelken, David, *Comparing Legal Cultures*, Aldershot, Dartmouth, 1997, pp. 33-35.

f.n. = footnote

Garrett,T.M., Baillie H.W., and Garrett, Rosellen, *Health Care Ethics: Principles & Problems*, 2nd ed., Prentice Hall, Englewood Cliffs, New Jersey, 1993.

Gellner, Ernest,"Globalization: Foreword"in Ahmed, Akbar S., and Donnan, Hastings, (ed.), *Islam, Globalization and Postmodernity*, Routledge, London and New York, London, 1994, pp. xi-xiv.

Ghanem, Isam, *Islamic Medical Jurisprudence*, Arthur Probsthain, London, 1982.

Ghanem, Isam, *Outlines of Islamic Jurisprudence*, Express Printing Services, 2nd ed., Dubai, U.A.E., 1981.

Ghanem, Isam, "The Responses of Islamic Jurisprudence to Ectopic Pregnancies, Frozen Embryo Implantation, and Euthanasia," *Med. Sci. Law*, (1987), vol. 27. No. 3. Printed in Great Britain.

Gibb, Hamilton A. R., *Modern Trends in Islam*, New York: Octagon Books, University of Chicago Press, New York, 1972. (The Haskell Lectures in Comparative Religion: University of Chicago, 1945).

Gibb, H.A.R., *Mohammedanism: An Historical Survey*, 1st ed., 1949, in the Home University Library, 2nd. ed., 1953, Paperback, Oxford University Press,1969.

Gibb, Hamilton A. R, *Studies on the Civilization of Islam*, Routledge & Kegan Paul Limited, London, 1962.

Gillon, Raanan, *Philosophical Medical Ethics*, Wiley & The British Medical Journal, London, 1994.

Goddard, Hugh, *Christians and Muslims: From Double Standards To Mutual Understanding*, Curzon Press, London, 1995.

Goitein, S. D., "The Birth-Hour of Muslim Law?" *The Muslim World*, vol. 50 1 . (1960), pp 23-29.

Goldziher, Ignaz., *Introduction to Islamic Theology and Law*, Princeton University Press, Princeton, New Jersey, 1981.

Goldziher, Ignaz, [1967], *Muslim Studies (Muhammedanisch studien)*, George Allen & Unwin Ltd., London, vol. 1 1967, vol. 2 1971.

Guillaume, Alfred. *Islam*, 1st. ed., 1954, 2nd ed.1956, (Pelican Book), Penguin Books, Harmondworth, Middlesex England, Hunt Barnard Printing, Aylesbury, Reprinted 1973.

Halliday, Fred], Islam*, and the Myth of Confrontation: Religion and Politics in the Middle East*, I. B. Tauris Publishers, London. New York, London, 1996.

Heer, Nicholas, (ed.), *Islamic Law and Jurisprudence*, University of Washington Press, Seattle and London, 1990.

Hitti, Phillip K., *Islam: A Way of Life*, Gateway Editions, Regency Gateway, University of Minnesota Press, 1970.

Hofmann, Murad, *Islam: The Alternative*, Garnet Publishing, Reading, 1993.

Hofmann, Murad Wilfried, *Islam 2000*, Amana Publications, Beltsville, Maryland, 1996.

Holm, Soren, "A common ethics for a common market?" in Richards, Tessa, (ed.), *Medicine in Europe*, BMJ Publications, London, 1992, pp. 118-123.

Holt, P. M. and Daly M.W., *A History of the Sudan: From The Coming of Islam To The Present Day*, Longman Group UK Ltd., 4th. ed., 1988, 4th. impression 1994, London New York, 1994.

Huber, Peter W., *Liability: The Legal Revolution and its Consequences*, Basic Books Inc. Publishers, New York, 1988.

Huff, Toby E. *The Rise of Early Modern Science: Islam, China, and the West* Press Syndicate of the University of Cambridge, CUP. Cambridge, 1995.

Ibid. and Id. Ibid. = same reference.above; Id. = same reference and same page as above.

Ibn Qayyim al-Jawziyya, *Medicine of the Prophet* ﷺ, Translated by Penelope Johnstone, The Islamic Text Society, Cambridge, 1998. (See Johnstone below).

Imber, Colin.,"Why you should poison your husband: A Note on Liability in Hanafi Law in the Ottoman Period,"pp. 206-216, in *Islamic Law and Society*, 1, 2 (1994)

Jackson, Sherman A., *Islamic Law And The State*, E. J. Brill, Leiden New York Koln, 1996.

Johnson, Douglas and Sampson, Cynthia (editors), *Religion: The Missing Dimension of Statecraft*, Oxford: Center for Strategic and International Studies, New York Oxford OUP 1994, Paperback editon, OUP, 1995.

Johnstone, Penelope, (Translation), *Ibn Qayyim al-Jawziyya's Medicine of the Prophet* ﷺ, The Islamic Text Society, Cambridge, 1998. (See above 'Ibn Qayyim').

Jones, Michael A., *Medical Negligence*, 2nd. ed., Sweet and Maxwell, London, 1996.

Kazi, A. K., and Flynn, J. G., translation of Shahrastani's, *Muslim Sects and Divisions*, Kegan Paul International, London, et. al., 1984. (See below Shahrastani).

Khadduri, Majid, *al-Imam Muhammad ibn Idris al-Shafi'i's al-Risala fi Usul al-Fiqh*, (Translated), 2nd. ed., The Islamic Texts Society, Cambridge, UK. 1987. (First published as *Islamic Jurisprudence: Shafi'i's Risala*, Johns Hopkins Press, 1961).

Khan, Muhammad Muhsin, *The translation of the meanings of Sahih al-Bukhari*, Kazi Publications, Lahore, Pakistan, 1979.

Kennedy, Ian, and Grubb, Andrew, *Medical Law: Text and Material*, 2nd. ed., Butterworths, London, 1994.

Kridelbaugh, William W., and Palmisano, Donald J.,"Compensation Caps for Medical Malpractice,"in *American College of Surgeons Bulletin*, vol. 78, No. 4, April, (1993), pp. 27-30.

Lewis, Charles J., *Medical Negligence: A Practical Guide*, Tolly, Croydon, Surrey, 3rd.ed. Tolly, Croydon, Surrey, 1994.

Lewis, Charles J., *Medical Negligence: A Practical Guide*, Butterworths, London et al., 4th ed., 1998.

Lloyd, G. E. R. (ed.), *Hippocratic Writings*, Penguin Classics, 1983.

Machiavelli, Nicolo, (1469-1527) *The Prince*, (Foreword by Norman Scott,

Professor of Modern History University of Oxford), Wordsworth Reference, Cumberland, Hertfordshire, 1993.

Makdisi, George, "Magesterium and Academic Freedom in Classical Islam and Medieval Christianity," pp. 117-133, in Heer, Nicholas, (ed.), *Islamic Law and Jurisprudence*, University of Washington Press, Seattle and London, 1990.

Makdisi, George, *The Rise of The Colleges: Institutes of learning in Islam and the West*, Edinburgh, Edinburgh University Press, 1991.

Malik, *Al-Muwatta' of Imam Malik ibn Anas: the first formulation of Islamic Law*, English translation: by Aisha Abdurrahman Bewley, London and New York, Kegan Paul 1989.

Mallat, Chibli, (ed.), *Islam and Public Law*, 1st. ed., Graham and Trotman, London Dordrecht Boston, 1993.

Marsh, S. B., and Soulsby, J., *Outlines of English Law*, Fifth edition (1994), Reprinted Stanley Thornes, Cheltenham, UK, 1995.

Mason, J. K., and McCall Smith, R. A., *Law and Medical Ethics*, 4th. ed., Butterworths, London Dublin Edinburgh, London, 1994.

Mayer, Ann Elizabeth, "The Shari'ah: A Methodology or a Body of Substantive Rules?" pp. 177-198 in Heer, Nicholas, (ed.), *Islamic Law and Jurisprudence*, London and Seattle, University of Washington Press, 1990.

McHale, Jean, and Fox, Marie, with Murphy, John, *Health Care Law: Text, Cases and Materials*, Sweet and Maxwell, London et. al., 1997.

McLaren, Anne, (Rapporteur), Opinion of The Group of Advisors on the Ethical Implications of Biotechnology to the European Commission No 9. 28 May 1997 'Ethical Aspects of Cloning Techniques' Reference: Opinion requested by the European Commission on 28 February 1997, pp. 1-7.

Medwar, P. B., "Transplantation of tissues and organs: Introduction," *Brit Med J*, 21:97, 1965.

Montgomery, Jonathan, *Health Care Law*, OUP., Clarendon, Oxford et. al., First Published and Paperback reprinted, Oxford, 1997.

Mussallam, Basim, *Sex and Society in Islam: Birth Control before the Nineteenth Century*, Cambridge London New York et. al., CUP., Cambridge, 1983.

Muslehuddin, Mohammad, *Islamic Jurisprudence and The Rule of Necessity and Need*, Islamic Research Institute, Islamabad, Pakistan, 1975.

Murray, Joseph E., "The Origins and Consequences of Organ Transplantation," *Bulletin of The American College of Surgeons*, vol. 80, no. 8, August 1995, pp. 12-25.

Muwatta' Malik, translated by Aisha Abdurrahman Bewley, see Malik.

New Eng. J. Med. = New England Journal of Medicine

Nielsen, J. S., "Islam and Europe: February 1996." Unpublished paper read at Janadiriya Meeting, Riyadh, Saudi Arabia, March, 1996; and personal communication.

Nielsen, J. S., Centre for the Study of Islam and Christian-Muslim Relations, Selly Oak Colleges, Birmingham, UK.
Nora, Paul F., (ed.), *Professional Liability/Risk Management: A Manual for Surgeons*, 2nd ed., American College of Surgeons. Chicago, 1991,1997.

O'Hagan, Timothy. *The End of Law*, Oxford, Blackwell, 1984.
Omran, Abdel Rahim, *Family Planning in the Legacy of Islam*, 1st. ed., Routledge London New York, London, 1992.
OUP. = Oxford University Press.

Parrott, N. R., "Transplantation" in *International Journal of Intensive Care*, London, Winter 1996 Vol. 3 No. 4, pp.126-133.
Powers, David, S.,"Legal Consultation *(Futya)*, in Medieval Spain and North Africa," pp. 85-106, in Mallat, Chibli, (ed.), *Islam and Public Law*, Graham and Trotman, London et. al., London1993.

Qadri, Anwar A., *Islamic Jurisprudence in the Modern World*, 1st. ed., 1963, 2nd. ed., SH. Muhammad Ashraf, Kashmiri Bazar, Lahore, Pakistan, 1973.

Qaradawi,Yusuf al-Qaradawi, *The lawful and The Prohibited in Islam*, American Trust Publications, Indianapolis, 1960.

Ramadan, Said, *Islamic Law: Its Scope and Equity*, 1st.ed., MacMillan London 1961), 2nd ed., Copy Right Dr. Said Ramadan 1970.
Richards, Tessa, (ed.), *Medicine in Europe: Articles from the British Medical Journal*, BMJ. London, 1992.
Rispler-Cham,Vardit, *Islamic Medical Ethics In The Twentieth Century*,: E.J. Brill Leiden NewYork Koln, Leiden, 1993.
Rosen, Lawrence. *The anthropology of justice: Law as culture in Islamic society*, Cambridge et. al., CUP. 1989.
Ryan, Kenneth J.,"Ethics and the transplant surgeon," Bulletin *(ACS) of the American College of Surgeons*, vol. 80, number 6, June 1995, pp. 8-14.

Sabiq, Sayed, *Fiqh as-Sunnah*, (tr. Muhammad Saeed Dibas and Jamal a-Din M. Zarabozo), AmericanTrust Publications, International Islamic Publishing House, Riyadh, Saudi Arabia, 1406 AH. (First published in Arabic in 1947) See Arabic titles.
Salmond, Sir John, *Jurisprudence*, 7th. ed., Sweet and Maxwell, London, 1924.
Schacht, Joseph, *An Introduction to Islamic Law*, OUP., 1st ed. 1964, Reprinted 1966, 1971, Clarendon Press, Oxford, 1971.
Schacht, Joseph, and Bosworth, C. E. (ed), *The Legacy of Islam*, 2nd ed., Oxford; OUP., 1979.

Schacht, Joseph, *The Origins of Muhammadan Jurisprudence*, Oxford: Clarendon Press Oxford, 1950.
Schimmel, Annemarie, *Islam: An Introduction*, New York, Suny, State University of New York Press, Albany, 1992.
Shafi'i, *Al-Risala: Translated*, See Khadduri, Islamic Text Society, Cambridge, 1987.
Shahrasani, (1086-1153 CE), Muhammad Abdul Karim ash-Shahrastani, *Muslim Sects and Divisions, Translation* of part of *al-Milal wa'n-Nihal*, by Kazi, A. K., and Flynn, J. G., Kegan Paul International, London, et. al., 1984.
Sheikh, M. S., *Islamic Philosophy*, Octagon Press, London, 1982.

Taylor, Noel Leigh, *doctors and the law*, The Law Society with Oyez Publications, London, 1976.
Teperman, Lewis W., "Transplantation," *Journal of the American College of Surgeons*, vol. 188, no. 2, February 1999, pp. 184-190

Weiss, Bernard G., *The Search For God's Law: Islamic Jurisprudence in the Writings of Sayf al-Din al-Amidi*, University of Utah Press, Salt Lake City, 1992.
Williams, Glanville, *Textbook of Criminal Law*, 2nd. ed., Stevens and Sons, London, 1983.
Winfield, P. H., *Textbook of the Law of Tort*, 4th. ed., Sweet and Maxwell. London, 1948.

Zubaidi, Ahmed Abdul Latif, *Mukhtasar Sahih al-Bukhari*, Translation by Muhammad Muhsin Khan, Maktabat Dar-us-Salam, Riyadh, et. al., 1994.
Zubair, Abdul Qadir, *An Outline of Islamic Law of Tort*, Islamic International Contact Publications, Lagos, Nigeria, 1990.

Arabic Titles

Abu Dawud, (202-275 AH), Suliman al-Ash'ath al-Sijistani, *Sunan Abi Dawud*, (ed.), Izzat ad-D'ass and'Adil as-Sayed, 1st. ed., Dar al-hadith, Beirut, (1393-1394 AH), 1973-1974.

Abu Dawud, (d. 275/888), Suliman al-Ash'ath al-Sijistani, *Sunan Abi Dawud*, al-Maktaba al-'Asriya, Beirut.

Abu-us-Sorour, Jamal. (ed.) *Proceedings of the First International Congress on Controls and Ethics of Human Reproduction in the Islamic World, Cairo, 10-13 December 1991,*
International Islamic Population Studies, Azhar University, El Walid Press, Cairo 1992.

Abu Suliman, Abdel Wahab Ibrahim,"*ad-Darura wa al-Haja wa atharuhuma fi at-Tashri' al-Islami" Fatwa* No. 42 Dated 13 / 4 / 1396 AH. (1976), in *Dirasat fi al-Fiqh al-Islami*, Book No. 26 p. 44; Markaz al-Bahth al-'Ilmi wa Ihya'a at-Turath al-Islami, Jamia'at Umm al-Qura, Macca, Kingdom of Saudi Arabia.

Abu Zahra, Muhammad, *Abu-Hanifa: His life, times, and opinions*, 2nd ed., 1369/1947, Dar al-Fikr al-Arabi, Cairo, Reprinted, 1977.

Abu Zahra, Muhammad, *Al-'Ilaqat ad-Duwalia fi Zil al-Islam*, Dar al-Fikr al-Arabi, Cairo, 1981.

Abu Zahra, Muhammad, *Ash-Shafi'i: His life, times, and opinions*, Dar al-Fikr al-Arabi, 2nd ed., Cairo, 1948.

Abu Zahra, Muhammad, *Ibn-Hanbal, His life, times, and opinions*, 1367/1947, Dar al-Fikr al-Arabi, Cairo, Reprinted, 1981.

Abu Zahra, Muhammad, *Malik, His life, times, and opinions*, 2nd. ed., 1952, Dar al-Fikr al-Arabi, Cairo, 1963-1964.

Abu Zahra, Muhammad, *Usul al-Fiqh*, 1377/1958, Dar al-Fikr al-Arabi, Cairo.

AH. = Muslim Lunar Calendar initiated by the second Caliph 'Umar ibn al-Khatab, starting at the date the Prophet left Makka for Madina *(Hijra)*, in the year AD. 622,
So, AH. = (AD. - 622) x 100/97, conversely AD. = AH. x 97/100 + 622.

Alamgir, *Al-Fatawa al-Hindiya (al-'Alimkeiria) fi Madhhab al-Imam Abi Hanifa an-Nu'man,* Shaikh Nizam and others, commissioned by Sultan Muhammad Orunck 'Alimkeir (1070 AH), al-Matba'a al-Amiriyya al-Kubra, Bulaq, 2nd. ed., Cairo, 1310 AH.

'Ali, Muhammad Ibrahim,"Al-Madhhab 'ind al-Hanafia," in *Dirasat fi al-Fiqh al-Islami Journal*, vol. 2.6, pp. 56-139.

Al-Salih, Sobhi, *'Ulum al-hadith wa Mustalahu*, 1st. ed., 1959, Dar al-'Ilm lil Malayien, Beirut, 15th ed., 1984.

Amin, Ahmad, *Duha al-Islam: vol. ii, (First Abbasid dynasty)*, Matba'at Lajnat al-Ta'lif wa al-Tarjama wa al-Nashr, Cairo, 1357/1938.

Ansari, (d. 925 AH), Zacharia ibn Muhammad ibn Zacharia al-Ansari, *Tuhfat al-Tullab ma'a Hashiyat al Sharqawi*, Mustafa al-Halabi, Cairo, (1360 AH).

Asfahani, Abu Bakr al-Asfahani, *Kitab al-Aghani*, Dar al-Thaqafa, Beirut, 6th ed., 1404/1983.

'Asqalani, (d. 852/1449), *Fath al-Bari bi Sharh Sahih al-Bukhari*, al-Matba'a al-Bahiya al-Masriya, and Dar Ihya' al-Turath al-Arabi, 4th. ed., Beirut, 1408/1988.

'Awadi, A. al-Awadi, "Human Life, its beginning and end in Islamic Law," *Kuwait Islamic Organization of Medical Sciences*, 1985.

Azimabadi, Muhammad Shams al-Haq al-'Azimabadi, *Aun al-Ma'bud: Sharh Sunan Abi Dawud,* al-Maktaba as-Salafia, al-Madina al-Munawara, 2nd.ed., 1288/1969.

Azimabadi, Muhammad Shams al-Haq al-'Azimabadi, *Aun al-Ma'bud: Sharh Sunan Abi Dawud, m'a Sharh Ibn Qayyim al-Jawzia*, Dar al-Kutub al-'Ilmia, Beirut, 1410/1990.

Bahwati, (d. 1051/1641), Mansur ibn Yunus al-Bahwati, *Kashaf al-Qina'a 'ala Matn al-Iqna'a*, al-Matba'a al-'Amirah ash-Sharafia, 1st ed., Cairo, 1319 AH.

Bahwati, *Sharh Muntaha al-Iradat: Daqai'q Awli al-Nuha li Sharh al-Muntaha*, 'Alam al-Kutub, Beirut.

Baihaqi, (d. 364/1066), Ahmad ibn al-Hussain ibn Ali al-Baihaqi, *as-Sunan al-Kubra*, Daral-Ma'arif al-Uthmania, Hyderabad, India, 1354 AH.

Baji, (d. 474/1081), Suliman ibn Khalaf al-Baji al-Andalusi, *al-Muntaqa, Sharh Muwatta' al-Imam Malik*, Mutba'at as-Sa'ada, Cairo.

Banna, (al-Sa'ati, d. 1371/1952), Ahmad Abdul Rahman al-Banna al-Sa'ati, *Al-Fath al-Rabbani li Tartib Musnad al-Imam Ahmad ibn Hanbal ash-Shaybani*, 2nd ed., Dar Ihya' al-Turath al-Arabi, Cairo, 1396 AH., (appears as Sa'ati below).

Bayh, Muhsin al-Bayh, *Khatta' at-Tabib al-Mujib lil Mas'oulia al-Madaniah*, Maktabat al-Jala' al-Jadidah, Al-Mansurah, Egypt, 1990.

Borno, Muhammad Siddiq ibn Ahmad ibn Muhammad al-Borno, *Al-Wajiz fi Idah Qawa'id al-Fiqh al-Kuliyah*, 1st. ed., 1983, Mua'ssasat al-Risalah, 5th. ed., Beirut, 1419/1998.

Bukhari, (d. 256/870) Muhammad ibn Ismail ibn Ibrahim ibn al-Mughirah ibn Bardzabah al-Bukhari al-Ju'afi.

Sahih al-Bukhari, Dar al-Fikr, Cairo, 1981

Sahih al-Bukhari, (ed.), M. M. Khan, Kazi Publications, Lahore, Pakistan, 1986.

Sahih al-Bukhari, (ed.), Mustafa Dieb al-Bogha, Dar Ibn Kathir, Damascus and Beirut, 4th ed., 1451/1990.

Sahih al-Bukhari, (ed.), Siddiqi, A., Islamic Bonds Publications, Kuwait, 1993.

Sahih al-Bukhari, (Mukhtasar) Summarised by Ahmad Abdul Latif az-Zubiedi, and translated by Muhammad Muhsin Khan, Maktabat Dar us-Salam, Riyadh, 1994.

Bukhari & Muslim,:

Jakni, Muhammad ibn Abdalla ibn Ahmad MaYa'ba al-Jakni, *Zad al-Muslim fi ma ittafaqa 'alayhi al-Bukhari wa Muslim*, Mu'assasat al-Halabi, Cairo, 1967.

Bultaji, Muhammad, *Munhaj 'Umar ibn al-Khattab fi al-Tashri,'* Dar al-Fikr al-Arabi, Cairo, 1390/1970.

Damad, (d. 1078 AH), Abdur Rahman Effendi Suliman, (Shiekhi Zada), *Majma' al-Anhur: Sharh Multaqa al-Abhur*, Dar at-Tiba'a al-'Amira, Uthmania Printers, 1327/1907.

Dasuqi, (d. 1815), Muhammad ibn Ahmad ibn 'Arafa al-Dasuqi, *Hashiyah 'ala al-Sharh al-Kabir*, Mutba'at Mustafa Muhammad, al-Maktaba al-Tijariya al-Kubra, Cairo, (1230 A.H).

Dirdir, (or Dardir, d. 1786), Ahmad ibn Muhammad ibn Ahmad ibn al-'Adawi al-Dirdir, *al-Sharh al-Kabir 'ala Mukhtasar Khalil*, Dar Ihya' al-Kutub Al-Arabia, al-Halabi, Cairo

Dhahabi, (d. 748 AH), al-Hafiz Muhammad ibn Ahmad ibn Uthman ibn Qaymaz al-Dhahabi, *al-Tib al-Nabawi*, (ed.), Ahmad Rif'at al-Badrawi, 2nd. ed., Dar Ihya' al-'Ulum, Beirut, 1406/1986.

Fatawa, or *Fatwa* (sing.):

Alamgiri, *Fatawi Hindiyah*, Shaikh Nizam and others, Luknow, [S.N], (1899-1900).

Al-Fatawa al-Islamiyya, High Council of Islamic Affairs, Cairo, Issued by Dar al-Ifta'a al-Masriyyah under the Grand *Imam*, the Minister of Religious Affairs, and the *Mufti* of the Republic, and the Secretary General of the High Council of Islamic Affairs, vol. 9, Cairo (1983).

Fatawa Ibn Taymiyya, Ahmad ibn Abd al-Halim, Dar al-Kutub al-Haditha, Cairo, 1966.

Fayrouzabadi, (d. 817), Muhammad ibn Jaqub al-Fayrouzabadi, *al-Qamus al-Muhit*, (ed.),Muhammad al-'Irq-sousi, Mua'ssasat ar-Risala, 4th. ed., Beirut, 1415/1994.

Ghazali, (d. 505/1111), Muhammad ibn Muhammad ibn Ahmad Abu-Hamid at-Tusi al-Ghazali, *al-Mustasfa min 'Ilm al-Usul*, 1st ed., al-Hallabi, al-Matba'a al-Amiriya, Bulaq, Cairo, 1322/1906; and *al-Mustasfa fi 'Ulum al-Usul*, Cairo, 1935 edition.

Ghazali, (d. 505/1111), Muhammad ibn Muhammad al-Ghazali, *Ihya' 'Ulum al- Din*, Dar al-Kutub al-'Ilmiya, Beirut, ad-Dar al-Masrriya al-Labnania, Cairo, (n. d.).

Ghazali, (d. 1997), Muhammad al-Ghazali *Laysa min al-Islam*, Dar al-Kutub al-Haditha, 3rd ed., Cairo, 1963.

Hakim, (d. 405 AH), Muhammad ibn Abd Allah al-Hakim al-Naisaburi, *al-Mustadrak 'l Sahihain fi 'l hadith*, , Dar al-Fikr, Beirut, (n.d.).

Hakim, (d. 405 AH), Muhammad ibn Abd Allah al-Hakim al-Naisaburi, *al-Mustadrak 'ala as-Sahihain fi'l-hadith wa Talkhis al-Hafidh adh-Dhahabi*, Dai'rat al-Ma'arif an-Nizamiyah, 1st ed., Hayderabad, India, vol. 1, 1334 AH.,and vol. 2, (1340 AH).

Halliday, Fred., (Sereis of three articles rendered in Arabic translation): "Fundamentalism, the Natural Response to Today's Problems." 10 Feb. 1997
"Nationalism and Fundmentalism." 11 Feb. 1997
"Islam is not a Military or an Economic Threat to the West." 12 Feb. 1997
in *Ash-Sharq Al-Awsat Newspaper*, all in pages 8, columns 1-5, :, London, et. al

Hattab, (d. 954/1547), Muhammad ibn Muhammad ibn Abdur-Rahman al-Hattab, *Mawahib al-Jalil li Sharh Mukhtasar Khalil*, together with al-Muwaq's, *at-Taj wa'l-Iklil li Mukhtasar Khalil*, 1st. ed., Matba'at as-Sa'ada, Cairo, 1329 AH.

Haythami (or al-Haytami), see below Ibn Hajar, *Tuhfat al-Muhtaj Sharho 'ala al-Minhaj*, al-Maktaba al-Tijaria al-Kubra, Matba'at Mustafa Muhammad, Cairo, 1304 AH.

Hijawi, (d. 960 AH), Abu al-Naja Musa ibn Ahmad ibn Salim al-Qudsi al-Hijawi, *al-Iqna'a ma'a Kashaf al-Qina,'* al-Matba'a al-'Amira al-Sharafiya, 1st ed., 1319 AH.

Hindi, (d. 975 AH), Ali al-Mutaqi ibn Husam al-Din al-Hindi al-Burhanfouri, *Kanz al-'Ummal fi Sunan al-Aqwal wa l' Af'al*, (ed.), Bakri Hayati and Safwa al-Saqa, Maktabat al-Turath al-Islami, 1st ed., Halab, Syria, 1391/1971-1395/1975. (16 vols., 1969-1977).

Haykal, Muhammad Hussein, *As-Siddiq Abu Bakr*, Matba'at Misr, (1361 A.H.).

Ibn 'Abd al-Salam, (d. 660 AH), Izz al-Din Abd al-Aziz al-Salami ash-Shafi'i, *Qaw'id al-Ahkam fi Masalih al-Anam*, (ed.) Taha Saad, Dar al-Jeel, 2nd ed., Beirut, 1400/1980.

Ibn 'Abidin, (d. 1252/1836), Muhammad Amin ibn Ali ibn 'Abidin, *Hashiyat Ibn 'Abdin: Radd al-Muhtar 'ala ad-Durr al-Mukhtar Sharh Tanwir al-Absar*, Mustafa al-Babi al-Halabi, 2nd. ed., Cairo, 1386/1966.

Ibn Abi Usaybia, (600-668 AH), Ahmad ibn al-Qasim ibn Khalifa ibn Yunus al-Sa'adi al-Khazraji Ibn Abi Usaybia, *'Uyun al-Anba'i fi tabaqat al-Atibba'*, (ed.), Nazar Rida, Dar Maktabt al-Hayah, Beirut, (n. d.).

Ibn al-Humam, (d. 861/1457 AH), Kamaluddin Muhammad ibn Abdel Wahid as-Siwasi al-Askandari, *Fath al-Qadir:Sharh al-Hidaya*, al-Matb'a al-Amiriyyah, Bulaq, Cairo, 1299 AH. (A compilation of six related books: al-Mirghanani, (d. 593 AH.), wrote *Bidayt al-Mubtadi'*, then he himself commented on it in, *Hidayat al-Muhtadi*; then Al-Babarti, (d. 786 AH.), wrote a commentary on the original

Bibliography and Bibliographical Abbreviations 333

al-Bidaya, and called it *al-'Inaya: Sharh al Bidaya*. Further on Ibn al-Humam, (d. 861 AH.) wrote his commentary on the commentary of al-Mirghanini *(al-Hidaya)*, and called his book *Fath al-Qadir:Sharh al-Hidaya*, this was completed by Ahmad Qadi Zadeh, (d. 988 AH), *Takmilat Fath al-Qadir: Nataj al-Afkar fi Kashf ar-Romouz wa al-Asrar*. Finally Sa'adi Jalabi Halabi commented on both *al-Hidaya* and *al-'Inaya* and it was called *Hashyat Sa'adi Jalabi Halabi*. (All six books are printed with *Fath al-Qadir*).

Ibn al-Muqaffa,' Abdullahi, *Kitab Kalila wa Dimna*, (ed.), Mustafa Lutfi al-Manfluti, Dar al-Kitab al-Arabi, Beirut, 1966.

Ibn al-Qaiyyim, (d. 751/1350), Muhammad ibn Abi Bakr ibn Qaiyyim al-Jawzia, *A'lam al-Muwqin'un Rabbi al-'Alimin*, Dar al-Fikr, Beirut, 1397 AH.

Ibn al-Sallah,'Uthman ibn Abd al-Rahman al-Shahrizouri, *'Ulum al-hadith*, (ed.), Nour al-Din 'Antar, Dar al-Fikr, Damascus & Beirut, 3rd. ed., 1984, Reprinted 1998.

Ibn Farhun, (d. 799/1397), al-Qadi Ibrahim ibn Ali ibn Farhoun, *Tabsirat al-Hukam fi Usul al-Aqdia wa Manahij al-Ahkam*, Mustafa al-Babi al-Halabi, Cairo, 1378/1958.

Ibn Hajar al-Haythami or (al-Haytami) (d. 947/15542), Ahmad ibn Muhammad, *Tuhfat al-Muhtaj Sharho 'ala al-Minhaj*, al-Maktaba at-Tijaria al-Kubra, Matba'at Mustafa Muhammad Cairo, (1304 AH).

Ibn Hanbal, (164-241 AH), *Musnad Ahmad Ibn Hanbal*, (ed.), Shu'aeib al-Arno'ut, Mua'ssasat al-Risala, Beirut, 1993

Ibn Hanbal, (164-241 AH), *Musnad Ahmad ibn Hanbal*, (ed.), Ahmad Muhammad Shakir, 2nd.ed., Dar al-Ma'arif, 1365/1946

Ibn Hazm az-Zahiri, (d. 456/1064), Ali ibn Ahmad ibn Sa'aid ibn Hazm al-Andalusi, *al-Muhalla*, (ed.), Ahmad Muhammad Shakir, al-Maktab al (at)-Tijari li't-Tiba'a wa'n-Nashr wa't-Tawzi', Beirut,? 1969[sic]; and also (with the same paging) in al-Matba'a al-Muniriya, Cairo, (1347 AH).

Ibn Hibban, (d. 354/965), 'Ala'ud-Din al-Farisi Ibn Hibban, *(al-Amir*: The Prince), *Sahih Ibn Hibban*, (ed.), Ahmad Muhammad Shakir, Dar al-Ma'arif, Cairo, 1371/1952.

(Ibn Hibban called his *Sahih, al-Musnad as-Sahih 'an at-Taqisim wa al-Anwa'a, min ghair wujud qat'a fi sanadiha wa la thubut jarhu fi naqiliha*).

Ibn Majah, (d. 273/886), (207-275? AH), Muhammad ibn Yazid al-Qizwini, *Sunan Ibn Maja*, (ed.), Muhammad Fua'd Abd al-Baqi, Dar Ihya' al-Kutub al-Arabia, Faisal Eisa al-Babi al-Halabi, Cairo, vol. 1 1372/1952, vol. 2 1373/1953.

Ibn Manzour, (d. 711/1311), Muhammad ibn Makram ibn Manzour al-Afriqi al-Masri, *Lisan al-Arab*, Dar Sadir, Beirut, 1990.

Ibn Muflih, (d. 884 AH), Muhammad ibn Muflih al-Maqdisi al-Hanbali, *al-Adab ash-Shar'ia wa'l-Minah al-Mari'a*, Distributed by Idarat al-Buhuth al-'Ilmia wa al-Ifta' wa al-Da'awa wa al-Irshad, Riyadh, Saudi Arabia, (n. d.).

Ibn Muflih, Muhammad, *Kitab al-Foro'u*, 2nd ed., Cairo, 1381/1962

Ibn Nujaim, Zien al-'Abidin ibn Ibrahim ibn Nujaim al-Hanafi, (d. 970/1613), *al-Ashbah wa'n-Nadha'ir*, Dar al-Kutub al-'Ilmiya, Beirut, 1400 AH., cited by Borno, 1998.

Ibn Nujaim, Zien al-'Abidin ibn Ibrahim ibn Nujaim al-Misri, *al-Bahr ar-Ra'iq Sharh Kanz ad-Daqiq*, Dar al-Ma'arifa, Beirut, (1311 AH).

Ibn Nujaim, *al-Bahr ar-Ra'iq: Sharh Kanz ad-Daqiq*, (Printed on the margin of al-Marghinani's, *Hidaya*), Mutba'at al-Halabi, Cairo, 1937.

Ibn Qadi Samawa, Mahmoud ibn Isra'il (d.823/1420) *Jami' al-Fosilien*, 1st ed., al-Matba'a al-Azhariya, Cairo, (1300 AH).

Ibn Qayyim al-Jawzia, (d. 751/1350), Muhammad ibn Abi Bakr az-Zar'i ad-Dimashqi, *Zad al-Ma'ad fi Huda Khayr al-'Ibad*, (ed.), Sho'ieb and Abdul Qadir al-Arno'ut, 1st ed. Mua'ssasat al-Risala, Beirut and Maktabat al-Manar al-Islamiyyah, Kuwait, Beirut, 1399/1979.

Ibn Qudama, (d. 620 AH), Abdullahi ibn Ahmad ibn Muhammad ibn Qudama al-Maqdisi, *al-Kafi fi fiqh Ahmad ibn Hanbal*, (ed.), Zuhier al-Shawish, al-Maktab al-Islami, 3rd ed., Beirut and Damascus, 1402/1982.

Ibn Qudama, *al-Mughni wa Mukhtasar al-Khirqi*, ('Umar ibn Hussain al-Khirqi), Maktabat al-Riyadh al-Haditha, Riyadh, 1401/1981.

Ibn Qudama, *al-Mughni,* Mutba'at al-Manar, Cairo, (1348 AH).

Ibn Qudama, *al-Muqni'a fi Fiqh Ahmad ibn Hanbal*, Matab'i ad-Dajwi, Cairo, 1980.

Ibn Rushd, (d, 595/1198), Muhammad ibn Ahmad ibn Muhammad ibn Ahmad ibn Rushd al-Qurtubi (the grandson), *Bidayat al-Mujtahid wa Nihayat al-Muqtasid*, Maktabat al-Kulliyat, Al-Azhar, as-Sanadiqiya, Cairo, (n. d.).

Ibn Rushd, *Bidayat al-Mujtahid*, Matba'at al-Ma'ahid, Jammalia, Cairo, 1353/1935.

Ibn Taymiyya, Ahmad ibn Abd al-Halim, *Fatawa,* Dar al-Kutub al-Haditha, Cairo, 1966.

'Illiesh, (d. 1299), Muhammad ibn Ahmad, *Sharh Minah al-Jalil 'ala Mukhtasar Khalil*, 1st ed., Dar al-Fikr Beirut, 1404/1984.

Jakni, Muhammad ibn Abdalla ibn Ahmad (Maya'ba al-Jakni), *Zad al-Muslim fi ma ittafaqa 'alayhi al-Bukhari wa Muslim*, Mu'assasat al-Halabi, Cairo, 1967, see Bukhari & Muslim.

Jarrahi, (d. 1162), Ismail ibn Muhammad al-'Ajaluni al-Jarrahi, *Kashf al-Khafa wa Muzil al-Ilbas 'amma Ishtahara min al-Ahadith 'ala Alsinat al-Nas*, (ed.), Ahmad al-Qulash, Maktabat at-Turath al-Islami, Halab, Syria, 1974; and Cairo edition,

Bibliography and Bibliographical Abbreviations 335

Jassas, (d. 370 AH), Ahmad ibn Ali ar-Razi al-Jassas, *Ahkam al-Qur'an al-Karim*, Matba'at al-Awqaf al-Islamia, Dar al-Khilafa al-Alia, 1335 AH.

Jindi, Anwar al-Jindi, *al-Islam wa Harakat al-Tarikh*, Dar Al-Kitab al-Labnani, Beirut, 1980

Kandhloy, Muhammad Zacharia al-Kandhloy, *Awjaz al-Masalik ila Muwatta' Malik*, Dar al-Fikr, Beirut, 1409/1989.

Kandhloy, Muhammad Yusuf al-Kandhloy, *Hayat as-Sahaba*, 1st ed., Dar al-Kitab al-Arabi, Beirut, 1408/1987.

Kasani, (d. 587/1327), Abu-Bakr ibn Mas'oud al-Kasani, *Badi"a as-Sani"a fi Tartib al-Shari'ah*, 1st ed., Matba'at al-Jammalia, Cairo, 1328/1910. (A commentary on Muhammad ibn Ahmad al-Samarqandi's treatise on Hanafi Law *Tuhfat al-Fuqaha*, ed., Abdul Jawad Khalaf).

Khalifat, Awad Muhammad, *Nasha't al-Harka al-Ibadia*, Matabi'Dar al-Sha'ab, 'Omman, Jordan, 1978.

Khirshi, Muhammad ibn 'Abdalla al-Khirshi, *Sharh un 'ala Mukhtasar Khalil*, al-Matba'a al-Amiriya, Bulaq, Cairo, (1317 AH).

Khirqi, Abu al-Qasim 'Umar ibn al-Hussain al-Khirqi, *Mukhtasar al-Khirqi ma'a al-Mughni*, (Ibn Qudama), Matba'at al-Manar, (1367 AH).

Madkour, Muhammad Sallaam, *al-Madkhal lil Fiqh al-Islami: History, Sources, and General Theory*, Dar an-Nahda al-Arabia, Cairo, 1386/1966.

Majallat al-Ahkam al-'Adlia wa Qanun al-Mu'amalat, Committee of Ahmad Jawdat and others, 1285-1293 AH., (1851 Acts). Matba'at Uthmania, Publisher Dar Sa'adat, Istanbul 1303 AH., see also, (Borno, *al-Wajiz*), above.

Malik, (d. 179/795), Malik ibn Anas ibn Malik, *al-Muwatta,'* (ed.), Farouq Sa'ad, 3rd ed., Dar al-Afaq al-Jadida, Beirut, 1403/1983.

Malik, *al-Muwatta,'* Dar ar-Rayan lil Turath, Cairo, 1408/1988.

Mirghinani, (d. 593 AH), Ali ibn Abi-Bakr ibn Abdul-Jalil ar-Rashidani al-Mirghinani, *al-Hidayah: Sharh Bidayat al-Mubtadi' (al-Bidayah)*, Matba'at Mustafa al-Babi al-Halabi, Cairo, 1355/1936.

Mu'ammar, Ali Yahya, *al-Ibadiya fi Mawkib at-Tarikh*, Maktabat Wahba, Mutba'at ad-Da'wa al-Islamiya, 1st. ed., Cairo, 1399/1979.

Mubarak, Qays ibn Muhammad Aal al-Sheikh Mubarak, *Al-Tadawi wal Masuliyya al-Tibbiyya fi al-Shari'ah al-Islamiyya*, 1st ed., Maktabat al-Farabi, Damascus, 1412/1991.

Musali, Abdalla al-Musali, *al-Ikhtiyar li Ta'alil al-Muhtar*, Mutba'at al-Qahira, 1356 AH.

Muslim, (206-261 AH), Muslim ibn al-Hajjaj al-Qatari al-Nisaburi, *Sahih Muslim*, (ed.), Muhammad Mu'adh Abd al-Baqi, Dar al-Fikr, Beirut, 1403/1983.

Muslim, (206-261 AH.), *Sahih Muslim,* (ed.), Musa Lashin and Ahmad Hashim, Izzedin Publications, 1st. ed., Beirut, 1987.

Musnad Ahmad Ibn Hanbal, (ed.), Shu'aib al-Arno'ut Mua'sasat al-Risala, Beirut, 1413/1993.

Muwaq, (d.897), Muhammad ibn Yusuf al-'Abdri al-Muwaq, *at-Taj wa al-Iklil li Mukhtasar Khalil,* printed with the commentary of al-Hattab, *Mawahib al-Jalil li Sharh Mukhtasar Khalil,* 1st. ed., Matba'at al-Sa'ada, Cairo, (1329 AH).

Nadwi, Ali al-Hassani an-Nadwi, *al-Sira al-Nabawiya,* 2nd. ed., Dar al-Shuruq, Jeddah, Saudi Arabia 1399/1979.

Nafarawi, Ahmad ibn Ghoneim ibn Salim al-Nafarawi, *al-Fawakih al-Dawani 'ala Risalat Ibn Zayd al-Qayrawani,* Matba'at al-Sa'ada, 1st. ed., Cairo, (1332 AH),

Najdi, Abdur Rahman ibn Muhammad ibn Qasim al-'Asimi an-Najdi, *Hashyat ar-Rawd al-Muraba': Sharh Zad al-Mustaqna'* , 2nd. ed., (1405 AH).

Najjar, Abd al-Wahab al-Najjar, *al-Khulafa' ar-Rashidoun,* Dar al-Qalam, Beirut, (1406/1986).

Nawawi, (d. 676/1277), Yahya ibn Sharaf an-Nawawi, *al-Majmu' Sharh al-Muhadhdhab,* Dar al-Fikr, Beirut. (n.d).

Nawawi, (d. 676/1277), Yahya ibn Sharaf an-Nawawi, *Sharh Irshad al-Sari,* (1305 AH).

n.d.= No date of publication.

Qarrafi, Ahmad ibn Idris ibn Abd al-Rahman al-Sanhaji al-Qarrafi, *al-Furuq,* Dar Ihya' al-Kutub al-Arabia, 1st. ed., al-Halabi, Cairo, (1344 AH).

Qattan, Sheikh Mana'a bin Khalil al-Qattan,"Al-Manzour al-Islami li Zira'at al-'Adda'" (Organ Transplantation). *Majallat al-Azhar,* No. 5 Jumada al-Uwla, (1418 AH), September 1997, pp. 756-765. Al-Qattan: Professor, at Imam Muhammad bin Sa'ud Islamic University and Supervisor of Postgraduate Studies (formerly Director of the High Institute of the Judiciary) Kingdom of Saudi Arabia.

Qays ibn Muhammad Aal al-Sheikh Mubarak, see above 'Mubarak.'

Ramli, (d.1004 AH), Muhammad ibn Ahmad ibn Hamza ibn Shihab ad-Din ar-Ramli, *Nihayat al-Muhtaj ila Sharh al-Minhaj,* Mustafa al-Babi al-Halabi, Cairo, 1357 AH.

Rida, Rashid, (ed.) *Majou'at al-hadith an-Najdia,* (six out of nine sections on *hadith* collected by Muhammad ibn Abdel Wahab), al-Maktaba as-Salafiya, al-Madina al-Munawara, Saudi Arabia, 1383 AH.

Rudwan, Fathi, *Fi Falsafat al-Tashri' al-Islami,* Dar al-Kitab al-Labnani, Beirut, 1975.

Sa'ati, (1371 AH), Ahmad Abdul Rahman al-Banna al-Sa'ati, (al-Banna), *Al-Fath al-Rabani li Tartib Musnad al-Imam Ahmad ibn Hanbal al-Shaybani,*

Bibliography and Bibliographical Abbreviations 337

together with *Kanz al-'Ummal*, Dar Ihya' al-Turath al-Arabi, 2nd. ed., Cairo, (1396 AH). (See Banna).
Sabiq, Sayed, *Fiqh as-Sunnah*, (1st Published 1365 AH.), Dar al-Fikr, Beirut, 1415/1995.
Sahnoun, (d. 240 AH), *al-Mudawwana al-Kubra:* (Riwayat Sahnun ibn Sa'id at-Tanukhi 'an Abdur Rahman ibn al-Qasim al-Muttaqi 'an Malik ibn Anas), Matba'at as-Sa'ada, Cairo, 1323/1905-6.
Salih, Abdel Ghaffar Ibrahim, *al-Qisas*, Mutba'at an-Nahda, Cairo, 1989.
Sana'ani, Muhammad ibn Ismail al-Sana'ani, *Subul al-Salam: Sharh Bulugh al-Muram*, Dar al-Kitab al-Arabi, Beirut, 4th.ed., 1987.
Sarakhsi, or Sarkhasi, (d. 438/1090), Muhammad ibn Sahl al-Sarakhsi, *al-Mabsut: Sharh Kitab al-Kafi*, (*Kutub Zahir al-Riwaya*) by Muhammad al-Hassan al-Shaybani: *al-Jami' al-Saghir, al-Jami' al-Kabir, al-Siyar al-Kabir, al-Siyar al-Saghir, al-Ziadat, wa Kitab al-Kafi*). Matba'at as-Sa'ada, 1st. ed., Cairo, 1324/1958, and Dar Sa'ada, Caio 1331 AH.
Ash-Shafi'i, (d. (150-204 AH), Muhammad ibn Idris, ash-Shafi'i, *Kitab al-Umm*, (ed.), Mahmoud Matarji, Dar al-Kutub al-'Ilmiya, Beirut, 1993.
Ash-Shafi'i, Muhammad ibn Idris, ash-Shafi'i, *Kitab al-Umm: Mawsu'at al-Imam ash-Shafi'i*, (ed.), Ahmad Badr ad-Din Hasoun, Dar Qutayba, Beirut, 1418/1996.
Shahawi, Ibrahim Dasuqi al-Shahawi, *Kitab al-Shahawi fi mustalah al-hadith. A study of the hadith Arabic text*, Jami'at al-Azhar, Cairo, 1386/1966.
Shahrastani, (479-548), (d. 548/1153), Muhammad Abdel Karim ibn Abi-Bakr Ahmad al (ash)-Shahrastani, *al-Milal wa'l Nihal*, (ed.), Abdel Aziz Muhammad al-Wakil, Mu'assasat al-Halabi, Cairo, 1387/1968.
Shinqiti, Muhammad ibn Muhammad al-Mukhtar al-Shanqiti, *Ahkam al-Jiraha al-Tibbiya*, Islamic University, al-Madina al-Munawara, 3rd ed., (1418/1997).
Sharawani, *Hawashi ash-Sharawani wa Ibn al-Qasim al-'Abadi 'ala Tuhfat al-Muhtaj Sharh al-Minhaj*, Dar Sadir, Beirut.
Shatibi, (d. 790/1388), Ibrahim ibn Musa al-Lakhami al-Qurnati al-Maliki ash-Shatibi, *Al-Muwafaqat fi ash-Shari'a*, Dar al-Ma'rifa, Beirut, and al-Maktaba at-Tijariya al-Kubra, Matba'at Mustafa Muhammad, Cairo, (1359/1975).
Shawkani, (d. 1250/1839), Muhammad ibn Ali ibn Muhammad al- (ash)-Shawkani, *Nayl al-Awtar: Sharh Muntaqa al-Akhbar*, al-Babi al-Halabi, Cairo, 1372 AH.
Shawkani, (d. 1250/1839), Muhammad ibn Ali ibn Muhammad al-Shawkani, *Risalat al-Qawl al-Mufeed fi Adilat al-Ijtihad wa al-Taqlid: a treatise refusing the doctrine that a Muslim must belong to one of the four madhahib*, Mustafa al-Babi al-Halabi, Cairo, 1347/1928. (1n 47 pages).
Sheikhi Zada, (d. 1087 AH), Abdur Rahman ibn Muhammad ibn Suliman, *Majma' al-Anhur: Sharh Multaqa al-Abhur*, Dar at-Tiba'a al-'Amira, Cairo.
Sheikhi Zada, (d. 1087 AH), Abdur Rahman Effendi Damad, also known as

Abdul Rahman ibn Muhammad ibn Suliman Sheikhi Zada, *Majma' al-Anhur: Sharh Multaqa al-Abhur*, Dar Sa'adat, 1327 AH.

Shirazi, Ibrahim ibn Ali al-Fairouzabadi al-Shirazi, (d. 1083 CE), *al-Muhadhab*, al-Babi al-Halabi, Cairo, (n.d.), cited by Omran

Shiriqi, Ibrahim ash-Shiriqi, *at-Tarikh al-Islami*, Ma'arif wa al-'Ulum Series, 2nd ed., al-Madina al-Munawara, 1391/1971.

Shubramulsi, (d. 1187 AH), Ali ibn Ali ash-Shubramulsi, *Hashiya 'ala Nihayat al-Muhtaj lil Ramli*, Mutba'at al-Qahira, Cairo, 1104 AH.

Suyuti, Jalal al-Din Abd al-Rahman ibn Abi Bakr al-Shafi'i al-Suyuti, (d. 911/1505), *al-Ashbah wa'l Nadha'ir*, Dar al-Kutub al-'Ilmiya, Beirut, 1st ed., 1399 AH., cited by Borno, 1998.

Suyuti, *al-Jami' al-Saghir fi Ahadith al-Bashir an-Nadhir*, Dar al-Fikr, Beirut, 1981.

Suyuti, *Sahih al-Jami' al-Saghir wa Ziyadatuhu: al-Fath al-Kabir*, (ed.), Muhammad Nasir al-Albani (d. 1999), Manshurat al-Maktab al-Islami, 1st ed., (Damascus ?), [sic], 1st ed., (1388/1969).

Tarabulsi, Ali ibn Khalil al-Trabulsi (d. 844/1441), *Mu'in al-Hukkam*, 2nd. ed., al-Halabi, Cairo, (1393/1973),

Tirmidhi,(d. 279/892), Muhammad ibn Eisa al-Salami al-Tirmidhi, *Sahih al-Tirmidhi*, (ed.), Muhammad Foa'd Abdul Baqi, al-Mutba'a al-Masriyah, al-Azhar, and Mustafa al-Babi al-Halabi, Cairo, 1350 AH.

Tirmidhi, (209-279 AH), *Sunan al-Tirmidhi: al-Jami' al-Sahih*, (ed.), Abdur-Rahman Muhammad 'Uthman, 2nd ed., Dar al-Fikr, Beirut, 1403/1983.

Tirmidhi, Sunan al-Tirmidhi: al-Jami' al-Sahih, (ed.), Ibrahim 'Atwa 'Awad, Dar Ihya' al-Turath al-Arabi, Beirut, (n. d.).

Zarkashi, (d. 794 AH), Muhammad ibn Bahadir al-Zarkashi, *al-Manthur fi al-Qawa'id*, (ed.), Taysir Fa'iq Ahmad Mahmud, 1st ed., Mu'assasat al-Khalij, Kuwait, 1402 AH., cited by Shinqiti, 1997.

Zarkashi, (d. 794 AH), Muhammad ibn Bahadir al-Zarkashi, *al-Manthour fi al-Qawa'id*, (ed.), Taysir Fa'iq Ahmad Mahmud, 1st ed., Wazarat al-Awqaf, Kuwait, 1404 AH., cited by Borno, 1998.

Zurqani, (d. 1122/1710), Muhammad ibn Abd al-Baqi ibn Yusuf ibn Ahmad az-Zurqani, *Sharh 'ala Mukhtasar Khalil*, al-Maktaba al-Tijaria, Mustafa Muhammad, Cairo.

Zurqani, (d. 1122/1710), Muhammad ibn Abd al-Baqi ibn Yusuf ibn Ahmad az-Zurqani, *Sharh...'ala Muwatta Malik*, Matba'at al-Istiqama, Cairo, (1379AH).

Index

A

abortion 202-3, 205, 210-5, 217-21, 223-5, 229, 236-8, 250, 272-3, 286, 295, 305, 319
Abu Bakr as-Siddiq 48, 86, 98
Abu Hanifah 20, 22, 36, 37, 39, 40, 42, 58, 75, 146, 148, 161, 165, 166, 167, 168, 171, 172, 177, 185, 186, 189, 194, 195, 196, 224
Abu Thawr 36
Abu us-Sorour 252 250, 252
Abu Yusuf 36, 39, 40, 42, 167, 172, 185, 189
Abu Zahra 14, 25, 52, 53, 54, 55, 57, 58, 60, 61, 91, 279, 292, 329
adh-dhara'i 14, 27
ahl ad-diwan 72, 76, 120, 122, 126, 143-4, 178, 284
Airedale NHS Trust v Bland 163, 176, 197, 279
'alaqa 202, 205, 210, 211, 212, 221, 226, 237
Alexis, Dr. Carrel 254
'Ali ibn Abi Talib 20, 32, 40, 41, 52, 53, 109, 130, 178, 205, 216
analogy (*qiyas*) 7, 14, 15, 25, 26, 28, 37, 38, 41, 44, 216, 242, 264
'aqila 27, 72, 73, 74, 93, 106, 107, 108, 117, 118, 119, 120, 122, 126, 139, 140, 141, 142, 143, 144, 196, 222, 223, 224, 232, 256, 284
'Arfaja ibn Sa'd 254
artificial insemination 243, 267
al-'Asqalani 21, 54, 96, 97, 98, 99
al-Awza'i 36
al-Azhar 14, 92, 243, 252, 260, 265-8, 276, 279, 333-4, 336-8
'azl (coitus interruptus) 101, 204, 205, 206, 207, 208, 209, 215, 217, 227, 228

B

bayt al-mal 106, 107, 117, 118, 122, 142, 143, 144
Ballantyne 52, 61, 246, 250, 321
BBC 193, 247, 253
Beatty v. Cullingworth 125

Blood, Diane 242
Bolam case 112
Bolam principle 112, 136
Bolam test 102, 112, 124, 127, 136, 152, 154, 283
Bolam v. Friern Hospital Management Committee 102, 111
Borno 58, 59, 122, 229, 253, 292, 318, 330, 333, 335, 338
Brazier 100, 122, 179, 199, 239, 250, 322
al-Bukhari and Muslim 11, 19, 23-4, 53, 55-6, 58, 90, 94-6, 125, 194, 207, 228, 250, 276, 277, 317

C

Challoner 252-3, 322
clones 246, 250, 309
cloning 2, 9, 233, 239-40, 244-7, 252, 274, 289, 309, 310-3, 326
coitus interruptus (see also *'azl*) 204, 206, 215
community welfare 7, 26, 72, 148
compensation 8, 32, 62-4, 70-5, 77, 90, 94, 102-3, 105-7, 110, 116-21, 128, 130, 132, 135-40, 143-5, 152, 156, 168, 188, 216-7, 223, 283-5
consensus (*ijma'*) 14-5, 21, 24-5, 28-9, 35, 38, 41, 44-7, 85, 100, 115, 118, 128, 132, 143, 172, 184, 188, 191, 225, 240
Coulson 16, 20, 38, 39, 41, 53, 54, 55, 56, 57, 58, 59, 322
Council of Grand Jurists in the Kingdom of Saudi 214

D

ad-Dardir 155, 157, 187, 199, 200, 211, 226, 228, 229, 230, 251, 330
Davies 122, 157, 194, 197-8, 237-8, 250-2, 264, 278-9, 292-3, 323
Declaration of Geneva, The 10, 296, 297, 298, 301, 305
Denning, Lord 104, 105, 115, 139, 150, 283
diagnosis 1, 141, 173, 174, 197, 271, 312
diya 26-7, 32, 70, 72-7, 92-3, 105-8, 117-20, 122, 130, 137, 139-46, 148-50, 156, 165, 167-72, 177-8, 184,-9, 191, 194-5, 196, 201, 222-4, 232, 256, 284-5

E

embryo 210, 213, 215, 217, 221,-2, 234, 236-9, 241-2, 246-7, 250-1, 253, 309-11, 322, 324
European Commission 245, 309, 310, 326
European Parliament 245, 253, 312, 313
euthanasia 2, 8, 118, 156, 159-65, 168-72, 175-6, 178-82, 189-94, 196-201, 242, 279, 285, 293
expiation 116, 120, 141-2, 144, 148, 188-90, 212, 223-4, 286

F

al-Fatawa al-Hindiya 35, 157, 211, 214, 228-31, 263, 278, 329
Fatawa al-Majma' al-Fiqhiyya 251
fatwa 4, 7, 34,-5, 50, 100-1, 211, 214, 228-9, 240, 243-4, 252, 266, 276, 278, 289-90, 319-20
fiqh 1, 4-9, 11, 13-14, 20-23, 25-26, 28, 30, 36, 39, 42, 44-46, 50-52, 59,-60, 62, 70-72, 77, 82-83, 88, 94, 100, 104-11, 113, 114, 116, 119-20, 124, 128, 130, 133, 137-9, 144-5, 148, 151, 153, 156-7, 161, 165-6, 176, 178, 184, 190, 192, 195, 198, 202-3, 209-11, 214-7, 220-1, 224-5, 229, 231, 233, 235-6, 240, 243-5, 248, 251-3, 256,-7, 260-2, 266-8, 273-4, 276, 278, 281-4, 286-90, 319-20
foetal 240, 251
foetus 202-3, 205, 211, 214-5, 217, 219-24, 232, 234, 237, 240, 247, 251
Friend 251, 253
fuqaha 2, 4, 7-8, 14-15, 18, 21-22, 24-25, 27-30, 32-36, 42-46, 50, 52, 69, 72-73, 76, 82, 84-85, 87-88, 100-2, 104, 107-10, 112-3, 115-21, 123, 127-8, 130-6, 138-40, 142-3, 146, 148-50, 165-7, 169, 171-2, 177-8, 183-7, 189-91, 202, 204, 206-7, 209-11, 213-8, 220-2, 224-5, 227-8, 235, 239-40, 242, 244, 248, 257-8, 260, 264-8, 271-3, 282-6, 289-90

G

al-Ghazali, Abu Hamid 15, 26, 52, 55, 56, 57, 58, 59, 82, 83, 85, 86, 90, 94, 97, 98, 205, 223, 227, 228, 231, 271, 276, 277, 279, 293, 331
al-Ghazali, Muhammad 41, 331
GMC 91, 151
Goethe 43
Great Ormond Street Hospital 151
Griffiths 180, 193, 199, 200, 201, 293
The Guardian Newspaper 151, 157, 158
guardian 102, 115, 133, 134, 140, 263, 303

H

hadith 5, 10-12, 19-24, 28, 30, 35-38, 40, 42-43, 52, 54, 57-58, 70, 74, 80, 86-88, 95-96, 106-8, 114, 118, 123-5, 134, 145, 147, 154, 156-7, 159, 168, 177, 194-7, 201, 204, 206, 207, 210, 214, 226, 227-8, 229, 242, 245, 248, 250-3, 257-9, 264-5, 268, 276-80, 314-17
haemodialysis 255, 274
Hanafi 35-36, 93, 109, 111-2, 116-7, 119, 125, 129, 132, 134, 140, 148-9, 153-4, 157, 161, 166-7, 171, 172, 177, 184, 185-6, 189, 193,

195-6, 198-202, 207-8, 211, 223, 230-1, 318
Hanbali 35, 39, 93, 113, 116, 118, 123, 125, 131-2, 142, 150, 153-4, 157, 170, 171-2, 177, 184, 188-9, 195-6, 197-201, 203, 207-8, 212, 223, 230-1, 263, 316-7
Harun ar-Rashid 20, 22, 40, 42, 58, 254
heart 19, 24, 30, 33, 48, 70, 90, 95, 105, 139, 173-4, 240, 256, 259-61, 268-72, 275, 277, 287
Hindi 12, 60, 91-92, 96, 98-99, 123, 155, 157, 211, 214, 228-31, 263, 276, 278-9, 293, 329, 331-2
Hippocrates 10
Hippocratic Oath 1, 9-10, 23, 51, 61, 295-6, 298
Hodges v. Harland & Wolf Ltd. 101
Hofmann, Murad 25
House of Lords 102, 104, 112, 117, 125, 163, 176, 221
Huber 71, 92, 324
Human Fertilisation and Embryology Act 219-20, 247
Hunter, John 255

I

Ibn 'Abidin 92-94, 110, 123, 125-6, 134, 146, 153-7, 186, 194-200, 208, 218, 228-32, 277-8, 332
Ibn al-Qayyim 55, 59, 83, 85, 87-88, 91-93, 95-99, 106, 108, 111, 114-6, 118-9, 121-6, 131, 142, 153-4, 156, 227
Ibn Hajar 35, 142, 154, 156, 200, 217, 230, 251, 293, 332-3
Ibn Hanbal 10, 23, 35-36, 38-39, 42, 54, 57, 59-60, 75, 91, 96, 107, 126, 143, 189, 198, 224, 229, 251, 273
Ibn Hazm 30, 55, 56, 61, 92, 153, 201, 206, 207, 227, 228, 333
Ibn Hibban 23, 54, 153, 333
Ibn Majah 12, 23, 52, 54-58, 60, 91-99, 122-6, 155-7, 193-5, 197, 201, 226,-31, 259, 275-80, 293, 315, 333
Ibn Muflih 125, 142, 154, 156, 189, 200-1, 230-1, 263, 278, 333
Ibn Qayyim 95, 325, 329, 333
Ibn Qudama 92, 93, 125-6, 130-1, 142, 153-4, 156-7, 188, 196-201, 212, 228-9, 231-2, 251, 279, 316, 334-5
ibn Qudama 334
Ibn Rushd 56, 75, 92-93, 108, 119, 121-3, 125-6, 130, 137, 140, 146, 154-5, 157, 178, 194-6, 198, 229, 231-2, 292, 334
Ibn Taymiyyah 228
Ibrahim al-Musali 254
ijma' 14-15, 24-26, 28, 44-45, 107, 117, 212
ijtihad 14-15, 25, 28, 30-32, 35, 37-38, 41, 44, 56, 59, 319-20
immunogenetics 255

istihsan 14, 26, 28, 37, 38
IUD 215, 216

J

Jackson 4, 40, 49, 57, 59, 60, 61, 325
James, Dr. Taylor 151, 157
Johnstone, Penelope 95, 96, 97, 114, 325
jurisprudence 11, 26, 36, 38-39, 44, 57-58, 60, 90-91, 134, 155, 157, 190, 229, 251, 253, 274, 276, 278-9, 281, 319-20

K

kaffara 116, 120, 141, 142, 190, 212, 223, 224
Kennedy and Grubb 101
Kharijite 40, 41, 207
kidney 254, 255, 256, 261, 262, 263, 274, 279

L

al-Layth 36
liability 2, 8, 62-63, 65, 67, 69, 70-72, 74-77, 83, 89, 92-94, 101, 103, 106-9, 113, 117-9, 126,-38, 141, 152, 155, 193, 273, 281, 283-4, 292
litigation 8, 66, 77, 102-3, 109, 120, 138, 144, 236, 284
liver 16, 22, 41, 44, 66, 73, 84, 110, 129, 169, 214, 217, 234, 254, 256, 261-2

M

MacNaughton 250
Madkour 14, 24, 34, 52-59, 153, 157, 209, 215, 228, 279, 335
Majam'a al-Fiqh al-Islami 215
Malik 22-24, 35-37, 42, 49, 53-54, 56-58, 60-61, 75, 83, 93-95, 97, 108, 110, 113, 116-7, 119, 123, 125-6, 130, 132, 137, 139-41, 149, 153-7, 168-9, 171-2, 177, 184-7, 189, 195-6, 198-9, 201-2, 207, 211-2, 222-5, 227, 230-1, 240, 268, 276, 279
Maliki 93, 108, 116-7, 119, 125, 130, 132, 137, 140, 149, 153-4, 157, 168-9, 171-2, 177, 184, 186-7, 189, 195-6, 198-9, 201, 207, 211-2, 222, 231, 240
Mason & McCall Smith 105, 122, 157, 159, 162, 164, 174, 176, 193-4, 196-7, 199, 201, 218, 230, 241, 250-1, 277, 279, 299
McLaren 252, 311, 326
McNair, J. 111, 113
medical practice 1, 4, 8-10, 62, 75-77, 88, 91, 106-8, 113-5, 121, 128, 171-2, 218, 283, 285, 301

medical practitioners 1, 2, 8, 83, 101, 113, 116, 119, 121, 127, 131, 134, 149, 219, 284
Messenger of Allah ﷺ 30, 38, 95, 191, 213, 254, 259
monozygotic twins 255, 310
Montgomery 68, 91, 103, 109, 112-3, 120, 122-4, 126, 135-6, 151, 155, 158, 162-3, 176, 179, 184, 192-4, 197, 199-201, 292-3, 326
Moore, Francis 255
mudgha 205, 210-2, 221, 237
Muhammad ibn al-Hasan 185
Musallam 144, 206-7, 227-8
al-Muwaq 95, 113, 131, 332, 335

N

Negligence 104, 122, 123, 124, 125, 128, 148, 154, 155, 194, 292
negligence 8, 63-64, 71-72, 91, 94, 97, 102-6, 108-9, 111-3, 115-6, 119-21, 127-8, 130, 136, 138-9, 141, 144, 146, 148-54, 161, 165, 171, 283-85
NEST 234, 250
Netherlands 160, 180, 183, 190, 193, 199-201, 285, 293
NHS 103, 120, 138, 144, 163, 175-6, 194-5, 197, 199, 279, 284
nuclear transfer 309-10
nutfa 205, 210-2, 217, 221, 223

O

Omran 56, 207-8, 214, 226-30, 243-4, 250, 252, 293, 327, 337
Owen, Ray 255

P

Palmer 199
pancreas 256
Parrott 255, 275, 327
People of the Book 49, 60, 281
Peter, Sir Medwar 255
plastic surgery 255
polygyny 250
pregnancy 2, 9, 202-4, 210-3, 214-26, 229-30, 232-3, 236-7, 286, 305, 320
The Prophet ﷺ 2-8, 11, 14-16, 18-25, 27, 28-30, 32-34, 36-44, 46-49, 53-58, 60, 64, 66-70, 72-76, 78-88, 91-92, 95-99, 105-8, 114, 116-8, 120, 123, 125, 130, 133-4, 139, 143-7, 149, 156, 164-5, 168-9, 177-8, 183, 191-2, 203-7, 210-1, 213-6, 222, 224, 226-8, 231-2, 237, 245, 251, 254, 256-60, 263,

265-6, 268, 270, 275, 288, 291, 314-5
public interest 7
PVS 174, 269, 270

Q

Qaradawi 60, 244, 252, 292, 327
qasama 26, 27, 72, 7475, 93, 122, 178, 222-3, 256, 284
qisas 74-75, 92, 118, 140, 146-9, 148-50, 157, 165-72, 177-8, 184-9, 191, 194, 196-8, 213, 222-3, 272, 285
qiyas 14-15, 24-26, 28, 30-32, 37-39, 41, 44, 51, 216
Qur'an 4-7, 12, 14-27, 29-34, 36-39, 41-42, 44,-51, 53-54, 59, 64-66, 70, 73, 81-83, 85, 88, 98-100, 105, 108, 116, 139, 142, 148, 156, 164-6, 168-9, 176-8, 183, 191, 203-6, 209-11, 213-4, 216, 224, 237, 241, 244, 248-9, 257-8, 260, 262, 264-6, 281-2, 286, 293, 314-7

R

rape 213, 215-6, 218-20, 225, 231, 301, 304-5, 319
responsibility 2, 8, 42, 48, 62-69, 71-72, 74-76, 83, 106, 117, 119, 125, 140, 142, 163, 183, 192, 224, 236, 302, 310
Rispler-Chaim, Vardit 34
Robert, Dr. Lanza 247
ruh 211-2, 216-8, 222, 237

S

Sabiq 52, 60, 156-7, 195, 198, 209, 231, 245, 251-2, 267-8, 276, 278, 327, 336
Sahih al-Bukhari 10, 21, 23, 56-59, 90-91, 95-96, 125, 157, 194, 227, 230, 277-8, 293, 322, 325, 328-30
Sahih Muslim 23, 56, 58, 60, 90-91, 93-99, 157, 194, 199, 201, 251, 276, 278-9, 335
as-Sarakhsi 56, 92, 94, 111, 112, 123-6, 129, 136, 140, 153-7, 185, 198-200, 230, 248, 253, 292, 337
Scarman, Lord 102, 112, 124, 136, 153-4
Schacht 20-21, 41, 45, 54, 59, 323, 327-8
Schimmel 58, 60, 328
Ash-Shafi'i 6, 11, 15, 18, 21-22, 24-25, 35-37, 39, 42, 52-55, 57, 75, 82, 92, 112, 124-6, 131, 133, 141, 144, 150, 154-7, 165, 167, 171-2, 194-8, 201, 212, 224, 227, 229, 231, 248, 253, 260, 277, 283, 292, 316, 329, 332, 337
Ash-Sharq Al-Awsat 11, 57, 250, 277, 279-80, 293
Ash-Shawkani 42, 56, 58, 96-99, 227, 337
Shahawi 5, 11, 20, 54, 57, 337

Shahrastani 15, 32, 52, 56-57, 248, 253, 282, 292, 325, 328, 337
Shari'ah 1, 3, 6-8, 10-14, 18, 25-27, 35, 37, 44-46, 48, 50-52, 55, 59-61, 65, 75, 108, 118, 125, 242-3, 245, 248, 252, 256, 282, 288-9, 314, 319
Shatibi 12, 27, 55, 57, 94, 256, 276, 337
Shi'ite 25, 35, 40-42, 46, 57, 207, 289
Shinqiti 259, 276-80, 337, 338
skin grafting 255
sperm 9, 204-5, 208, 210, 221, 228, 233-5, 237, 240, 242-4, 273
stem cells 240, 246, 247, 251
Sufyan ibn 'Uyaynah 24, 36
Sunday Times, The 193, 242, 250, 251, 252, 253, 280
Sunnah 4,-8, 14-19, 21-26, 29-31, 33, 36-42, 44-45, 51-52, 59-60, 75, 82, 139, 156-7, 166, 169, 183, 195, 198, 204, 209, 214, 231, 244, 248-52, 276-8, 282, 286, 293, 315, 317
As-Suyuti 11, 56, 58, 91, 96, 193, 198, 251-2, 276, 279, 316, 318, 338

T

ta'zir 119, 267
termination of life 9, 192, 285
termination of pregnancy 2, 9, 202, 210-3, 215-7, 219-22, 225, 320
ath-Thawri 35-36, 42
the loop 215, 273, 286
The Times 8, 87 94, 122, 141, 155, 158, 164, 193-4, 197, 199, 201, 232, 253, 280
Thorn, George 255
At-Tirmidhi 20, 23, 58, 91, 96-97, 99, 194, 226, 231, 315, 338
tortfeasor 65, 72-73, 143-5, 166, 167, 168, 184-8, 222-4, 242
transplantation 2, 9, 150, 174, 239-40, 251, 254-7, 260-2, 264, 266-8, 272-6, 261, 268, 279-80, 312, 319
treatment 1, 8, 49, 68, 74, 77-78, 80-88, 97-98, 100, 104, 106, 114-6, 118-9, 128, 133-6, 139, 141-2, 160, 163, 172, 175-6, 197, 216, 234-5, 241, 255, 257, 259-60, 270, 273, 277, 283, 286, 296-7, 303, 307-8, 312

U

'Umar ibn Abd al-'Aziz 22
'Umar ibn al-Khattab 31, 49-50, 61, 73, 75-76, 80, 93, 96, 130, 142, 145-6, 178, 198, 205, 229, 277
al-Umm 11, 52-55, 57, 92, 124-6, 153-7, 194-8, 201, 229, 253, 277, 292, 337
uterus 208, 215-6, 235, 240, 243-4, 252, 273, 286, 311

V

vicarious liability 70, 72, 106, 126, 284

W

Weis 251, 253
Western law 7, 13, 76, 282, 286, 288
Whitehouse v. Jordan 112, 122, 124-5

Y

Yawm al-Kilab 254
Yu, Dr. Voronoy 255

Z

az-Zurqani 150, 155, 157, 217, 338

بعيداً عن السياسة
د. إحمد عبد العزيز .. الطبيب الكبير الذي عاد لمقاعد الدراسة يدرس القانون ويتخصص في الشريعة ويعد رسالة الدكتوراه عن استجابة الفقه الإسلامي للمستجدات في عالم الطب !

بقلم الأستاذ / محجوب محمد صالح
رئيس تحرير جريدة الأيام

الدكتور أحمد عبد العزيز يعقوب عرفه أهل السودان رقماً في عالم الطب ، عرفوه الجراح الكبير الذي أضاف الى زمالة الجراحة زمالة في الباطنية ، والذي تخصص في أمراض القلب ، والذي أدار بنجاح مستشفى الخرطوم – أكبر مستشفيات السودان – مثلما أدار السلاح الطبي؛ لكن الذي لا يعرفه الكثيرون أنه عاد طالباً بعد أن تجاوز الخمسين من العمر ليدرس القانون فينال فيه البكالوريوس من جامعة القاهرة فرع الخرطوم ثم نال دراسات فوق الجامعية في كلية الحقوق بجامعة الخرطوم وأخيراً توج ذلك كله في شهر يوليو من العام الماضي بحصوله على الدكتوراه في القانون من جامعة لندن .

تستوقفنا رسالة د. أحمد للحصول على الدكتوراه في القانون لأنها تمثل قمة في (التأصيل) الذي ينبني على العلم والذي يتأسس على المعرفة . إن موضوع الرسالة هو :

«استجابة الفقه الإسلامي للمستجدات في مسؤولية الطبيب المهنية » ـ (اطلاعات في الفقه المقارن والقانون المعاصر) .

جمع فيه د. أحمد بقدرة فائقة بين ميداني تخصصه الطب والقانون وغاص في أعمال الفقه الإسلامي بدراية وقدره بحثيه متميزة لعرض موقف الفقه الإسلامي من أنواع المسؤولية التي تقع على عاتق الطبيب وهو يؤدي مهنته وقارن بينها وبين القوانين الأخرى وخرج بنتيجة بحثية ممتازة مدعمة بالأسانيد ومستنده الى الفقه المقارن .

إن الموضوعات التي تعرض لها د. أحمد في رسالته موضوعات متنوعة متشبعة بالغة التعقيد استطاع أن يتابع كل مدارس الفقه الإسلامي في معالجته لها ، ثم يقارن بين ذلك وبين قوانين الدول الأخرى خاصة القوانين الانجليزية الأمريكية والذي يطالع الرسالة يدرك مدى الجهد الذي بذل في البحث والرجوع الى المصادر الاصلية والتنقيب من كافة زوايا الموضوع واعتماد الموضوعية والعلمية منهجاً للدراسة المقارنة .

في البداية يتوقف د. أحمد عند الفقه الإسلامي مستعرضاً مصادره من الكتاب والسنة والإجماع والقياس ويثبت موقف المذاهب الأربعة محدداً مناهجها ثم يعرج بعدها على موضوعه الأساسي ليحدد أسس المسؤولية الطبية في الإسلام ويربط بينها وبين (الضمان) أي التعويض عن الضرر سواء كان الضرر نتيجة لخطأ غير مقصود أو لأهمال من الطبيب .

د. أحمد عبد العزيز لم يهتم بالطب كعلم فحسب بل أهتم به كمهنة أيضاً لها ضوابطها وقواعدها وأسسها التنظيميه فكان عضواً في الجمعية الطبيه وفي نقابة الأطباء وفي المجلس الطبي بل تولى رئاسة هذا المجلس في مرحلة من مراحله ولعل هذا كان من أسباب اهتمامه بالجانب التنظيمي والقانوني بالنسبة لمهنة الطب وعندما ادرك أحمد ان أي دراسة عليا للقوانين والقواعد التي تحكم مهنة الطب تحتاج

بداية لدراسة جامعية في القانون لم يستنكف وهو في خمسينات عمره ان يعود طالباً جامعياً من جديد . فالتحق بكلية القانون في جامعة القاهرة فرع الخرطوم في اواخر الثمانينيات حيث حصل على البكالريوس في القانون ، ثم تابع الدراسة في كلية القانون بجامعة الخرطوم ليحصل على دبلوم عال في الشريعة ، ثم شفعه بدرجة الماجستير من جامعة الخرطوم ومن ثم التسجيل في جامعة لندن للحصول على الدكتوراه في القوانين كانت حصيلتها هذه الرسالة المتميزة التي تكرم ووضع بين يدي نسخة منها قبيل عطلة الاضحى المبارك فكانت افضل (عيدية) يمكن ان تقدم ، إذ وجدت من الوقت ماكمنى من أن أمر على صفحاتها الاربعمائه وأنا منبهر بهذه الآفاق الرحبة التي تتفتح أمام كل من يطالعها .

الرسالة معنية باستجابة الشريعة الاسلامية للتطورات في علم الطب فهي تعالج مسؤولية الطبيب في المشاكل التقليدية ثم يعرج على المستجدات والمتغيرات الحديثة في دنيا الطب من زراعة الاعضاء والاستنساخ واطفال الانابيب والاجهاض وتجميد وحفظ الحيوانات المنوية ، ومايتفرع من ذلك كله من مشاكل عملية واخلاقية وقانونية وحضارية :
القانون والمستجدات العلمية :

رسالة د. أحمد معنية إذاً بمدى استجابة الفقه الاسلامي لكل هذه التطورات على ضوء إرث عظيم من الاجتهاد الفقهي ... إن التطورات التكنولوجية تتواصل وتتعاظم وتنعكس على الممارسات الطبيه اليومية والتي تشهد وسائل ومعالجات جديدة وكلها تواجه بالتحدي الاطباء ورجال القانون والمجتمع بأسره ، والتطور في اساليب الفحص والتشخيص والعلاج فرض على الطبيب ان يدخل في ممارسات جريئه يترتب عليها مخاطر محسوبة وغير محسوبه ، والتقدم في الأبحاث والاكتشافات العلمية تجاوز قدرات وطاقات وابعاد القوانين القديمة ، لذلك نجدهم في الغرب اليوم يثيرون قضايا اخلاقية وقانونية ترتبط بالموقف من هذه المستجدات ويديرون حواراً مكثفاً حول هذه الموضوعات ، والمجتمع الاسلامي لايختلف عن هذه المجتمعات ..هذه التحديات تفرض نفسها عليه ، وأمور الصحة تهم كل الناس لانها مرتبطة بحياتهم ومجتمعهم والناس يشرعون ويضعون القوانين وفق معتقداتهم وعاداتهم وتقاليدهم وثقافتهم ومن الطبيعي ان يتلفت المسلم ليبحث عن مشروعية الاستنساخ أو الاجهاض أو أطفال الأنابيب وأن يتسائل عن رأي الشرع فيه ويتوقع من الفقهاء أن يفتوا في أمر هذه المستجدات وفق رصيد ضخم من التراث الفقهي الاسلامي ولن يتأتى لهم ذلك مالم يتعمقوا في الدراسة وفي الفهم ويدركوا أبعاد القياس وأسس الاجتهاد ويقارنوا بين حصيلة اجتهاداتهم والقوانين الاخرى – ولذلك تصبح العلاقة بين العمل والقانون مسألة هامة وملحة وتأتي هذه الرسالة (المتميزه) في الفقه ، وفي الطب ، وفي القانون المقارن لتملأ فراغاً كبيراً في هذا الجانب المهم لانها تتميز بالموضوعية والعلمية وبالعمق وبالغوص في اعماق الفقه الاسلامي جنباً الى جنب مع دراسة القوانين الوضعية والمقارنة بينها واستنباط الحلول والإجتهاد في الفروع ... يقول د. أحمد في مقدمة رسالته أنه بدءاً يخاطب بها الاطباء المهتمين بالجانب الفقهي للعمل الطبي ولكنه ايضاً يخاطب الفقهاء رغم إنه لاينتمي إليهم . يخاطبهم عملاً بنصيحة الرسول الكريم :
(نضر الله وجه أمرىء سمع مقالتى فوعاها وبلغها كما سمعها ، فرب مبلغ أوعى من سامع ، ورب حامل فقه لمن هو افقه منه ، ورب حامل فقه ليس بفقيه ،) ... وكم أتمنى لو استطاع د. أحمد أن يترجم وينشر رسالته هذه لتعم الفائدة ولأنها حقاً تمثل (تأصيلاً) يعتمد على العلم والدراسة وعلى المقارنة لايبتغى به الاوجه الحقيقية والاسهام المخلص في التقنين الدقيق لمهنة الطب .

الأيام ١١ مارس ٢٠٠١م
ص ١٢ (الأخيره)